Look Smarter Than You Are with Oracle Hyperion Planning

An Administrator's Guide

interRel Consulting
Tracy McMullen
Edward Roske

1st Edition

interRel Press, Arlington, Texas

Look Smarter Than You Are with Oracle Hyperion Planning: An Administrator's Guide

interRel Consulting
Tracy McMullen
Edward Roske

Published by:

interRel Press
A Division of interRel Consulting Partners
Suite 304
1000 Ballpark Way
Arlington, TX 76011

Library of Congress Cataloging-in-Publication Data
Roske, Edward; McMullen, Tracy
      Look Smarter Than You Are with Oracle Hyperion Planning: An Administrator's Guide

Edward Roske, Tracy McMullen 1st ed.
      p. 724 cm.
      Includes index.
      ISBN 978-0-557-40981-5

Trademarks
Various trademarked names appear throughout this book. Rather than list all the names and the companies/individuals that own those trademarks or try to insert a trademark symbol every time a trademarked name is mentioned, the author and publisher state that they are using the names only for editorial purposes and to the benefit of the trademark owner with no intention of trademark infringement.

This book is dedicated to Jim Dorrian and Bob Earle. For those who don't know, they invented Essbase, the database on which Oracle Hyperion Planning resides.

Bob and Jim, for creating the greatest multi-dimensional database known to man, we thank you.

Edward Roske, Tracy McMullen

ABOUT THE EDITORS/AUTHORS

Edward Roske, Oracle ACE Director, fell in love with Hyperion at first sight. In 1995, Edward was working for the Moore Business Forms printing facility in Mundelein, Illinois. While his official title was "Coordinator of Finance", his role focused on coordinating the linking of many, many Microsoft Excel sheets. When someone in his area deleted a row in a supporting workbook and #REF errors showed up in the summary workbook, Edward personally tracked the errors down cell-by-cell. When he saw his first demonstration of Arbor Essbase (as it was known at the time), he quit his job to become a full-time Essbase consultant (in the process becoming one of those rare individuals who quit stable jobs to consult on products with which they have absolutely no experience).

Edward is a pioneer. He was one of the first Hyperion Planning Certified consultants in the world. He was also one of the first people in the world to become certified in Essbase back in the mid-90's. While at Moore, he also obtained his first patent proving that there are still new ideas waiting to be discovered and exploited for financial gain.

In May of 1997, Edward left his senior consulting position with a Chicago-based firm to co-found interRel Consulting with Eduardo Quiroz. Proving that being humble will get you nowhere, Edward helped write interRel's original motto: "Reaching for perfection, we deliver the impossible in record time." He has been the CEO of interRel Consulting since its inception, growing it to be a multi-million dollar firm with consultants from coast to coast.

Edward still keeps his Hyperion Planning and Oracle Essbase skills sharp. He has overseen successful Hyperion implementations at over 100 companies. His cube optimizations have resulted in calculation improvements of more than 99.99%.

Continuing his quest to become the world's foremost EPM-vangelist, Edward has been a regular speaker at annual Hyperion user conferences since 1995 and he is noted for his humorous slant to technically boring information. He is the Essbase Domain Lead for the Oracle Applications Users Group (OAUG) and chair of the Hyperion track for the Oracle Developer Users Group's (ODTUG) annual Kaleidoscope conference. Edward also has one of the most visited Hyperion blogs at http://looksmarter.blogspot.com/.

Though not especially relevant, if Edward ever found a busload of nuns and orphans in need of help, he would totally save them.

ABOUT THE EDITORS/AUTHORS

Tracy McMullen, Oracle ACE Director and Hyperion Planning Domain Lead for the Oracle Applications Users Group, has been leading the development of Enterprise Performance Management and Data Warehousing applications for over 10 years. Roles on projects have ranged from developer to architect and project manager on technologies from Hyperion and Business Objects to Cognos and Oracle. She's seen all of the business intelligence tools and Hyperion is her favorite.

Tracy started her career at Arthur Andersen Business Consulting on a project programming in RPG (fun stuff!). Thankfully, her next project introduced her to the world of multi-dimensional databases with a Cognos PowerPlay implementation for an oil and gas client (many years ago Tracy was certified in Cognos PowerPlay and Impromptu). Next, she helped clients from various industries revolutionize their information delivery with Hyperion and other technologies. After years of successful business intelligence implementations, a few shredded documents (not shredded by Tracy, for what it's worth) changed her career path from future Partner to cancer destroyer.

Tracy joined The University of Texas M.D. Anderson Cancer Center where she led the charge in implementing budget and planning solutions utilizing Hyperion Planning. Fate stepped in once again with relocation to the South Texas Coast and Tracy found her new home with interRel Consulting as Director of Special Projects (which really means she does a million different things from consulting to training to project management to sales).

Tracy is a Hyperion Certified Consultant for Oracle Essbase, Hyperion Certified Solutions Architect for Hyperion Planning and a Certified Project Management Professional (PMP). Tracy has been a regular instructor at interRel, user conferences and other professional seminars since 2000 on topics including information delivery, business intelligence, data warehousing, and Hyperion implementations.

If you want to learn more from Tracy, you can visit her blog at http://looksmarterthanyouare2.blogspot.com/. She's also published articles in Oracle Magazine, IOUG Select Journal, and the ODTUG Technical Journal. Her strong technical background is complemented by comprehensive practical experience in project management, a skill important not only on the job but at home as well where she manages her kids on a daily basis (ok, she attempts to manage with moderate success).

ABOUT INTERREL CONSULTING

Integrated solutions are key to providing our clients the timely information they need to make critical business decisions. Our philosophy, experience, and methodologies are integral components of our application development, project management, optimization and training. As a result of our experience and commitment to excellence, interRel has become one of the premier providers of analytical solutions using Oracle BI and Hyperion solutions.

interRel solves business problems through utilizing Business Intelligence (BI) and Enterprise Performance Management (EPM) technologies. Our EPM Assessment is designed to identify an organization's current EPM current state relative to the corporate strategy.

interRel has been in business since 1997, and we take pride in delivering our solutions with small teams composed of members with an average of over eight years of Oracle Hyperion and BI related tools, application and consulting experience.

Exclusive EPM/BI consultancy

- 100% of our revenue is from Oracle EPM / BI products
- 100% of our Consultants specialize in Oracle EPM Systems (Hyperion)
- 100% of our Senior Consultants are Hyperion Certified
- Senior Consultants have 8+ years of experience
- "Junior" Consultants have 5+ years of experience

Oracle Hyperion Community - Training, Free Webcasts, and More

Through our various outlets, our focus is always to interact and help others in the Oracle Hyperion community.

If you like this book, join us in person for a hands-on training class. interRel Consulting offers classroom education on a full spectrum of Oracle EPM solutions, including standard course offerings such as *Essbase and Planning Accelerated Fundamentals*, tailored for new Administrators, as well as unique advanced courses like *Hyperion Calc Scripts for Mere Mortals* and *Oracle Data Integrator (ODI) for Hyperion*. All classes are taught by knowledgeable, certified trainers whose experience averages more than 8 years per instructor. This interactive environment allows attendees the opportunity to master the skill set needed to implement, develop and manage Hyperion solutions successfully.

All classes are held at our headquarters in Dallas and offer CPE accreditation. interRel Consulting also provides custom training on-site to clients.

interRel Consulting proudly offers free twice-weekly webcasts. These webcasts include the full scope of Oracle BI and EPM System (Hyperion) products, including Essbase, Planning & Hyperion Financial Management. Webcasts are primarily held every non-holiday week and twice in most weeks. Topics include 'Tips, Tricks & Best Practices,' which gives you an insider's guide to optimize the usage of your solution. The 'Administration' series focuses on making your job easier and giving a snapshot of the Accelerated Fundamentals course outline while the 'Overview' webcasts discuss the highlights of a solution and how it can be used effectively. All webcasts include interactive examples and demonstrations to see how the products really work.

Awards & Recognitions

- 2008 and 2009 Back-to-Back Oracle Titan Award winner for "EPM & BI Solution" of the year
- 2008 Oracle Excellence Award winner with Pearson Education
- 2009 Oracle EPM/BI Innovation Award winner
- One of the fastest growing companies in USA (Inc. Magazine, '08 and '09)
- The only company in the world *of any kind* with two Oracle ACE Directors and one Oracle ACE

interRel's commitment to providing our customers with unsurpassed customer service and unmatched expertise make interRel the partner of choice for a large number of companies across the world. Learn more at www.interrel.com.

ACKNOWLEDGEMENTS

Those contributing significant content to this book include Rodrigo Becerra, Troy Seguin, Heather Wine, Rob Donahue and Christopher "CTI" Solomon of interRel Consulting.

Thank you to Markus Shipley, Doug Burke, Kelli Stein, and Vanessa Roske for their tireless editing and ever-helpful feedback. Big shouts out to Laura Gregor, David Mitchell, Steve Press, and Gauthier Vasseur for being long-time, strong supporters. We would like to thank some of the product and domain folks at Oracle for their insight and advice: thanks to Shubhomoy Bhattacharya, Guillaume Arnaud, Shankar Viswanathan, Al Marciante, Alan Fuller, Aneel Shenker, John O'Rourke, Rich Clayton, Floyd Conrad, and Mike Nader.

Edward also wants to say "thank you" to Melissa Vorhies Roske, Vanessa Roske, and Eliot Roske for giving up their time with him on evenings and weekends, so he could make his publishing deadline. His family puts up with a lot, so if you want to so them your appreciation, remember that nothing says "thank you" quite like a college scholarship to an Ivy League school.

Tracy McMullen would like to thank Blanche and Randy McMullen Sr. for always lending a helping hand. Thanks to mom and dad for their never-ending support and Randy, Taylor and Reese for their patience and understanding.

We give our sincerest gratitude to all the people above and the others we didn't have room to mention. We hope that they feel that this book is partly theirs as well (just without the fame, glory and most importantly, the royalties).

DISCLAIMER

This book is designed to provide supporting information about the related subject matter. It is being sold to you and/or your company with the understanding that the author and the publisher are not engaged by you to provide legal, accounting, or any other professional services of any kind. If assistance is required (legal, expert, or otherwise), seek out the services of a competent professional such as a consultant.

It is not the purpose of this book to reprint all of the information that is already available on the subject at hand. The purpose of this book is to complement and supplement other texts already available to you. For more information (especially including technical reference information), please contact the software vendor directly or use your on-line help.

Great effort has been made to make this book as complete and accurate as possible. That said, there may be errors both typographic and in content. Therefore, use this book only as a general guide and not as the ultimate source for specific information on the software product. Further, this book contains information on the software that was generally available as of the publishing date.

The purpose of this book is to entertain while educating. The authors and interRel Press shall have neither liability nor responsibility to any person living or dead or entity currently or previously in existence with respect to any loss or damage caused or alleged to be caused directly, indirectly, or otherwise by the information contained in this book.

If you do not wish to abide by all parts of the above disclaimer, please stop reading now and return this book to the publisher for a full refund.

TABLE OF CONTENTS

FOUNDATIONS

Scene 1:
Eddie and The Consultants: An Oracle Hyperion Planning Musical

Brace yourself for the shocking truth: computer books are boring. So to make your job learning how to be an administrator of Oracle Hyperion Planning a bit more interesting, we've decided to weave a musical comedy throughout this book. Bear with us, because we assure you that this will be far more entertaining than it sounds at the moment; however, if musicals "just aren't your thing", you can skip through the few scattered musical interludes and go straight for the Planning content. Don't complain to us when it's boring, though.

PROLOGUE

In 2006 and 2007 at the last of the late, great Hyperion Solutions conferences, the employees of interRel performed (for a standing-room-only audience) what was called by many, the best musical ever. *Eddie and the Consultants: A System 9 Musical* was the story that everyone in the business world could relate to... sort of a cross between *My Fair Lady* and *Office Space*.

Set way back when Hyperion System 9 was the current version (maybe 50 years ago or so), it was the story of Eddie, a young lad from Accounting, and Penny, a young lass from IT, both unable to communicate in the other's language of love. Over the course of a week-long Hyperion System 9 implementation (note: implementations normally take slightly more than a week but this was a work of comedic fiction), the fearless couple faced technical issue after functional issue *and* the super villain Dr. Dementor who was determined to crush the project with his trusty deathray. Despite all of these obstacles, they finally were brought together by a love that couldn't be bound by the confines of mere software and deathrays. By the end of the story, not only were Eddie and Penny in love, the world's leading EPM (Enterprise Performance Management) software had been successfully implemented, leaving a world in which we could all live *truly* happily ever after (or so we thought).

There were, of course, others in the musical beyond of love-addled stars. Meet the complete cast of *Eddie and the Consultants*:

INFORMATION TECHNOLOGY
PENNY, Our gorgeous, unlucky-in-love heroine
TRIXIE, Penny's best friend

ACCOUNTING
CFO, Take no prisoners executive
EDDIE, Our dashingly handsome, lovelorn, genius hero
JACK, Former Excel guru (recently killed by a bus)
SILENT BOB, Eddie's best friend, the strong/silent type

ALL-POWERFUL CONSULTANTS
SUPERMANAGER, Project manager extraordinaire
MR. ANACHRONISM, Sees the future *as foretold by prophecy*
THE TRANSLATOR, Has a really useful Bachelor's degree in
Communications to translate between Accounting and IT
AQUAMAN, Talks to fish, swims, and frankly, doesn't do much else

OTHERS
HYPERION SOFTWARE, Talking and dancing software with arms
DR. DEMENTOR, Super villain with a trusty death ray

A SEQUEL

Eddie's Story

The portion of Hyperion System 9 that the happy couple implemented was a godsend. Under Eddie and Penny's leadership, their company was doing all their reporting and analysis out of Hyperion (now Oracle) Essbase... but...

...the company was still budget crunching in Microsoft Excel. The CFO was convinced the spreadsheet-intensive budgeting model, designed by Jack who of course was no longer with the company, was the only way to budget. Odd that the CFO didn't question whether it should take 3 months per quarter to come up with numbers that were no longer accurate once the budget was complete, but there you have it.

Eddie, ecstatically in love and contemplating marriage, was told it was time to start budgeting for the quarter. Knowing he only had 3 months to complete the process before this forecast was due and the next forecast needed to start, he thought he'd cut a few corners. He looked at the Excel template and realized that several of the rows and columns of the spreadsheet were totally irrelevant to his department, so he deleted them. After all, why would anyone need spreadsheet cells in specific locations for totaling into linked consolidation spreadsheets?

Oblivious to the consequences, Eddie started entering numbers into his much smaller spreadsheet template. He dutifully checked the totals on his circa 1940's adding machine while his CFO sang him his favorite motivational tune: *Adding Machine* (parody of *Chain Gang*):

[Adding machines make the click, ding sounds in the song instead of pick axes.]
OH DON'T YOU KNOW
THAT'S THE SOUND OF MY MEN
USING ADDING MACHINES
OH DON'T YOU KNOW
THAT'S THE SOUND OF MY MEN
USING ADDING MACHINES

DURING PLAN, THEY WORK SO HARD
EVEN AFTER THEIR BRAINS ARE FRIED
WORKIN' ON THOSE BUDGETS AND FORECASTS
KEEPING THEIR TIES ALL TIED
I HEAR THEM MOANIN' THEIR LIVES AWAY
BUT I THINK, THEY LIKE WHEN I SAY

OH DON'T YOU KNOW
THAT'S THE SOUND OF MY MEN
USING ADDING MACHINES
OH DON'T YOU KNOW
THAT'S THE SOUND OF MY MEN
USING ADDING MACHINES

Since his spreadsheet was so much smaller than it was originally designed to be, Eddie finished his budget in minutes and the CFO never got to the remaining song verses. Sending the filled-in Excel template off to some nameless consolidation person in IT to deal with, Eddie dashed off to the jewelry store to find just the right engagement ring.

Penny's Story

Penny was not having nearly as great a day as Eddie. In addition to her day job, Penny had recently become the nameless person in IT responsible for consolidating the budget templates.

The original Excel model was built by Jack and thanks to an ill-timed step in front of a speeding bus, Jack was no longer around. Penny tried to take over the maintenance of his Excel WFH (Workbook From Hell), but from what she could tell, Jack must have built the spreadsheets while under the influence of some *very* strong narcotics. No other explanation for the labyrinth of linked workbooks made sense.

Forgetting the disaster of cell formulas all over the place, the budget process itself was a convoluted mess of insanely time-consuming steps apparently designed to make data very unlikely to tie. She opened her e-mail to find that Eddie had sent her his department's budget template. She opened his spreadsheet only to discover that he deleted some rows. Too late: it had already linked itself into the summary spreadsheets. The entire house of budget cards came crashing down around her as her screen filled with #REF errors.

She was assuming that the funeral dirge playing in her head was the first stage in her psychotic break.

Penny started to curse Jack, spreadsheets, budgets, and the fact that Eddie's parents ever conceived a boy who would asininely delete rows in the worst Excel mess ever, when she heard footsteps approaching. Expecting to see the Grim Reaper, she looked up to see Eddie. Stunned at how someone's timing could be so vastly wrong, she saw Eddie get down on one knee and utter the words she had waited years to hear: "Will you marry me?"

How in the name of Bill Gates could Eddie possibly propose at a time like this when it was going to take her days, weeks perhaps, to fix the budget model? Without thinking of the long-term marital consequences, Penny took the ring from Eddie's outstretched hand... and threw it at his forehead all the while yelling at him about his broken template.

What's next for our heroes?

Eddie was in shock. He thought he had found his one true love, but he realized that any relationship that couldn't survive one mangled budget certainly couldn't survive a marriage. With their relationship (and the budget) in a shambles, Eddie decided the only course of action was to put Penny in his past and sulk back to the relative safety of his debits and credits.

Is their relationship doomed to the scrap heap of time on top of all the other failed partnerships between Accounting and IT? Will Penny and Eddie ever make it beyond this devastating setback? And what about the budget? Can it possibly be completed with only two days to go?

BIG NEWS

That's where you come in. Congratulations, fearless reader. You've been cast as the new Penny in *Eddie and the Consultants: A Planning Implementation.* Join us for this rollicking musical sequel (in book form without notes, sets, scores, costumes, or any of the other stuff you'd normally see in a musical) where you'll play the part of Penny as you learn Oracle Hyperion Planning.

Note!

This book covers both versions 9.3.1 and 11.1.1.x. We've highlighted those features and functions that are new or different in the 11.1.1 version. You may find other minor differences in the interface but overall planning in the 9.3.1 and 11.1.1 versions are similar.

Scene 2:
Introduction to Oracle Hyperion Planning

Penny sat quietly at her desk, hands folded in her lap, holding back the tears that were filling her eyes. Her love life *and* the quarterly budget were a complete mess. Eddie proposed and she threw the ring back in his face. What was she thinking? Well, he did break Jack's poorly designed Excel budget workbook, so he sort of deserved it. But still, how could she get out of this budget mess of DJ (Dead Jack) and Eddie's creation?

There had to be an answer. She remembered back to the System 9 implementation, when times were good, people were singing (some better than others) and she was finally in a relationship. Her mind went back to something one of the all-knowing consultants told her about Hyperion: "Penny, Enterprise Performance Management lets you do reporting, analysis, modeling, budgeting, and consolidations all in one system."

Wait a minute... budgeting? That's right, one of the key components of Oracle EPM is Oracle Hyperion Planning. The CFO had not-so-brilliantly opted to stick with dearly departed Jack's Excel model instead of implementing Planning like the genius-in-retrospect consultants recommended. It is time to call the

Note!

When we say "Planning" with a capital "P," we're referring to Oracle Hyperion Planning. If it's a lower-case "p," then we're talking about the concept of planning and budgeting. It's confusing, I know. Blame Hyperion for naming their planning product "Planning."

Meanwhile, back at the Hall of Consultants ...

While Aquaman - having nothing better to do since he's... well... *Aquaman* - is making a vegan faux-ham sandwich, SuperManager is lecturing to the other consultants, Mr. Anachronism and The Translator.

"...and while that other superhero got all the credit for saving the world, I daresay that he couldn't have done it without my project plan," says SuperM.

"I think what SuperManager is trying to say is that behind every great project – saving the world for instance – is a great, underappreciated project manager," says the Translator. "Wouldn't you agree, Mr. Anachronism?"

Just then the phone rings, interrupting their stories of self-congratulations. It is Penny and she needs to learn more about Planning from the consultants. SuperM reassures Penny in a confident tone. "Penny, let me tell you about this unstoppable, unbeatable planning and forecasting solution that can *save* your budget."

Oracle Hyperion Planning is a centralized, Web-based planning, budgeting, and forecasting solution. Never fear, Excel gurus, Microsoft Office integration is also possible. Features include workflow and process management, flexible modeling, powerful reporting and analysis, Business Rules, task lists, and more. You can use do both Top-Down (Target) and Bottom-up planning as well as have multiple versions for iterative planning cycles. Everything is web based: web-based data entry and annotations, web-based management of planning cycle, web-based forms development, web-based security, and web based outline maintenance.

Penny immediately realizes this is her chance to save the budget and possibly her future with Eddie. "Show me how to implement Oracle Hyperion Planning," she demands, somewhat impolitely for normally image-conscious IT professionals.

"Patience, my administrative padawan, we will get there," Mr. Anachronism says calmly in a Star Wars reference that flies right over Penny's head. "We must first begin with some important

terms and concepts that you'll need to know before building
Planning applications."

YOU GOT SERVED...

The Translator steps forward, swooshing his dark cloak
behind him. "I am The Translator," he announces in dramatic
fashion, "and along with my trusty companions, SuperManager and
Mr. Anachronism, I will cover some terminology that's key to your
understanding of Oracle Hyperion Planning." The Translator pulls
up   Microsoft   PowerPoint,   opens   a   file   called
Hyperion_Planning_Glossary_Version_1959_Autosave.PPT,   and
begins to explain.

Throughout Planning, you will hear slightly techie sounding
things like "Server", "Client" and "Web Client." Don't let this scare
you into thinking that you need any sort of background in computer
science or networking because we'll tell you all you need to know
about everything (yes, everything).

In its simplest terms, a server is just another word for a
computer. However, unlike the computer you use at work or at
home, a server is a computer that generally doesn't have anyone
sitting in front of it. It's just sitting there all alone in a dark room
(heartbreaking, we know) doing its own thing while humming away.
But before you let this story of computer abandonment send you
into a depressive fugue you should know that this computer is hard
at work 24/7 (and not just surfing match.com for a SWF or "Server
White Female"). The server's job is to get files, data, software
applications (like Planning), and web pages from it to you.

Don't want to think in computer terms? Well let's go get
some lunch and maybe that will bring some clarity to the issue.
When you go to your favorite restaurant, you see some people eating
and some people working. The people eating the food are *clients* of
the restaurant, and the people working at the restaurant
(specifically the waiters) are the *servers* of the food. So in the same
way that a server at a restaurant brings you food, a computer server
brings data to your computer (aptly named, the client).

There's just one more term that needs some explanation and
that term is Web Client. We now know that the computer you're
using is named the client...so therefore a web client is simply a
program that you access in a web browser.

APPLICATIONS AND PLAN TYPES DEFINED

You will plan in one or more Planning applications. Depending on the design of your environment, you may have a single Planning application with multiple plan types (also called databases). You may plan in multiple applications, each with a single plan type. For example, you might use an application called ENTBUD that contains plan types BUDREV (detailed revenue planning by product or customer), BUDSAL (detailed salary planning by employee), and BUDSUM (summary plan type to budget other expenses by account and consolidate all budget data together). Why such '80s sounding, 16-bit names? You are limited to 8 characters when naming Planning applications and plan types.

Each application and plan type will have a number of components:

- Data Forms – predefined templates for entering plan data over the Web or in Excel with Smart View
- Data Form Folders – folders used to organize data forms within a Planning application
- Task Lists – guided list of steps or tasks for completing a budget
- Business Rules – objects that are executed to perform predefined calculation logic or other operations on data; common Business Rules include those to rollup data from base data to totals, perform allocations from upper level data to lower levels, perform driver based calculation logic, copy data, and clear data.

DIMENSIONS DEFINED

Planning utilizes a multi-dimensional data structure. Underlying data is stored in a multi-dimensional database called Essbase. Data is organized into dimensions or groupings of related data elements grouped into a hierarchical format.

To oversimplify, a *dimension* is something that can be put into the rows or columns of your report or data form (or it applies to the whole page). Different databases have different dimensions.

Have a look at this really simple Profit & Loss Statement:

	Actual	**Budget**
Sales	400,855	373,080
COGS	179,336	158,940
Margin	221,519	214,140
Total Expenses	115,997	84,760
Profit	**105,522**	**129,380**

It only has two dimensions. Down the rows, we have our "Measures" dimension (often called "Accounts"). Across the columns, we have our "Scenario" dimension, the dimension that contains Actual, Budget, Forecast, and the like.

The only two dimensions so far are Scenario and Measures. The more detailed breakdowns of Measures (Sales, COGS, Margin, et al) are the members of the Measures dimension. Actual and Budget are members in the Scenario dimension. A *member* identifies a particular element within a dimension.

If we pivot the Measures up to the columns and the Scenario dimension over to the rows, our report will now look like this:

	Sales	COGS	**Margin**	Total Expenses	**Profit**
Actual	400,855	179,336	221,519	115,997	105,522
Budget	373,080	158,940	214,140	84,760	129,380

While it doesn't look very good, it does illustrate a couple of important points. First, a dimension can be placed into the rows, the columns, or the page (as we'll see in a second). If it's really a dimension (as Scenario and Measures both are), there are no restrictions on which dimensions can be down the side or across the top. Second, notice that the values in the second report are the same as the values in the first report. Actual Sales are 400,855 in both reports. Likewise, Budgeted Profit is 129,380 in both reports. This is not magic.

Three Dimensions

A spreadsheet is inherently two dimensional (as are most data forms and reports for Planning). It has rows and columns. This is great if your company only produces a Profit & Loss Statement one time and then files for bankruptcy, but most companies will tend to have profit (be it positive or negative) in every month. To represent this in Excel, we use the spreadsheet tabs (one for each month):

All Products and Markets.xls	Actual	Budget
Sales	31,538	29,480
COGS	14,160	12,630
Margin	17,378	16,850
Total Expenses	9,354	6,910
Profit	8,024	9,940

Jan / Feb / Mar / Apr / May / Jun / Jul / Aug / Sep / Oct / Nov / Dec /

We've now introduced a third dimension, Time. It could be across the columns (if you wanted to see a nice trend of twelve months of data) or down the rows, but we've put it in the pages. That is, if you click on the "Jan" tab, the whole report will be for January.

If you're looking for Actual Sales of 400,855, you won't find it now because that was the value for the whole year. We could get it by totaling the values of all twelve tabs onto a summary tab.

Four Dimensions and More

Right now, this spreadsheet is not broken down by product or market. Within Excel, it's problematic to represent more than three dimensions (since we've used the rows, columns, and tabs). One way is to have a separate file for each combination of product and market:

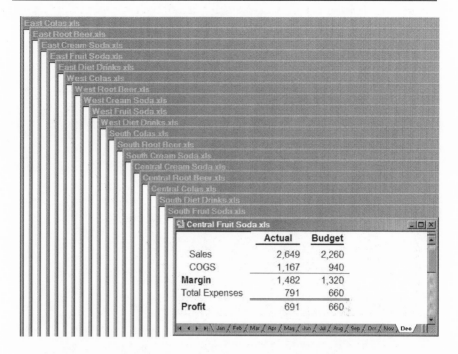

As you can see, this is getting ridiculous. What if we want to pivot our market dimension down to our columns so that we could compare profitability across different regions? To do this, we'd either have to have a series of linked spreadsheet formulas (which would break as soon as we added or deleted a new product or market) or we could hire a temporary employee to print out all the spreadsheets and type them in again with the markets now in the columns.

Now that you understand dimension, let's discuss some terms related to the elements within a dimension. A member or member name is the short, computery name for the member of an Essbase dimension (like "100-10"). An alias is the longer, more descriptive name for a member (like "Cola"). Members are grouped into hierarchies within a dimension.

All in the Family

Since we're discussing dimensions, we'll also cover some "family" topics. The most common way to refer to members in a dimension relative to each other is by using "family tree" relationships.

⊟ **Product**
  ⊟ 100 (+) (Alias: Colas)
    — 100-10 (+) (Alias: Cola)
    — 100-20 (+) (Alias: Diet Cola)
    — 100-30 (+) (Alias: Caffeine Free Cola)
  ⊟ 200 (+) (Alias: Root Beer)
    — 200-10 (+) (Alias: Old Fashioned)
    — 200-20 (+) (Alias: Diet Root Beer)
    — 200-30 (+) (Alias: Sasparilla)
    — 200-40 (+) (Alias: Birch Beer)
  ⊟ 300 (+) (Alias: Cream Soda)
    — 300-10 (+) (Alias: Dark Cream)
    — 300-20 (+) (Alias: Vanilla Cream)
    — 300-30 (+) (Alias: Diet Cream)
  ⊟ 400 (+) (Alias: Fruit Soda)
    — 400-10 (+) (Alias: Grape)
    — 400-20 (+) (Alias: Orange)
    — 400-30 (+) (Alias: Strawberry)
  ⊟ Diet (~) (Alias: Diet Drinks)
    — 100-20 (+) (Alias: Diet Cola)
    — 200-20 (+) (Alias: Diet Root Beer)
    — 300-30 (+) (Alias: Diet Cream)

The members directly below a member are called its children. For example (we'll reference Essbase's Sample.Basic application), a Product dimension has five children: Colas, Root Beer, Cream Soda, Fruit Soda, and Diet Drinks. If we ever wanted to refer to those members on a report or data form without hard coding them, we could say "give us all the children of Product."

The advantage to this (aside from the saving in typing) is that if a new product line needs to be added (say, "Water"), we don't have to modify our reports and data forms. Any report or data form designed to display the children of Product will pick up the new "Water" product and add it to the list automatically.

If Colas, Root Beer, and the other rug rats are all the children of Product, what relation is Product to its children? Assuming you didn't fail "Birds and the Bees 101," you'll know that Product must be the *parent* of Colas, Root Beer, and the rest. In other words, the parent of any member is the one that the member rolls-up into. Qtr2 is the parent of May. Year is the parent of Qtr2.

Since Colas and Root Beer are both the children of Product, Colas and Root Beer are siblings. This is simple, but what relationship do January and May have? Well, their parents are siblings so that makes them... cousins. Correct, but "cousins" while technically correct isn't used that often. In general, people say that January and May are at the "same level."

What if you want to refer to all the members into which May rolls (not just the one right above)? Well, those are its ancestors which in this case would be Qtr2 and Year. Correspondingly, the descendants of Year would include all four quarters and all twelve months.

Note that there are members that don't have any children. If our database doesn't go below the month level, May is barren. We refer to childless members as being "level-0". If you want all bottom, child-less members of a dimension, just ask for the level-0 members. For example, the level-0 members of the Year dimension are the months.

Level-0 (bottom level) members also are sometimes referred to as "leaves," because they're at the edges of the family tree. SuperManager sometimes refers to level-0 members as "the ones who have to sit at the little table in the living room on Thanksgiving," but we think he is the only one, because that's rather a lot to say.

All of the parents of the level-0 members are referred to as level-1. Since the level-0 members of the Year dimension are the months, then the level-1 members are the quarters. For the Market dimension, the level-1 members are the regions: East, West, South, and Central.

Just as the parents of the level-0 members are level-1 members, the parents of level-1 members are level-2 members, their parents are level-3 members, and so on up the hierarchy. There are many places in Essbase that you can specify, for example, "All the level-2 members of the Product dimension," so remember that levels count up from the bottom of a dimension starting at 0.

If you want to count down the hierarchy, use generations instead of levels. The dimension itself is considered generation-1 (or "gen1," for short). Its children are gen2. For the Year dimension, the gen2 members are the quarters.

Yes, the quarters are both level-2 and generation-2. Why do we need both levels and generations? Well, in some dimensions with many, many levels in the hierarchy, you'll want to count up from the bottom or down from the top depending on which is closer. We've seen a dimension with 17 levels in the hierarchy, and it was nice definitely to have both options available. The children of gen2 members are gen3 and so on down the hierarchy.

Note!

Why do generations start counting from 1 and levels from 0? It's because generation 0 is considered to be the outline itself making its children, the dimensions, generation 1.

While counting with generations is pretty straight-forward, levels can sometimes be a bit tricky. Look at this portion of the Measures dimension:

For this dimension, Gen1 is Measures. Gen2 is Profit and Inventory. Gen3 is Margin, Total Expenses, Opening Inventory, Additions, and Ending Inventory.

So far this is looking pretty easy, but let's switch our focus to the levels. The level-0 members are Sales, COGS, Marketing, Payroll, Misc, Opening Inventory, Additions, and Ending Inventory. The level-1 members are Margin, Total Expenses, and Inventory. What are the level-2 members? Profit (because it's the parent of level-1 members Margin and Total Expenses) and Measures (because it's the parent of level-1 member Inventory).

The trickiness is that Measures is *also* a level-3 member because it's the parent of Profit, a level-2 member. This means that if you ask Essbase for level-2 members, you'll get Measures, but you'll also get Measures if you ask for level-3 members. Notice that this counting oddity does not occur with generations.

Note!

This unevenness of some dimensions is also known as a ragged hierarchy.

STANDARD PLANNING DIMENSIONS

Your planning application will be designed and tailored for your specific planning process. However, there are some common dimensions that you will find in all applications.

Period

All of us experience the constant effects of time and likewise every Planning application has a Period dimension that includes

periods like months, weeks, and quarters. Here is an example of a
time periods dimension:

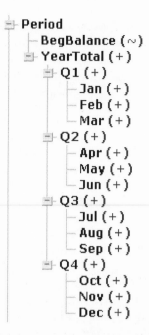

Other common names for this dimension include Periods,
All Periods, Time (Edward's personal favorite), Time Periods, and
Year Total. As you can tell from the plus signs above next to each
member, this dimension generally aggregates from the bottom-up.

Year

It is standard for a Planning application to have two time
dimensions. One dimension will house the quarters, months, days,
and so forth. A separate dimension, generally called "Years" or "FY"
(for Fiscal Year), will contain the calendar year. Here's an example
of a Years dimension:

⊟··Years (Alias: Current Year)
  ├···FY03 (~) (Alias: 2003)
  ├···FY04 (~) (Alias: 2004)
  ├···FY05 (~) (Alias: 2005)
  ├···FY06 (+) (Alias: 2006)
  ├···FY07 (~) (Alias: 2007)
  ├···FY08 (~) (Alias: 2008)
  ├···FY09 (~) (Alias: 2009)
  └···FY10 (~) (Alias: 2010)

Unlike the Period dimensions that usually contain quarters and months, Years dimensions typically do not aggregate. Most often, the top member of a Years dimension is set to equal the data in the current year. In the above image, the tilde (~) signs (also called "no consolidate" tags) denote which years are not to be added into the total. As you can see, only FY06 has a plus next it, and therefore, is the only one to roll into Years (because 2006 was the Best. Year. Ever!). As such, Years equals FY06.

Measures / Accounts

Just as every Planning application has a Time dimension, every Planning application has a dimension that lists the metrics for the database. While common practice is to call this dimension Measures, other frequently used names include Accounts and Metrics.

The Measures dimension below contains some profit and loss accounts, inventory metrics, and three calculated ratios:

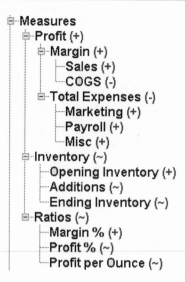

```
⊟ Measures
   ⊟ Profit (+)
      ⊟ Margin (+)
         ├ Sales (+)
         └ COGS (-)
      ⊟ Total Expenses (-)
         ├ Marketing (+)
         ├ Payroll (+)
         └ Misc (+)
   ⊟ Inventory (~)
      ├ Opening Inventory (+)
      ├ Additions (~)
      └ Ending Inventory (~)
   ⊟ Ratios (~)
      ├ Margin % (+)
      ├ Profit % (~)
      └ Profit per Ounce (~)
```

You'll notice that under "Profit," there are two members for "Margin" and "Total Expenses." Each one of these members has members below it. It's quite common for a Measures dimension to have many levels of hierarchy. A financial reporting application, for instance, might have hierarchy all the way down to a sub-account level.

While most every application will have a Measures dimension, what the Measures dimension contains will differ wildly:

- A financial planning application will have accounts for income statement, balance sheet, and sometimes cash flow.
- An inventory planning application will have measures for beginning inventory, ending inventory, additions, returns, adjustments, and so forth.
- A sales planning application will have measures for sales dollars, units sold, and average sales price.
- A human capital planning application will have metrics for payroll, unemployment, payroll taxes, sick days, vacation days, years of employment, and so on.

The Measures dimension is the most important dimension in any application (take that *Periods*) since it lets you define what metrics you're going to plan and analyze, but you can safely expect every Measures dimension to be unique for every application.

It's worth pointing out that the Measures dimension shown above is very odd. It's not normal to see inventory statistics along with profit and loss accounts in the same database. The important thing to realize is that Planning (and Essbase) can handle things beyond just financial metrics.

Scenario

The "Scenario" dimension usually houses members such as Actual, Budget, Forecast, and several variances (differences between one scenario and another). While the most popular name for this dimension is Scenario (or Scenarios), other names could include Category or Ledger (we recommend sticking with Scenario).

You can apply different planning methods to different scenarios and associate different time periods and exchange rates. For example, the annual Budget scenario may allow data entry for a specific window of time for all periods while the Forecast scenario may allow data entry for the upcoming 18 months only.

Version

The "Version" dimension is used to differentiate between different drafts of budget and plan data. Versions allow multiple iterations of a plan like Initial, Draft1, Draft2, and Final. You can model possible outcomes based on more optimistic or less optimistic assumptions like Best Case and Worst Case or use Versions to manage the dissemination of plan data like Internal and External. Versions are independent of scenarios; for example, you can have a Budget Draft 1, Budget Draft 2, and a Budget Final.

Versions are either defined as Target or Bottom Up. Target versions allow data entry at any level in the hierarchy of dimensions. Business Rules can allocate data down to lower levels if created by the Planning administrator.

 Workflow tasks are not allowed for target versions. You can copy one target version to another which will copy data for all levels and members.

Note!

Bottom up budgets only allow data entry at the bottom members of every dimension (remember we described these members as level-0 members). Summary members are display only and aggregate from bottom level members. You can copy from one bottom up version to another (such as from 2nd Draft to Final).

Entity

The "Entity" dimension differentiates between organizational entities. Commonly, this dimension is called Entities (the name Planning prefers), Organization (the name we prefer),

Departments, Cost Centers, Companies, Locations, and other industry-specific names (like Stores or Branches). Process management primarily follows the entity hierarchy structure.

Currency

If you enabled Planning's built in multi-currency functionality, you will also see a Currency dimension, listing the available currencies for the application. A hidden dimension that you won't see in Planning but will in reporting and analysis is "HSP_Rates".

Note!

It is possible to implement currency conversion in Planning without using the built-in functionality. In most cases we recommend you build in your own currency conversion logic since Planning currency conversion can be very slow and will impede your ability to optimize your application.

Planning Sample Application

The Translator turns to Penny and says, "Now that you know some of the terms and definitions of Oracle Hyperion Planning, let us see Planning in action. First let us review the dimensions within the sample application."

Within the Planning sample application, revenue is planned by products by region and expenses are planned by account by region. The Planning sample application has the standard dimensions discussed above along with some custom dimensions and members. The Account dimension contains the following hierarchies and members:

The Entity dimension contains the following organization structure:

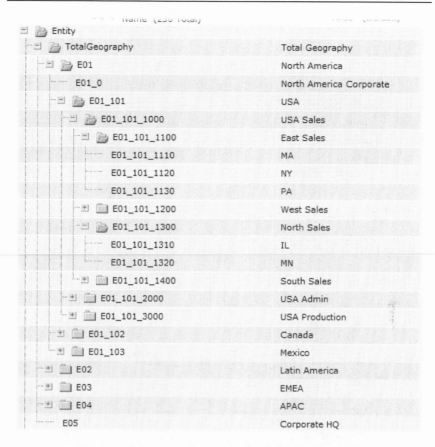

Name (250 Total)	Alias (Default)
Entity	
TotalGeography	Total Geography
E01	North America
E01_0	North America Corporate
E01_101	USA
E01_101_1000	USA Sales
E01_101_1100	East Sales
E01_101_1110	MA
E01_101_1120	NY
E01_101_1130	PA
E01_101_1200	West Sales
E01_101_1300	North Sales
E01_101_1310	IL
E01_101_1320	MN
E01_101_1400	South Sales
E01_101_2000	USA Admin
E01_101_3000	USA Production
E01_102	Canada
E01_103	Mexico
E02	Latin America
E03	EMEA
E04	APAC
E05	Corporate HQ

Finally, the Segments dimension contains the products and services for planning revenue:

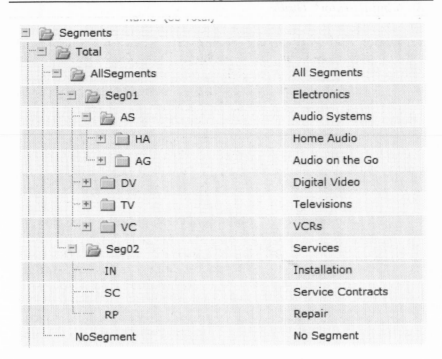

Segments	
Total	
AllSegments	All Segments
Seg01	Electronics
AS	Audio Systems
HA	Home Audio
AG	Audio on the Go
DV	Digital Video
TV	Televisions
VC	VCRs
Seg02	Services
IN	Installation
SC	Service Contracts
RP	Repair
NoSegment	No Segment

THE PLANNING UNIT

We'll provide you one last definition before we move to the next topic. A planning unit is the combination of entity, scenario and version. Planning uses them to track the budgets and they are the basis for workflow and approvals in process management (more on this in the Review and Approve scene). An example of a planning unit would be Budget, Draft1, West Region. We'll discuss planning units in more detail during the course of the book, but we wanted you to know the term when you encounter it.

ALL THE MOVING PIECES

Before we conclude this scene, let's review all of the components involved with Oracle Hyperion Planning.

The Enterprise Performance Management (EPM) Workspace is the single environment that brings together reporting and applications over the web (including Hyperion Planning). Through the Workspace, you can access applications and reporting and analysis from one interface.

Planning is the central component for budgeting and forecasting in Oracle's EPM solution. The administrator manages the Planning applications and environment via the web client within the EPM Workspace. End users can work with Planning data via the Workspace (web client) or Smart View (the Microsoft Office Add-in for Oracle EPM products).

Planning stores all of the data or "numbers" in an underlying Essbase database. Essbase is an online analytical processing (OLAP, also known as multi-dimensional) database. It provides enterprise-wide information analysis and delivers high-speed reporting of information. Essbase includes a powerful calculation engine for business rules and business modeling and write back capabilities to any level; important features in budgeting and forecasting applications. Data is organized into dimensions, providing a business view of the information.

Shared Services provides the foundation for many Oracle EPM products. Shared Services delivers a security model, consistent installation and configuration interfaces and processes, and starting in version 11.1.1, life cycle management for Oracle EPM solutions. Shared Services also manages the core services (the underlying "plumbing") for Oracle EPM including session management, authentication and authorization, repository services, and logging and usage.

Enterprise Performance Management Architect provides a single interface to build, deploy, and manage all financial applications for Planning, Financial Management and Essbase. EPMA is one of the ways that you can create and manage Planning applications. It also makes a handy place to share data and dimensions among different EPM applications.

Financial Reporting is a reporting and analysis module within Oracle Business Intelligence Enterprise Edition Plus (OBIEE+) that is primarily utilized for highly formatted financial and operating reports against Essbase, Planning, and Financial Management sources.

Planning can work with a number of ETL (extract-transform-load) and data relationship tools including ODI (Oracle Data Integrator), DIM (Data Integration Management, Informatica repackaged) and DRM (Data Relationship Management formerly known as Hyperion Master Data Management). Hyperion Application Link is a legacy tool that was used to build dimensions and load data to Planning applications in earlier versions of Planning.

"Huh?" Penny stares blankly at the consultants in what turns out to be a rather endearing way. "There are an amazing lot of moving pieces to Planning."

"Yes," The Translator smiles in a rather non-endearing way, "but don't worry. During the course of this musical/book, we'll go through each one of the components in much more detail. You'll be an expert in no time, singing the song of security management in Shared Services and dancing the dance of Planning administration via the web. Now that we've made it through some key terms and concepts for Planning, it is time to get your hands dirty and experience Hyperion Planning from the point of the view of the end user." The Translator turns with a familiar swoosh of his super cloak, covering his face, indicating the close of the scene.

Scene 3:
Plan Over the Web

After sitting through the first scene with The Translator, Penny is ready get into the details. How do users enter plans over the web? (No linked Excel spreadsheets? It is too good to be true.) The consultants jump into a detailed demonstration of the end user experience in Hyperion Planning to show Penny those details through the eyes of Eddie.

Note!

For the full blown end user experience, check out *Look Smarter Than You Are with Hyperion Planning: An End User's Guide*.

Note!

The steps in this section assume that you have set up the Planning Sample application. Instructions are included in Appendix A of this book.

THE PLANNING WEB CLIENT

As the name would imply, the Planning Web Client provides access to Planning via the Internet. This is great because it means that no matter what computer you're using, as long as there is an Internet connection to your company's Planning server you will always be able to access Planning. This is also bittersweet because, well... no matter what computer you're using, as long as there is an Internet connection you will always be able to access Planning. But you love not being able to escape your jobs and responsibilities, right?

Having constant access to Planning (providing the server doesn't go down) is possible because all the required Planning software resides on the server. The Web interface (Planning over the Internet) provides a massive advantage because it is possible to provide application access to many people in many locations without having to install any software on the client computers.

Alright, so we know that we'll be accessing Planning via a Web Client, but what's more important is what we'll be doing once we access Planning. So what types of actions do end users perform in this magical Planning Web Client? In a nutshell, you'll be using the Web Client to enter data, update and change data, run Business Rules and more. You will also use the Web Client to perform workflow tasks. We'll delve deeper into workflow later on, but for now just know that workflow is how we review and approve budgets.

There are two ways to access the Planning Web Client: via the Workspace and by directly logging into the Planning web client. Most companies utilize the Workspace because you can access multiple Planning and Financial Management applications, reports, dashboards, external content and much more all in one Workspace. If you log into the Planning web client, you can access that application only.

WHAT IS THE WORKSPACE?

Enterprise Performance Management (EPM) Workspace is the single place for you to access Oracle EPM content including Planning. Think of Workspace as Grand Central Station in New York...once you're there you can hop onto your train of choice and go straight to your destination: Planning applications, dashboards, reports, adhoc analysis and more. Right now, our destination is the Planning application.

Access the Planning Web Client via the Workspace

Logging on to Workspace and accessing the Planning Web Client is easy. The first step is to open up your Internet browser, such as Internet Explorer or Firefox.

1. Type in the following URL:
    http://*servername*:19000/workspace/

If you're not sure what the Workspace *servername* or the Workspace URL is, e-mail your Planning administrator and ask her very nicely to please provide you with the information you need.

Once you've entered the correct URL, the Workspace Log In page should pop up. It will look a little something like this:

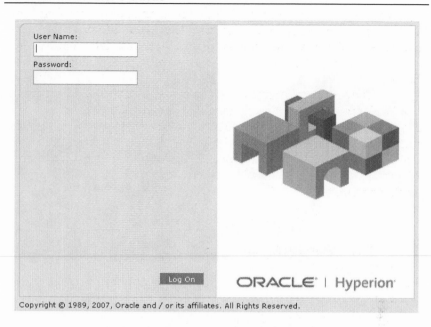

2. In the User Name text box, enter your system user ID.
3. In the Password text box, enter your system password.
4. Click Log On.

Excellent...you have just logged on to Workspace. From here you will access the Planning Application of your choosing.

To access a specific Planning application,

5. Select Navigate (steering wheel icon) >> Applications >> Planning >> application name. The applications you have access to are displayed. To follow along with this book, choose the Planning Sample application:

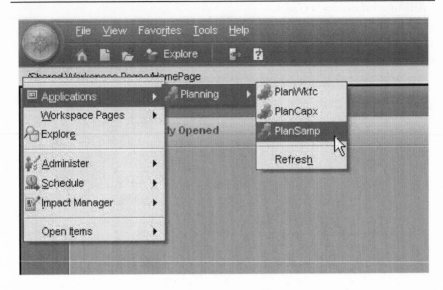

You can also access Planning directly instead of going through Workspace.

Access Planning Directly

To log on to Planning without going through the Workspace,
1. Type in the following URL:
    http://*servername*:8300/HyperionPlanning/LogOn.jsp
    The window below will pop up:

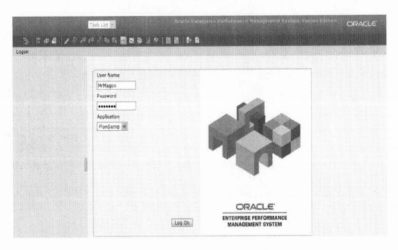

2. In the Application drop-down list, select the Hyperion Planning application with which you want to work:

3. In the User text box, enter your system user ID.
4. In the Password text box, enter your system password.
5. Click Log On.

Congratulations, because you're now the first person in your family who can access Planning via Workspace and directly. In a way, you're like Jackie Robinson and Neil Armstrong all rolled into one. Now that you've logged on to Planning by whichever means suited your fancy, it's now time to learn how to navigate your way around Planning.

On the left hand side of the screen, the *View Pane* displays the data forms and folders for the application:

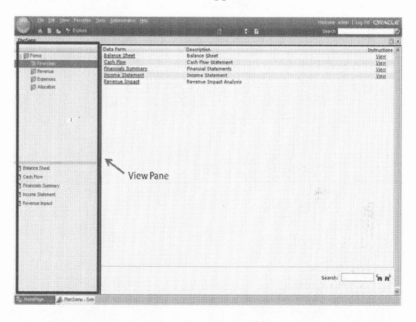

You can either show or hide the View Pane by clicking on View >> View Pane:

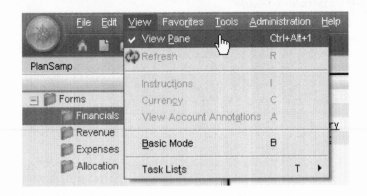

ADVANCED MODE VS. BASIC MODE

While you're hanging out in the *View* menu, notice that Planning has two modes: *Advanced Mode* and *Basic Mode*. At the moment, you're probably in Advanced Mode. In Planning you have an option of working in either mode.

How will you know when to work in which mode? When you want to work mainly with data forms and data form folders in a Windows-Explorer-type view, Advanced Mode is the best option. Use Basic Mode when you want to follow a guided step process using Task Lists.

To alternate between Advanced and Basic Mode click on View >> Advanced/Basic Mode:

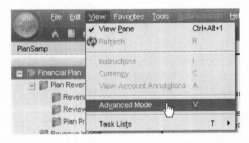

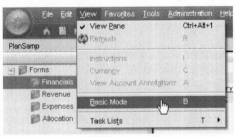

Go ahead and switch between Advanced Mode and Basic Mode and see how each mode looks different.

Did you notice the difference between the View Pane when you switched between the two modes? The process of opening data forms is different depending on whether you're in Advanced or Basic Mode.

To open a data form in Advanced Mode:

1. Click View >> Advanced Mode.
2. Expand the "Forms" folder and select the "Financials" folder.
3. To open up the Balance Sheet data form you can select it in the View Pane or by selecting Balance Sheet from the main Data Form page:

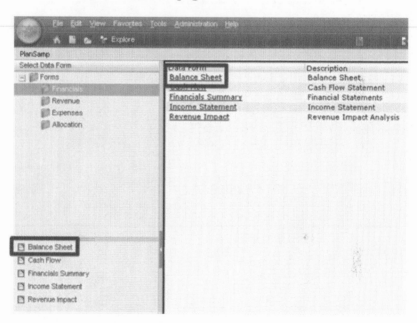

The form will open and that's all there is to it!

Note!   As the administrator, you will primarily work in Advanced Mode.

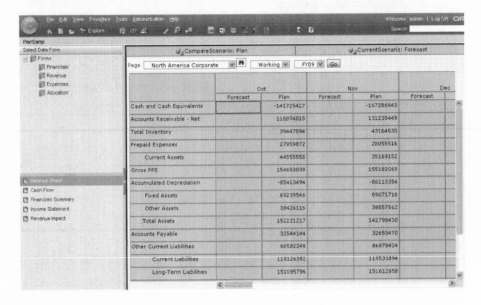

To open a data form while in Basic Mode:
1. Click on View >> Basic Mode.
2. Select the Financial Plan task list from the View Pane.
    This will give you an overview of the Task List.
3. Select View Task List to view the Task List:

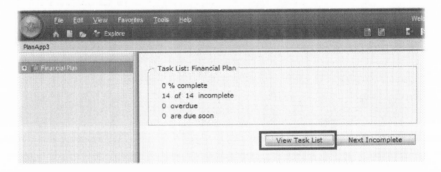

You are brought to the Task List where you can see what percentage of your tasks have been completed, how many tasks are still remaining, and the number of tasks overdue or due soon. From here we see that nothing has been completed yet (assuming you are accessing the task list for the first time). Quickly, before anyone realizes you haven't done anything:
4. Click on the Revenue Assumptions folder in the View Pane:

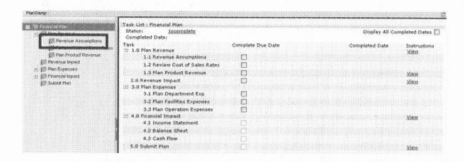

As expected, the Revenue Assumptions data form opens:

Page MA ▾	Plan ▾	Working ▾	FY09 ▾	Units ▾ Go				
	Jan	Feb	Mar	Q1	Apr	May	Jun
Bookshelf Audio System	7386	8182	8869	24437	6246	7170	9371
Home Theater Audio System	3682	3134	3587	10403	2622	2886	5453
Personal Audio							
Boom Box	38607	32768	34186	105561	29858	29727	48365
Personal CD Player	12303	10415	13163	35881	11930	9470	15162
MP3 Player	7185	10402	10599	28186	10945	11970	12587
DVD Player	19707	18572	13575	51854	16418	23926	28758

Opening data forms is easy. Entering data in data forms is just as easy.

ENTER PLAN DATA

Before we enter data, let us review some of the data form components:

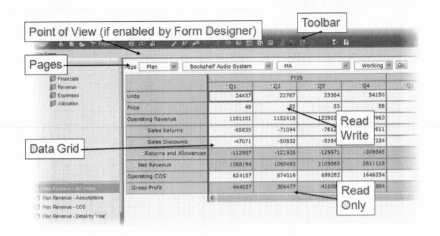

A data form will contain one or more dimensions in the rows and columns of the form. You may see a list of members or a hierarchy of members that you can collapse or expand. The Plan Revenue – All Years data form has Fiscal Year and Period in the columns of the data form and Accounts in the rows. Notice that you can expand and collapse the hierarchies for both Period and Accounts within this data form, allowing you to view and plan data at a summary or detailed level.

Not much unlike your mother, a data form has a Point of View, except that in Planning, the Point of View on a form is a fixed set of members for dimensions that are not in the Page, Rows or Columns. For example, if the data form should always use the Budget scenario, you will probably add it to the Point of View. You can't change Point of View (often called POV, for short) selections.

A data form may also contain one or more Page drop down boxes. A Page component is a drop down list of members from a dimension. In the Plan Revenue – All Years data form, the Page dimensions include: Scenario, Segment, Entity, and Version. You as the end user and star of a hit musical can choose the desired member from the Page drop down and select the *Go* button to refresh the form. If the Page drop down contains a long list of members, a search icon resembling a pair of binoculars will display allowing you to search for a desired member.

Once you've selected the page options, you are ready to enter data into valid data cells by typing some numbers (or in some cases, text) into the data form.

You will see that there are three primary types of cells in a data form, each indicated by a different shade of color.

White Cells	Valid data cells available for input.
Yellow Cells	"Dirty" cells; A cell that is "dirty" indicates that data has been changed but not saved.
Green/Gray Cells	Read-only cells. You cannot edit or input data into these cells.

Open up the Revenue Assumptions data form and practice entering some data (follow along with us). In our example, there is no data in the "Personal Audio" row under "Jan" (Row 4, Column 1).

1. Type "25", press Tab (or click on another cell) and you'll see a few things happen.

Notice how the color of the cell changed? This change from white (well, more of a cream color, but let's just call it white) to yellow means that the cell is now a dirty, little cell. Another thing that you should have noticed is that the number "25" now appears under "Q1".

2. Type in "50" for "Feb" of the "Personal Audio" row and you'll see Q1's total add up to "75" automatically:

Simple enough, right? What do you think would happen if we manually entered a number under Q1 when there was no data for Jan, Feb, and Mar? Let's try it.

3. Delete your data for Jan and Feb by selecting each respective cell and pressing either 'backspace' or 'delete' on your keyboard.

4. Type "120" under "Personal Audio", "Q1". Planning is smart enough to divide it up equally between the three months:

This is called time spreading. We'll discuss spreading capabilities in more detail shortly.

A quick note on navigating the data forms: if you want to move horizontally, say from "Jan" to "Feb" to "Mar" while in the same row, then press *Tab*. If you want to move vertically, say down the month of Jan for each row, then press *Enter*. Tab moves you from left to right, and Enter moves you from top to bottom.

You've seen how to enter numerical values but does Planning allow the data entry for text values? Yes, in two different ways enabled by the Planning Administrator.

Enter Smart List Data

You can choose text values from predefined drop down lists within a data form. These predefined lists are called Smart Lists and are created by the Planning Administrator. See the example below where Eddie can identify the Sales Risk as Low, Medium or High for products by region:

| Page | MA ⌄ | Sales_Risk ⌄ | FY10 ⌄ | Go |

	Jan	Feb	Mar	Apr	
Bookshelf Audio System	Low				
Home Theater Audio System	Low				
⁻Home Audio					
Personal Audio	Low				
Boom Box	High				
Personal CD Player	High				
MP3 Player	Low ⌄				
⁻Audio on the Go	High Medium **Low**				
⁻Audio Systems					

You can use Smart List values in Business Rules and in reports.

Enter Text and Dates

You can also enter free form text values or dates in data forms if enabled by the Planning Administrator. Simply type in the empty cell. Be aware, keep it brief because display options aren't that great for text cells:

| Page | MA ⌄ | Sales Manager ⌄ | FY10 ⌄ | Go |

	Jan	Feb	Mar	Apr	
Bookshelf Audio System	Bob				
Home Theater Audio System	Bob				
⁻Home Audio					
Personal Audio	Larry				
Boom Box	Larry				
Personal CD Player	Junior				
MP3 Player	Junior				
⁻Audio on the Go					

Tip! Leave the essays at home. Text cells are not the right place for the novel you always been meaning to right. Text cells are for short bits of information

Refresh a Data Form

Let's face it, we've all made mistakes. What if you enter data but you don't want to save what you've done? Should you delete all of the values that you typed in? Try this and notice how the cells are still marked as "dirty" even though we deleted all of the data. If you want to make these cells "clean" again or go back to the original data values in the form without saving, you need to refresh the data form.

To refresh a data form (and not save data changes),

1. Click on View >> Refresh:

A warning will pop up telling you that you're about to lose any unsaved data. Go ahead and click *OK* and the data form should look as good as new (making your mistakes something you'll have to live with but thankfully, no one else will).

Save a data form

To save data, all you need to do is click on File >> Save:

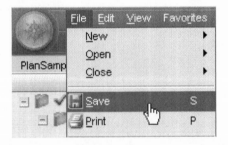

In general, Save will recalculate the form's subtotals and possibly run Business Rules associated to the form (this depends on how you design the form). If you have changed data and you try to leave the form without saving, you will receive a prompt to save. Click "OK" to save, "Cancel" to discard.

View Instructions

Now before you get as excited as a planner in heat looking for every white cell you can find to enter data, it might help to have some instructions on what to do. As the Planning Administrator, you may want to include some instructions as a guide to help end users prepare the budget data. To view Instructions, select View >> Instructions:

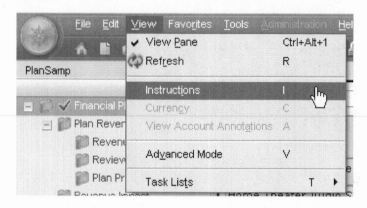

1. Open the Plan Revenue – All Years data form.
2. Select View>>Instructions to view the data form instructions.

Logging Off

When you've had enough of all this Planning nonsense and you're ready to log off here's how you do it:
1. *Select File >> Log Off.*

Planning will try and make you second guess yourself by asking if you're sure you want to log off. Don't let it get the best of you with its Jedi minds tricks. Just click *Yes.*

Penny is excited about the possibilities but is a bit concerned about all of the different data forms, rules, dependencies and due dates that will need to be completed to create the overall budget. This is going to be way to confusing for some of her less intelligent users. She needs the budgeting steps to be easy-peasy with no confusion. Eddie's forgiveness is at stake.

SuperManager, capable of reading minds, reads Penny's thoughts. (Did she really just think "easy-peasy"?) "Penny," SuperManager proudly says in a deep booming voice, hands on his hips and chest puffed out in superhero fashion. "I'm here to save you yet again. Oracle Hyperion Planning has a feature called Task Lists that lets you define important steps and due dates in the planning process. We wouldn't want Eddie to get confused in the planning process and miss the budget deadline," SuperManager chuckles (for no apparent reason).

USE TASK LISTS

As it is with most things in life, a little bit of guidance and help can go a long way. We've already seen that data form instructions help you in your Planning process. Think of task lists as having your own personal tour guide through the budgeting and forecasting process.

The wizard-like task list will itemize the steps users need to complete as they work through the budget. It even has helpful instructions and due dates for those who do not spend their entire lives strapped to a computer doing budgeting. Administrators and interactive users can create and manage tasks and task lists. There are quite a number of tasks that a task list can contain:

- Data Forms - This task opens up a data form where you can change and add data.
- Business Rules - This task list launches a Business Rule.
- Link to Workflow - This will take you to Workflow, where you can review and approve plans.
- URL - This task opens up a specified web address. You may need to go to another website to access tools for the planning process.
- Descriptive - This task provides a description of what you need to do in the planning process.

Whether you're in Advanced or Basic Mode you'll be able to access task lists, albeit slightly differently depending on the mode. We'll walk through the task list experience from Basic mode using the Planning Sample task list, Financial Plan.

Task Lists in Basic Mode

To use a Task List in Basic Mode:

1. If you're currently in Advanced Mode, go ahead and switch back to Basic Mode (View >> Basic).
2. Click on View >> Task Lists and you will see an option to select either Task List, Report or Status:

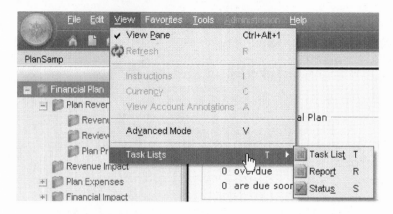

3. Select *Task List.*

This brings you to the Task List summary view where you see the listed task list steps, their status (complete or incomplete), due date, completed date, and any defined instructions:

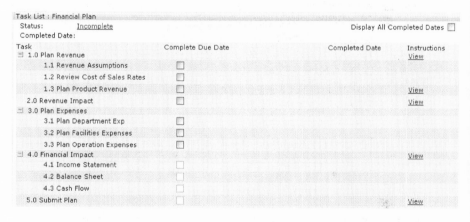

According to the task list pictured above no one at the company is very productive because not a single item has been completed (note that this is not representative of your company, we're sure). Let's work on completing a task - entering Revenue Assumptions - so you can meet the budget deadline and not get fired.

4. Look over at the View Pane (if you don't see it, click View >> View Pane) and select the Revenue Assumptions data form (step 1 in the Financial Plan task list):

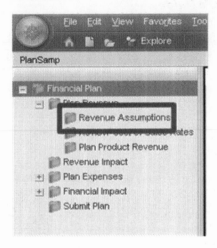

5. Click the "Personal Audio" cell for "Jan", type in "500" and press Enter:

Page	MA		Plan	Working	FY09	Units	Go
		Jan	Feb	Mar	−Q1	Apr	
Bookshelf Audio System		7386	8182	8869	24437	6246	
Home Theater Audio System		3682	3134	3587	10403	2622	
Personal Audio		500			500		

6. Save your work by either clicking File >> Save, or by clicking the "Save" icon (it's the one shaped like a floppy disk because, well, back in some other century people used those for saving data) on the toolbar at the top of the screen:

You are almost done; just one last step.

7. See the little "complete" check box at the bottom left hand of the screen? Check that:

Now go back to the Task List so you can show the CFO that you are making progress in the budget. (This is job security we're talking here, people.) You can always navigate your way back to the task list summary view by one of the following methods:

8. Click on View >> Task Lists >> Task List
    OR
    Use a shortcut and click on the "Task List" icon from the toolbar.

Once you're back at our Task List you see that Revenue Assumptions is listed as complete and if you click on "Display All Completed Dates" it will inform you of the date and time that the task was completed:

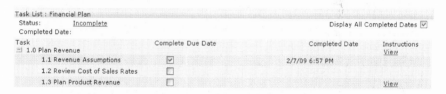

If you want a summarized status of the tasks that have been completed, the tasks that are overdue, and the tasks that are due soon, look at the Task Status.

To view the Task Status,

1. Click View >> Task List >> Status.
    OR
    Click the "Status" icon from the toolbar:

The Task List Summary status will display, showing you the percent complete, number of incomplete tasks, number of overdue tasks, and number of tasks with upcoming due dates:

Task List: Financial Plan

7 % complete
13 of 14 incomplete
0 overdue
0 are due soon

| View | Next |

Now that you've saved your job and mastered Task Lists in Basic Mode, it's time to learn about accessing and using Task Lists in Advanced Mode.

USE RIGHT-CLICK MENUS

Like any good Windows application, Planning can provide context-sensitive right-click menus based on where you're right-clicking. In addition to task lists, the Planning Administrator (you, assumedly) may design some custom right-click menus to help guide you through the planning process. Right-click menus are assigned form by form and can contain tasks like opening data forms, launching Business Rules, and navigating to Workflow.

To access a right-click menu, simply right-click (tricky, so you might want to bookmark this page for future reference) in the row or column members and choose a menu option. Let's check out the menu provided in our Planning Sample application.

1. Open the Plan Revenue – All Years data form from the Plan Revenue folder in the View Pane.

2. Right-click in the form and note the two custom menu options - Revenue Assumptions and Cost of Sales Rate:

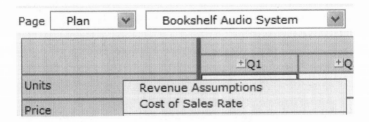

Both menu options will open another data form.

3. Select Revenue Assumptions and the data form will open.

Penny thanks SuperManager for his help with Task Lists and right-click menus. SuperManager says, "Penny, you can now handle Planning all by yourself for the rest of time with no people to support you," and then attempts to fly out a window only to realize that his superpowers apparently due not extend beyond Hyperion and into the world of flying. "I, uh, meant to do that," he says, falling out the window onto the ground below. "But before I leave, I should tell you about adjusting and spreading."

ADJUST AND SPREAD

Have you ever finished your budget only to be told by someone above you in the org chart that you need to increase revenue or decrease expenses?   Rather than go back to the beginning every time you need to revise, Planning provides the ability to adjust data in cells by either a specific amount or a percentage. You can adjust one cell or multiple cells. Let's go through a quick example:

1.   Navigate to the Revenue Assumptions data form.
2.   Set your Page selections to the following members (MA, Plan, Working, FY09):

3.   Select the "Bookshelf Audio System" cell for the month of "Jan".
4.   Select Edit >> Adjust. This will bring up the Adjust Data window:

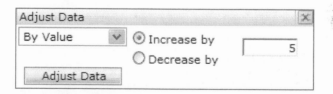

You have the option to increase or decrease the data by a specific amount or by a percentage.

5.   Keep the "Increase by" button and "By Value" option, selected, but change the value from "5" to "20" and then click Adjust Data:

	Jan	Feb	Mar	⁻Q1
Bookshelf Audio System	7406	8182	8869	24457
Home			3587	10403
Pers				
Boon			34186	105561
Pers			13163	35881

Adjust Data ☒

By Value ▾   ⦿ Increase by   [20]
             ◯ Decrease by

[Adjust Data]

You'll see the amount for Jan and Q1 increase by 20.

What if you made a mistake and want to go back to the original data set before you adjusted? To undo what you just did, all you have to do is refresh the page. Do this by either clicking View >> Refresh or by using the shortcut Refresh icon.

> 6. Go ahead and click Refresh. A window will appear asking if you're sure you want to do this and lose any unsaved data.
>
> 7. Click OK.

If you're worrying about how long it will take to adjust each cell individually, relax. It is possible to adjust multiple cells or data values at once. Just highlight multiple cells before selecting adjust data.

Time Spreading

As we mentioned earlier, Time Spreading allows you to enter data at a summary level (like at the quarter- or year-level) and then have Planning automatically push the data down to the time periods underneath. Let's explore time spreading in more detail than we did under the Enter Data section.

While working in a data form, you can:

- Spread the value in a summary time period back to its base time periods.
- Spread values among members based on the proportional values of existing data.
- Spread values based on a calendar's weekly distribution in a quarter: 4-4-5, 5-4-4, 4-5-4, or None (this depends on how the Planning Administrator set up the application)

To spread, or distribute, data based on the Periods dimension:

> 1. On the data entry form, select the cell for the summary time period whose new value you want to spread.

2. Enter the new value.
3. When you leave the cell, the new values should spread
   to the time periods beneath the summary time period.

So how will the data values spread? It depends on the type
of account or measure for which you are planning. For Revenue,
Expense, and Saved Assumption Accounts (Flow), values entered at
upper levels are spread to the children based on a percentage of the
values already there. It sort of goal seeks, in a way. If there are no
existing values, values are spread evenly or based on weekly
seasonal distributions (4-4-5, 5-4-4, 4-5-4).

For Asset, Liability, Equity Accounts, and Saved
Assumption with Time Balance First, values entered at upper levels
are placed in the first child. Other children remain unchanged. For
example, if you change Qtr 1 from 30 to 50, January will change to
50. February and March will remain unchanged. If there are no
existing   values   in   any   of   a   member's
children,   values   entered   at   upper   levels   will   be   placed
in all children.

For Asset, Liability, Equity, and Saved Assumption
Accounts with Time Balance (Last), values entered at upper levels
are placed in the last child. Other children remain unchanged. For
example, if you change Qtr 1 from 30 to 50, March will change to 50.
January and February will remain unchanged. If there are no
existing   values   in   any   of   a   member's
children,   values   entered   at   upper   levels   will   be   placed
in all children.

Let's see an example of Time Spreading in action. Notice
below we have October through December, rolling up to Q4.

Oct	Nov	Dec	Q4
10,000	2,500	2,500	15,000

Next we type 20,000 into Q4. The values are spread back
based on existing data distribution in the first row of the data form.

Oct	Nov	Dec	−Q4
13,333	3,333	3,333	20,000
44	44	44	44

Now you try it!

1. Open the Plan Revenue – Assumptions data form.
2. Set your Page selections to the following members: MA, Plan, Working, FY09.
3. Select the cell for "Q1", "Personal Audio".
4. Type in "3000".

Notice "3000" is split evenly for the three months that roll up to Q1.

5. Select the cell for "Q1", "Bookshelf Audio System".
6. Type in "30,000".

Notice "30,000" is split proportionally based on the existing data values.

7. Select File >> Save to save the data form.

You can temporarily lock a cell so that it is not impacted by spreading (Planning will ignore the locked cell or cells) by selecting Edit >> Lock Cells.

Note!

Months that have already been locked by administrators cells with supporting detail, and other read-only cells will also be skipped.

You've seen some cool capabilities in spreading values over Time but what about spreading over other dimensions like Entity or Product? What about spreading over both Entity and Product? Assuming you're on Planning 9.3.1 or later, you have two alternatives: Grid Spreader and Mass Allocate.

Grid Spread

Have you ever wanted to go to the bottom-right cell of a spreadsheet, update Net Income to be a bit higher, and have your spreadsheet automatically spread the change back throughout the spreadsheet? The Grid Spread feature allows you to do exactly that.

Grid Spread allows you to increase or decrease numbers throughout your form no matter from what dimension they're derived and it takes into consideration the data values already present. When using Grid Spread, the calculations are performed right then and there on your computer (the client), and you're able to see the calculation results so you can decide whether to save or not to save (to paraphrase Hamlet).

Grid Spread is enabled on a form by form basis:

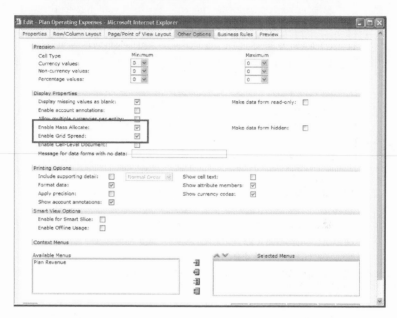

There are three types of spreads: Regular, Chunky, and Extra Creamy. Wait, those are for peanut butter. There are three types of *Grid* Spreads: Proportional Spread, Even-Split, and Fill.

A proportional spread divides data across members and dimensions in proportion to the values that are already there. The best way to understand this is with an example.

Mr. Anachronism says to Penny mysteriously, "I see in the future a new initiative to further rollout Oracle EPM to the other North American business units. All powerful, all knowing, impotent consultants..."

The Translator interrupts, "I think the word you're looking for there is 'omnipotent.' Impotent does now mean what you think it means."

Not having majored in Communications, Mr. Anachronism chooses to trust The Translator on this one, so he corrects himself, "All powerful, all knowing, *omni*potent consultants will be brought in to assist with the implementation. To pay for this, Consulting Services will need to increase in the month of January for the great liberal state of Massachusetts. Oh, and one day, many years away, they'll actually elect a republican senator. No, I'm serious. They will."

To budget for Mr. Anachronism's vision:

1. Open the Plan Operating Expenses data form within the Expenses folder.
2. Set your page options to the following members (MA, Working, Plan, FY09):

3. Select the cell for "Consulting Services", "Jan". (But it is greyed out, you cry in angst! Just select it.)
4. Select Edit >> Grid Spread.
5. The first item we see, "Cell Value: 12,620" shows us the cell value that we selected prior to opening the Grid Spread option.
6. Look at the "Adjust Data" section next. Adjust the data "By Value", Increase by "3000":

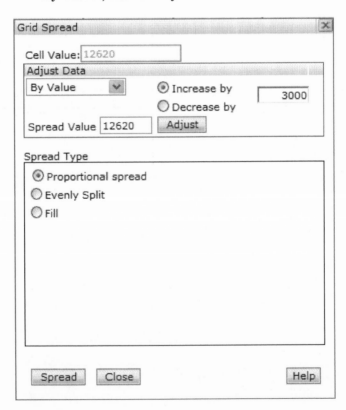

7. Click Adjust, which updates the Spread Value from "12,620" to "15,620".

8. Select the Spread Type Proportional Spread and then click Spread:

Page MA ▼		Working ▼	Plan ▼	FY09 ▼ Go
	Jan	Feb	Mar	Q1	Apr
Individual Contractors	4934	2367	1404	8705	
Consulting Firms	10686	5201	2786	18673	
Consulting Services	12620	7568	4190	24378	
Advertising					
Promotions					
Advertising and Public Relations					
R&D: Consulting					
R&D: Materials					
External R&D					
R&D: Internal Labor					
R&D: Internal Materials					
Internal R&D					
Engineering Expense					

Grid Spread ⊠

Cell Value: 12620

Adjust Data

By Value ▼   ⊙ Increase by   [3000]
               ○ Decrease by

Spread Value [15620]   [Adjust]

Spread Type
⊙ Proportional spread
○ Evenly Split
○ Fill

You'll now see the data in your data form change in proportion to each cell's previous value.

9. Select File >> Save to save the data form. This step is also necessary to correctly calculate the summary values on the sheet like Consulting Services

Voila! You accomplished in seconds what would have taken some serious building and modeling time using Excel functions. Let's next take a look at how Grid Spreader can evenly spread values.

Note! Like Time Spreading, Grid Spread will skip read only cells, locked cells and cells with supporting detail.

Performing an even split causes the values to be split evenly among the target cells. Follow along with our example.

1. If necessary, open the Plan Operating Expenses data form.

2. Set your page options to the members MA, Working, Plan, FY09.

3. Select the cell for "Consulting Services", "Jan".
4. Select Edit >> Grid Spread.
5. The first item we see, "Cell Value: 15,620," notifies us of the cell that we selected prior to opening the Grid Spread option.
6. Type "10,000" directly in the Spread Value text box.
7. Select the Even Split and then click Spread:

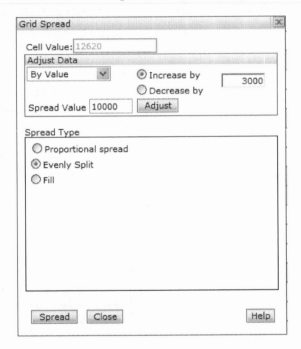

Notice the values "5000" are entered into both Individual Contractors and Consulting Firms cells for Jan.

8. Select File >> Save. The total for Consulting Services now equals "10,000".

	Jan
Individual Contractors	5000
Consulting Firms	5000
−|Consulting Services	10000

With spreading options like this, could budgeting get any easier?

Mass Allocate

But what if you want to spread your data far and wide including to cells in the database not even shown in the form? The answer is in Mass allocate which, while similar to Grid Spread in that you can spread data across one or more dimensions, is far more powerful. Unlike Grid Spread where the spreading is limited to what you see on the form itself, Mass Allocate creates a Business Rule that runs behind the scenes on the Essbase server.

Data will automatically spread (no chance to view ahead of time before saving). The grid is reloaded and the result is presented to the end user. Allocation options available for Mass Allocate include proportional, relational spread, fill, and even split.

To use Mass Allocate:

1. Put the cursor in the source cell containing the value you wish to allocate to lower level cells.
2. Select Edit >> Mass Allocate.
3. Options:
    a. Increase or decrease values by a specified amount with Adjust.
    b. Increase or decrease values by a specified percentage with Adjust.
    c. Replace values with a new value by entering it in the Spread Value text box.
4. Choose Spread Type - Proportional, Relational, Evenly split, or Fill:

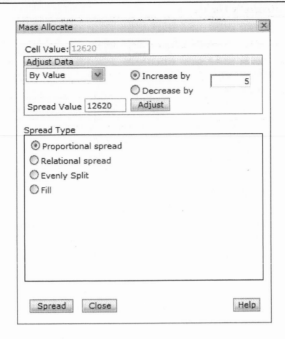

5. Click Spread.

Sharp-eyed readers will notice that Mass Allocate offers a fourth type of spreading that Grid Spread does not. The Relational Spread type allows you to spread data based on data in another member. For example, you want to plan for an expense of $50,000 at a corporate level but then allocate it down to business units based not on plan, but rather on last year's actual revenue. Relational spread is the way to do this. You will define a source member and relative member when using relational.

In order to use Mass Allocate, the Planning Administrator must assign end users a Mass Allocate role in security since allocating numbers throughout an application is considered a powerful job indeed. We wouldn't users wandering off, mass allocating willy-nilly. Here's what that role looks like in Shared Services:

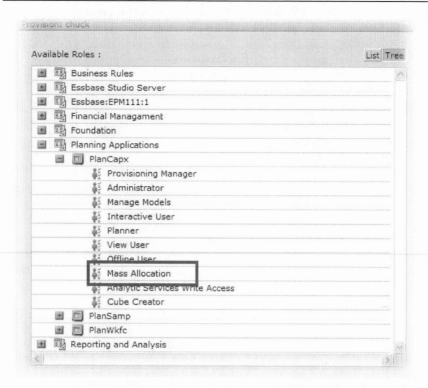

Like Grid Spread, Mass Allocate is also enabled on a form by form basis:

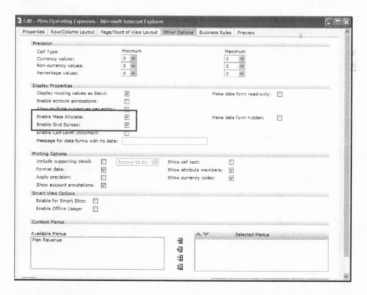

We enabled Mass Allocate for the Plan Operating Expenses data form and assigned the Mass Allocate role for the Planning Sample application (you can do the same to follow along with us; for the detailed steps check out the appendix).

To spread data using Mass Allocate,

1. Open the Plan Operating Expenses data form.
2. Set your page options to the members MA, Working, Plan, FY09.
3. Select the cell for "Consulting Services", "Jan".
4. Select Edit >> Mass Allocate.
5. The first item we see, "Cell Value: 10,000" shows us the cell that we selected prior to opening the Mass Allocate option.
6. Type "8000" directly in the Spread Value text box.
7. Select Relational Spread.

In real life we would most likely choose Actual, Final, FY08 as the relative members for spreading.

Spread Type

Currency	Local	Local	
Segments	NoSegment	NoSegment	
Entity	E01_101_1110	E01_101_1110	
Version	Working	Final	
Scenario	Plan	Actual	
Year	FY09	FY08	
Account	506100	506100	
Period	Jan	Jan	

Evenly Split

Sadly, the sample data in the Planning sample application contains just a sample of the data we need to allocate correctly. To make the spreading actually work, we're going to have to choose some other members to run through the steps.

8. Select the relative members for spreading (Plan, Final, FY09).
9. Click Spread.

The data is automatically spread and saved to the underlying Essbase database:

| Page | MA | ▼ | ⋈ | Working ▼ | Plan ▼ | FY09 ▼ | Go |

	Jan	Feb	Mar	=(
Individual Contractors	2527	2367	1404	
Consulting Firms	5473	5201	2786	
=Consulting Services	8000	7568	4190	

Rules for Mass Allocate

- Allocates data to all the source cell's descendants
- Allocates across multiple dimensions
- Spreads data even to cells not displayed on the data form
- Does not require that you have access to the target cells
- Cannot be undone after you mass allocate values
- Can use customized spreading patterns, created by an administrator
- Must be enabled on a form
- Must assign separate role in Shared Services for Mass Allocate

Note!

Planning provides powerful features for analyzing and budgeting scenarios. But what if end users need to document their assumptions? Surely Planning can do this.

"Planning provides a number of features to attach supporting information or commentary, add additional line item details, and provide notes and comments to the plan," says Mr. Anachronism before Penny can even ask (because he knew she was going to ask it one day). "Let's now take a look at data form attachments, supporting detail, cell text, and some other stuff I just know is going to impress you."

ATTACH DOCUMENTS TO DATA FORMS

Sometimes you have some supporting information outside of Planning and you'd like to attach those documents to your planning data. Beginning in Planning 11, you can attach documents to cells on a form. Items you can attach include existing Financial Reporting reports and books, Web Analysis documents, Answers queries and Dashboards, Word documents, Excel spreadsheets, and

PDFs. The Planning Administrator must enable attachments for data forms (on a form by form basis).

We'll walk through a basic example to show you how to attach documents in Planning. We've enabled the data form Plan Department Expenses to allow attachments:

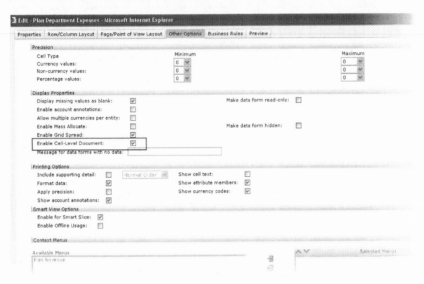

To attach a document to a data form,
1. Log into the Workspace or, if you are already logged in, click on Explore to navigate to the Workspace repository (this is where most of your reports, queries and other documents are housed for reporting and analysis).
2. Select File >> Import >> File:

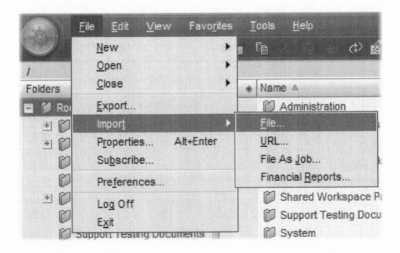

3. Browse and select the desired file to import (we created a dummy Excel spreadsheet called Travel Detail Expense Plan.xlsx):

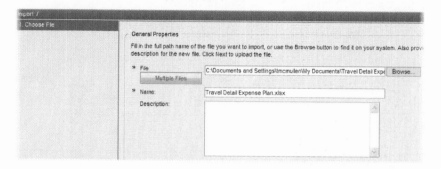

4. Click Next.
5. Optional: Set any advanced properties for the imported file such as keywords for searching:

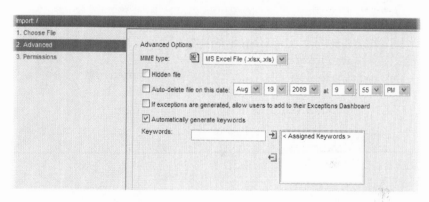

6. Click Next.
7. Optional: Assign any permissions for the file:

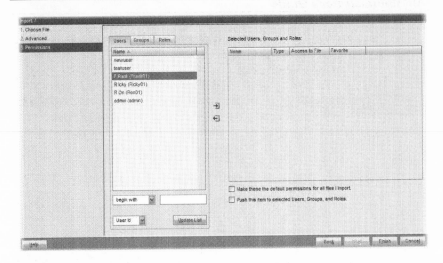

8. Click Finish.
9. From the Navigation icon, click Applications>> Planning>> Planning Sample (the name of your Planning Sample Application) to navigate back to the Planning application or, if you already have the application open, simply click the tab for that application.
10. Open the Plan Department Expenses data form and right-click on the cell for "YearTotal", "Travel Expenses" to show the Add/Edit Document option:

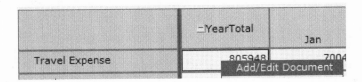

11. Highlight and click on Add/Edit Document and a dialog box will appear.
12. Click on the magnifying glass icon to select a document from Workspace to attach:

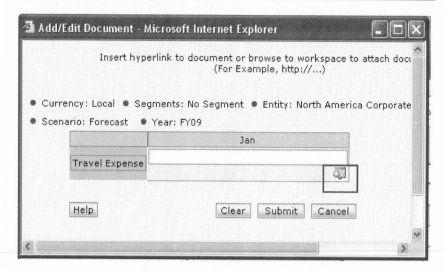

13. Locate the Travel Detail Expense Plan.xlsx in the Workspace repository, select it, and click *OK*:

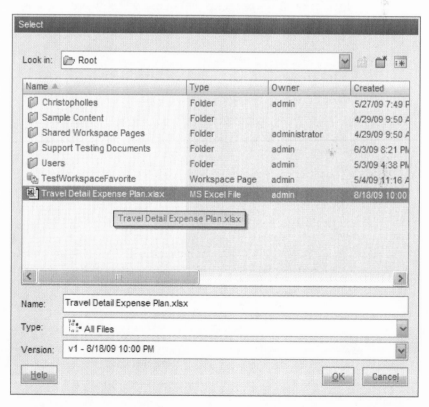

14. After the hyperlink from the Workspace is inserted, click Submit:

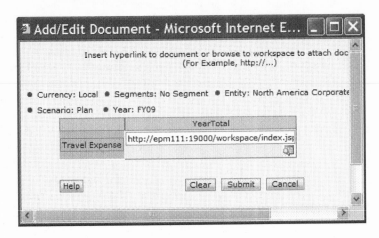

15. A small icon will appear at the right hand corner of the cell to indicate an attached document. It's supposed to look like a paper clip (if paper clips were basically square):

	⁻⁾YearTotal
Travel Expense	805948
Meals Expense	48607
⁻⁾Travel	854555

16. Right-click on the icon and select Open Document:

	⁻⁾YearTotal	Jan	F
Travel Expense	805948	70045	
Meals Expense	48607	Add/Edit Document	
⁻⁾Travel	854555	Open Document 74375	

Since our attached document was an imported Excel file, Microsoft Excel will launch and you will be prompted to open the file. If the document you attach is a Financial Reporting report or other EPM document, the document opens within the Oracle EPM Workspace as another tab.

ADD SUPPORTING DETAILS

What you shouldn't do is come up with your budget outside of Planning and then copy the summary values in. If you want to show where a summary number comes from, Supporting Detail in Planning lets you list out your assumptions and drivers you use to calculate the required number on the form.

Some people refer to Supporting Detail as "line item detail" because it allows end users to provide detail below the bottom-level in the Planning model. For example, there may be an account called Travel and you want to include details for each trip that makes up the travel account. You can build a hierarchy of supporting detail under a cell or cells using different methods for aggregation (+ - * / ~). Cells with supporting detail will be shaded a deep blue color.

To access Supporting Detail, select the desired cell or grouping of cells in a single row and select Edit >> Supporting Detail from the menu.

To enter support detail:

1. Select the cell or cells within the data form to add supporting detail.
2. Select Edit >> Supporting Detail:

3. Add or type a description (up to 1500 characters) for each line within the supporting detail.
4. Use the buttons to create or change multiple lines of supporting detail. Hierarchies of members can be

created using the buttons Add Child, Add Sibling, Move, Delete, Delete All, Promote, Demote, Move Up, Move Down, Duplicate Row and Fill:

5. Set mathematical operators for each line.
6. Type the data value to set or calculate.
7. Click Save.

"Penny, I see in Eddie's future a trip to the annual Budgeteer's Conference in Las Vegas (Vegas, baby!)," Mr. Anachronism says. He closes his eyes and grimaces a moment. "There's more... it is a bit foggy since this vision really should be staying in Vegas, but during the conference, I see you entering a cheesy Las Vegas style wedding chapel. Elvis is standing before you holding a bible. Near him is someone in a tuxedo. It's ..."

Penny knocks over her coffee nervously, the hot liquid spilling next to Mr. Anachronism, breaking his trance. "So what you are saying is that Eddie needs to add detail behind the travel expenses for any upcoming business trips, documenting airfare, lodging, meals, etc.?"

"Yes," Mr. Anachronism grumbles as he wipes the coffee off his cloak. "if the Planning application doesn't have members to do so, he will need to use supporting detail. And going forward, please don't surprise me while I'm seeing the future."

To practice entering Supporting Detail:
1. Open the Plan Department Expenses data form.
2. Select the following page options (MA, Working, Plan, FY09):

Notice that if you are following along with the book exercises, your page selections "remember" your last selection.
3. Select the cells for "Jan", "Feb", and "March" for "Travel Expenses".
4. Select Edit >> Supporting Detail. The Supporting Detail window will display:

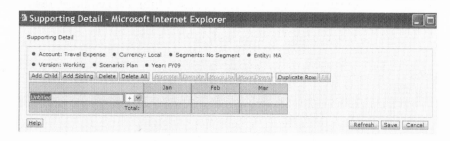

5. In the first line, type in "Airfare" and set the consolidation to "+".
6. Click Add Sibling.
7. In the second line, type "Lodging" and set the consolidation to "+".
8. Click Add Sibling.
9. In the third line, type "Other Travel" and set the consolidation to "+".
10. Click Add Child.
11. In the fourth line, type "Rental Car" and set the consolidation to "+".
12. Click Add Sibling.
13. In the fifth line, type "Miscellaneous" and set the consolidation to "+".
14. Next add the data values for each line for Jan, Feb and Mar:

		Jan	Feb	Mar
Airfare	+ ⌄	8000	6000	2000
Lodging	+ ⌄	8000	5000	1000
Other Travel	+ ⌄	2500	1500	700
Rental Car	+ ⌄	2000	1000	500
Miscellaneous	+ ⌄	1000	500	200
	Total:	18500	12500	3700

Notice how the line items for Rental Car and Miscellaneous roll up to total Other Travel and then into a total for all the lines. The numbers in the Total line are what will be stored back in the Essbase database.

15. Click Save.

The data is saved and the data form is refreshed, displaying blue cells to indicate supporting detail.

(i) The data has been saved. [x]

| Page | MA | ✓ [M] | Working ✓ | Plan ✓ | FY09 ✓ Go |

	−YearTotal	Jan	Feb	Mar	−Q1
Travel Expense	374162	19000	12500	3700	35200
Meals Expense	97475	8557	5060	3053	16670
−Travel	471637	27557	17560	6753	51870

Keep the following tips in mind when using supporting detail: 1) the underlying Essbase database, dimensions and members do not change; 2) supporting detail can be added to both target and bottom up versions; 3) you can copy supporting detail from multiple cells in Excel or other applications and paste into the Supporting Detail dialog box; and 4) unfortunately there is no way to upload supporting detail.

ADD CELL TEXT

Once in a while, you'll want to comment on an individual value in your form. Maybe a variance is off and you want to explain why or maybe you've up your travel for January to $2000 and you need to explain why "Going to Cabo" is a legitimate business expense.

Cell Text lets you add commentary to your plan. Cell-level text comments can be added to any intersection at any level in a data form.

To enter cell text, you must have at least read access to the cell. All users who have read access to the cell can read the cell text comment. The cell text can be printed within the data form and is also available in Financial Reporting reports using the Planning ADM driver.

To enter a cell text comment:
1. Open the Plan Department Expenses data form.
2. Select the following page options (MA, Working, Plan, FY09):
3. Select a cell or range of continuous cells; for this example select "Travel Expenses", "YearTotal".
4. Select Edit > Cell Text:

5. Type the text up to 1500 characters.

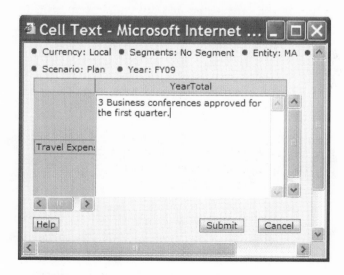

6. Click *Submit*.

The cell text is attached to the cell and is noted with a triangle in the upper right hand corner:

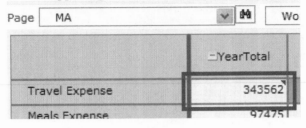

To view the cell text, simply select Edit >> Cell Text.

Keep cell text comments as short as possible (they will display better for printing and reports).

Tip! Define standards for all planners for where cell text comments will be posted (e.g. post at YearTotal vs. individual months).

ADD ACCOUNT ANNOTATIONS

Another text option the Planning administrator may use is account annotations. Account annotations are a way for you, the end user, to add text descriptions or comments to accounts if you want to customize the account to your specific needs. The main consideration is that the same account annotation will display for all dimensions except entity, scenario, and version, also known as the planning unit. The account annotations can vary by planning

Note! Account Annotations are rarely used. We're only showing you them since you'll probably run into them on the menu at some point and wonder "What If?"

unit.

The Planning Administrator will enable account annotations by data form. To use account comments, the form's design must meet these criteria:

- The Accounts dimension must be assigned to a row axis.
- Only users with write access to the account for the given planning unit can add comments.
- The Accounts, Entities, Versions, and Scenarios dimensions cannot be assigned to the column axis.
- The Entities dimension can be assigned to the row, page, or POV axis.

- The Versions and Scenarios dimensions must be assigned to either the page or POV axis.

If the account annotations have been enabled, you can access them by clicking View >> Edit Account Annotations:

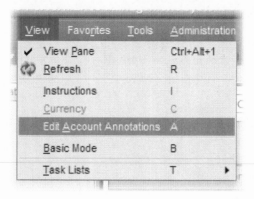

In account rows, in the column to the right of the account member names, enter a comment or URL of up to 1500 characters. You can include URL links to the following file types on a server or FTP site: .TXT, .DOC, .XLS, and .PDF. Below we added interRel Consulting as the description for the consulting firm.

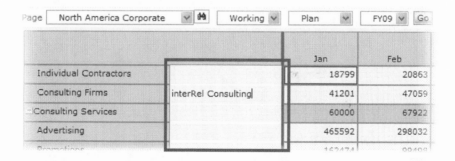

During the planning cycle and once the plan is in place, end users need to present updated plan information in various status meetings. Because Planning is so gosh-darn easy, end users find a few different alternatives available within the Planning menus to help them print and export the necessary data forms.

MISCELLANEOUS FEATURES

Just as the consultants are about to wrap up the Planning demonstration, Aquaman calls. "Hello, Penny. Aquaman calling. I noticed that you've contacted all of the other consultants for Planning advice and you haven't called me. Surely I can provide some really useful Planning information?"

"Uh, well, gee, um," Penny stammers, not wanting to hurt Aquaman's feelings. Aquaman is not exactly the best resource for information or help since Planning generally doesn't involve communicating with fish or swimming really, really quickly.

"For example," Aquaman continues. "Have you seen the View Member Formula feature? There's also a neat 11x feature that lets users hide rows and a couple of other things. I could tell you about those and more while waiting for Shark Week to start on the Discovery Channel."

Those features do seem interesting. Maybe Aquaman is good for something.

Beginning in version 11, end users can now hide or show rows and columns with zeroes and/or missing data. This is a straightforward feature to use and helpful when many of the rows on a large data form contain zeroes or no data at all.

	Jan	Feb	Mar
Property Taxes	362529	227113	100854
Property Insurance	151905	93172	46782
Facility Rent			
Building Exp			147636
Building Services			3101
Janitorial Services	28728	17416	9312
Security Services	13656	8710	3453
Business Fees and Licenses			

Page: North America Corporate | Working | Forecast | FY09 | Go

Show member properties in outline / Hide rows with no data / Hide rows with zeros and no data

While it doesn't provide the best printing capabilities, you can print data forms as PDF files and include supporting detail, cell text, and account annotations. Printing data forms requires Adobe Acrobat Reader 4.0 or later. To print a data form, select File >> Print.

In addition to printing, you can also export forms into Microsoft Excel. Most of the time you will use Smart View to access data forms in Excel but if you simply wanted to export the data

form content to a static Excel spreadsheet, select File >>
Spreadsheet Export.

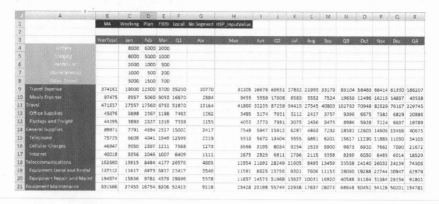

View Member Formulas

Have you ever wondered "where in the heck did this number
come from?" The Planning Administrator will usually create a
number of calculations for the Planning application that
automatically derive numbers based on your plan inputs. In many
cases, she does this using member formulas. Beginning in version
11, you can view the logic behind the member formulas calculations.
In the example below, we have enabled View Member Formulas on
the Income Statement data form (do the same to follow along with
the steps below).

1. Open the Income Statement data form.
2. Click on the *f* icon to view the logic for the calculated
   member:

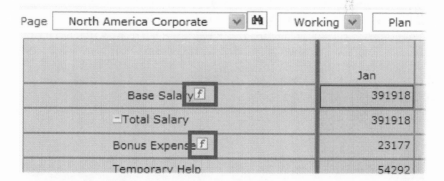

The member formula window will display with the member
calculation logic:

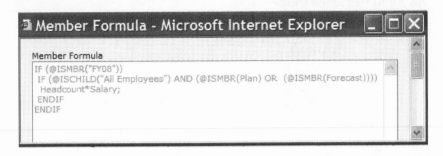

Ideally, the Planning Administrator will add in comments to help you understand the calculation syntax since it can be a bit Essbasy. For example, Penny, could add the following words to help Eddie decipher the member formula: "/*If it is FY08, then check to see if the member is a child of the member 'All Employees' and is also either in Plan or Forecast. If it is, then multiply headcount and salary. Otherwise, do nothing.*/"

3. Click Close to close the member formula window after marveling at its self-documenting greatness.

Add Rows to a Form

You are now an expert at entering data in data forms. But what if an account that you need to plan for is not on the data form? Can you add the member to the data form so that you can enter plan data? Yes, if the administrator has given the end user write access to the data form and enabled the ability for end users to add rows to data forms. (Realistically, this probably won't happen because the Planning Administrator has designed the form with specific requirements in mind and doesn't want end users to muck up her data form.)

When you add a row to a data form, you are not only adding it for yourself but all other users of that data form. Still, this may be something that you want to do so we'll review the steps.

To add a row within a data form from an end user perspective, click Edit >> Add Row:

Type in the row's member name in the Edit Form and click *Save*.

Once you add a row to a form, you can't delete it. You must contact the Planning Administrator to remove rows.

RUNNING BUSINESS RULES

"Thanks, Aquaman. Those are some helpful features. You're a lot more useful than your mother says. I see now why they call you King of Atlantis, but I've really got to go talk with the CFO about implementing Hyperion Planning..." Penny stands, ready to hang up the phone.

"Wait, my newfound and virtually only friend!" Aquaman cries frantically. "I haven't told you about one of the most important features: running Business Rules."

Penny tosses her notes down and flops into her uncomfortable chair. She's going to be late at this point but she can see that Aquaman is desperate to tell her about Business Rules. Who knows? Maybe it is something really important. "OK, Aquaman, tell me about Business Rules."

If you need to run either simple or complex calculations on your Planning data then Business Rules are going to be your weapon of choice. Business Rules perform calculations on data like aggregating data from detail levels to summary levels, allocating data from summary levels to detailed levels, copying data, clearing data and more. Business rules in most cases are created by the Planning Administrator.

Business Rules Assigned to a Data Form

Some Business Rules are attached to data forms and will automatically run when you save a data form. You can also launch a Business Rule associated with a data form by double clicking on the rule in the view pane.

The Calculate Currencies and Calculate Data Form Business Rules are two Business Rules that are created by Planning for every form. The Planning Administrator will choose whether or not to use them on a form by form basis. The Planning Administrator can also create custom Business Rules that can be run from this same listing.

1. Open the Income Statement data form under the Financial folder.
2. Notice the two Business Rules associated with the form:

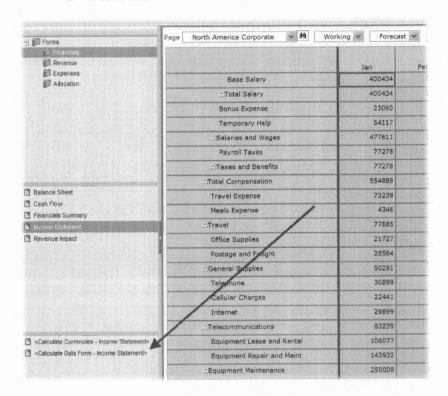

3. Double-click on <Calculate Data Form – Income Statement Business Rule to run the Business Rule>.
4. The Business Rule will launch, showing the following message upon completion:

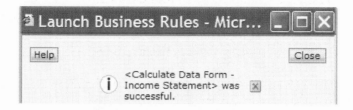

5. Click Close.

If no Business Rules are assigned to a data form, the message "No Business Rules available" will display.

Launch Business Rules

Some Business Rules may not be associated with a specific data form. Use the Launch Business Rules page to select and launch any Business Rule for your Planning application. The list of Business Rules that the current user has access to are shown by plan type. Unfortunately our Planning Sample application doesn't have any independent Business Rules for us to test but the basic steps are as follows.

To launch a Business Rule,

1. Select Tools > Launch Business Rules.
2. Under Plan Type, select the desired plan type(s) to view their corresponding Business Rules.
3. From the Business Rules box, select the Business Rule you would like to run.
4. Click Launch to run the calculation process.

Depending on the Business Rule, it may run a few seconds or a few minutes. A message will display letting you know the Business Rule has run successfully (or if it failed in misery with errors).

Run Time Prompts

Sometimes you may be prompted to enter some information for the Business Rule. What market should be calculated? What period should be calculated? What percent should be used in the bonus calculation?

Business Rules have the ability to prompt users for values when running the Business Rule. This is conveniently called a "run time prompt". Say you needed to re-calculate your department budget after submitting data. A single Business Rule is created for all the departments, and all you have to do is select your specific department when prompted by the Business Rule. The rule will run for your department.

Take a look at the run time prompt below:

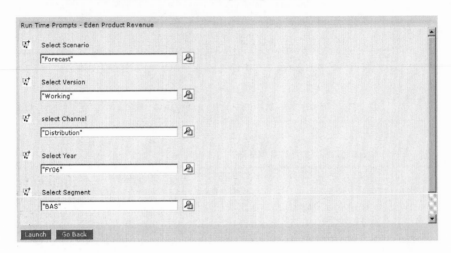

Notice the user is prompted to select a Scenario, Version, Channel, Year and Segment. A Member Search icon is available to search the dimensions for a specific member or members. If you know the desired member name exactly, simply type it in. Click *Launch* to run the Business Rule.

The administrator dictates the rules for run time prompts. They can be single or multiple members, numeric value, Smart List value, or text value. Members available for runtime prompts are limited by your security and limitations further defined by the Planning Administrator.

SET PREFERENCES

Planners can also set a number of preferences to make Planning behave like it's your own personal budgeting product.

To access user preferences:

1.   Click File >> Preferences:

The Oracle EPM Preferences dialog box is where you can access and make changes to several preference options including General, Authentication, Explore, Interactive Reporting, SQR Production Reporting, Financial Reporting, Web Analysis, Consolidation, and Planning. Since this is a book devoted to Planning we will focus on the General and Planning preferences.

The General Preferences section is an area that all users have access to. The Default Startup Options under the General Preferences tab gives the user the option of which content to load upon logging in to Workspace, as well as giving you the option of whether to be prompted before saving unsaved files. It also displays your e-mail address (which you cannot change in this section) and accessibility options.

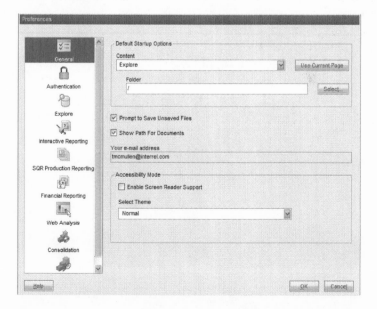

If you click on the Planning section, you'll see that the Planning user preferences are divided up into 4 tabs: Application Settings, Display Options, Printing Options, and User Variable Options.

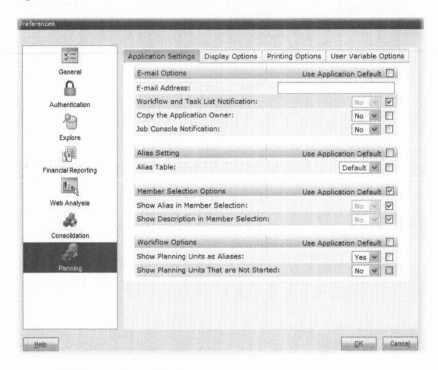

Application Settings

The Application Settings tab is where you would go if you needed to specify general application settings. You can enable e-mail notification so that you automatically receive e-mail notification when you become the new owner of a planning unit. You can also control display of member names or their aliases, set options for member selections, and set workflow options.

Application Settings	Display Options	Printing Options	User Variable Option

E-mail Options	Use Application Default ☐
E-mail Address:	
Workflow and Task List Notification:	No ☑
Copy the Application Owner:	No ☐
Job Console Notification:	No ☐

Alias Setting	Use Application Default ☐
Alias Table:	Default ☐

Member Selection Options	Use Application Default ☑
Show Alias in Member Selection:	No ☑
Show Description in Member Selection:	No ☑

Workflow Options	Use Application Default ☐
Show Planning Units as Aliases:	Yes ☐
Show Planning Units That are Not Started:	No ☐

To enable e-mail notification for yourself:
1. Select Applications Settings tab under Planning Preferences.
2. In the Email Address text box, enter your e-mail address.
3. Select the Workflow and Task List Notification check box.
4. Optional: You can select Copy the Application Owner if you want the owner of the application to receive a copy of your e-mail notifications. Do her a favor and *don't* check this box.
5. Click OK.

You now automatically receive e-mail notification when you become the new owner of a planning unit. The application owner will be listed as the source of the e-mail notifications. The Subject line of an e-mail notification is in this format: NEW OWNER: Abc Plan (Scenario, Version, Entity).

If you have multiple alias tables, you can select the alias table on the Application Settings tab of Planning Preferences. You can also choose how you would like to see members in any Member Selection boxes: member name or alias.

Display Options

Planning Display options allow you to set up the formatting for numbers on a data entry form, overriding the formatting that has already been set up for a currency. You can set aspects of page selection (remember last page selected) and change the limit for warnings on large data forms.

Application Settings	Display Options	Printing Options	User Variable Options

Number Formatting	Use Application Default ☐
Thousands Separator:	Currency Setting ▾ ☐
Decimal Separator:	Currency Setting ▾ ☐
Negative Sign:	Currency Setting ▾ ☐
Negative Color:	Currency Setting ▾ ☐

Page Options	Use Application Default ☐
Remember selected page members:	Yes ▾ ☑
Allow Search When Number of Pages Exceeds:	100 ☐
Indentation of Members on Page:	Indent level 0 members only ▾ ☐

Other Options	Use Application Default ☐
Remember most recent page visited:	Yes ▾ ☑
Warn if data form larger than cells specified	1500 ☐
UI Theme:	tadpole ▾
Text Size:	Normal ▾
Date Format:	Automatically Detect ▾ ☐

The Number Formatting options are pretty straightforward. The Page Options allow you to dictate how pages should be displayed on data forms. Do you want to remember the last page selected? In most cases, yes. If you don't like to see a long list of members in a page drop down, you can decrease the number of members displayed and use the search mechanism instead:

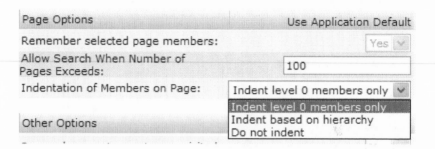

You can indent level-0 members only, indent based on hierarchy, or use no indentation at all when viewing members in the page on a data form:

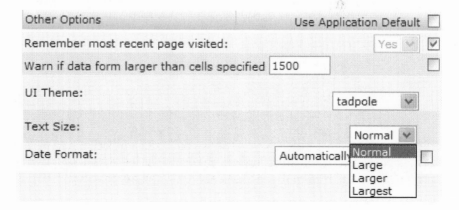

In Other Options, you can choose to remember the last page visited (e.g. if you last opened Plan Revenue – All Years data form, when you log back into Planning, that is the form that will open initially). If you have some forms that are rather large and the message indicating "You have a really big form; are you sure you want to open?" is getting annoying, increase the cells specified. If you are getting up there in age and your eyesight isn't quite what it used to be, change the text size to Large, Larger or Largest:

Printing Options

Use the Printing Options tab to format how printed forms appear when printed. These settings can be overwritten when you actually print the data form:

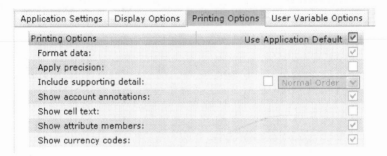

SET USER VARIABLES

The final tab in the Planning Preferences section is the User Variable Options. User Variables allow data forms to be filtered for just the members end users want to see. For example, an end user may have read access to all entities but write access for the IT department. When he plans expenses, he really only cares about the IT entity. So the administrator sets up a User Variable called My Entity and designs the Expenses data form to select this variable. The end user sets his My Entity variable to "IT Department" and the form only shows "IT Department" and not the other 500 entities.

Let's walk through an example of using a form that has a user variable.

1.   Open the data form Revenue Impact under the Financials folder.
2.   You should get the following error message (assuming someone else hasn't set the user variable):

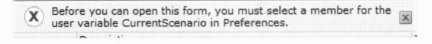

You cannot open a data form that contains a user variable if you haven't selected a member for that variable. Let's do this now.

3.   Select File>>Preferences and select the Planning preferences.
4.   Select the User Variables tab.
5.   For the user variable CurrentScenario, click the Member Selection icon:

6. Select the member Plan and click *Submit:*

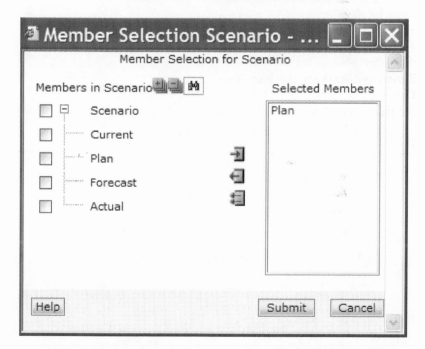

You can type "Plan" into the text box if you know the exact spelling of the member name.

7. Repeat the steps above selecting "Actual" for the user variable CompareScenario:

Application Settings	Display Options	Printing Options	User Variable Options

User Variable Options

Dimension	User Variable Name	Selected Member	
Scenario	CompareScenario	Actual	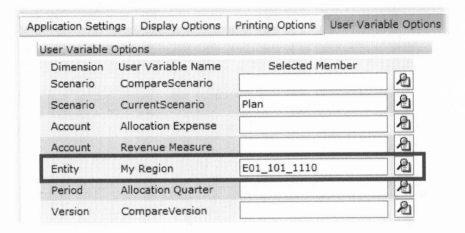
Scenario	CurrentScenario	Plan	
Account	Allocation Expense		

While we're here, let's also set the user variable for My Region. This is not required for the Revenue Impact form, but we want you to know how to do it.

8. Repeat the steps above selecting E01_101_1110 for the My Region user variable:

Application Settings	Display Options	Printing Options	User Variable Options

User Variable Options

Dimension	User Variable Name	Selected Member	
Scenario	CompareScenario		
Scenario	CurrentScenario	Plan	
Account	Allocation Expense		
Account	Revenue Measure		
Entity	My Region	E01_101_1110	
Period	Allocation Quarter		
Version	CompareVersion		

9. Click OK.
10. Reopen the Revenue Impact data form and notice the form defaults to Plan and Actual scenarios:

	Q1		Q2		Q3		Q4	
	Plan	Actual	Plan	Actual	Plan	Actual	Plan	Actual
Gross Revenue	31278918	29036993	33476920	30249688	33546284		65063515	
Pretax Income From Operations	12156596	10874746	13616222	11888596	12804913		23631275	
Net Income	12156596	10874746	13616222	11888596	12804913		23631275	
Change in Cash	12156596	10874746	13616222	11888596	12804913		23631275	

	Q1	Q2	Q3	Q4	Q1	Q2	Q3	Q4
Units	19195	22566	20277	38560				
Price	52	46	73	73				
Operating Revenue	998679	1046043	1483325	2799020				
Sales Returns	-58665	-67957	-91040	-163774				
Sales Discounts	-41642	-48237	-64031	-114109				
Returns and Allowances	-100307	-116194	-155070	-277883				
Net Revenue	898372	929848	1328255	2521137				
Operating COS	602928	726525	872869	1659689				
Gross Profit	295444	203324	455386	861248				

Penny immediately realizes that user variables will provide a huge time savings when it comes to data form development. (More on how to create user variables to come in the Create an Application act.)

Now that we've seen all of the possibilities over the web, let's review Microsoft Office capabilities with Planning.

PLAN IN EXCEL

Penny is overwhelmed with Oracle Hyperion Planning. She's sure that with Planning, Eddie can budget and forecast faster and more accurately than ever before. She has one last worry though. What if Eddie doesn't want to plan over the web? He loves Excel. He really loves Excel.

"Never fear, Penny." The Translator swooshes his cape once again. (Seriously? The cape swooshing is getting a bit old). "You can access Planning from Excel (and Word and PowerPoint) using the Smart View Add-in."

Smart View is NOT just another Excel add-in for Hyperion or Oracle EPM. Its capabilities are far greater than any other Hyperion Excel add-in you've seen to date. Smart View provides a common Microsoft Office interface to Essbase, Financial Management, Planning, Enterprise, Financial Reporting, Interactive Reporting, SQR Production Reporting, Web Analysis, and Oracle Business Intelligence Enterprise Edition (OBIEE+). This means you can use Microsoft Excel to plan and Microsoft Excel, Word, or PowerPoint to view, manipulate, report and share data.

Combining the powers of Planning and Smart View allows planners to update Planning data in forms, calculate data using Business Rules, and utilize most of the other features available through the Planning web client, all through Microsoft Excel. (If you are a financially minded individual, Excel is as valuable as your left hand.) The chart below shows the similarities and differences between the Planning web client and Smart View:

	Planning Web Client	**Smart View Add-in for Planning**
Enter data	Yes	Yes
Launch Business Rules	Yes	Yes
Supporting detail	Yes	Yes
Cell text	Yes	Yes
Adjust function	Yes	Yes
Mass allocate and grid spread	Yes	No*
Linked formulas with Excel	No	Yes
View instructions	Yes	Yes
Workflow	Yes	No*
Copy / Paste	Yes	Yes
Client install required	No	Yes
Composite forms	Yes	No*
User variable updates	Yes	No*
Task lists	Yes	No*

Note!

*Beginning in 11.1.2, these features will be supported as Smart View begins to become the primary interface to Planning. For details on Smart View and Planning, see *Look Smarter Than You Are with Hyperion Planning: An End User's Guide*.

Penny jumps to her feet. "I've seen enough. This is the solution we need for enterprise budgeting and forecasting." Penny dashes from the room, barges into the executive washroom, and shows Hyperion Planning to the CFO who immediately agrees to implement the solution. "This is the best idea I've ever had! Now it's up to you Penny. Only you can save us all. Now please leave the room while I sing you an inspirational ditty." A disco ball and wild colored lights start as the CFO sings a parody of *I Believe in Miracles*:

> I BELIEVE THAT PENNY, CAN IMPLEMENT
> PLANNING! (LIKE CONSULTANTS DO)
> AND WHEN SHE'S FINISHED SHE'LL RECONCILE
> WITH EDDIE!
>
> YOU'RE GOING TO HELP EDDIE.
> IT'S SO GREAT THAT HE NEEDS YOU.
> IT'S GREAT THAT HE NEEDS YOU SO BADLY.
> BECAUSE BY NEXT WEEK, HE'LL HAVE FALLEN
> BACK IN LOVE MADLY.
>
> YESTERDAY, YOU WERE A PATHETIC IT GEEK
> NOW YOU'VE GOT A WEEK TO SINK OR SWIM, NO
> PRESSURE YOU SEE, CAUSE
> I BELIEVE IN PENNY, SHE CAN DO, ANYTHING
> (ANYTHING IT'S TRUE)
> I BELIEVE IN PENNY AND HYPERION PLANNING...

CREATE AN APPLICATION

Scene 4:
Create an Application

Up to this point, you've been using an existing application. This is kind of liking driving a car. It's an important skill, and while you get an idea of what must be under the hood, you don't know how to actually build a car. In this section, we'll get out of the driver's seat and get into the role we were destined to fulfill: Planning Administrator. Clear your mind of all thoughts since learning to build an Oracle Hyperion Planning application is more complicated than anything else you've done in the last few minutes.

REQUIREMENTS AND DESIGN

Before you start the process of building an application, you need to go through detailed requirements and design sessions. You will ask many questions to help you understand how to best create the Planning application (or applications) to meet your budgeting and forecast needs. Questions for each subject area include:

- How do you budget, plan, and forecast today?
- What is the timing and frequency?
- Who is involved?
- At what level of detail will you plan?
- What are the dimensions?
- What data should be loaded into Planning?
- What reports are needed?
- How will users plan?

You'll be asking these questions and many others, but since this is not a book on reengineering your planning process, we're going to assume that you've collected all of the requirements for each subject area. Now you're ready to think about Planning application design.

WHAT IS AN APPLICATION AND PLAN TYPE?

Application Defined

A Planning application is a set of dimensions and members used to meet a specific set of planning needs. You can design many planning applications to meet budgeting and forecast needs:

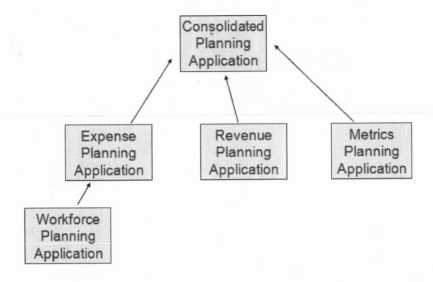

Plan Types Defined

A Planning application can have up to 5 plan types (also known as Essbase databases) at least through version 11.1.1.3:

- 3 Customizable Plan Types, E.g., Revenue, Net Income, Balance Sheet
- 4th plan type, Workforce Planning (if initialized)
- 5th plan type, CapEx (if initialized)

Workforce Planning and Capital Expenditure Planning are additional modules that you can purchase that provide prebuilt structures and objects to facilitate workforce and capital expenditure planning processes. Before you go off and build your own custom Planning applications for employee-level or asset-level budgeting, you should really look at these pre-built modules.

You may design a single Planning application with multiple plan types instead of multiple planning applications:

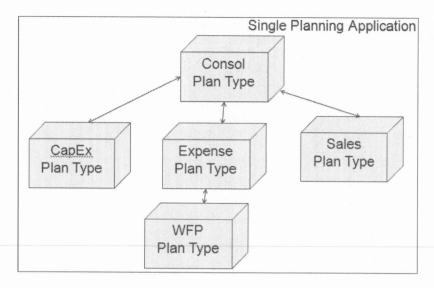

Planning application and plan type names are limited to a maximum of 8 characters. You cannot change the number of plan types or the plan type names after the application is created.

Within a Planning application, you can define and manage 20 possible dimensions. If you enable multi-currency within an application, you will have seven required dimensions and then up to 13 custom dimensions.

Tip!

You do not want to create a Planning application with 20 dimensions. Forget performance for a second: the real concern with an application of this size is that it would be too complex for your end users to ever grasp what was going on.

If you can count, you may have noted that we actually have eight dimensions listed above. HSP_Rates is a dimension that is created in the underlying Essbase database but is not a dimension that you maintain in Planning. It is created and managed based on currency settings and exchange rate tables. Therefore, eight dimensions are created even though you only manage seven of them.

If you do not enable multi-currency, there are six required dimensions.

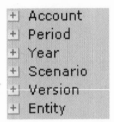

In addition to the required dimensions, you may add up to 13 additional dimensions. You can assign these custom dimensions to a specific plan type or to all plan types.

For example, a planning application design might include three plan types: P&L, Revenue, and Salary. The Salary plan type may include a custom dimension "Employee" so that salary can be planned by employee. For the other plan types, P&L and Revenue, the Employee dimension does not apply.

In the example below, the salary plan type includes the 7 required dimensions plus the Employee dimension:

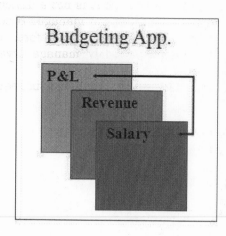

**7 Required
Dimensions:**
• Accounts
• Entity
• Scenario
• Version
• Time Period
• Year
• (Currency)

**Additional
Dimensions:**
• Employee

Revenue budgets are submitted by sales by product and channel so two custom dimensions, Product and Channel, are created for the Revenue plan type. Product and Channel do not apply to salary or P&L planning, so the two dimensions are not included in those plan types.

In the example below, the revenue plan type includes the 7 required dimensions plus the Product and Channel dimensions:

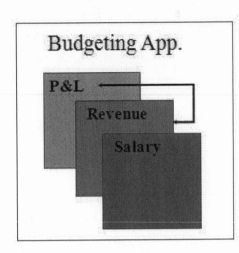

7 Required Dimensions:
- Account
- Entity
- Scenario
- Version
- Time Period
- Year
- (Currency)

Additional Dimensions:

- Product
- Channel

Hopefully by now you can see that it is better to only include in a plan type those dimensions that apply to a subject area or set of accounts. Next let's talk about the time basis for your application.

Time Basis

When you create an application you will define the Time Basis for the application and the base level for the Time Periods dimension (the level zero members). Options include:

- 12 Months – Automatic quarter roll-ups
- Quarters – No monthly data
- Custom – Weeks, Days, etc.

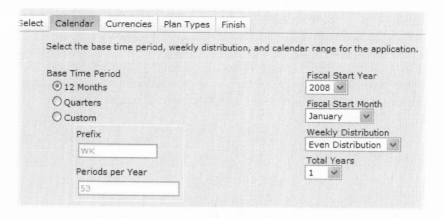

If you choose Custom Time Periods, the periods are numbered automatically. For weeks, a prefix of "WK-" with 53 periods per year is added. For days, a prefix of "Day-" with 366 Periods per year is added. Custom Time Periods can be used for odd calendars like 13 periods or 53 weeks:

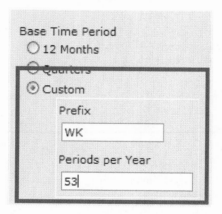

 Custom Time Period prefixes may not have spaces.
Note!

If you choose the base time period of 12 months, you will define how data will be distributed when users enter data at upper levels of the time dimension. Time spreading takes place automatically in the data form for the Period dimension. Remember in the Plan Over the Web scene, we tested time spreading by entering a value into a quarter and saw that Planning automatically distributed it to the quarter's months. Here is where you define how data is distributed. Available options include even, 445 weekly distribution, 544 weekly distribution, and 454 weekly distribution. If you use one of the 4, 4, and 5 types of distribution, it will put slightly more into blank months that have 5 weeks versus those that have 4. The default option is even distribution:

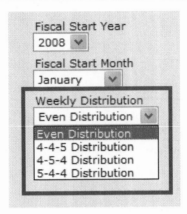

You will also define the Fiscal Start Year and the number of years for the application. If the base time period is set to 12 Months, then you will define the Fiscal Start Month. You can't change the start year or fiscal month once the application is created, though you can add more years to the Planning application.

Multi-Currency

If you decide to use Planning's built-in currency functionality, you will check the option to enable Planning multi-currency. When you check this option, two dimensions will be added to the application, HSP_Rates and Currency. You cannot "turn off" multi-currency once enabled. You will set the Default Application Currency which cannot be changed once the application is created. All new entities will be assigned this currency by default.

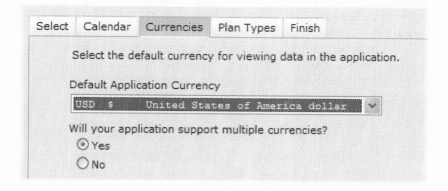

Note! Do not enable multi-currency unless you know for sure that you need it. There are many good reasons to get by without it if you have some Essbase expertise. How to set up currency conversion outside of Planning is beyond the bounds of this book since it would mean teaching a ton of Essbase.

Penny's Application Design

Penny and the Consultants complete the requirements and design process, creating the following high level Planning design:

- Plan type 1 – Sum (consolidated financial reporting plan type)
- Plan type 2 – Rev (sales and revenue focused plan type with custom dimension Segments)
- No workforce planning or capex modules (although we'll be implementing them for the next budget cycle)
- Standard 12 month calendar
- Fiscal period beginning January
- Start year – 2008
- 5 years within the application
- NO Multi-currency application

Now that the design is complete, we are ready to create a Planning application!

Note!

You cannot change the following after an application is created:

- Starting year and start month
- Multi-currency vs. single currency
- Plan types
- Name of application and database

EPMA VS. CLASSIC

Planning applications can be created and maintained in two different ways: Planning Classic using the Planning web client and Enterprise Performance Management Architect (EPMA).

Classic application creation/maintenance uses the Planning web client to create and manage Planning applications. The "Classic" method uses the steps and processes available before EPMA was introduced. It's actually a well designed interface and the vast majority of the companies implementing Planning use the classic method.

EPMA provides a single interface to build, deploy, and manage all financial applications for Planning, Financial Management and Essbase. Within EPMA you can manage, link, and synchronize all of your Oracle EPM applications.

From an application creation perspective, there are two differences between Classic and EPMA deployed applications: 1) where you create applications and 2) where you maintain dimensions and member properties. Everything else is the same.

For this book, we will follow the Classic creation method not only because it's the most widely used, but because EPMA functionality changed drastically from version 9 to 11. Don't fret, though. You can go to Appendix B (Intro to EPMA) on page 573 to understand those application creation and maintenance steps.

CLASSIC APPLICATION CREATION

If you have implemented Planning in earlier versions, you've completed application creation steps in a number of different places. Some steps (like creating and registering data sources) were manual and used a Planning Desktop client. Thankfully the process is much easier in recent versions.

For this book, we assume you have completed the installation and configuration processes for Planning, Essbase, Shared Services, and Smart View.

Before we get started, you need to create an empty relational database somewhere (e.g. Oracle schema/database, SQL Server database). You will need the following information to create a Planning application:

- Relational database server and database name
- Relational database ID and password (Full control access for the database or schema at a minimum)
- Essbase server
- Essbase supervisor ID and password

CREATE A DATA SOURCE IN 9.3.1

Some of the steps for creating an application differ between versions 9.3.1 and 11.1.1. If you're on Planning 11.1.1, skip to page 111.In Planning 9.3.1, you will use the Shared Services Configuration utility to create and register a data source for Planning.

1. Open the Configuration Utility. The navigation menu structure may be different depending on your installation. Our navigation path looks like the following:

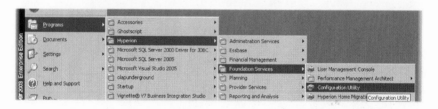

2. Choose English. If you don't know how to read English, then it explains why this book isn't working for you.
3. Expand Planning and check Data Source Configuration:

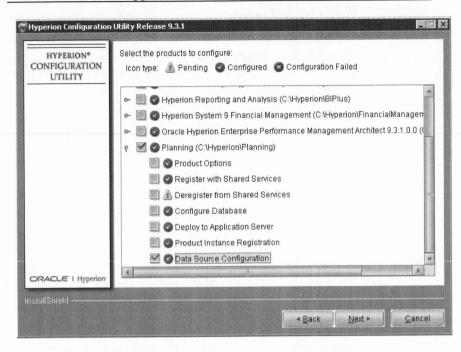

4. Click Next.
5. Click Create Data Source:

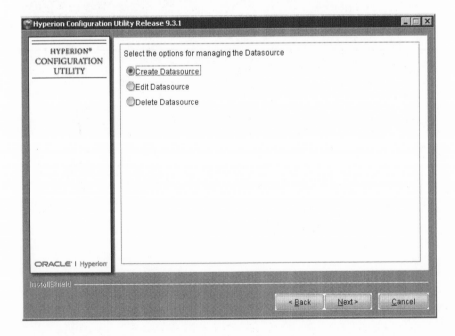

6. Click Next.
7. Enter a data source name and description for the data source. (While the illustrations below use a name of trainxx, to follow along with this book, name your data source ENTPLN):

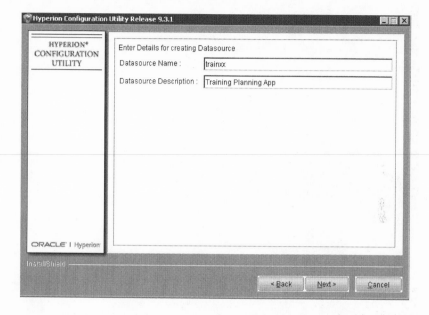

Tip!

We recommend you give the data source the same name as you'll be giving the Planning application.

8. Click Next.
9. Select an Instance (one instance is typically created and will contain all Planning applications):

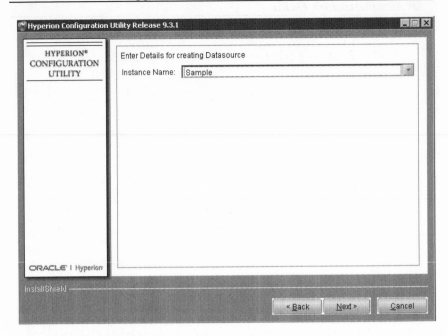

10. Click Next.
11. Select a database:

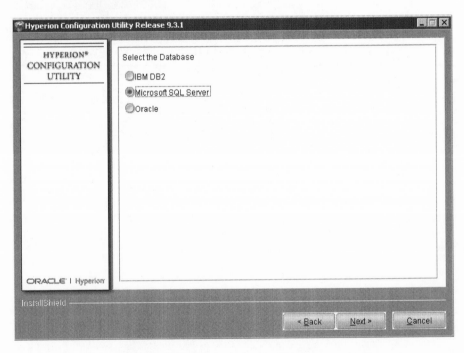

12. Click Next.
13. Enter the relational database connection information:

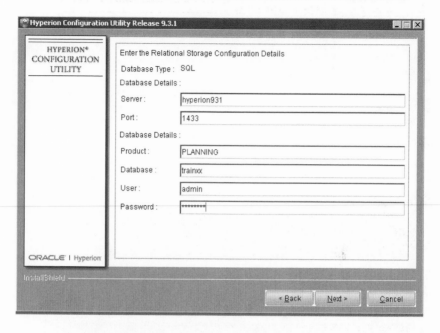

14. Click Next.
15. Enter the Essbase connection information:

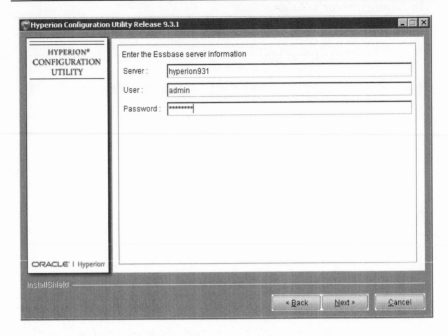

16. Click Next.
17. The following window will display:

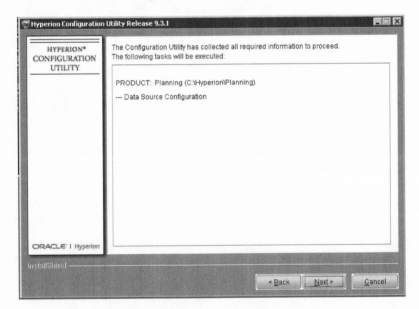

18. Click Next.
19. Once you see a successful message, click Next, No, and Finish to exit the configuration utility:

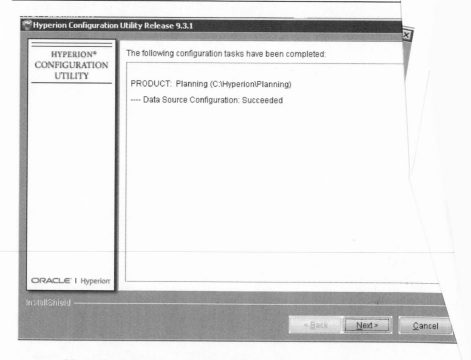

Now that you've created a data source, you are ready to create the application. (Skip ahead to page 115 since if you just did the steps above, you must be on 9.3.1.)

CREATE A DATA SOURCE IN 11.1.1

While the steps to create an application in version 11.1.1 are similar, there are a few differences in where the action takes place. In 9.3.1, you create and manage data sources in the Shared Services Configuration Utility. In version 11.1.1, you create and manage data sources in the Workspace Classic Administration.

1. Open the Workspace (http://servername/Workspace).
2. Log into the EPM Workspace, providing an ID and password:

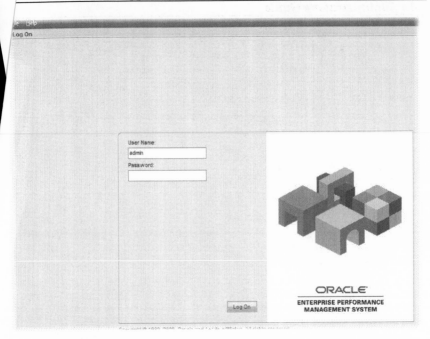

3. Select Navigate (steering wheel icon) >> Administer >> Classic Application Administration >> Planning Administration:

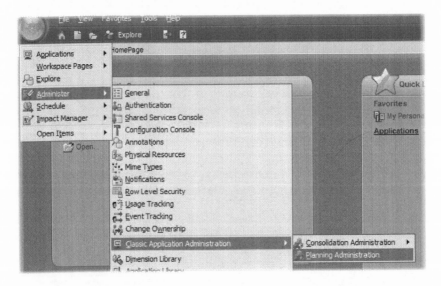

4. Click Manage Data Source.

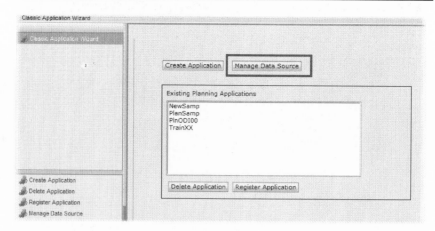

5. Click Create Data Source:

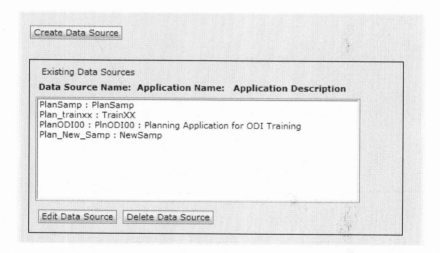

6. Click Next.
7. Enter a data source name and description. Penny decides to call her data source Entpln, the same name as the application name.
8. Enter the relational database connection information including server, port (in most cases default will work), database, user id and password.
9. Enter the Essbase connection information including server, supervisor user id and password.
10. Click Validate for both connections to ensure accurate information and no connectivity issues:

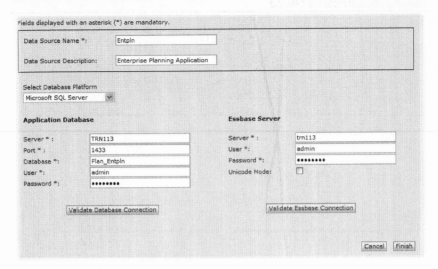

11. Click Finish. The data source should be added to the Data source listing:

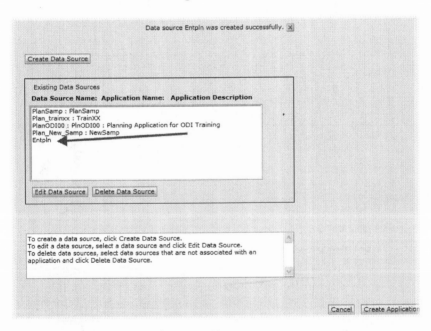

If you need to edit or delete data source connections, use the appropriate button (Edit, Delete) under Manage Data Sources. Now you are ready to create an application.

CREATE AN APPLICATION

For both version 9.3.1 and version 11.1.1, you will use the application creation wizard to create the Planning application.

To create an application,

1. Select Navigate icon >> Administer >> Classic Administration >> Planning.
2. Click Create Application:

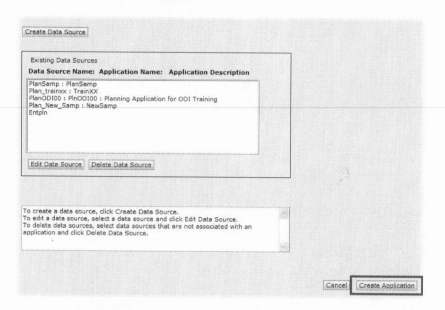

3. Select your data source – Entpln.
4. Specify the application name – Entpln.
5. Specify the description.
6. Choose the Shared Services project – Planning application.
7. Choose the instance – in our example, default.
8. In version 11.1.1, choose the calculation mode: Calculation Manager or Business Rules. In version 9.3.1, Calculation Manager is not available. Business Rules will be used by default.

To follow along with this book, select Calculation Manager:

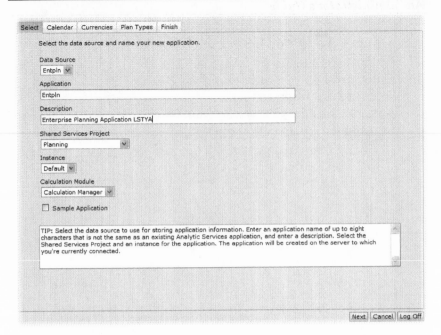

9. Click Next.

10. Enter the calendar information per requirements:

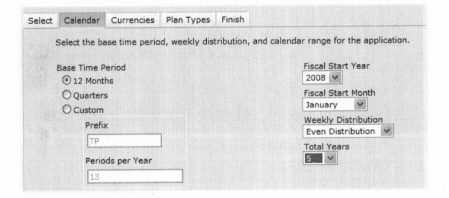

11. Click Next.

12. Select No for multiple currencies:

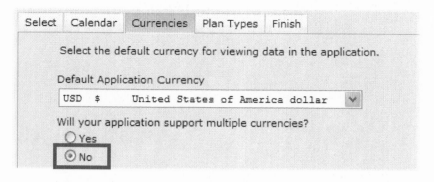

13. Click Next.
14. Enter the plan type names (Sum, Rev):

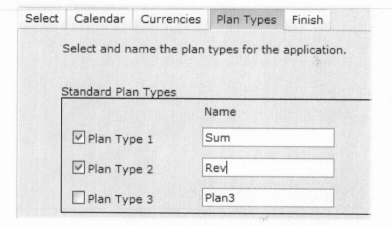

15. If you see options for Workforce (WFP) or Capital
    Expenditure (Cap ex) plan types, do not check workforce,
    capital expenditure, or any other module options that you
    happen to see.
16. Click Next.
17. Review the application definition information:

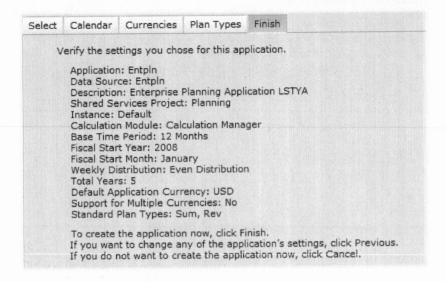

Select	Calendar	Currencies	Plan Types	**Finish**

Verify the settings you chose for this application.

Application: Entpln
Data Source: Entpln
Description: Enterprise Planning Application LSTYA
Shared Services Project: Planning
Instance: Default
Calculation Module: Calculation Manager
Base Time Period: 12 Months
Fiscal Start Year: 2008
Fiscal Start Month: January
Weekly Distribution: Even Distribution
Total Years: 5
Default Application Currency: USD
Support for Multiple Currencies: No
Standard Plan Types: Sum, Rev

To create the application now, click Finish.
If you want to change any of the application's settings, click Previous.
If you do not want to create the application now, click Cancel.

18. Click Finish when ready.

19. Look for a successful message:

Congratulations!
You have successfully created a new Planning application.

Click here to create another application

So what happens when you click the Finish button? Planning creates the relational database tables in the underlying relational database and creates the underlying Essbase application; however, the Essbase databases have not yet been created.

20. Click Log Off.

21. Log back into the Workspace.

22. Select Navigate >> Applications >> Planning >> Entpln
    (your newly created Planning application!).

Troubleshooting Application Creation

If the application creation was not successful, you probably received a message to check out the log. To find the Planning log, navigate to the main Oracle EPM logs directory (most Hyperion / Oracle EPM logs are placed in this common directory). In version 11, the Planning log is located in the *installdirectory*\logs\services directory:

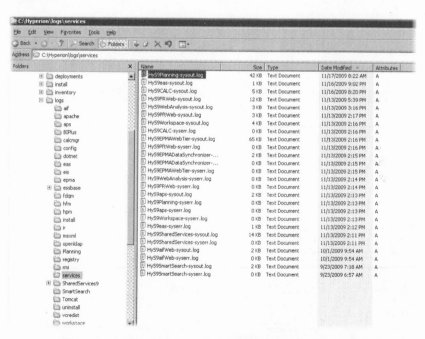

Once you open the log, you still may not understand why the application creation process failed. This is less of failing of you, your parents, or your country's educational system and more the fault of really difficult to read Java-centric log files. For example, review the log file entry below. Can you figure out the issue?

```
>>>>Caption = Classic Application wizard    ::: Text = Opening Classic Application wizard
Unable to find JDBC_CATALOG key for application: EntPln
Connection to the datasource created successfully.
Unable to create Analytical application. Exiting Application Creation.
Exception in Application Creation :Unable to create Analytical application. Exiting Application Creation.
java.lang.IllegalStateException: Unable to create Analytical application. Exiting Application Creation.
    at com.hyperion.planning.HspManageApplication.createApp(Unknown Source)
    at com.hyperion.planning.appdeploy.HspManageAppSession.createApplication(Unknown Source)
    at HspCreateApp.Handle(Unknown Source)
    at HspCreateApp.doPost(Unknown Source)
    at javax.servlet.http.HttpServlet.service(HttpServlet.java:709)
    at javax.servlet.http.HttpServlet.service(HttpServlet.java:802)
    at org.apache.catalina.core.ApplicationFilterChain.internalDoFilter(ApplicationFilterChain.java:252)
    at org.apache.catalina.core.ApplicationFilterChain.doFilter(ApplicationFilterChain.java:173)
    at HspValidationFilter.doFilter(Unknown Source)
    at org.apache.catalina.core.ApplicationFilterChain.internalDoFilter(ApplicationFilterChain.java:202)
    at org.apache.catalina.core.ApplicationFilterChain.doFilter(ApplicationFilterChain.java:173)
    at org.apache.catalina.core.StandardWrapperValve.invoke(StandardWrapperValve.java:213)
    at org.apache.catalina.core.StandardContextValve.invoke(StandardContextValve.java:178)
    at org.apache.catalina.core.StandardHostValve.invoke(StandardHostValve.java:126)
    at org.apache.catalina.valves.ErrorReportValve.invoke(ErrorReportValve.java:105)
    at org.apache.catalina.core.StandardEngineValve.invoke(StandardEngineValve.java:107)
    at org.apache.catalina.connector.CoyoteAdapter.service(CoyoteAdapter.java:148)
    at org.apache.jk.server.JkCoyoteHandler.invoke(JkCoyoteHandler.java:199)
    at org.apache.jk.common.HandlerRequest.invoke(HandlerRequest.java:282)
    at org.apache.jk.common.ChannelSocket.invoke(ChannelSocket.java:754)
    at org.apache.jk.common.ChannelSocket$SocketConnection.runIt(ChannelSocket.java:684)
    at org.apache.jk.common.ChannelSocket.processConnection(ChannelSocket.java:876)
    at org.apache.tomcat.util.threads.ThreadPool$ControlRunnable.run(ThreadPool.java:684)
    at java.lang.Thread.run(Thread.java:595)
java.lang.RuntimeException: Create application failed.
    at com.hyperion.planning.appdeploy.HspManageAppSession.createApplication(Unknown Source)
    at HspCreateApp.Handle(Unknown Source)
    at HspCreateApp.doPost(Unknown Source)
```

At first glance, you may not understand the error messages. If you look closer, you can see the issue occurred when Planning was trying to create the Essbase application ("Unable to Create the Analytic Application"). Since the issue is with Essbase, let's now look at the Essbase server log to see if we can find more information. The Essbase server log file is stored in the *installdirectory*\logs\essbase directory:

```
ESSBASE.LOG - Notepad
File  Edit  Format  View  Help

[Mon Nov 16 21:08:00 2009]Local/ESSBASE0///Info(1051187)
Logging in user [admin] from [100.100.100.26]

[Mon Nov 16 21:08:00 2009]Local/ESSBASE0///Info(1051035)
Last login on Monday, November 16, 2009 9:07:57 PM

[Mon Nov 16 21:08:00 2009]Local/ESSBASE0///Info(1051001)
Received client request: List Applications (from user [admin])

[Mon Nov 16 21:08:00 2009]Local/ESSBASE0///Info(1051160)
Received validate Login Session request

[Mon Nov 16 21:08:00 2009]Local/ESSBASE0///Info(1051001)
Received client request: Logout (from user [admin])

[Mon Nov 16 21:08:00 2009]Local/ESSBASE0///Info(1051037)
Logging out user [admin], active for 0 minutes

[Mon Nov 16 21:08:07 2009]Local/ESSBASE0///Info(1051164)
Received login request from [100.100.100.26]

[Mon Nov 16 21:08:07 2009]Local/ESSBASE0///Info(1051187)
Logging in user [admin] from [100.100.100.26]

[Mon Nov 16 21:08:07 2009]Local/ESSBASE0///Info(1051035)
Last login on Monday, November 16, 2009 9:08:00 PM

[Mon Nov 16 21:08:07 2009]Local/ESSBASE0///Info(1051001)
Received client request: Create Application with Front End Type (from user [admin])

[Mon Nov 16 21:08:07 2009]Local/ESSBASE0///Error(1051041)
Insufficient privilege for this operation
```

In this case, the Essbase ID "admin" that was used in the Planning data source connection did not have supervisor privileges in Essbase and therefore could not create an application in Essbase. To fix this issue, the admin was provisioned for supervisor access, resulting in successful application creation.

Other common issues in the application creation process are due to insufficient access for the relational database, incorrect server information, and others (that unfortunately we don't have time to address in this musical).

Navigate to the Application

To open the new Planning application,

1. Log back into the Workspace.
2. Select Navigate >> Applications >> Planning >> Entpln:

You'll see the Opening... status window and then you should be directed to the new Planning application:

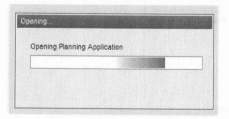

Create the Databases in Essbase

To complete the planning application creation process, you need to create the plan types (a.k.a. databases) in Essbase.

1. Select Administration >> Manage Database:

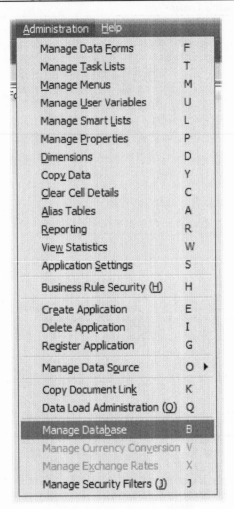

2. Check the option for Database (we haven't assigned any
   security yet so no need to refresh security filters).
3. Click Create button:

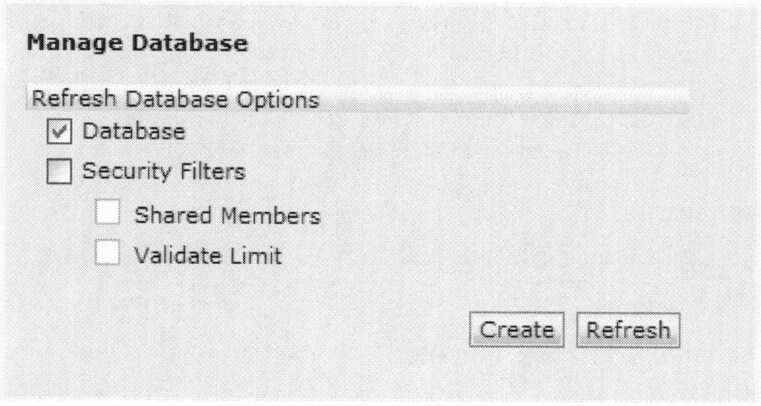

Manage Database

Refresh Database Options
- [✓] Database
- [ ] Security Filters
  - [ ] Shared Members
  - [ ] Validate Limit

[Create] [Refresh]

4. Click Create (again):

WARNING: You are about to recreate all Essbase cubes (databases) for this Application. This will delete all Essbase cubes (databases), outline, calculation scripts and data associated to this application. This step cannot be undone. To preserve your data, please back up your databases and outline, and export data from all databases. To preserve your calculation scripts, please copy them to another directory. Click 'Create' to proceed.

[Cancel] [Create]

5. Click Finish when complete (and be shocked that any computer program would bother showing you how long something took *in milliseconds*):

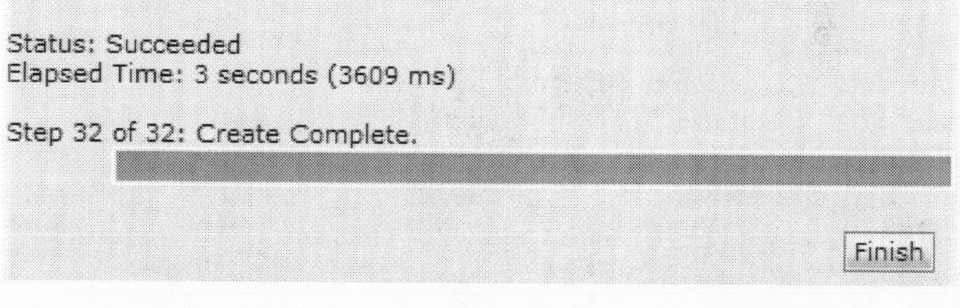

Status: Succeeded
Elapsed Time: 3 seconds (3609 ms)

Step 32 of 32: Create Complete.

[Finish]

The step you just completed created the underlying Essbase block storage option (BSO) databases, one for each plan type. Planning does not support aggregate storage option (ASO) databases.

When the database is created, an Essbase outline is also created. The Essbase outline contains *all* of the hierarchical information for your application. Unlike a relational database where the hierarchy is applied to data already stored in tables, in Essbase, the outline directly controls *how* data is stored and indexed. When you modify the dimensions and members, the Create and Refresh to Essbase will update the underlying Essbase outline. When the outline is updated, the database is restructured.

Note!

Essbase allows one and only one outline per database.

Building and ordering dimensions, adding hierarchies, adding members with member attributes, creating member formulas and more outline components all drive the performance of your Essbase database / Planning plan type. But first and foremost, your outline needs to reflect your business requirements for budgeting and forecasting.

Note!

Don't ever hit Create again on the same application.

Manage Database

Once the application and plan types (a.k.a. databases) are created in Essbase, you will need to continually refresh to Essbase as changes are made. You are pushing changes that you make in the Planning web client to the Essbase database. Remember, all of the metadata information captured via the Planning web client is stored in a relational database, items like data form definitions, task list definitions, application security assignments, and dimension and member definitions. Essbase stores the data or numbers themselves. For Planning to work correctly, the Essbase outline must be in sync with the metadata information stored in the underlying Planning relational repository. "Manage Database" is how you sync.

Depending on the changes you've made, you can select the information to sync to the Essbase database:

- Database (Sync dimensions, hierarchies, members and member properties from Planning to Essbase)
- Security Filters (Create / sync security filters for member access)

- Additionally you can apply security to Shared Members and validate the limit of security filters (4KB per row)
- Currency Conversion CalcScript (if using Planning's multi-currency; Essbase runs the calculations for currency conversion)

You will select "Create" once in an application's life (we just did that). After the databases are created, you will select "Refresh" all other times.

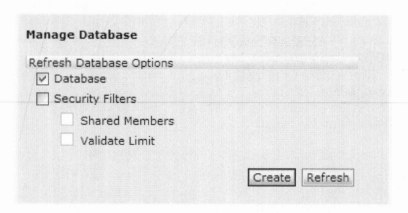

Note!

If you click "Create" by mistake, you will lose all Essbase components that you may have created including data, load rules, and calc scripts.

All users should be logged off of the application when performing a refresh. If a user is logged in and performing an action within Planning, your application refresh to Essbase could fail.

You can schedule application refreshes (often performed nightly). Use Microsoft Windows Scheduled Tasks tool or other to run the AppSchedule R Command line. The AppSchedule.exe is stored in the UTILS folder in the Planning directory. The syntax is as follows:

```
AppSchedule.exe ([Server Name]), Domain Name,
Application Name, user name, password, procedure
AppSchedule.exe ABCServer, USDomain, interRelBD,
demoadmin, password, /R
```

/C for create application or /R for refresh application.

"Congratulations, Penny! You created your first Planning application." The Consultants fill the room with cheering and clapping.

"Wow, that didn't take as long as I thought it would," Penny says with relief. "Now let's call Eddie so he can start budgeting."

The cheering abruptly stops, ending in an uncomfortable silence.

"You tell her," says SuperManager to Mr. Anachronsim.

"No, you tell her," says Mr. Anachronsim to The Translator.

The Translator nods, his cape suspiciously not swooshing. "Penny, we still have many more steps to go before we are ready to call Eddie. Next up is to complete the dimension building process for your Planning application."

Scene 5:
Build Dimensions

SuperManager tries to reassure Penny. "Rome wasn't built in a day," he says, patting her on the back. "Then again, they didn't have my project plan." Penny nods her head, a bit disappointed but still determined to plug through whatever it takes to save the budget and win over Eddie. "Let's build some dimensions!"

DEFINE CALENDAR

Recall that we defined the calendar specifications during the application creation. Planning will always create a Period dimension and Year dimension. They are always two separate dimensions. Planning does not support mixed calendar basis (Jan 2009, rolling to Quarter 1 2009, rolling to FY09 and Jan 2010, rolling to Quarter 1 2010, rolling to FY10).

```
TIME
  + YR 2009
    + Q1 2009
      + Jan 2009
      + Feb 2009
      + Mar 2009
      + Q2 2009
      + Q3 2009
      + Q4 2009
  + YR 2010
      + Q1 2010
      + Q2 2010
      + Q3 2010
      + Q4 2010
```

The default roll up structure is based on the base time periods that are defined by the budget administrator when the application is set up. As the budget administrator, you can change the names and descriptions of the periods and add new summary time periods in the hierarchy.

To view and manage any dimensions in Planning Classic, select *Administration >> Dimensions* after you have opened the application. Let's take a look at the Year dimension.

View and Edit Year

While you can't change the start year, you can add years to your Planning application and add aliases (or descriptions) to members.

To edit Year members,

1.   Select Administration >> Dimensions:

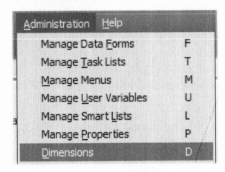

2.   Choose Year from the dimension drop down.
3.   Check FY09 and click the Edit Year button:

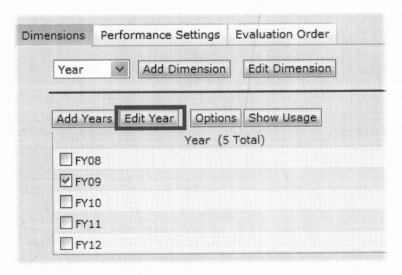

4. Add an alias to FY09 called PY (PY is short for "Prior Year"):

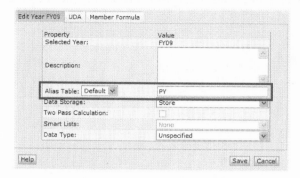

5. Click Save.
6. Repeat the same steps, setting FY10 to CY (Current Year):

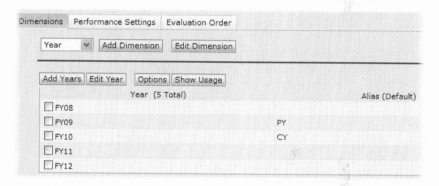

7. Click Save.

You can also edit the dimension member year itself, adding an alias or renaming the member.

To edit the Year dimension member:

1. Select Edit Dimension when Year is selected in the dimension drop down.
2. Update the Dimension member name, alias or other properties (more on the member properties in just a moment):

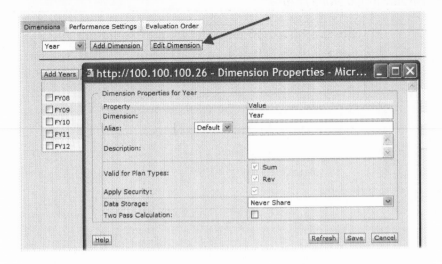

If you have Essbase experience, you may identify an issue with a dimension named "Year". We'll see in a few pages.

To add years to a Planning application:
1. Select the Year dimension from the dimension drop down in the Dimension editor.
2. To add years, click Add Years button.
3. Enter the number of years to add:

To set the current period and year:
1. Select Period or Year dimension from the dimension drop down in the Dimension editor.
2. Click the Options button.
3. Change the period and year as necessary:

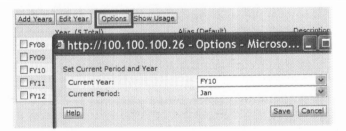

Update the Period Dimension

Remember the application creation wizard built the Period dimension for us, but we can still update it. Now let's review and update the Period dimension.

1. Select Administration >> Dimensions:

2. Choose Period from the dimension drop down:

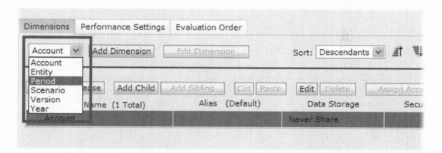

3. Expand and review the Period dimension that was created by the Planning Application Wizard:

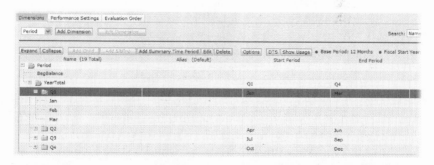

Notice that we see the hierarchy of months, quarters and years. Aliases (long descriptions or alternate names that can be given to members) are blank. We see that each Period rollup has a Start Period and an End period.

Penny knows the CFO is a stickler for seeing the full month names on all reports. She decides the most efficient way to provide this in reporting is to add the month names as aliases in Planning.

4. Select Jan.
5. Click the Edit button. The Member Property window displays with a number of options.
6. In the Alias drop down, select Default (this is probably your only available choice).
7. Type in "January":

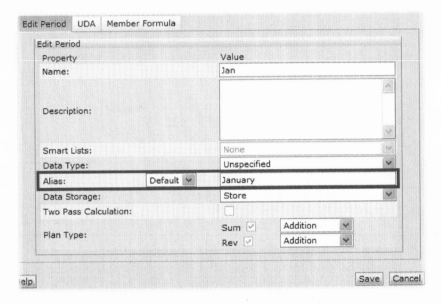

8. Click Save.
9. Repeat the same steps to assign the full month names to the default alias table.

Turn on DTS

Dynamic time series (DTS) allows end users to retrieve dynamic 'to-date' totals from the Planning database. To enable DTS, a dimension must be tagged with the Time dimension property and luckily for you, Planning already assigned this property to the Period dimension. Now you can assign a description to the generation identifying an alternative display for end users like "year-to-date", "quarter-to-date", "history-to-date", etc.

1. Click the DTS button:

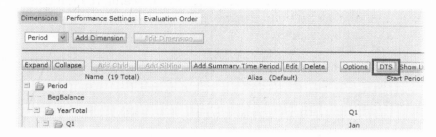

2. Check the options for QTD and YTD and identify the correct generations for each (QTD is generation 2 and YTD is generation 1):

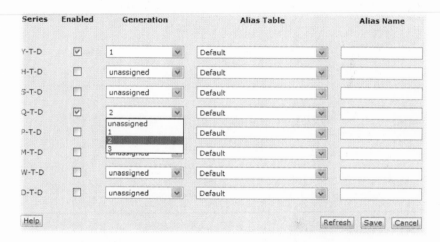

You can define aliases for the DTS series. For example, you may want to display on reports and data forms "YearToDate" instead of "Y-T-D".

3. Click Save.

Did you get the following error message?

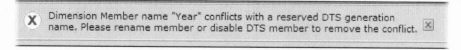

Dimension Member name "Year" conflicts with a reserved DTS generation name. Please rename member or disable DTS member to remove the conflict.

Year is a reserved word in Planning and Essbase when you turn on DTS. So in order to enable DTS for our Planning application, you must rename the Year dimension.

4. Click Cancel to get out of the DTS screen.
5. Select the Year dimension from the dimension drop down in the Dimension editor.
6. Select Edit Dimension when Year is selected in the dimension drop down.
7. Change the Year member name to FiscalYear:

Dimension Properties for Year

Property		Value
Dimension:		FiscalYear
Alias:	Default ✓	
Description:		
Valid for Plan Types:		✓ Sum ✓ Rev
Apply Security:		✓
Data Storage:		Never Share ✓
Two Pass Calculation:		☐

Help   Refresh Save Cancel

8. Click Save.

To push the changes we've made so far to Essbase (we have to rename the dimension member in Essbase so DTS can be successfully added),

9. Select Administration >> Manage Database:

Manage Database

Refresh Database Options
☐ Database
☐ Security Filters
☐ Shared Members
☐ Validate Limit

Create   Refresh

10. Check database and click Refresh.
11. Click Refresh.
12. Click Finish.

Now go back into the Period dimension and enable and set
the DTS settings.

13. Select Period from the dimension drop down in the
Dimension editor.
14. Click the DTS button:

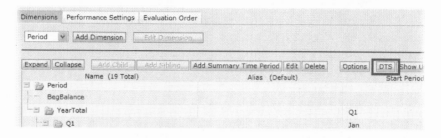

15. Check the options for QTD and YTD and identify the
correct generations for each:

Series	Enabled	Generation	Alias Table	Alias Name
Y-T-D	☑	1	Default	
H-T-D	☐	unassigned	Default	
S-T-D	☐	unassigned	Default	
Q-T-D	☑	2	Default	
P-T-D	☐	unassigned / 1 / 2 / 3	Default	
M-T-D	☐	unassigned	Default	
W-T-D	☐	unassigned	Default	
D-T-D	☐	unassigned	Default	

| Help | | | Refresh | Save | Cancel |

16. Click Save.

You should be able to successfully save the DTS settings.

Now before we move on to the other dimensions, let's take a
break from the keyboard to learn about dimension types and
member properties.

DEFINE DIMENSION TYPES AND MEMBER PROPERTIES

Remember when we updated the aliases for FY09 and
FY10? Alias is one of the possible member properties in Planning

(and Essbase, for that matter). All dimensions and members will have properties associated with them. You might also recall how we turned on DTS for the Period dimension (the one Planning assigned as the "Time" dimension). A dimension can also have a dimension type that allows certain functionality in Planning.

Dimension Types

A dimension can be assigned a dimension type which enables specific functionality and member properties for time and financial intelligence within Planning. Valid dimension types for Planning applications include:

- Accounts
- Time
- Country
- Attribute

Planning will assign the Accounts, Time, and Country dimension types by default. The Country dimension type is used for the multi-currency modules.

Planning dimensions will have a number of properties in addition to dimension types. In most cases, these properties are applicable for all members as well as top level dimension nodes.

Description

The Description property allows administrators to add an additional description to a member. Only administrators view description properties.

Alias

The Alias property provides an alternate name or description for the member. This property is viewed by end users and is assigned by alias table. You can use multiple alias tables to store different member names for end users to use in planning and reporting. For instance, you might want to have an alias table for "English" and another for "Spanish" so your users can practice their espanól when looking at members in forms and reports.

Data Type

Members in Planning may have a specific data type assigned: Unspecified, Currency, Non-Currency, Percentage, Smart List, Date and Time. We'll further define these data types when we discuss the Accounts dimension; this is typically when you select a Data Type other than "Unspecified".

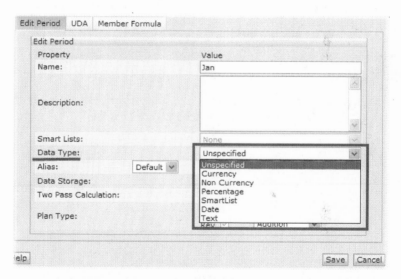

Data Storage

The Data Storage property tells Essbase how the member should be stored back in Essbase. Valid data storage options include:

- Store - Store the data value with the member.
- Never share - Do not allow members to be shared implicitly; Planning creates a lot of "Never Shared" members by default so that you can easily send information into summary members for "Target" versions.

- Label Only - Create members for navigation and grouping. These members usually won't make sense from a logical consolidation standpoint.
- Shared Member - Share data between two or more members.
- Dynamic Calc and Store - Do not calculate the data value until a user requests it, but store the data value immediately after the retrieval. This type was designed to be used for infrequently calculated formulas.
- Dynamic Calc - Do not calculate the data value until a user requests it, and then discard the data value.

When should you set a member to Store in Planning? When you will need to load data or input data to that member. Set a member to store if that member has a large number of children. Most of the time, your large sparse dimensions will be set to Store. (What is a sparse dimension? We'll get there in a few scenes, because it's a somewhat advanced topic.)

In most cases, use the Dynamic Calc property for your variances, ratios, averages, and other formulas. You can also set upper level members of a hierarchy to dynamic calc when those members have just a few children. Often times you set upper levels of the Accounts and Time dimensions (and other dense dimensions) to Dynamic Calc to help reduce your database size.

For performance reasons, you should virtually never use the Dynamic Calc and Store property. We recommend sticking to Dynamic Calc unless you have little used sparse members with very complicated formulas.

You should assign Never Share to a member that is the only child of its parent (or could potentially be the only child of its parent). Essbase has a built-in feature called Implicit Sharing, a mischievous gremlin of a function that can cause confusion in your Essbase databases. Essbase tries to be smart for us. When a parent only has one child, the data values for both the parent and the child will always be the same, right? So Essbase decides to only store one value, the child value, which reduces your database size. But this causes issues in loading or inputting data for the parent, who dynamically pulls the data value from the child.

```
⊟ Product <5> {Caffeinated, Intro Date, Ounces, Pkg Type
   ⊞ 100 (+) <3> (Alias: Colas)
   ⊞ 200 (+) <4> (Alias: Root Beer)
   ⊞ 300 (+) <3> (Alias: Cream Soda)
   ⊟ 400 (+) <1> (Alias: Fruit Soda) (Never Share)
       400-10 (+) (Alias: Grape) {Caffeinated: False, Intro
   ⊞ Diet (~) <3> (Alias: Diet Drinks)
```

When should you use Label Only? Use Label Only for members like "Scenario", "Ratios", or "Drivers" whose sole purpose in life is to organize the dimension and hierarchy: members for which it never makes sense to add their children together. A member marked as Label Only will automatically pull the value of its first child when referenced. Because of this, when we make a member Label Only, we will often make its first child have a plus and the other children have a tilde to designate that only the first child is rolling to the member. This is entirely to help indicate what's going on in Essbase to a user who might not know that a Label Only member pulls the value from its first child.

In this example below, it makes no sense to add Actual and Budget together, so we flag Scenario as Label Only:

```
⊟ Scenario (Label Only)
    Actual (+)
    Budget (~)
    Variance (~) {Dynamic Calc} {Two Pass}
    Variance % (~) {Dynamic Calc} {Two Pass}
```

Valid for Plan Type

We've already discussed that a single planning application may have multiple plan types or databases. Penny's database has two plan types: Sum and Rev. Depending on the dimension, a dimension (or member) may or may not be required for all plan types. As the administrator, you have some flexibility in defining the dimensions and members that are valid and available in the plan types. You can specify how the member should roll up within the hierarchy using the Consolidation property once a member is assigned to one or more plan types.

For the Year and Period dimensions, all members are assigned to all plan types. The budget administrator cannot change this assignment (notice the check marks are grayed out):

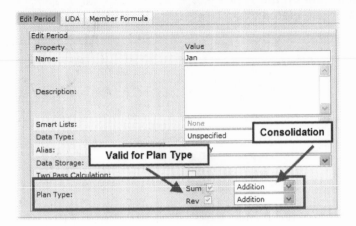

You can, however, assign the consolidation property. What's a consolidation property?

Consolidation Operators

Consolidation operators tell Essbase how to roll up the members in the outline. Valid consolidation operators for Planning include:

- Addition (+)
- Subtraction (-)
- Multiplication (*)
- Division (/)
- Percent (%)
- Ignore (~)
- Never (^)

Note!

Never consolidate (^) will not aggregate a member up across any dimension in the Essbase database (e.g. prices, index) while no consolidate (~) will not aggregate a member up for the dimension in which it resides but will aggregate for all other dimensions (e.g. Product, Customer).

Two Pass

The two pass member property tells Essbase "Come back and calculate this member at the end." Why is this important? Let's look at an example.

The Accounts dimension is calculated first (we'll learn this shortly) so Profit % is calculated based on input sales and profit. Once we roll up the Time dimension, the monthly Profit % is added together and placed in Q1's Profit %:

A	B	C	D	E	F
1	Jan	Feb	Mar	Q1	
2 Profit	100	100	100	300	
3 Sales	1000	1000	1000	3000	
4 Profit %	10%	10%	10%	30%	
5					
6					

Hmmm... something's not right there. We want Profit % to recalculate once the quarter and year totals for Profit and sales have been calculated. Tag the Profit % member with the two pass member property and Essbase circles back to calculate the correct percent after it's finished everything else:

A	B	C	D	E	F
1	Jan	Feb	Mar	Q1	
2 Profit	100	100	100	300	
3 Sales	1000	1000	1000	3000	
4 Profit % (tagged as two pass calc)	10%	10%	10%	10%	
5					
6					

UDAs

You can create user defined attributes for members on the UDA tab. UDAs provide a way to reference groups of members for analysis, calculations, or data loading. For example, say you want to perform a bonus 10% calculation for all managers managing "Large" markets and 5% bonus calculation for all managers managing "Small" market accounts.

While UDAs can be used to filter, what they can't do is easily give a subtotal for "Large" and "Small" markets (alternate hierarchies or attributes would be a solution to meet this requirement).

Member Formulas

Because Planning sits on top of Essbase, you have an amazingly powerful calculation engine at your electronic fingertips. One way to build in calculations for Planning is through member formulas that are calculated back in Essbase. You can use a number of functions and operators to create all sorts of business rules and calculations.

Mathematical functions define and return values based on selected member expressions. These functions include most standard statistical functions. An example with a mathematical function would be the member formula for the "Variance":

```
@VAR (Actual, Budget);
```

Conditional operators allow tests based on criteria. A member formula to calculate "Commission" might use conditional checks:

```
IF (Sales > 1000)
     Sales * .02;
ELSE
     10;
ENDIF
```

In English-speak, if Sales is greater than 1000, then Commission is equal to Sales times 2 percent; otherwise, Commission is equal to 10.

Functions can also be used in member formulas. The member formula for the "Market Share" member uses an index function:

```
Sales % @PARENTVAL (Markets, Sales);
```

In other words, Market Share is equal to the Sales for the current member as a percent of the current member's parent data value for the Markets dimension.

The member formula for the member "Mar YTD" uses a financial function:

```
@PTD(Jan:Mar);
```

The member formula for "Payroll" shows you an example of how to use conditional or Boolean criteria:

```
IF (@ISIDESC (East) OR @ISIDESC (West))
     Sales * .15;
ELSEIF (@ISIDESC(Central))
     Sales * .11;
ELSE
     Sales * .10;
ENDIF
```

To put it in English, for all of the members under and including East and West, Payroll is equal to Sales times 15 percent; for all members under and including Central, Payroll is equal to Sales times 11 percent; and for all other members, Payroll is equal to Sales times 10 percent.

Tip!

The syntax for member formulas is almost identical to the syntax used in calc scripts. The calc script scene provides more detail on Essbase calc syntax.

Note!

Member formulas must end with semicolons. If the member name has spaces, you must enclose the member name in double quotes.

Now that you are fully fluent in Planning and Essbase dimension types and member properties, we'll turn our attention to building out the remaining dimensions, starting with adding a UDA to the Period dimension.

ADD A UDA

Let's create a UDA now to highlight Holiday versus Non-Holiday months for the Periods dimension.

1. Within the Planning web client, select Administration >> Dimensions.
2. Select the Period dimension.
3. Navigate to and select the member Nov.
4. Click Edit.
5. Select the UDA tab.
6. Select the Add button.
7. Type in the UDA value "Holiday Season":

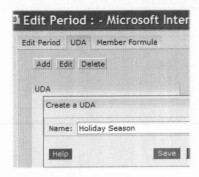

8. Select the Save button.
9. Click Cancel (to close the Add UDA window).
10. Select the desired UDA and assign by selecting the arrow icon:

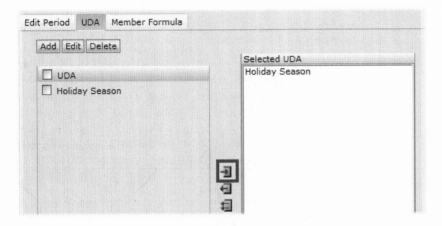

11. Click Save.
12. Select the member Dec and click Edit.
13. Select the UDA tab.
14. Select the "Holiday Season" UDA and assign by clicking the arrow icon:

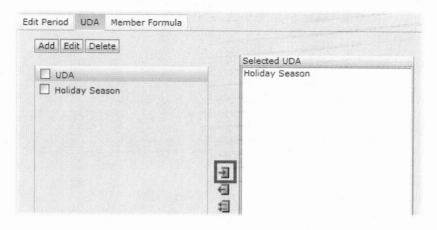

15. Click Save.

Remember UDAs provide additional ways to categorize dimensions. They are best used on dense dimensions or for behind the scenes use on sparse dimensions (more on dense and sparse on page 423). UDAs can be referenced in load rules, calc scripts and reporting and analysis (no data forms though). You may create a business rule to calculate planned sales by month; you expect all "Holiday Season" months to increase 25% while non "Holiday Season" months will increase 10%. To perform this logic, you can reference the UDA in a calc script or business rule.

BUILD ENTITY

The Entity dimension is typically the dimension containing your organization or geographical hierarchy for reporting and analysis. Workflow approvals and signoffs will take place by the Entity dimension and currencies will be assigned to entity members if you are using Planning's built in multi-currency functionality.

The Entity dimension is required for all plan types, but members and hierarchies may vary by plan type. For example, you may have a detailed revenue plan type that only requires the sales business units, whereas the summary plan type requires all entities. A member will automatically be valid for any plan type for which its parent is valid.

Add Members to the Entities Dimension

Warning! Be careful not to click Add Dimension. Once you add a dimension to an application, it isn't easy to delete it:

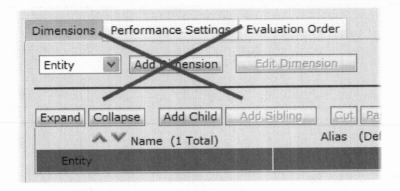

To add members to the Entity dimension:
1. If not in the Dimension editor, select Administration >> Dimensions.
2. Select Entity from the dimension drop down.
3. Click on the Add Child button:

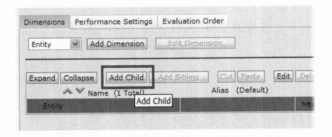

4. Type in "TotalGeography" for the member name.
5. Type in "Total Geography" for the alias.

Notice that a number of the properties already have default values assigned. That will save you some time (which is one of the few things that they're not making more of). Data storage is set to NeverShare. Base currency is set to USD (the only currency defined in single currency application in Penny's case). The Sum and Rev plan types are both checked with a consolidation operator of Addition assigned. Data type is set to unspecified.

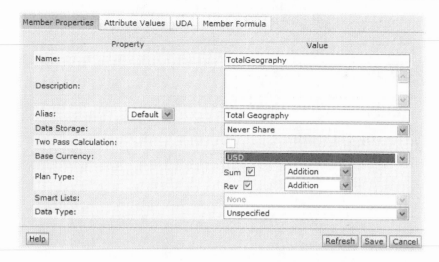

6. Click Save.
7. Repeat the same steps to add the hierarchy and members to the Entities dimension per the table below, using Add Child, Add Sibling buttons:

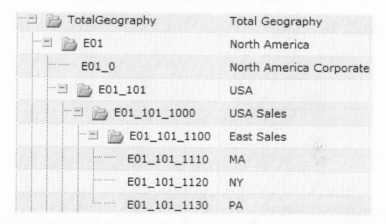

Set the properties for each of the members according to the following table.

Member Name	Alias	Storage	Plan Type	Consol
E01	North America	Never Share	Sum, Rev	+
E01_0	North	Never	Sum,	+

	America Corporate	Share	Rev	
E01_101	USA	Never Share	Sum, Rev	+
E01_101_1000	USA Sales	Never Share	Sum, Rev	+
E01_101_1100	East Sales	Never Share	Sum, Rev	+
E01_101_1110	MA	Never Share	Sum, Rev	+
E01_101_1120	NY	Never Share	Sum, Rev	+
E01_101_1130	PA	Never Share	Sum, Rev	+

Notice that you didn't have to change any of the properties other than member name and alias. Do you see why we love default properties?

You may be asking why members are tagged Never Share instead of Store. This is to prevent implied shares when a member only has one child. Watch out for members that have only one child.

After you have made a number of changes to the application, it is always good to sync those changes with Essbase (in other words, "save often").

To push the changes we've made so far to Essbase:
1. Select Administration >> Manage Database.
2. Check database and click Refresh.
3. Click Refresh.
4. Click Finish.

BUILD ALTERNATE HIERACHIES

You've just built a single hierarchy with entities rolling up by geography. But what if you also wanted to create a hierarchy that rolled up base entities by function? Do you have to build another application? Nope. All you need is an alternate hierarchy.

An alternate hierarchy is a set of shared members in a separate hierarchy within the same dimension; shared members do not store data but reference the original base member. So if you want to roll up entities by geography or function, you can do that. If you want to have a legal entity hierarchy and a management reporting hierarchy, you can do that. If you want to roll up products by category as well as product manager, you can do that. Alternate hierarchies help you as the administrator build in easy to use reporting structures to meet the needs of end users.

Penny needs to build an alternate hierarchy to group entities by function. Follow along with us now. To build an alternate hierarchy and add shared members to the entity dimension:

1. If not in the Dimension editor, select Administration >> Dimensions.
2. Select Entity from the dimension drop down.
3. Click on the Add Child button.
4. Type in "Function" for the member name.
5. Repeat the same steps to add the hierarchy and members to the Entities dimension per the table below, using *Add Child, Add Sibling* buttons:

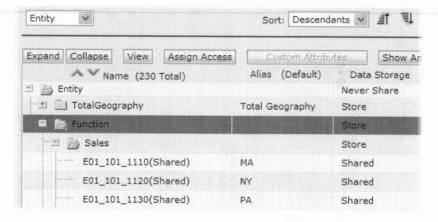

Set the properties for each of the members per the following table.

Member Name	Alias	Storage	Plan Type	Consol
Sales		Store	Sum, Rev	~ Ignore
E01_101_1110	MA	Shared	Sum, Rev	+
E01_101_1120	NY	Shared	Sum, Rev	+
E01_101_1130	PA	Shared	Sum, Rev	+

Sales is set to ~ because we do not want to double count numbers in the dimension member Entity.

If you run into the following message, click OK. Shared members will always inherit properties from the base member:

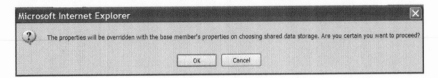

Notice that if you click Edit to view and edit the properties of a shared member, the only things that you can change are assigned plan types and the consolidation method:

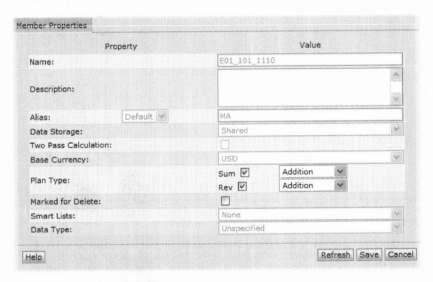

Alternate Hierarchy Rules

Helpful
Info

- Shared members must be in the same dimension and must reside below the nonshared member.
- Shared members cannot have children.
- An unlimited number of shared members is allowed.
- Shared members cannot have UDAs, member formulas, or attributes.
- Shared members may have aliases.

Now that you know the basics of Entity building, let us build the Account dimension.

BUILD ACCOUNT

The process to build the Account dimension is the same process as the Entity dimension. The only difference is that we have a few more properties to assign.

Source Plan Type

As the administrator, you can define which accounts are valid for which plan types. If an account is valid for more than one plan type, a source plan type must be specified. The plan types valid for a member are determined by the plan types assigned to the parent. For example, in Penny's design the expense accounts will not be added to the Rev cube:

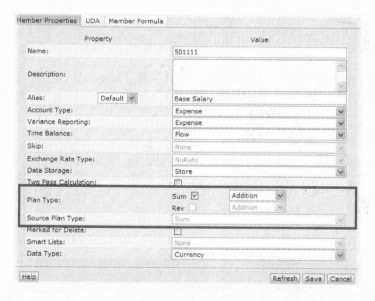

Expense accounts will only exist in the Sum cube, but revenue accounts will exist in both Rev and Sum. Because the account exists in two places, we have to determine the source plan type – where data will be stored. In Penny's design, the revenue accounts will be stored in the Rev plan type and the Sum plan type will reference Rev data values using an @XREF function.

Member Properties	UDA	Member Formula		
	Property		Value	
Name:			411100	
Description:				
Alias:	Default ∨		Operating Revenue	
Account Type:			Revenue	∨
Variance Reporting:			Non-Expense	∨
Time Balance:			Flow	∨
Skip:			None	∨
Exchange Rate Type:			NoRate	∨
Data Storage:			Store	∨
Two Pass Calculation:			☐	
Plan Type:			Sum ☑ Addition ∨	
			Rev ☑ Addition ∨	
Source Plan Type:			Rev	∨
Marked for Delete:			☐	
Smart Lists:			None	∨
Data Type:			Currency	∨
Help			Refresh Save Cancel	

Variance Reporting

The Variance Reporting (also known as Expense Reporting in Essbase circles) property is a simple flag that tells downstream calculations and reports whether a positive variance is good or bad. If you're over your target on revenue, everyone is happy. Of course, the opposite is true when you spend too much on Office Supplies. Well, not everyone will be upset, but you don't want to be making enemies in the Finance Department when it comes time for them to cut you the bonus check for those positive-variance Revenues, right?

Let's walk you through an example. If you budget $1,000,000 in revenue and you make $1,100,000, that's a favorable variance of $100,000. Expenses are quite the opposite: if you budget $1,000,000 in marketing expenses and you spend $1,100,000, that's an unfavorable variance of $100,000. In general, you want expense data to have lower actuals than budget.

To allow for this, Planning (and Essbase) uses a property called Variance Reporting. Tag all of your expense accounts with "Expense" and Essbase will calculate the variance correctly when using the @VAR or @VARPER functions. Essbase will show a positive variance when Actual data is higher than Budget for revenue or metric accounts. Essbase will show a negative variance for those expense accounts tagged with the "Expense Reporting" property:

	Jan	FY2007		
	Actual	Budget	Variance	
Net_Rev	100	75	25	
Op_Expense	100	75	-25	
Op_Income	#Missing	#Missing	#Missing	

The Variance Reporting Expense property is set to Expense for all measures where budget should be higher than actual:

Member Properties	UDA	Member Formula	
Property		**Value**	
Name:			
Description:			
Alias:	Default ▾		
Account Type:		Revenue	▾
Variance Reporting:		Non-Expense	▾
Time Balance:		Expense	
		Non-Expense	
Skip:		None	
Exchange Rate Type:			

If you choose an account type of "Saved Assumption", you can specify the variance reporting property. If you choose any of the other account types, the variance reporting property will be automatically assigned.

Time Balance Property

The Time Balance property is only available in the dimension tagged as Accounts, and is used to tell Planning/Essbase how a given member should be aggregated up the Time dimension.

For example, should Headcount for January, February, and March be added together for Q1 (quarter 1)? This definitely wouldn't make sense.

	Actual	FY2007			
	Jan	Feb	Mar	Q1	Q2
Headcount	100	125	122	347	#Mis

In most cases you want **Q1** to equal the March headcount (though some might want the average across the periods), or in other words, the last headcount in the period. To get Planning to do this, you tag Headcount with the Balance option (in Essbase circles this is the Time Balance Last or "TB Last" setting) so that it will take the last member's value when aggregating time:

Time Balance:	Balance
Skip:	Flow
	First
Exchange Rate Type:	Balance
	Average
Data Storage:	Fill
Two Pass Calculation:	Weighted Average - Actual_Actual
	Weighted Average - Actual_365

Depending on your requirements, you could also assign Time Balance First or Time Balance Average.   Here is Q1's headcount now nicely equaling its last child, Mar (short for March):

	Actual	FY2007			
	Jan	Feb	Mar	Q1	Q2
Headcount	100	125	122	122	#M

What if we have just closed January? Then, showing the March headcount wouldn't be accurate because March is blank. A sub-property associated with Time Balance allows us to define how we handle missing & zero values. In this example, we would want to ignore any blanks (or #missing). So we set Headcount to Balance, and then select Skip "Missing":

Time Balance:	Balance
Skip:	None
Exchange Rate Type:	None
	Missing
Data Storage:	Zeros
Two Pass Calculation:	Missing And Zeros

Now Qtr1 will correctly show the January value:

	Actual	FY2007			
	Jan	Feb	Mar	Q1	Q2
Headcount	100	#Missing	#Missing	100	#M

Another example of Time Balance utilization is for inventory analysis members:

Tip!

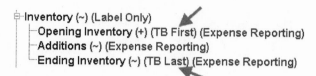

Fill is another Time Balance option that will automatically "fill" or distribute the value set at a parent to all of its descendants. Weighted average Time Balance options provide a waited daily average accounting with or without Leap Year.

If you choose an account type of "Saved Assumption", you can specify the time balance property. If you choose any of the other account types, the time balance property will be automatically assigned. Saved Assumptions are fun that way.

Account Type

The Account Type will dictate how an account will flow over time and how the account's sign will calculate when performing variance calculations. Each account member will be assigned an account type:

- Expense – Flow and Expense
- Revenue – Flow and Non-Expense
- Asset – Balance and Non-Expense
- Liability – Balance and Non-Expense
- Equity– Balance and Non-Expense
- Saved Assumption – User Defined Time Balance and User Defined Variance Reporting

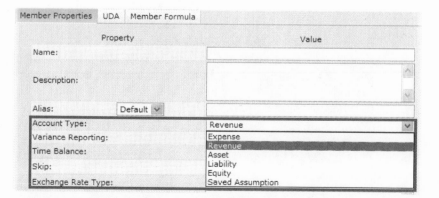

The Saved Assumption account type is often used to store drivers like headcount, square feet, or units sold. Once Saved Assumption is selected, you define variance reporting and time balance properties for the member.

Data Type

The Data Type property determines how values are stored in account members, and if multi-currency is used, the exchange rates used to calculate values. Valid data type options include Unspecified, Currency, Non Currency, Percentage, Smart List, Text, and Date. For the most part the data type names are self explanatory with the exception of Smart Lists. Smart Lists are controlled drop down selections of text values for a member (more on Smart Lists starting on page 362).

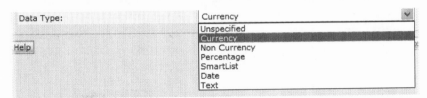

And yes, Planning can display date and text account members. An account member with a data type of "Text" allows users to enter free form text comments or information for the account at the intersection of other dimension members. In your Capital Expense application, you create an account called "Asset Model Number" for users to input a specific model number that can be entered by item.

Exchange Rate Type

The Exchange Rate Type is only enabled if Data Type is set to Currency and the application is multi-currency.
- Average - uses account's average exchange rate
- Ending - uses account's ending exchange rate
- Historical - uses account's exchange rate that was in effect when the earnings for a Retained Earnings account were earned or the assets for a Fixed Assets account were purchased (for example)

Penny's head is swimming with new account properties. There's only one way to help this sink in. Let's create the Accounts dimension.

Add Members to the Accounts Dimension

Before we start building out the account dimension, let's review a few considerations for the Accounts dimension member (the top level node). 1) You can rename the Account dimension; 2) it must be valid for all plan types; 3) security is activated automatically; 4) the Account member can be tagged as Two Pass; 5) by default, the Account dimension is dense; and finally 6) custom attributes are not allowed for the Account dimension unless it is changed to sparse.

What do the terms dense and sparse mean? It is too complex to cover now. Hold on to your boots; we'll cover dense and sparse in the Calculate with Calc Scripts scene.

Recall that we mentioned the hierarchy building process is the same across dimensions.

To build the account dimension,

1. If not in the Dimension editor, select Administration >> Dimensions.
2. Select Account from the dimension drop down.
3. Click on the Add Child button.
4. Type in "Income Statement" for the member name.
5. Repeat the same steps to add the hierarchy and members to the Account dimension according to the image and table below, using *Add Child* and *Add Sibling* buttons:

Set the properties for each of the members according to the following table. All data types are set to Currency. Variance Reporting and Time Balance properties should be inherited from the Account Type property. Two pass should not be selected.

Member Name	Account Type	Storage	Consol	Plan Types	Source Plan

Member Name	Account Type	Storage	Consol	Plan Types	Source Plan
Account		Label Only			
Income Statement	Revenue	Dynamic Calc	+	Sum, Rev	Sum
300000	Revenue	Dynamic Calc	+	Sum, Rev	Sum
400000	Revenue	Dynamic Calc	+	Sum, Rev	Sum
411000	Revenue	Dynamic Calc	+	Sum, Rev	Rev
411100	Revenue	Store	+	Sum, Rev	Rev
411200	Revenue	Store	+	Sum, Rev	Rev
500000	Expense	Dynamic Calc	-	Sum	
501111	Expense	Store	+	Sum	
502100	Expense	Store	+	Sum	
503100	Expense	Store	+	Sum	

The detailed revenue accounts will be sourced from the Rev plan type:

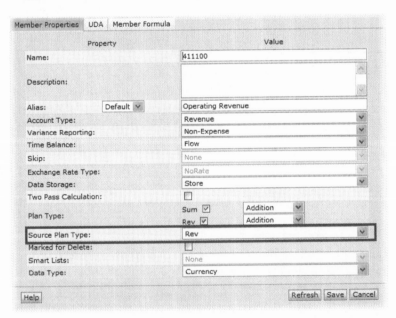

Remember for the expense accounts check only the option for the Sum plan type. The expense accounts are not required in the Rev plan type:

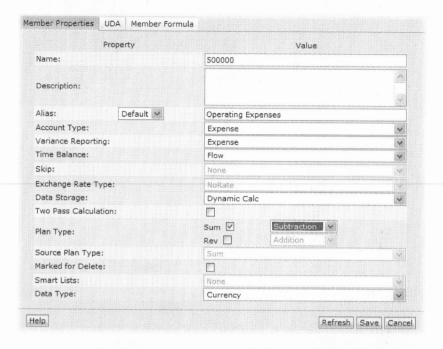

One last note – did you notice how each dynamic calculated member rolled up to another dynamically calculated member? Never (or only on really rare occasions where you have a damned good reason) should a dynamically calculated member roll up to a stored member. Stored members can and should roll into dynamically calculated members.

Name (11 Total)		Data Storage
⊟ 📁 Account		Label only
⊟ 📁 Income Statement		Dynamic Calc
⊟ 📁 300000	Net Income	Dynamic Calc
⊟ 📁 400000	Gross Profit	Dynamic Calc
⊟ 📁 411000	Gross Revenue	Dynamic Calc
411100	Operating Revenue	Store
411200	Revenue Synergies	Store
⊟ 📁 500000	Operating Expenses	Dynamic Calc
501111	Base Salary	Store
502100	Travel Expense	Store
503100	Office Supplies	Store

Now refresh Essbase with the new changes.

1. Select Administration >> Manage Database.
2. Check Database.
3. Click Refresh.
4. Click Refresh (yep, you click a Refresh button twice).
5. Click Finish once update is complete.

REVIEW THE OUTLINE IN ADMINISTRATION SERVICES

Administration Services (also known as *Essbase* Administration Services – EAS – or *Analytic* Administration Services – AAS – depending on your version) is a central administration tool for managing and maintaining all of Essbase. The goal of Administration Services is to make Essbase applications easier to maintain in a modernized interface that is fully cross-platform supported. Although in the case of Planning, you won't be making any changes to the outline in EAS. You should only make changes in the Planning web client (or EPMA for non-Classic applications). You will use EAS for some Planning tasks, like calculation scripts, data loading, and application management. We'll cover most of these topics throughout the remainder of the musical.

For now, we will use the Administration Services console to see what is created "under the covers" of Planning. As a Planning administrator, it is important to know and understand the "Essbase" aspect of Planning.

1. Launch the Essbase Administration Services console (your location may differ):

2. Enter your ID and password:

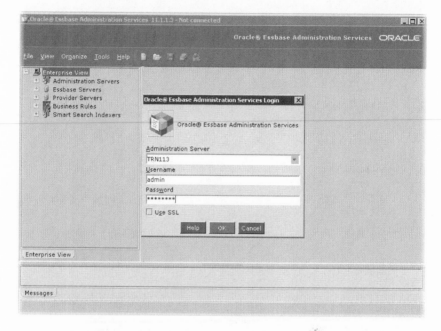

3. Expand the server to view the list of applications.
4. Select the Entpln application.
5. Expand and you'll see that two databases have been created:

6. Expand Sum.
7. Right-click on the Sum outline and select *Edit*:

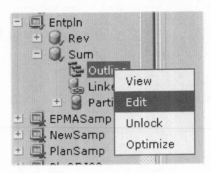

The outline will open in the Outline Editor.

8. Review the dimensions, hierarchies, and properties built from Planning:

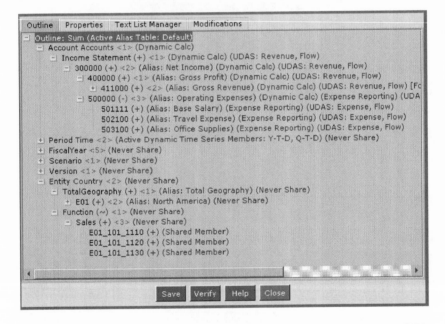

9. Right-click on the account "411000" and select Edit Member Properties.
10. Click on the Formula tab:

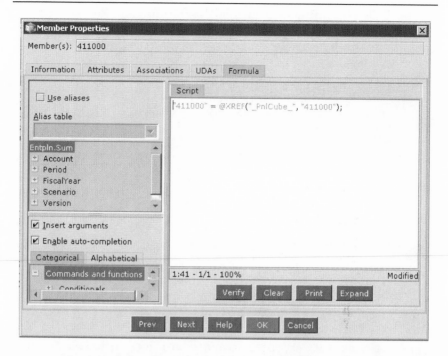

A member formula with an @XREF function was automatically added to the account, **"411000"** = **@XREF("_PnlCube_"**, **"411000");** . Since the source plan type for the revenue account members is the Rev plan type, any data will be shared using the @XREF function to externally reference the Sum plan type (the location alias for Sum is _PnlCube_):

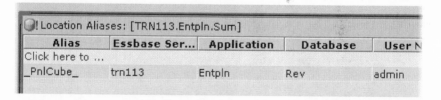

Repeat the same steps to view properties for account "411100" and note the same @XREF function is added. The data storage for this member in the Sum cube has also been set to dynamic calc automatically even though you specifically set the "Store" data storage.

Now let's take a look at the Rev plan type:

11. Expand Rev in the Administration Services Console.

12. Right-click on the Rev outline and select Edit.

13. The outline will open in the Outline Editor.
14. Review the dimensions, hierarchies, and properties built from Planning:

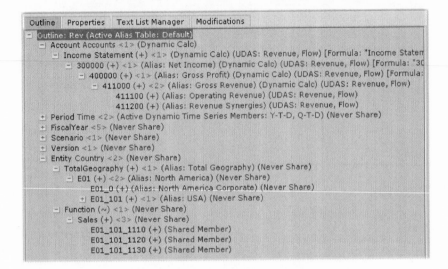

Notice the expense accounts are not included in this database (provided you've been following along correctly).

15. Right-click on the account "411000" and select Edit Member Properties.
16. Click on the Formula tab. There are no member formulas because the source data value is stored here.

Once you've reviewed the underlying Essbase outlines, close the outline (Click Close) and close Administration Services.

Note!   Remember you cannot edit anything in the Administration Services console. Any properties changed here will be overwritten the next time you "refresh to Essbase."

We've covered the standard Planning dimensions of Entity and Account. How about those dimensions that are unique to your Planning process and requirements like Customer and Employee? Let's now turn our attention to custom dimensions.

BUILD CUSTOM DIMENSIONS

Within Planning, you can add up to 13 User-Defined Dimensions into a Planning application. Examples include Customers, Employees, Products, and Projects. Once you add a user defined dimension, you can't delete it without hacking a bunch of underlying relational tables and voiding your warranty. Custom dimensions may be assigned to a specific plan type. For example, the Employee dimension may exist in a salary plan type while Product exists in a sales plan type. Once you assign a custom dimension, all members in that custom dimension are available in that plan type.

By now you are an expert at building dimensions so try to build the Segments dimension below without the detailed steps (just in case, we've listed those steps below):

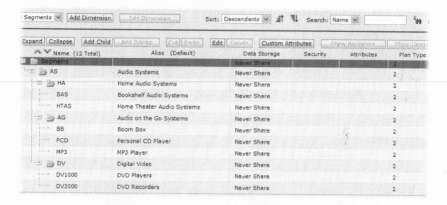

Add Segments Dimension

If you're not ready to branch out on your own just yet, here are the steps to follow:
1. Select Administration >> Dimensions.
2. Select the Add Dimension button.

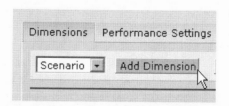

Be careful clicking *Add Dimension*. Once you add dimensions to an application, you CANNOT easily delete them. There's no Undo for the Add Dimension button.

3. Type in "Segments" for the Dimension name.
4. Do not check the Sum plan type.
5. Check the Rev plan type.

6. Do not check Apply Security (we won't secure based on this dimension).
7. Accept default for data storage - Never Share:

Add Dimension		
Property		Value
Dimension:		Segments
Alias:	Default	
Description:		
Valid for Plan Types:		☐ Sum ☑ Rev
Apply Security:		☐
Data Storage:		Never Share
Two Pass Calculation:		☐
Help		Refresh Save Cancel

8. Click Save.

Why did we only select the Rev plan type? Per Penny's design, revenue will be planned by segment but not expenses.

9. Click *OK* when you are prompted "Are you sure you want to create a new dimension?"
10. Select Segments from the Dimension drop down list in the Dimension Editor.
11. Build the following hierarchy for the new product dimension using *Add Child* or *Add Sibling*. All properties should be set to Never Share, +, and all others should accept defaults:

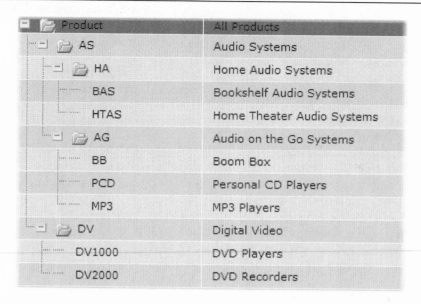

☐ 📁 Product	All Products
☐ 📁 AS	Audio Systems
☐ 📁 HA	Home Audio Systems
BAS	Bookshelf Audio Systems
HTAS	Home Theater Audio Systems
☐ 📁 AG	Audio on the Go Systems
BB	Boom Box
PCD	Personal CD Players
MP3	MP3 Players
☐ 📁 DV	Digital Video
DV1000	DVD Players
DV2000	DVD Recorders

12. Refresh Planning to Essbase (Administration >>
Manage Database).

Now that Penny has built the Segments dimension, she
needs to group the base products by Product Manager. One report
requires products down the rows and product managers across the
columns (a cross tab report of product and product manager).

Should she build another dimension called "Product
Manager" into the database listing the managers and then load data
by product by product manager? While this solution addresses the
reporting requirement, the issue with this solution is that by adding
a dimension, she is increasing the database size. You will hear a
reoccurring theme in both Planning and Essbase: minimize the
number of dimensions. This is both for performance and usability.

How about assigning a UDA of Product Manager to each
product? UDAs cannot create crosstab reports. In fact, when you
select a UDA in reporting and analysis, the base members will
display, not the actual UDA. You cannot obtain subtotals by UDA.

How about an alternate hierarchy, adding a Product
Manager member under Segments, listing product managers, and
then creating shared members for the products, rolling up to them?
The alternate hierarchy will create totals by product manager and
provide analysis paths from product manager to product. However,
because product manager and product are in the same dimension,
you cannot create a cross tab report. (One of the golden rules of

Essbase is that members from a single dimension may exist in only the row or only the column or the point of view.)

So is there a good solution to meet Penny's product manager requirement? Yes, in attribute dimensions.

BUILD AN ATTRIBUTE DIMENSION

In early versions of Essbase, you were limited in the number of dimensions that you could have per database (by practicality, if nothing else). Most databases were five to nine dimensions, and any more than that was seriously stretching Essbase's capabilities. But users complained that they needed to be able to analyze data by more dimensions.

For instance, if you had a product dimension, you might want to also analyze Product Start Date, Sales Manager, Packaging, Size, Weight, Target Group, and more as dimensions too. Since all these "dimensions" are really just alternate ways of divvying up the Product dimension (in this example), attribute dimensions were born.

Attribute dimensions are dimensions that can be placed in the rows or columns (as we discussed above) with some special considerations. Just like regular dimensions, they define characteristics about the data that is loaded to Essbase. They have hierarchies and members just like any other dimension.

One of the special qualities of attribute dimensions is that adding them to the outline does not impact the size of the Essbase database. You can add a virtually unlimited number of attribute dimensions. We've seen cubes with over 100 attribute dimensions.

Another big benefit of attributes is that they can be used to develop really nice cross tab reports. For example, we can create a report with flavors across the columns and package types down the side. You can't do this with shared members from the same dimension, but attribute dimensions give you a great way to do detailed product and customer analysis that isn't possible otherwise. You can even analyze sum totals, minimums, maximums, averages and counts of members in attribute dimensions which certainly isn't possible with UDAs.

But wait - before you get too excited, let's learn a bit more about attributes. There are four types of Attribute dimensions: Text, Numeric, Boolean, and Date.

Text attributes are the default type and are used to describe text characteristics.

When *AND, OR NOT,* <, >, =, >=, <=, <>, *!=, IN,* and *NOT IN* operations are performed on text dimensions, Essbase makes logical comparisons for text attribute dimensions. Not always the most logical thing to do, but it's there all the same.

Numeric attribute dimensions contain numeric values at level 0. You can perform *AND, OR NOT,* <, >, =, >=, <=, <>, *!=, IN,* and *NOT IN* operations on numeric attribute dimensions. You can group numeric values into ranges (using the : symbol) and include these numeric values in calculations.

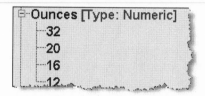

Boolean attribute dimensions contain exactly two members (that are defined by the user): True and False, Left and Right, Yes and No, Up and Down, Dog and Cat, or any other two members that you want. Once the two Boolean member names are defined, you must use the same names for all Boolean attribute dimensions in the database. When you perform *AND, OR NOT,* <, >, =, >=, <=, <>, *!=, IN,* and *NOT IN* operations on Boolean attribute dimensions, Essbase translates true to 1 and false to 0.

Date attribute members must contain date members at level-0 that are formatted properly. Valid date formats are mm-dd-yyyy or dd-mm-yyyy. All dates must be after 01-01-1970 and before 01-01-2038.

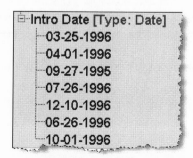

AND, OR NOT, <, >, =, >=, <=, <>, *!=, IN,* and *NOT IN* operations can be performed on Date attribute dimensions. Date values can be also included in calculations.

There are five ways to calculate attribute data: Sum, Count, Average, Minimum, and Maximum. Sum is the default when you don't specify which one to use, but you can use the other calculations as though it was yet another dimension:

	A	B	C	D	E	F
1			Year	Product	Market	Actual
2			Bottle	Can	Pkg Type	
3	Sales	Sum	$ 270,593	$ 130,262	$ 400,855	
4		Min	$ 11,750	$ 30,469	$ 11,750	
5		Max	$ 46,956	$ 62,824	$ 62,824	
6		Avg	$ 27,059	$ 43,421	$ 30,835	
7		Count	10	3	13	
8						
9						

Note! Attribute dimensions are always dynamically calculated which could mean slower performance any time an attribute is referenced in data forms and retrievals.

Attribute Dimension Rules in Planning

Helpful Info

- Consider the implication of Dynamic Calculations as reporting on Attribute dimensions can be slow.
- Define attribute dimensions on sparse dimensions only.
- You cannot tag attribute members as a shared members.
- You cannot tag attribute members as two-pass calculation.
- You cannot assign a UDA to attribute members.
- You cannot use consolidation symbols or formulas.

Let's put some of your newfound Attribute dimension knowledge to work in our Entpln application.

Create an Attribute Dimension and Members

1. In the Planning web client, select Administration >> Dimensions (if necessary).
2. Select the Segments dimension from the Dimension drop down.

3. Select the Segments dimension in the Dimension Editor (if you highlight any other member in the hierarchy, the Custom Attributes button is disabled).

4. Select the Custom Attributes button:

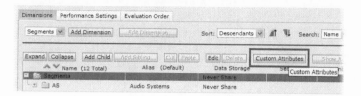

5. Select the Create button in the left panel to create a new attribute dimension.

6. Enter the name of the custom attribute: "Product Manager".

7. Select Text as the Data Type:

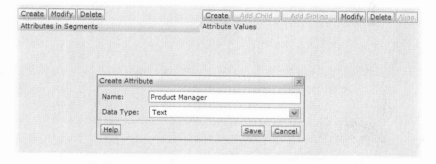

8. Click Save button.

9. Click Cancel (to close the Create Attribute window).

10. Add the Attribute values by selecting Create in the right panel:

11. Type in "Senior Managers" and click Save.

12. The Create Attribute Value window remains open. Type in "Junior Managers" and click Save.
13. Click Cancel to close the Create Attribute Value window.
14. Check the box next to "Senior Managers".
15. Click Add Child and add the following children to the Senior Managers parent ("Grace", "Marlon").
16. Click Add Child and add the following children to the Junior Managers parent ("Marilyn", "Frank"):

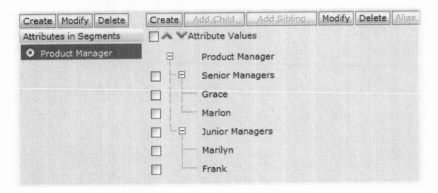

17. Click Save.

For each member, add an alias:
   o   Frank: Frank Sinatra
   o   Grace: Grace Kelly
   o   Marlon: Marlon Brando
   o   Marilyn: Norma Jean

18. In the Attribute values section, check the option next to the desired name; e.g. "Frank".
19. Click the Alias button:

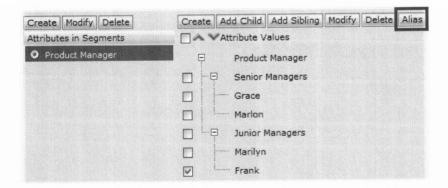

20. Enter the Alias name and click Save:

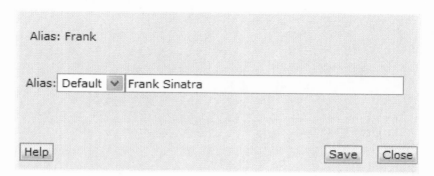

21. Click Close.
22. Repeat the same steps to assign the remaining aliases for Product Manager.
23. Click Close when attribute values are complete.

Associate Attribute Values to Base Members

Now that we've created the attribute values for product manager, we need to assign a product manager to the actual product.

24. Select the BAS member in the Product dimension and click the Edit button.
25. Select the Attribute Values tab.
26. Assign the appropriate attribute value (Marlon) by selecting the radio button and using the arrow keys to move the member to the Assigned Attribute value window:

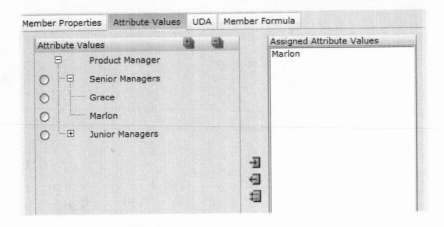

27. Click Save.
28. Repeat the same steps for remaining attribute values.
    o Assign the "Marlon" attribute to the "BAS" Segment
       member
    o Assign the "Marlon" attribute to the "HTAS"
       Segment member
    o Assign the "Frank" attribute to the "BB" Segment
       member
    o Assign the "Frank" attribute to the "PCD" Segment
       member
    o Assign the "Marilyn" attribute to the "MP3" Segment
       member
    o Assign the "Grace" attribute to the "DV1000"
       Segment member
    o Assign the "Grace" attribute to the "DV2000"
       Segment member
29. Refresh your changes to Essbase (Administration >>
    Manage Database).

In the Dimension Editor for Segments, the attributes
column should now list "View". You can click View to view the
assigned attribute:

Note! In 9.3.1 and 11.1.1, varying attributes are not supported for Planning though 11.1.1 does support varying attributes in Essbase directly.

We walked through an example of creating a text attribute dimension but remember that you can create numeric, date, and Boolean attributes.

In some cases, the design decisions are clear cut on when to use UDAs vs. alternate hierarchies vs. attribute dimensions. In other scenarios, the answer will be less obvious. Let's review some design decision points.

When should you use Attributes?

Use attributes when you need to create crosstab reports (when for instance you want to put Product in the rows and Product Start Date across the columns or Product Packaging Type in the rows and Product Start Date in the columns). Also use attributes when you need to hide a level of detail in most reports but still want it available upon request.

Attributes are very helpful when performing comparisons based on certain types of data or when performing calculations based on characteristics.

Finally, use attributes when you need to add dimensionality to the database without increasing the size of the database. Attributes are "available on request." By default they do not show up in end user Ad-hoc Analysis. In Smart View, attributes can be brought into the query using the Query Designer or Report Designer (as well as free form typing).

When should you NOT use Attributes?

Do not use attributes when you need to define characteristics that vary over time in Planning. For example, let's say we have "Employee Status" as an attribute dimension based on the "Employee" dimension. Jack was run over by a bus in October and his employee status was changed from "Active" to "Inactive" to reflect his untimely death. If we run reports for the month of January, it will look like Jack was "inactive/no longer with us" for that month. Jack was alive and kicking for months January through September, but Essbase has no way of knowing this because employee status is solely tied to the Employee dimension.

If you need to track how an attribute changes over time, you must make it a stored dimension. Varying attributes are not supported by Planning at the moment. You can parallel something like attributes changing over time using Smart Lists, though (more on that on page 362).

Do not use attributes when you need to calculate a value by placing a formula on a member (member formulas aren't allowed on attribute members). Watch out for attributes when you need to improve retrieval performance (attributes are dynamically calculated and can be slow at times).

BUILD SCENARIO

The Scenario dimension in a Planning application is used to apply and track different planning methods and create new forecasts. This dimension typically has members like "Actual", "Budget", and "Forecast". Scenarios can be associated with different time periods and different exchange rates. For example, the Budget member allows data entry for all 12 months during the annual plan. Once the budget is complete, the time periods for data entry are closed or ready only. The Forecast is completed quarterly and the next 2 rolling quarters are open for data entry. Start period, start year, end period and end year are the Scenario properties that control data entry.

If you are using multi-currency, you can associate different scenarios with different exchange rates and define whether or not to include BegBalance in the currency conversion process.

Users are assigned read, write or none access to Scenario members for data entry and for reporting and analysis. The Actual scenario is almost always assigned read.

You can also build calculated members into the Scenario dimension. Often times you want to compare Scenarios: Actual versus Budget or Budget versus Forecast and variance members are the way to meet this requirement.

Beginning in version 9.3.1, you can build hierarchies into the Scenario dimension. For example, you might build the following structure to track and highlight budget adjustments.

Penny is ready to build the Scenario dimension for her application:

1. *Select Administration >> Dimensions.*
2. Select Scenario dimension from the drop down.
3. Click Add Child/Sibling to add the scenario dimensions.
4. Add the following members and properties to the Scenario dimension (change Current to Actual by clicking Edit for the Current member):

Member	Start Year	Start Period	End Year	End Period	Storage	Enable for Process Mgmt.
Actual	2008	Jan	2012	Dec	Never Share	N
Budget	2010	Jan	2011	Dec	Never Share	Y
Forecast	2011	Apr	2012	Mar	Never Share	N

If a property is not noted above, accept the default value.

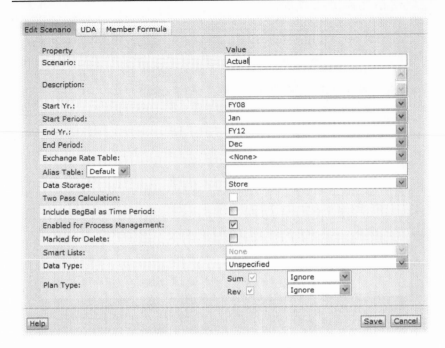

 Note! Data can still be loaded outside of forms via load rules or other data loading mechanisms to periods not in the start and end range. The start and end range limit data entry in Planning data forms in both the web and Smart View.

Notice in the Dimension Editor for Scenario, you can quickly copy an existing scenario and its properties to a new scenario member:

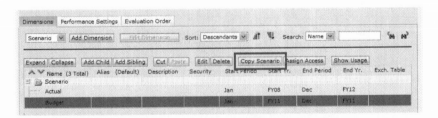

Next Penny needs to add in a variance calculation for Actual and Budget. Whenever possible you want to take advantage of

Essbase's calculation engine and build calculations into the database.

Add a Variance Member and Formula

1. In the Dimension Editor, select the Scenario dimension from the drop down option.
2. Add a member "Variance" to the Scenario dimension with the following properties:
   o Dynamic calc
   o Do not enable process management

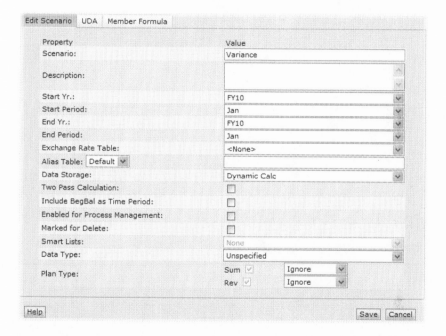

Other properties like start and end period don't apply for this member because it is a dynamically calculated member. Users won't be submitting data for Variance.

3. Select the Member Formula tab.
4. Add a member "Variance" to the Scenario dimension with the following member formula syntax: @VAR(Actual, Budget);

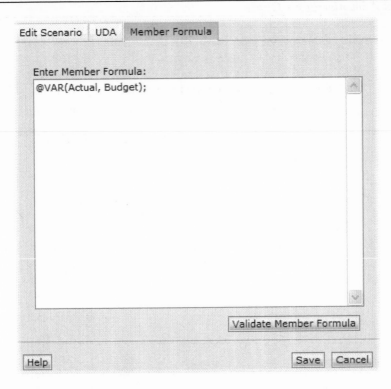

The @VAR function was used to calculate variance because this function looks at the variance reporting property for the member to determine whether an actual versus budget variance should be positive or negative.

    5. Click Validate Member Formula to check the syntax.

You should have received the following error message.

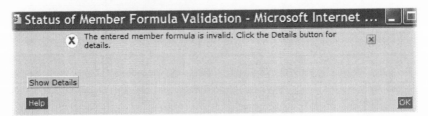

Why? Budget and Actual don't exist yet in Essbase. We haven't run a database refresh yet so the formula won't validate.

    6. Refresh   the   database   (Administration>>Manage Database).

Once the refresh is successful, you are ready to add the Variance calculation.

7. Select Administration >> Dimensions.
8. Select the Scenario dimension.
9. Add (or edit) the member "Variance" to the Scenario dimension with the following properties:
    o Dynamic calc
    o Do not enable process management

For the remaining properties, accept the default values.

10. Click the Member Formula tab.
11. Add a member "Variance" to the Scenario dimension with the following syntax: @VAR(Actual, Budget).
12. Click Validate Member Formula.
13. Click Save to save the member formula.
14. Click Save to save the new member.
15. Refresh the database (Administration >> Manage Database).

The resulting Scenario dimension should look as beautiful as the following image:

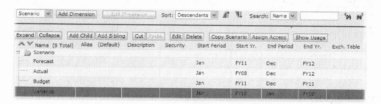

BUILD VERSION

The Version dimension and its members are independent of Scenario members. Version members are available to all scenarios. Possible versions include:

- Preliminary and Final versions allow multiple iterations of a plan.
- Sandbox1, Sandbox2, Sandbox3 versions allow users to have multiple versions to play around with the plan before copying to a Final version.
- Best Case and Worst Case versions model possible outcomes based on more optimistic or less optimistic assumptions.
- Internal and External versions help manage the distribution of plan data.

So in most cases you will have an Actual Final version, but for Budget you may have a Sandbox1 Budget, Sandbox2 Budget and a Final Budget that is reviewed and approved in workflow. Planning provides built in capabilities for end users to copy one version to another.

Versions are defined as either Target or Bottom Up. A target version allows data entry at any level in the dimensions across the application. Business rules can then be created to allocate target data to lower level members. A few considerations for target versions include:

- Workflow Tasks are not allowed for target versions.
- Copying target version to target version will copy all levels and members.
- Children of target members must be blank (for example, #missing) for the data input to be allowed at the parent.
- Target members must be set to Store.

A bottoms up version allows end users to enter data at level-0 members but not upper levels. Summary members are read only and aggregate from level-0 members. Users may copy one bottom up version to another (such as Sandbox to Final).

For Penny's application, let's build out the Version dimension:

1. Select Administration >> Dimensions.
2. Select Version dimension from the drop down.
3. Click Add Child/Sibling to add the Scenario dimensions.
4. Add the following members and properties to the version dimension (rename BUVersion 1 to Final):

Member	Storage	Version Type
Final	Never Share	Bottom up
Sandbox	Never Share	Bottom up
Target	Never Share	Target

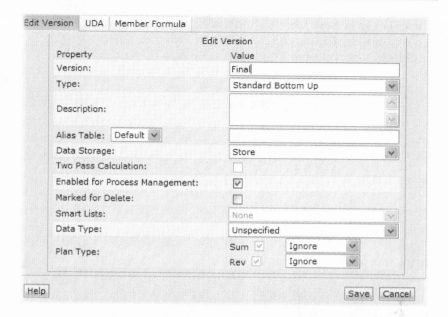

The resulting Version dimension should look as follows:

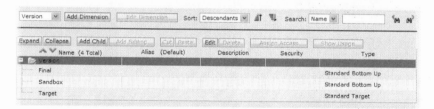

5. Refresh the database (Administration >> Manage Database) to push changes to Essbase.

Now that you've defined all of the dimensions manually, you may be starting to worry. Are you going to have to manually build your Entity dimension, one by one by one?

Fortunately for your sanity, you aren't. You have a number of alternatives to build dimensions automatically from another source like a flat file or relational table. In the early days of Planning we used Hyperion Application Link (HAL). Nowadays, the supported methods are Oracle Data Integrator (ODI) and Data Integration Management (DIM). Both ETL (extraction, transformation, and load) solutions provide adapters to build dimensions in Planning Classic applications. We could write a whole other book on ODI [note to self: write a book on ODI] so we won't include those steps here (though you can check out the appendix on page 649 for a good introduction). What we will cover in this book is how to use the Outline Load Utility, available in Planning 11.1.1, to build a dimension from a flat file.

OUTLINE LOAD UTILITY

Introduction to the Outline Load Utility

The Outline Load utility was introduced to Planning in version 11.1.1 and you can use it to load metadata and data. You load .CSV metadata files in parent-child format directly into Planning. The Outline Load Utility can update and build the following dimensions and outline components: Account, Period, Year, Scenario, Version, Currency, Entity, user-defined dimensions, attributes, UDAs, exchange rates, Smart Lists, Dates and Text measures.

The syntax and parameters are as follows:

```
OutlineLoad [-f:passwordFile][/S:server]
/A:application /U:userName [/M]
[/I:inputFileName/D[U]:loadDimensionName|/
DA:attributeDimensionName:baseDimensionName] [/TR]
[/N] [[/R] [/U]] [/C] [/F] [/K]
[/X:exceptionFileName] [L:logFileName] [/?]
```

Available parameters for the Outline Load Utility include:

-f:*passwordfile*	Pass in encrypted password file
/S:*server*	Server
/A:*application*	Application
/U:*username*	User to log into the application
/M	Generate fully qualified header records for loadable dimensions
/I:*inputfilename*	Name of the flat file containing header record and data records in CSV format
/D:*loaddimensionname*	Dimension to be updated with flat file
/DU:*userdefinedload dimensionname*	User defined dimension to be loaded; New dimension will be created if it doesn't exist
/DA[T]:*attributeload dimensionname: basedimensionname*	Text attribute dimension to be loaded:base dimension; New attribute is created if it doesn't exist
/DAN:*attributeload dimensionname: basedimensionname*	Numeric attribute dimension to be loaded:base dimension; New attribute is created if it doesn't exist

/DAB:attributeloaddimensionname:basedimensionname	Boolean attribute dimension to be loaded:base dimension; New attribute is created if it doesn't exist
/DAD:attributeloaddimensionname:basedimensionname	Date attribute dimension to be loaded:base dimension; New attribute is created if it doesn't exist
/TR	Used when loading data via the Outline Load utility
/N	"Dry run"; doesn't actually load data from flat file
/O	Maintain order of members in load file
/H	Order input records in the parent child order; /-H loads members in the order within the flat file (faster)
/R	Delete all members before performing the load
/U	Delete all planning units with the /R option
/T	Inherit unspecified plan type settings from parent when adding new members
/C	Perform a cube refresh after metadata load
/F	Create security filters when performing cube refresh
/K	Lock the dimension (recommended)
/X:exceptionfilename	Exception file name
/L:logfilename	Log file name
/DX:Hsp_Rates	Load Hsp Rates dimension and create exchange tables
/?	Display usage text

To follow along with Penny and run a build process for the Entity and Account dimension, please download the files at http://www.interrel.com/Pages/Publishings.aspx.

Update the Entity Dimension from Flat File

Here is the Entity.CSV metadata file for the Entity dimension. If you ever loaded metadata into Planning using HAL, you will find this file very similar to a file you uploaded with HAL. Fields can be in any order, but headers are case sensitive and must match exactly:

Parent	Entity	Alias: Default	Data Storage	Plan Type (Sum)	Aggregation (Sum)	Plan Type (Rev)	Aggregation (Rev)
Entity	TotalGeography	Total Geography	Store	1	+	1	+
TotalGeography	E01	North America	Store	1	+	1	+
E01	E01_0	North America Corporate	Store	1	+	1	+
E01	E01_101	USA	Store	1	+	1	+
E01_0	E01_101_1000	USA Sales	Store	1	+	1	+
E01_101_1000	E01_101_1100	East Sales	Store	1	+	1	+
E01_101_1100	E01_101_1110	MA	Store	1	+	1	+
E01_101_1100	E01_101_1120	NY	Store	1	+	1	+
E01_101_1100	E01_101_1130	PA	Store	1	+	1	+
E01_101_1000	E01_101_1200	West Sales	Store	1	+	1	+
E01_101_1200	E01_101_1210	CA	Store	1	+	1	+
E01_101_1200	E01_101_1220	CO	Store	1	+	1	+
E01_101_1200	E01_101_1230	WA	Store	1	+	1	+
E01_101_1000	E01_101_1300	North Sales	Store	1	+	1	+
E01_101_1300	E01_101_1310	IL	Store	1	+	1	+
E01_101_1300	E01_101_1320	MN	Store	1	+	1	+

1. Create an Entity.CSV file with the same rows and columns as the sample file above (or download at http://www.interrel.com/Pages/Publishings.aspx). Place this file on the C drive of the Planning server (in real life you will place this folder in a more secure, clearly defined location).

Valid headers for the Entity dimension (and other dimensions) include:

Required Header Name	Required Values (if any)
Entity	
Parent	
Alias: Default	
Data Storage	Store, Dynamic Calc, Never Share, Shared, Label Only
Description	
Formula	
Two Pass Calculation	True, False (or 1, 0)
Base Currency	
UDA	
Smart List	
Data Type	Unspecified, Currency, Non-Currency, Percentage, Smart List, Date, Text
Operation	Update (default), delete level 0, delete idescendants, delete descendants
Plan Type (*Plan1*)	True, False (or 1, 0)
Aggregation (*Plan1*)	+-*/%~ Never
Plan Type (*Plan2*)	True, False (or 1, 0)
Aggregation (*Plan2*)	+-*/%~ Never

Required Header Name	Required Values (if any)
Plan Type (*Plan3*)	True, False (or 1, 0)
Aggregation (*Plan3*)	+-*/%~ Never

The only required column is the Entity name.

2. Create a batch file and place it in the C:\Hyperion\products\Planning\bin directory (or whichever directory contains your Planning utilities if you've installed it differently). The .BAT file should contain the following syntax :

```
OutlineLoad /A:Entpln /U:admin /M /I:c:\entity.csv
/D:Entity /L:c:\outlineLoad.log
/X:c:\outlineLoad.exc
```

Depending on the folder structure on your Planning server you may need to update the file paths to match your specific directory structure.

3. Double click on the batch file to execute the utility from within the batch. (To create a batch file for each dimension, you simply "Save As" each file and change the parameters as needed.)

Notice the syntax above doesn't include anything about a password. You will be prompted to enter the password for the user defined in the syntax. Beginning in version 11, you can use a password encrypted file to supply the password.

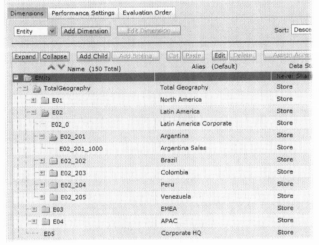

4. Execute the batch file with the OutlineLoad.cmd script to update the Entity dimension.

You can also run the script / syntax live from the command line. Now let's take a look at the log:

```
[Fri Jan 01 13:35:29 CST 2010]Successfully located and opened input file "c:\Entity.csv".
[Fri Jan 01 13:35:29 CST 2010]Header record fields: Parent, Entity, Alias: Default, Data Storage, Plan Type (sum),
Aggregation (Sum), Plan Type (Rev), Aggregation (Rev)
[Fri Jan 01 13:35:43 CST 2010]Located and using "Entity" dimension for loading data in "Entpln" application.
[Fri Jan 01 13:35:43 CST 2010]Load dimension "Entity" has been unlocked successfully.
[Fri Jan 01 13:35:43 CST 2010]A cube refresh operation will not be performed.
[Fri Jan 01 13:35:43 CST 2010]Create security filters operation will not be performed.
[Fri Jan 01 13:35:43 CST 2010]Examine the Essbase log files for status if Essbase data was loaded.
[Fri Jan 01 13:35:43 CST 2010]Planning outline data store load process finished. 144 data records were read, 144 data records
were processed, 144 were successfully loaded, 0 were rejected.
```

According to the log, the Entity dimension was updated successfully. Let's take a look at the Entity dimension in the Planning web client:

Update the Account Dimension from a Flat File

Here is the Account.csv metadata file for the Account dimension. Remember, fields can be in any order, but headers are case sensitive:

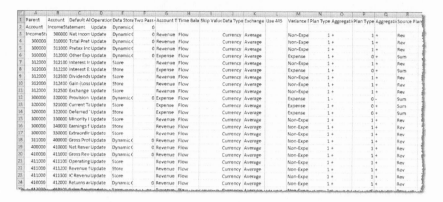

1. Create an account.csv file with the same rows and columns as the sample file above (or email us for a copy). Place this file on the C drive of the Planning server (in real life you will place this folder in a more secure, clearly defined location).

Valid headers for the Account dimension are similar to the Entity headers with a few more properties for accounts (only the Account name is required):

Required Header Name	Required Values (if any)
Account	
Parent	
Alias: Default	
Data Storage	Store, Dynamic Calc, Never Share, Shared, Label Only
Description	
Formula	
Two Pass Calculation	True, False (or 1, 0)
Base Currency	
UDA	
Smart List	
Data Type	Unspecified, Currency, Non-Currency, Percentage, Smart List, Date, Text

Required Header Name	Required Values (if any)
Operation	Update (default), delete level 0, delete idescendants, delete descendants
Plan Type (*Plan1*)	True, False (or 1, 0)
Aggregation (*Plan1*)	+-*/%~ Never
Plan Type (*Plan2*)	True, False (or 1, 0)
Aggregation (*Plan2*)	+-*/%~ Never
Plan Type (*Plan3*)	True, False (or 1, 0)
Aggregation (*Plan3*)	+-*/%~ Never
Source Plan type	*Plan type name*
Account Type	Expense, Revenue, Asset, Liability, Equity, Saved Assumption
Time Balance	Flow, First, Balance, Average, avg_actual, avg_365_fill
Use 445 / Use 544 / Use454	True, False (or 1, 0)
Skip Value	None, Missing, Zeros, Missing and Zeros
Exchange Rate Type	Non, Average, Ending, Historical
Variance Reporting	Non-Expense, Expense

2. Create a batch file that contains the following syntax:

```
OutlineLoad /A:Entpln /U:admin /M /I:c:\Account.csv
/D:Account /L:c:\outlineLoad.log
/X:c:\outlineLoad.exc
```

Depending on the folder structure on your Planning server you may need to update the file paths to match your specific directory structure.

3. Double click on the batch file to execute the utility from within the batch.
4. Enter the password when prompted.

Once the script is complete, review the OutlineLoad.log and verify a successful load.

```
[Fri Jan 01 14:13:33 CST 2010]Successfully located and opened input file
"c:\Account.csv".
[Fri Jan 01 14:13:33 CST 2010]Header record fields: Parent, Account, Alias: Default,
Operation, Data Storage, Two Pass Calculation, Account Type, Time Balance, Skip Value,
Data Type, Exchange Rate Type, Variance Reporting, Plan Type (Sum), Aggregation (Sum),
Plan Type (Rev), Aggregation (Rev), Source Plan Type
[Fri Jan 01 14:13:33 CST 2010]Located and using "Account" dimension for loading data
in "Entpln" application.
[Fri Jan 01 14:13:38 CST 2010]Load dimension "Account" has been unlocked successfully.
[Fri Jan 01 14:13:38 CST 2010]A cube refresh operation will not be performed.
[Fri Jan 01 14:13:38 CST 2010]Create security filters operation will not be performed.
[Fri Jan 01 14:13:38 CST 2010]Examine the Essbase log files for status if Essbase data
was loaded.
[Fri Jan 01 14:13:38 CST 2010]Planning Outline data store load process finished. 120
data records were read, 120 data records were processed, 120 were successfully loaded,
0 were rejected.
```

Now let's take a look at the Account dimension in the Planning web client:

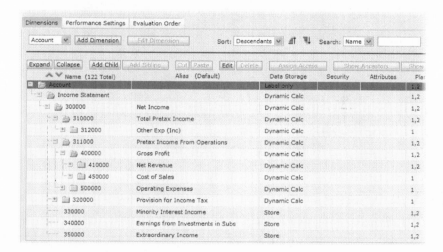

What if the outline load utility ran into errors? You should find some helpful messages to help determine which records errored out and why. See the sample exception file below:

```
[Fri Jan 01 13:55:34 CST 2010] Error occurred loading data record 6:
312000,312100,Interest
Income,Update,Store,,Revenue,Flow,,Currency,Average,Non-Expense,1,+,1,+,Rev
[Fri Jan 01 13:55:34 CST 2010] java.lang.RuntimeException: Unable to set source plan
type of member 312100 to Rev.  The parent does not exist in this plan type.
[Fri Jan 01 13:55:34 CST 2010] Error occurred loading data record 8:
312000,312300,Dividends from LT Inv in
Subs,Update,Store,,Revenue,Flow,,Currency,Average,Non-Expense,1,+,1,+,Rev
[Fri Jan 01 13:55:34 CST 2010] java.lang.RuntimeException: Unable to set source plan
type of member 312300 to Rev.  The parent does not exist in this plan type.
[Fri Jan 01 13:55:34 CST 2010] Error occurred loading data record 9:
312000,312400,Gain (Loss) on
Disposal,Update,Store,,Revenue,Flow,,Currency,Average,Non-Expense,1,+,1,+,Rev
[Fri Jan 01 13:55:34 CST 2010] java.lang.RuntimeException: Unable to set source plan
type of member 312400 to Rev.  The parent does not exist in this plan type.
[Fri Jan 01 13:55:34 CST 2010] Error occurred loading data record 10:
312000,312500,Exchange Rate Gain
(Loss),Update,Store,,Revenue,Flow,,Currency,Average,Non-Expense,1,+,1,+,Rev
[Fri Jan 01 13:55:34 CST 2010] java.lang.RuntimeException: Unable to set source plan
type of member 312500 to Rev.  The parent does not exist in this plan type.
[Fri Jan 01 13:55:45 CST 2010]Planning Outline data store load process finished with
exceptions:  exceptions occured, examine the exception file for more information. 125
data records were read, 125 data records were processed, 121 were successfully loaded,
4 were rejected.
```

According to the log, the Account dimension was updated successfully, although 4 records were rejected. We see that one member "312000" is missing. Since it does not exist in the file or in the outline, no children can be added to this member.

To view flat file format and header definitions for other dimensions and Planning components, see the Planning Administrator Guide (search "Outline Load utility").

Penny's eyes start to close and her chin droops to her chest. "Are we there yet?" she grumbles.

"Almost," assures The Translator. "I realize you are achieving dimension overload. For now we'll define a few dimension settings and come back and explain them in later scenes."

SET DENSE AND SPARSE SETTINGS

In Planning applications, each dimension will be assigned a specific setting, dense or sparse, that impacts how the underlying database is created. This dense/sparse setting is one of the things you can tune for performance. For now, just follow us and set the following dense and sparse settings for your application.

To set dense and sparse in Planning:

1. Select Administration >> Dimensions.
2. Select Performance Settings tab.
3. Select Sum.
4. Set dimensions in the following order (use the up and down arrow keys to move dimensions) with dense and sparse settings: Period-Dense, Account-Dense, Entity-Sparse, Version-Sparse, Scenario-Sparse, FiscalYear-Sparse:

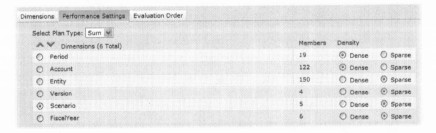

5. Select Rev.
6. Set dimensions in the following order with dense and sparse settings: Period-Dense, Account-Dense, Segments-Sparse, Entity-Sparse, Version-Sparse, Scenario-Sparse, FiscalYear-Sparse:

Dimensions	Performance Settings	Evaluation Order		

Select Plan Type: Rev ⌄

Dimensions (7 Total)	Members	Density	
○ Period	19	⦿ Dense	○ Sparse
○ Account	17	⦿ Dense	○ Sparse
⦿ Segments	12	○ Dense	⦿ Sparse
○ Entity	150	○ Dense	⦿ Sparse
○ Version	4	○ Dense	⦿ Sparse
○ Scenario	5	○ Dense	⦿ Sparse
○ FiscalYear	6	○ Dense	⦿ Sparse

> 7. Refresh to Essbase (Administration >> Manage Database).

Can you set dense and sparse settings in the Essbase Administration Services console for Planning applications? No!

And with that, it's time for a celebration involving lots of tasty beverages, because Penny has reached a major milestone. Now that the dimensions are complete, she is ready to load some data.

Scene 6:
Load Data

You can load data into Hyperion Planning through several alternatives. End users can submit data via data forms over the web and in Excel using Smart View. Users can also submit data via the Smart View Essbase provider or Essbase Excel Spreadsheet Add-in if a role of Adhoc Write is assigned to end users. To perform bulk data loads, the following alternatives exist:

- Free-form data loading directly to Essbase
- Data load rules against flat files and SQL tables to Essbase
- Oracle Data Integrator (ODI)
- Data Integration Management (DIM)
- Outline Load Utility
- Enterprise Performance Management Architect Data Synchronizations for EPMA deployed applications

In this scene, we'll focus on loading data directly to Essbase from flat files with rules files. This method is remarkably efficient (since it's using Essbase's native load method) though the editor is remarkably antiquated (since the user interface hasn't really been updated in 15 years).

DATA LOAD RULES OVERVIEW

We can use data load rules to perform transformations and define information in a text file for Essbase to load data. We have to define what columns map to what dimensions, which columns contain data, and any necessary header information for a specific data load file.

When should you use a data load rule?

- You need to ignore fields or strings in a data file.
- You need to change the order of fields by moving, joining, splitting or creating.
- You need to map the data in the data source to the database by changing strings.
- You need to change the data values in the data source by scaling data values or adding them to existing values in the data source.
- You need to set header records for missing values.

- You need to reject an invalid record and continue loading data.
- You want to add new dimensions and members in the database along with the data load.
- You want to change existing dimensions and members in the database along with the data load.

So what we are really saying is that in most cases you will use a data load rule to load data to Essbase.

Load rules are created and managed in Administration Services. Here is what a data load rule will look like in the Data Prep Editor:

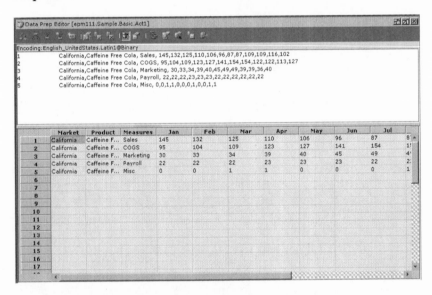

The best way to learn about load rules is to create one.

CREATE A DATA LOAD RULES FILE

Unlike the Outline Load Utility, there isn't a specific file format or header section required for the data coming into the data load rule. That is what the rules file is for: to map the data file information to the Essbase dimension structure. We will first review the general steps for creating a load rule and then jump into a specific example for the Entpln application:

1. In Administration Services, navigate to the *Rules Files* option under the application or database.
2. Right-click and select Create Rules File:

3. Select File >> Open Data File.
4. Browse to and open the data file.
5. Once the data file is open, select Options >> Data Source Properties.
   The Data Source properties window will open.

Data source properties will tell Essbase the data source delimiters, what field edits have been made in the rules file, and what header rows may exist.

On the Delimiter tab, specify Comma, Tab, Spaces, Custom, or Column Width delimiter for the data file (if someone with a perverse sense of humor gave you a data file with ! or ~ as the delimiter, Essbase can handle this with the custom option):

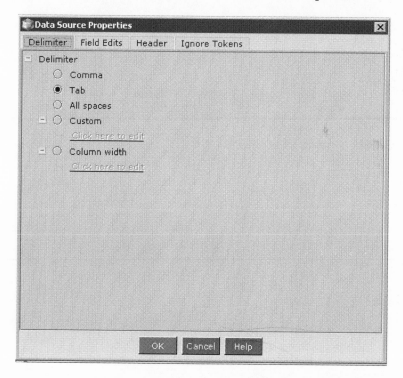

Specify how many lines to skip or define any records that may have header information and field information on the header tab:

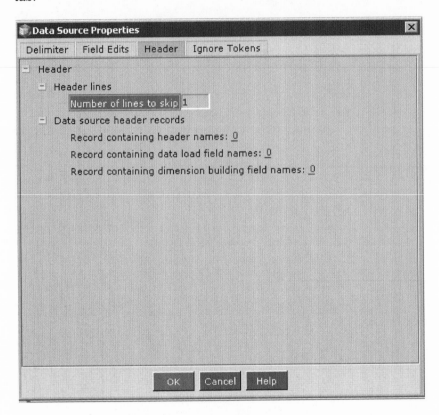

Next, associate the outline,

6. Select Associate Outline icon or Options >> Associate Outline.
7. The Associate Outline window will open.
8. Select the desired database.

To define the data load settings,

9. Select Options >> Data Load Settings.
10. The Data Load Settings window will open:

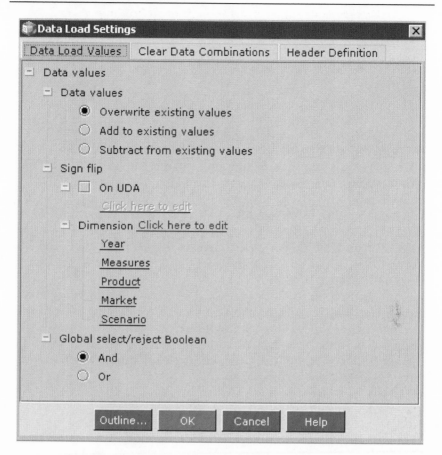

On the Data Load Values tab, define whether this rules file should overwrite, add to, or subtract from existing values. In most cases, you want to overwrite, but there are some exceptions.

Here's one: the source file you load to Essbase contains daily transaction data but your Essbase database contains aggregated monthly data. You would want to specify "Add To Existing Values" for the following text file to get Essbase to calculate the total for the month (and make sure not to load the same file twice). If the data load rule is set to overwrite, then only the final value in the file will be stored:

```
01/01/2007, Jan, California,Caffeine Free Cola, Sales, 145
01/02/2007, Jan, California,Caffeine Free Cola, Sales, 123
01/03/2007, Jan, California,Caffeine Free Cola, Sales, 132
01/04/2007, Jan, California,Caffeine Free Cola, Sales, 145
01/05/2007, Jan, California,Caffeine Free Cola, Sales, 102
01/06/2007, Jan, California,Caffeine Free Cola, Sales, 116|
```

You can also specify whether to flip a sign based on an assigned User Defined Attribute on the Data Load Values tab. If your source file contains debits and credits, you will want to load only positive values because you will be handling the sign flipping in Essbase using Unary Operators. To do this, you can assign a UDA of "Flip Input" (or something else descriptive of the task) to all of your accounts that will be arriving as negative values. Check the "Sign Flip on UDA" check box and select the "Flip Input" UDA. The sign will be flipped for all records in the data file for the accounts tagged "Flip Input".

To clear data for a specific intersection before loading the data file, utilize the Clear Data Combinations tab. This is helpful if you load actual data on a daily basis and want to automatically clear out the month being loaded before loading the daily data. In the example below, the rules file will clear all January Actual data before loading the new data file:

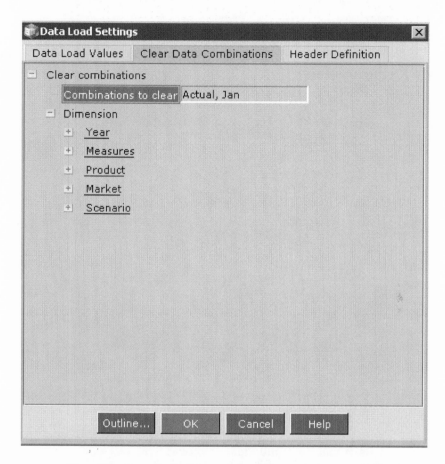

The Header Definition tab allows you to define any dimension not represented in the data file. In the example below, we've defined a header of 'Actual' because there isn't a column in the file that identifies the scenario. Essbase needs to know exactly where you want to load data for every dimension. Should it load data to Actual or Budget?

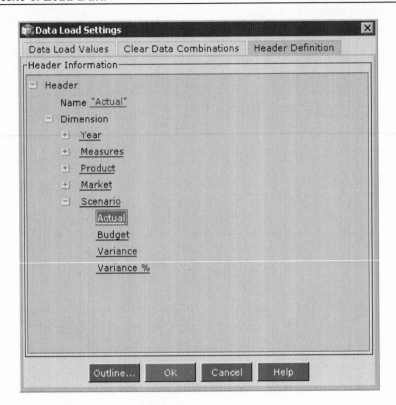

Note!   A data load rules file must reference every dimension, either in the fields section or in the header section.

Next, define the Field properties, mapping the columns to dimensions or members and identifying data values.

11. Select Field >> Properties.
12. The Field Properties window will open.

The Global Properties tab allows you to translate text to upper / lower case, add prefixes and suffixes, convert spaces to underscores, and perform a find and replace. This is used to make sure that the values specified in the data load match what is in the outline, especially if you've used a dimension build file to add prefixes or suffixes to member names.

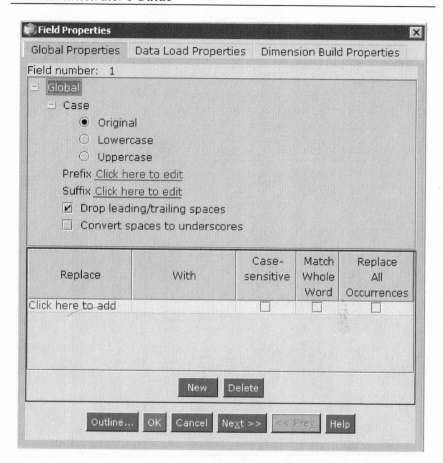

For example, let's say your Account number structure and Product number structure have the exact same number. Essbase won't allow you to have a member with the same name so you built your Product dimension to include a prefix "Product_". Now your source file only has the product number. You need to add the prefix "Product_" to the Product column so that data will load to the correct product member.

The members in the data file must match the members in your outline exactly! If the Account dimension has the member "Net Revenue" but our data file has "NetRevenue" with no space, data will not be loaded for those records. But (whine) it's close. Can't Essbase figure it out? Nope. Members in the data file must match member names in the outline.

Tip!

Next we will select the Data Load Properties tab. (Ignore the Dimension Build Properties tab since we are focusing on data loading).

13. Select the dimension that maps to the field
    or select a specific member
    or select "Data Field"
    or select "Ignore field during a data load":

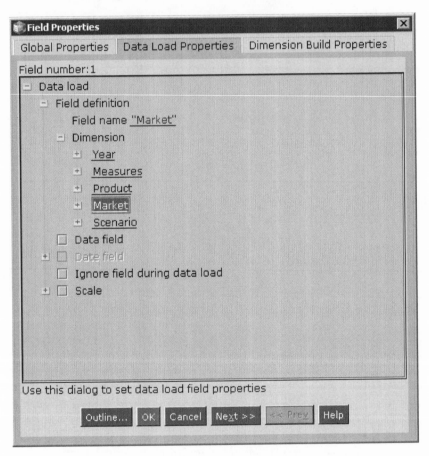

Tip!

When navigating in the field property window, double-click to select a particular item. Make sure the item shows up in blue next to Field Name. If you single click, the item will not be selected. This can be an annoying little feature that will test your memory and patience… "but I know I set that property" and you probably did, but you single clicked instead of double clicking.

Note!

You can only have one column assigned "Data Field" within a data load rules file.

14. Click Next to move to next field.
15. Click OK once all of the fields have been defined.

Note!

There are two modes for rules files: dimension building and data loading. When working on a dimension build rules file, select the Dimension Building mode:

When working on a data load rules file, select the Data Load mode:

Here is an example of a data load rules file where the first three columns map to a dimension and the remaining columns map to a specific member in the Period dimension:

Encoding:English_UnitedStates.Latin1@Binary

Map Column to Dimension   **Map Column to Specific Member**

	Market	Product	Measur...	Jan	Feb	Mar	Apr	May	Jun	Jul
1										
2										
3										
4										
5										
6										
7										
8										
9										
10										
11										
12										
13										
14										

The last step before saving is validating the rules file. Rules files are validated to ensure the member and dimension mapping defined in the rules file maps to the associated outline. Validation cannot ensure that the data source will load properly. For example, you've defined the rules file, setting source file and data load properties, assigned field columns, and everything validates successfully. But what if your source file contains the member "Forecast" but "Forecast" doesn't exist in the outline? Any records containing members that do not exist in the outline will not be loaded to Essbase. These invalid or "fallout" records are sent to an exception file that you can review after the load has finished.

16. Select the Validate icon (or select Options >> Validate).

My Data Load Rules File won't Validate – What Should You Check?

Helpful
Info

- Is the field name valid?
- Are the file delimiters correctly placed?
- Is there a member in the field name?
- Is the dimension name used in another field name or the header?
- Are you using a member as member combination in one place and a single member in another?
- Is more than one field defined as the data field?
- Is the dimension used for sign flipping in the associated outline?
- Is the rules file associated with the correct outline?

17. Select the Save icon (or select File >> Save).

Within a rules file you can filter records from a source file using either Select or Reject. Say your data file had all accounts but you only wanted to load data for revenue accounts. You could define a filter using wildcards to only load data for the revenue account range.

To add a filter to your load rule,
1. Select Record >> Select or Reject.
2. Define the type: String or Number.
3. Type in the value.
4. Select the criterion: equals, does not equal, greater than, greater than or equal to, less than, less than or equal to, contains, or does not contain.
5. Check whether it is case sensitive.
6. Click OK.

Don't forget that starting in Essbase 9.3, you have the ability to use substitution variables in rules file. Say you receive a current month file every month but the file doesn't actually specify the month. Historically, you've updated the header of the rules file for each new month. Now you can use your &Curmo substitution variable in the header definition (no updates required each month).

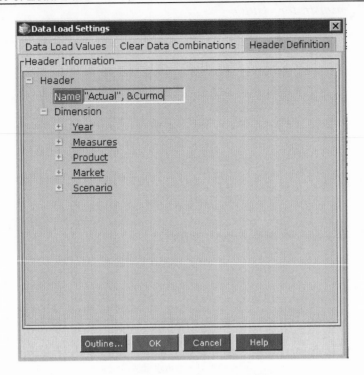

Now that the data load rules file is created, you are ready to load data!

We will use the following data file for Penny's application. To follow along with us, email us for a copy of this file or create your own (all dimensions referenced in the file with months going across the columns):

FiscalYear	Entity	Scenario	Version	Account	Jan	Feb	Mar	Apr	
FY09	E01_0	Budget	Sandbox	501111	390000.00		240000.00		120000.00	1
FY09	E01_0	Budget	Sandbox	501130	23000.00		14000.00		6200.00 8300.00	1
FY09	E01_0	Budget	Sandbox	501140	54000.00		34000.00		15000.00	2
FY09	E01_0	Budget	Sandbox	501240	70000.00		43000.00		20000.00	2
FY09	E01_0	Budget	Sandbox	501250	33000.00		33000.00		33000.00	3
FY09	E01_0	Budget	Sandbox	502100	19000.00		11000.00		5900.00 5900.00	1
FY09	E01_0	Budget	Sandbox	502200	4300.00 2600.00	1500.00 1200.00	4900.00 2800.00	3
FY09	E01_0	Budget	Sandbox	503100	22000.00		13000.00		7600.00 6500.00	2
FY09	E01_0	Budget	Sandbox	503200	28000.00		17000.00		10000.00	7
FY09	E01_0	Budget	Sandbox	504100	30000.00		18000.00		10000.00	9
FY09	E01_0	Budget	Sandbox	504200	22000.00		13000.00		7600.00 6500.00	2
FY09	E01_0	Budget	Sandbox	504300	30000.00		19000.00		9100.00 10000.00	
FY09	E01_0	Budget	Sandbox	505100	100000.00		63000.00		34000.00	3
FY09	E01_0	Budget	Sandbox	505200	140000.00		88000.00		40000.00	5
FY09	E01_0	Budget	Sandbox	506110	35000.00		21000.00		12000.00	1
FY09	E01_0	Budget	Sandbox	506120	78000.00		47000.00		25000.00	2
FY09	E01_0	Budget	Sandbox	506210	470000.00		300000.00		150000.00	1
FY09	E01_0	Budget	Sandbox	506220	160000.00		99000.00		50000.00	5
FY09	E01_0	Budget	Sandbox	506311	96000.00		61000.00		25000.00	3
FY09	E01_0	Budget	Sandbox	506312	29000.00		18000.00		7200.00 11000.00	
FY09	E01_0	Budget	Sandbox	506321	660000.00		420000.00		170000.00	2
FY09	E01_0	Budget	Sandbox	506322	240000.00		150000.00		60000.00	9
FY09	E01_0	Budget	Sandbox	506410	200000.00		130000.00		53000.00	7
FY09	E01_0	Budget	Sandbox	506420	5200.00 3300.00	1300.00 2000.00	3300.00 5200.00	4
FY09	E01_0	Budget	Sandbox	506430	32000.00		20000.00		9100.00 11000.00	
FY09	E01_0	Budget	Sandbox	506510	150000.00		87000.00		49000.00	4
FY09	E01_0	Budget	Sandbox	506520	7100.00 4400.00	2100.00 2400.00	6000.00 6200.00	6
FY09	E01_0	Budget	Sandbox	506530	43000.00		25000.00		16000.00	1
FY09	E01_0	Budget	Sandbox	506550	160000.00		96000.00		59000.00	4
FY09	E01_0	Budget	Sandbox	506570	2800.00 1700.00	910.00 880.00	2800.00 2200.00	2
FY09	E01_0	Budget	Sandbox	507300	23000.00		14000.00		7800.00 7000.00	2
FY09	E01_0	Budget	Sandbox	507400	86000.00		52000.00		27000.00	2
FY09	E01_0	Budget	Sandbox	509110	360000.00		220000.00		100000.00	1
FY09	E01_0	Budget	Sandbox	509120	150000.00		92000.00		46000.00	4
FY09	E01_0	Budget	Sandbox	509210	13000.00		8000.00 3200.00	4700.00 7900.00	1
FY09	E01_0	Budget	Sandbox	509220	28000.00		17000.00		9200.00 8800.00	2
FY09	E01_0	Budget	Sandbox	509230	13000.00		8500.00 3400.00	5000.00 8500.00	1
FY09	E01_0	Budget	Sandbox	509310	5700.00 3700.00	1400.00 2200.00	3600.00 5700.00	5
FY09	E01_0	Budget	Sandbox	509320	7500.00 4700.00	2100.00 2700.00	5600.00 6900.00	6
FY09	E01_0	Budget	Sandbox	509330	21000.00		13000.00		6800.00 6300.00	2
FY09	E01_0	Budget	Sandbox	501300	15000.00		9300.00 4500.00	5000.00 13000.00	
FY09	E01_0	Budget	Sandbox	510200	29000.00		18000.00		8600.00 9600.00	2
FY09	E01_0	Budget	Sandbox	511900	-25000.00		-16000.00		-7400.00	
FY10	E01_0	Budget	Sandbox	501111	390000.00		240000.00		120000.00	

Create the ldrev Rules File

1. In Administration Services, select your Ent.pln Rev database.
2. Right-click on the database, and Create>>Rules File.
3. Select File >> Open data file from within the rules file editor:

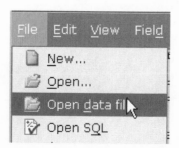

4. Browse to and select the data load file RevDataFile.txt.

The data file will open in the Rules File Data Editor:

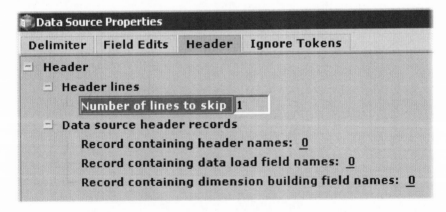

5. Select Options>>Data Source Properties
6. Define data source properties:
   a. Delimiter: Tab
   b. Number of Lines to skip: 1

Data Source Properties

Delimiter	Field Edits	Header	Ignore Tokens

Header

  Header lines

    Number of lines to skip   1

  Data source header records

    Record containing header names: **0**

    Record containing data load field names: **0**

    Record containing dimension building field names: **0**

7. Define the Data Load Settings by selecting Options>>Data load settings. Fortunately we can accept the defaults.
8. Click OK to close.
9. Define the field properties for the appropriate dimensions by selecting Field >> Properties. Select the Data Load tab and double click on the appropriate

dimension or member for each individual field (e.g. Field1 is Fiscal Year, Field2 is Entity, and so on):

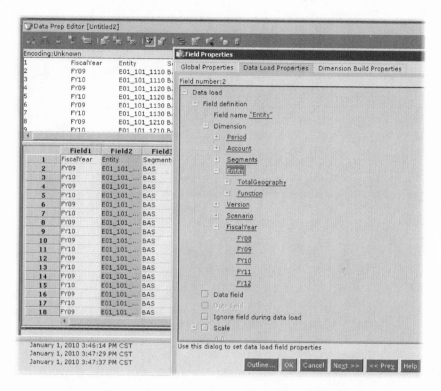

We could have alternatively used the data file column headings because the names match the dimensions or members exactly.

The resulting load rule should look like the following:

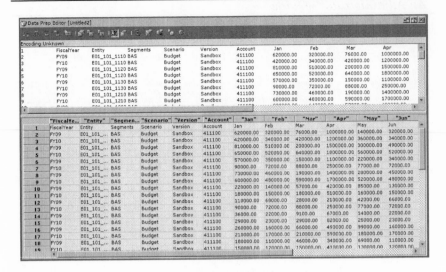

10. Validate the rules file by selecting the Validate button.

11. Save the rules file as ldrev by selecting File>>Save.

Create the ldsum Rules File

1. Create (or email us for) a data file to load expenses to the Sum plan type:

FiscalYear	Entity	Scenario	Version	Account	Jan	Feb	Mar	Apr
FY09	E01_0	Budget	Sandbox	501111	390000.00	240000.00	120000.00	
FY09	E01_0	Budget	Sandbox	501130	23000.00	14000.00	6200.00	8300.0
FY09	E01_0	Budget	Sandbox	501140	54000.00	34000.00	15000.00	
FY09	E01_0	Budget	Sandbox	501240	70000.00	43000.00	20000.00	
FY09	E01_0	Budget	Sandbox	501250	33000.00	33000.00	33000.00	
FY09	E01_0	Budget	Sandbox	502100	19000.00	11000.00	5900.00	5900.
FY09	E01_0	Budget	Sandbox	502200	4300.00 2600.00	1500.00 1200.00	4900.00	2800.
FY09	E01_0	Budget	Sandbox	503100	22000.00	13000.00	7600.00	6500.
FY09	E01_0	Budget	Sandbox	503200	28000.00	17000.00	10000.00	
FY09	E01_0	Budget	Sandbox	504100	30000.00	18000.00	10000.00	
FY09	E01_0	Budget	Sandbox	504200	22000.00	13000.00	7600.00	6500.0
FY09	E01_0	Budget	Sandbox	504300	30000.00	19000.00	9100.00	10000.
FY09	E01_0	Budget	Sandbox	505100	100000.00	63000.00	34000.00	
FY09	E01_0	Budget	Sandbox	505200	140000.00	88000.00	40000.00	
FY09	E01_0	Budget	Sandbox	506110	35000.00	21000.00	12000.00	
FY09	E01_0	Budget	Sandbox	506120	78000.00	47000.00	25000.00	
FY09	E01_0	Budget	Sandbox	506210	470000.00	300000.00	150000.00	
FY09	E01_0	Budget	Sandbox	506220	160000.00	99000.00	50000.00	
FY09	E01_0	Budget	Sandbox	506311	96000.00	61000.00	25000.00	
FY09	E01_0	Budget	Sandbox	506312	29000.00	18000.00	7200.00 11000.	
FY09	E01_0	Budget	Sandbox	506321	660000.00	420000.00	170000.00	
FY09	E01_0	Budget	Sandbox	506322	240000.00	150000.00	60000.00	
FY09	E01_0	Budget	Sandbox	506410	200000.00	130000.00	53000.00	
FY09	E01_0	Budget	Sandbox	506420	5200.00 3300.00	1300.00 2000.00	3300.00	5200.
FY09	E01_0	Budget	Sandbox	506430	32000.00	20000.00	9100.00 11000.	
FY09	E01_0	Budget	Sandbox	506510	150000.00	87000.00	49000.00	
FY09	E01_0	Budget	Sandbox	506520	7100.00 4400.00	2100.00 2400.00	6000.00	6200.
FY09	E01_0	Budget	Sandbox	506530	43000.00	25000.00	16000.00	
FY09	E01_0	Budget	Sandbox	506550	160000.00	96000.00	59000.00	
FY09	E01_0	Budget	Sandbox	506570	2800.00 1700.00	910.00 880.00	2800.00	2200.
FY09	E01_0	Budget	Sandbox	507300	23000.00	14000.00	7800.00	7000.
FY09	E01_0	Budget	Sandbox	507400	86000.00	52000.00	27000.00	
FY09	E01_0	Budget	Sandbox	509110	360000.00	220000.00	100000.00	
FY09	E01_0	Budget	Sandbox	509120	150000.00	92000.00	46000.00	
FY09	E01_0	Budget	Sandbox	509210	13000.00	8000.00 3200.00	4700.00 7900.	
FY09	E01_0	Budget	Sandbox	509320	28000.00	17000.00	9200.00 8300.	

2. In Administration Services, select your Entpln.Sum database.
3. Right-click on the database, and Create>>Rules File.
4. Select File>>Open data file and navigate to and select the ExpenseDataFile.txt.

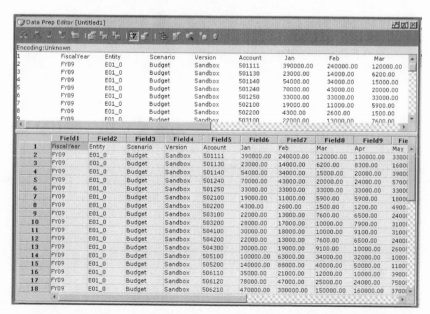

5. Select Options>>Data Source Properties
    a. Define data source properties:
    b. Delimiter: Tab
    c. Number of Records to skip: 1
6. Accept the defaults for Data Load Settings (under Options>>Data load settings).
7. Define the headers necessary (any dimensions that are not present in the data file).
8. Define the field properties for the appropriate dimensions by selecting Field >> Properties (e.g. Field1 is Fiscal Year, Field2 is Entity, and so on).
9. Select the Data Load tab and double click on the appropriate dimension or member for each individual field.

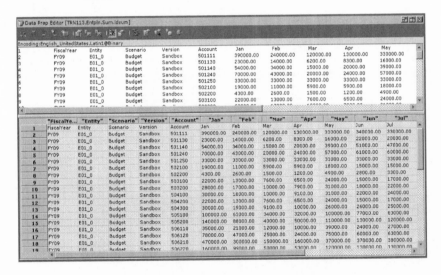

10. Validate the rules file by selecting the Validate button.
11. Save the rules file as "ldsum" by selecting File>>Save.

LOAD DATA

We have the data file, we have the data load rules file. Let's load some data! (Is it sad that we are really excited about getting to this step? Ok, yes, we are complete geeks.)

To load data using a rules file,

1. Within Administration Services, select the Entpln.Revdatabase and choose Actions >> Load data for

"Entpln" from the menu (or right-click on the database and select Load Data).

2. The Load Data window will open:

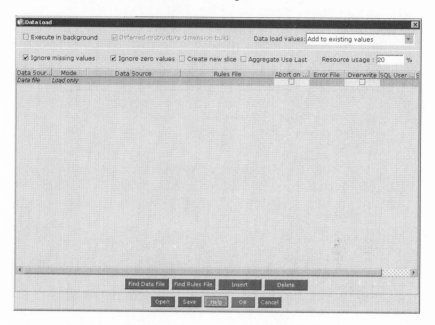

You can disregard some of the options as they are only applicable to ASO databases: Create new slice, Aggregate Use Last, and Resource Usage.

3. Select Find Data File and navigate to the RevDataFile.txt.
4. Select Find Rules File and navigate to the ldrev.rul data load rules file.

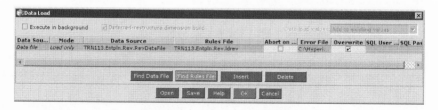

5. Specify the error file location and name.
6. Check the "Overwrite" check box if you want the error file to replace an error file that may already exist.

Abort on error during data load will stop the data load process if an error is found with the data file. If this is not selected,

Essbase will load the valid records and send the invalid records to the error file.

Execute in the background will run the process in the background on your desktop, freeing up Administration Services to perform other tasks. If this is not selected and your data load takes 3 hours, you can't do anything else in Administration Services until the data load is complete (while the break would really do you some good, this will most likely frustrate the heck out of you).

Tip!

You can load more than one load file with the same or different rules file if needed. Click the *Insert* button to insert a new record for specifying load information.

7. If we were loading directly from a relational source instead of a text file, we would need to specify the SQL connection information. That doesn't apply to us since we are using a text file.
8. Click *OK* to load data.

You should see a successful message but if not, check out the error file to find the problem. Log files unless specified differently are stored in the Essbase install EAS\client folder.

9. Repeat the steps above to load the ExpenseDataFile.txt using the ldsum.rul rules file.

Penny is anxious to see the data. She excitedly launches Smart View but is crestfallen when she doesn't see any data. The old refrain about "guys don't do pull ups for girls with no roll ups" briefly passes through her brain, and then she remembers: this is an Essbase block storage database that requires calculation or aggregation to see data values at upper levels. She immediately turns to the consultants. "How do I calculate the database?"

Scene 7:
Calculate with Calc Scripts

The Translator jumps to his feet, the annoying cape swooshing dramatically. "Before we can calculate the databases, we need to review some Essbase fundamentals." Get ready to impress your coworkers with complicated concepts like "dense" and "sparse" and "optimized block structure".

DENSE AND SPARSE

Remember back to late last night when we finally finished building dimensions and we set the dense and sparse settings at the very end. You blindly trusted our settings. Now let us explain what exactly dense and sparse are and how these settings affect your database. We'll start with defining a member combination. A member combination is the intersection of members from each dimension. See the following examples of member combinations for the following sample outline:

```
Year Time (Active Dynamic Time Series Members: H-T-D, Q-T-D) (Dynamic Calc)
    Qtr1 (+) (Dynamic Calc)
    Qtr2 (+) (Dynamic Calc)
    Qtr3 (+) (Dynamic Calc)
    Qtr4 (+) (Dynamic Calc)
Measures Accounts (Label Only)
    Profit (+) (Dynamic Calc)
    Inventory (~) (Label Only)
    Ratios (~) (Label Only)
Product {Caffeinated, Intro Date, Ounces, Pkg Type}
    100 (+) (Alias: Colas)
    200 (+) (Alias: Root Beer)
    300 (+) (Alias: Cream Soda)
    400 (+) (Alias: Fruit Soda)
    Diet (~) (Alias: Diet Drinks)
Market {Population}
    East (+) (UDAS: Major Market)
    West (+)
```

Example member combinations:
- Qtr1->Profit->100->East->Actual
- Year->Profit->100->East->Actual

- Jan->Sales->100-10->New York->Budget
- Jan->Sales->100->New York->Budget

Tip!

The symbol "->" is known as a cross dimensional operator in Essbase (more on this later). For now, when you see the "->", think of the word "at". We are referencing the data value at Qtr1 at Profit at 100 at East at Actual.

Dense data is data that occurs often or repeatedly across the intersection of all member combinations. For example, you will most likely have data for all periods for most member combinations. You will most likely have data for most of your accounts for member combinations. Time and accounts are naturally dense.

Sparse data is data that occurs only periodically or sparsely across member combinations. Product, Market, and Employee dimensions are usually sparse:

Products

Markets					
X					
		X			
X					
	X				
				X	

Sparse

Time

Measures					
X	X		X		
X	X	X	X	X	
X	X	X		X	
	X	X	X	X	
X		X	X	X	

Dense

You as the administrator will assign a dense / sparse setting to each dimension. This will dictate how the Essbase database is structured.

To set dense and sparse for Planning dimensions (remember these steps from the last scene):

1. Select Administration >> Dimensions
2. Select Performance Settings tab.
3. Select the plan type.
4. Set dimensions in the following order (use the up and down arrow keys to move dimensions) with dense and sparse settings:

Dimensions (6 Total)	Members	Density	
○ Period	19	⦿ Dense	○ Sparse
○ Account	13	⦿ Dense	○ Sparse
⦿ Entity	9	○ Dense	⦿ Sparse
○ Fiscal Year	6	○ Dense	⦿ Sparse
○ Scenario	5	○ Dense	⦿ Sparse
○ Version	5	○ Dense	⦿ Sparse

Select Plan Type: Sum

Dimensions | Performance Settings | Evaluation Order

Why can't you change the dense / sparse setting for the Product Manager dimension or any other attribute dimensions? If you answered "attribute dimensions are always sparse", pat yourself on the back. You're coming along, my fledgling administrator.

BLOCK STRUCTURE

The Essbase database is composed of a number of blocks. A block is created for each intersection of the sparse dimensions. In the example below, Market and Product are sparse. See a block for each sparse member combination in the example below:

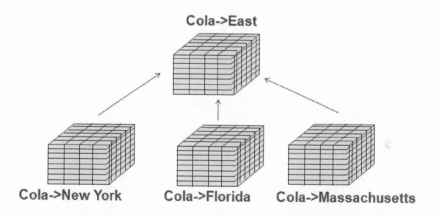

Cola->East

Cola->New York   Cola->Florida   Cola->Massachusetts

There are four types of blocks:

- Input blocks are blocks where data is loaded or input.
- Calculated blocks are blocks that are created through consolidation or calculation.
- Level zero blocks are blocks that are created from the level zero members of all dimensions.

- Upper-level blocks are all blocks that contain at least one upper level member (non-level zero).

Each block is made up of cells. These cells are created for each intersection of the dense dimensions. In the example below, Time, Measures, and Scenario are dense dimensions. See the cells for each dense member combination in the example below (we've highlighted one specific cell "Profit" at "Jan" at "Actual"):

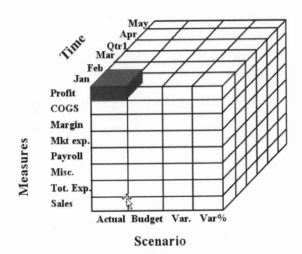

OUTLINE CONSOLIDATION

Essbase is built to perform outline consolidations. You assigned a consolidation attribute to each member that tells Essbase how to perform the consolidation, whether it should add to the total, subtract from the total, and so forth. Unary operators include +, -, *, /, %, and ~. The consolidation will use these operators and follow the path of the hierarchies for each dimension.

So what do outline consolidation and dense/sparse have to do with each other? Essbase will perform dense calculations first and then sparse calculations. The default calculation order for Essbase is the following:

- First, Accounts
- Second, Time
- Third, remaining dense dimensions
- Fourth, remaining sparse dimensions
- Two Pass Calculation (covered in a later scene)

Let's follow the path of an Essbase consolidation to help you better understand. In the example below, the highlighted cells indicate cells loaded with data.

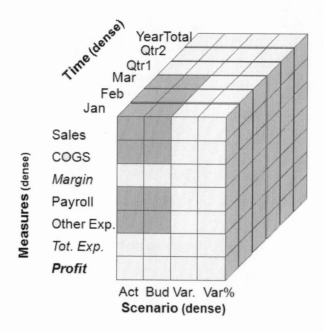

Next you see those cells populated with the Accounts dimension calculation (see Profit, Margin, Tot. Exp).

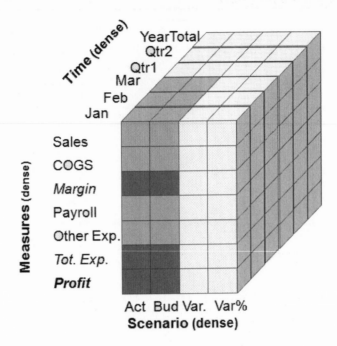

Finally the cells in the upper portion of the block represent those cells populated with the Time dimension calculation (Qtr1, Qtr2, YearTotal).

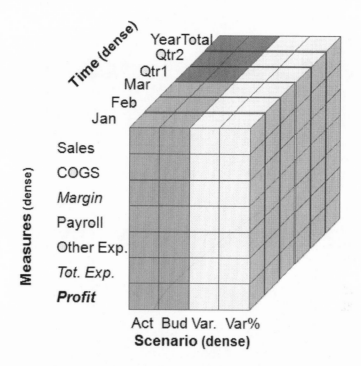

Why don't the variance and variance % members show calculated data values? 99% of the time you will tag these two members with the dynamic calc property so data will never be stored and in most cases, you won't need to calculate the Scenario dimension (and in most cases, this is a sparse dimension instead of a dense dimension; but we're getting a bit ahead of ourselves).

Here is another view of this dense calculation. Data is loaded to Sales and COGS members for each month. We are looking at the block for Vermont, Cola, and Actual (there's that cross dimensional symbol that means "at").

Vermont -> Cola -> Actual

Accounts	Jan	Feb	Mar	Qtr1
Sales	124.71	119.43	161.93	
COGS	42.37	38.77	47.28	
Margin				

First we consolidate the Accounts dimension, calculating the Margin member.

Vermont -> Cola -> Actual

Accounts	Jan	Feb	Mar	Qtr1
Sales	124.71	119.43	161.93	
COGS	42.37	38.77	47.28	
Margin	82.34	80.66	114.65	

Next we consolidate the Time dimension, calculating the Qtr1 member.

Vermont -> Cola -> Actual

Accounts	Jan	Feb	Mar	Qtr1
Sales	124.71	119.43	161.93	406.07
COGS	42.37	38.77	47.28	128.42
Margin	82.34	80.66	114.65	277.65

Once the Dense calculation is complete, the sparse calculation is next. The Vermont -> Cola -> Actual block and the New York -> Cola -> Actual block are added together to create the East -> Cola -> Actual block.

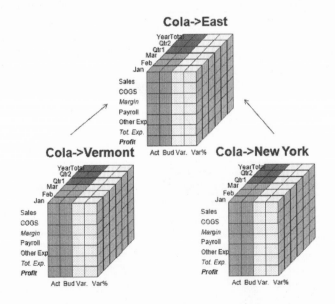

DEFAULT CALC

Finally we get to the calculation part. After loading data or submitting data via a data form, block storage databases require a separate calculation step to roll up values from level zero members to upper level members. The default calc is the simplest method for calculating Essbase databases, performing outline consolidations and calculating formulas as they appear in the outline. The default calc runs a "Calc All" calc script against the Essbase database.

Outline consolidations (sometimes called "unary operators") are those little plus, minus, divide, multiply, percent, and "no consolidate" signs that you place on individual members in the outline:

```
Measures
  Profit (+)
    Margin (+)
    Total Expenses (-)
  Inventory (~)
```

In the example above, you see that "Margin" has a plus sign next to it and "Total Expenses" has a minus sign. These are unary operators. When a default calculation occurs on the database, the data in these two members will consolidate together and be saved in the Profit member. "Inventory" has a tilde next to it (AKA "No Consolidate") so it won't be added to the data from "Profit" and stored in Measures.

The other type of calculation that occurs during a default calculation is the members in the outline with formulas will have their formulas evaluated:

```
Ratios (~)
  Margin % (+) [Formula: Margin % Sales;]
  Profit % (~) [Formula: Profit % Sales;]
```

When the default calculation occurs, the formula on "Margin %" will evaluate and take margin as a percentage of sales.

To launch the default calc for the Sum plan type,
1. Open Essbase Administration Services.
2. Navigate to and select the Entpln.Sum database.
3. Right-click and select Execute Calculation.

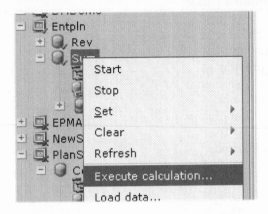

4. Select Default calc.

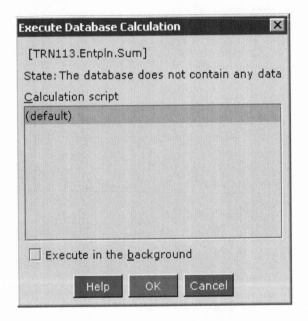

5. Check "Execute in Background" (this frees up the Administration Services console for other tasks):

6. Click OK.

Data will be consolidated for all dimensions and members in the Sum plan type.

7. Repeat the steps above to launch the default calc for the Entpln.Rev database.

In an earlier scene, we discussed using outline consolidations and member formulas for members. Quite often, these tools provide all the calculation power an application will need. However, as member formulas start to reference other levels or other dimensions, they can get very complex, very quickly. In Penny's current application, the Budget member has no formula.

Let's say the CFO is in charge of setting goals for the remainder of the year. He doesn't want the goals to be reasonable or obtainable (else everyone would reach them too easily and where's the motivation in that?), so he directs Penny to set every "Budget" member to be exactly fifty percent greater than the "Actual" number from last year. The problem is that this calculation would be very complex, and probably not a good thing to store directly in the outline as it may change frequently, so we'll need to override the default calculation. Calc scripts to the rescue...

WHAT IS A CALC SCRIPT?

At this point, you're probably asking yourself "What the heck is a calc script?" If you're not, then you're skipping the headings that introduce each section. A calc script is short for "calculation script" and it allows you to override the standard outline calculations and take complete control of how your database derives its numbers. While most of the time calc scripts are run at regular intervals to do simple things like aggregate subsets of your database, they can also be run sporadically such as at the start of budgeting season when you want to run your allocation processes with each what-if iteration.

A calc script is really just a sequential series of commands, equations, and formulas. It is stored in a standard text file with a .CSC extension, so you can even open one in Notepad if you want to. Here's the calc script that will set all of your budget values to 50% above your actuals:

```
/* Creates Initial Budget */
SET UPDATECALC OFF;

CLEARDATA Budget;
Budget = Actual * 1.5;
CALC ALL;
```

You might have noticed that this calc script actually does a few things beyond just creating the budget, but we'll get to those in due time.

There are a lot of reasons to use a calc script. If you're not happy with the order in which Essbase calculates the members and dimensions, a calc script can easily override the default order. If you don't want to calculate the entire database, a calc script can be written to only calculate the current month. If you want to clear data or copy data from one place to another, calc scripts can do the job. Want to create formulas that aren't in the outline? Calc scripts are there for you. Calc scripts will even let you perform allocations and multi-pass calculations. When one of the end-users passes you a multi-stage allocation calculation that would make most Excel gurus run home crying to their mommies, you can just tie on your cape and write an Essbase Calc Script to save the day.

CREATE A CALC SCRIPT

Normally, people edit their calc scripts in Administration Services. It is possible to create and modify calc scripts in your favorite text editor, but only nerds do this. Since I'm a nerd, I'm completely okay with that. [Other Author's Note: Edward wrote that last line. I, Tracy McMullen, am definitely not a nerd (not that there's anything wrong with nerds).]

There are some definite advantages to using your own text editor. Text editors tend to let you see more lines at once, allow better find and replace functionality, have better line numbering, and provide greater printing options than Administration Services' built-in Calc Script Editor. If you create your calc script in an external editor, it is very easy to copy and paste the body into Administration Services, or you can save your calc script as a text file in the appropriate database directory (if you do this, remember to save the file with a .CSC extension).

My First Calc Script

For now, let's pretend that you're not a nerd for a second and use Administration Services to create your first calc script.

1. In Administration Services, select the database.
2. Right-click on the database and select *Create >> Calculation Script*:

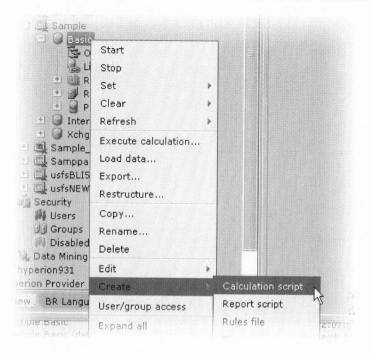

Tip!

You can also create a calc script by going to the menu and choosing *File >> New >> Scripts >> Calc Script Editor*.

3. The Calculation Script Editor window will display:

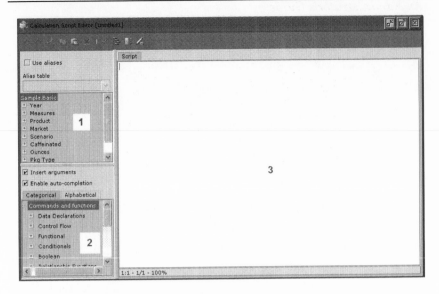

This editor has three main panes:

1. Outline. This pane helps you to select members from the outline and add them automatically to the calc script being edited.

2. Functions. This pane lets you select functions and commands and add them to the calc script being edited. The check boxes above this pane determine if arguments to the functions and commands will be inserted as well.

3. Data entry. This is where you actually type your calc script.

While you could live without panes one and two (though it would be a royal pain), all of the power of calc scripts is entered into pane three.

The calc editor (as we'll call it from now on) has a toolbar at the top of the screen just below the menu:

While most of the buttons are the same ones you'd see in fancy Windows applications like Notepad, the rightmost three icons are calc editor specific. The check mark icon validates the syntax of your calc script. The outline icon associates an outline with your calc script. You'll need to do this if you don't see an outline in the outline pane (pane one, remember?). The final icon (the green down arrow next to a cash register receipt) runs the calc script that's open in pane 3. We're not going to be using the toolbar for right now, but go right ahead if you'd like to. It's a free country.

Note!   If you are in Cuba, then you're not actually in a free country but rather are under the ironclad grip of a communist dictatorship. Hopefully this won't stop you from using the toolbar, though.

Simplest Calc Script

While it's small in stature, it's powerful in nature. This single line will aggregate all of the dimensional hierarchies in your outline, calculate all of the formulas attached to members, perform time balancing on time balanced members, and does it all quickly using "intelligent calculation". We'll be covering more sophisticated calc scripts throughout this scene, but you should remember that no matter what you create, you will always have the power of default.

```
CALC ALL;
```

For the Sum database, create a CalcAll calc script.
1. Open the Essbase Administration Services console.
2. Navigate to the Sum database.
3. Right-click on Sum and select Create >> Calc Script:

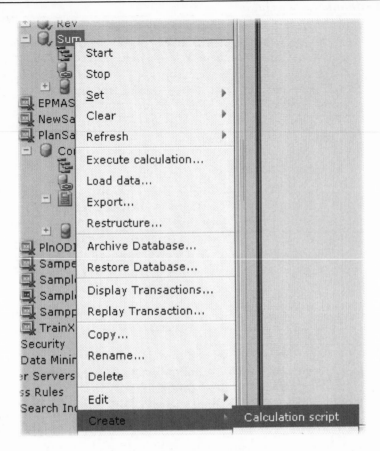

4. The Calc Script editor will open.
5. Type "CALC ALL;" into the data entry pane.
6. Go up to the menu and choose Syntax >> Check Syntax (or press *Ctrl-Y*):

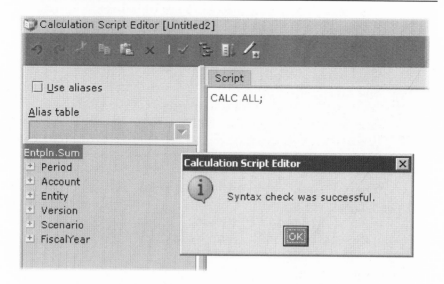

7. After you see the validation message, go up to the menu to Options >> Execute Script (or just press *F5*) to calculate Entpln.Sum:

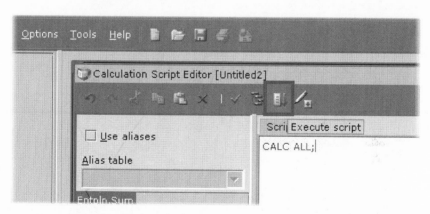

Since this is essentially the default calc, don't worry about saving this calc script.

Calc Script Syntax

There are a few simple rules to follow when writing a calc script:

1. End every statement with a semicolon.
2. You do not talk about fight club.

3. You can break a statement onto multiple lines, but the end of the statement must have a semicolon.
4. If a member name contains spaces or starts with a number, surround it with "double quotes."
5. Start comments with /*
6. End comments with */
7. Each statement must have a semicolon at the end.
8. Calc scripts are not case-sensitive.
9. Spaces between member names, commands, and functions do not matter.

There are many more rules, but these are the important ones that people tend to forget causing them to wonder for hours why their calc scripts aren't working. Here's a calc script that demonstrates several of those syntax rules:

```
/* Calculate Budget */

"Annual Budget" =
  "aCTual" * 1.1;
```

Notice that the first line is a comment and it has the appropriate start and end characters. "Annual Budget" has a space in the member name, so it's surrounded by double quotes. At the end of the entire statement (although not at the end of the comment), there's a semicolon. (You can tell the calc script language was written by a programmer, because only programmers end sentences with semicolons ;) Finally, observe that the second instance of Actual uses wacky cases just to show you that calc scripts are indeed *not* case-sensitive (unless you have explicitly told Essbase to behave otherwise).

SIMPLE CALCULATIONS

One of the simplest calculations you can perform is to tell Essbase to do the calculation for a single member. In a production system, this is the leanest, meanest calc script you can write, and is used when you want the script to finish in the quickest possible time.

Calculate Single Members

Imagine for a moment that the "Variance" member in Penny's application was stored and not dynamically calculated. We've just loaded data and we want to tell Essbase to calculate the formula on "Variance" and leave the rest of the outline alone. All we have to do is spell the member name and add a semicolon:

```
Variance;
```

How do you think you'd modify the calc script to calculate both Variance and Variance %? Hopefully it's something like this:

```
Variance;
"Variance %";
```

Notice that we have to use double quotes around "Variance %" due to the space in the name.

Tip! If you want to be safe about it, put double quotes around all member names (even "Variance"). It doesn't hurt anything, and it does help you identify your member names quickly during troubleshooting exercises.

The technique of specifying a member name on a line by itself can be applied to members that do not have formulas but do have members aggregating into them. Imagine that we have just loaded data in Penny's application to the great state of Massachusetts. Now we want to roll-up the MA numbers to the top of the Entity dimension:

```
"East Sales";
"Entity";
```

The nice thing about this script is that it doesn't bother rolling up totals that haven't changed. There's no MA in the West Sales (thankfully) so we know we don't need to modify the totals for West Sales.

It's also possible to temporarily override the formula in the outline for a member. Let's return to our earlier example where we were an evil budget manager trying to set our budgets slightly higher than our actuals so no one could ever meet their numbers. To do this in a calc script, we just set up an equation with Budget on the left-side of the equal sign:

```
Budget = Actual * 1.5;
```

This script will set the budget to be 50% greater (notice that we're multiplying times 1.5) than actuals. If you're really in need of a raise, you could set the profit of your company to double what it should be:

```
Profit = Profit * 2;
```

Forgetting that the above calc script is probably illegal (thanks, Senator Sarbanes, wherever you are), it is interesting in that it puts the member "Profit" on both sides of the equation. It's also useful to understand that every time you run it Profit will double, so make sure you only run scripts like this once.

Tip!

There are better ways to increase your company's profitability than writing an illegal calc script.

Intelligent Calculation

Before we go any further, you have to learn the command to turn off intelligent calculation. Intelligent calculation allows Essbase to remember which blocks in the database need to be calculated based on new data coming in, and which haven't been impacted (and don't need calculation). Intelligent calculation is wonderful when you're running a default calc.

But (there is always a "but") intelligent calculation is the devil's work when you're running a calc script. Think about the budget calc script from earlier:

```
Budget = Actual * 1.5;
```

Do we want this calc script only to operate on so called "dirty blocks" or do we want all budgets throughout the entire system to be set 50% above actuals? If we leave intelligent calculation turned on during the running of our calc, Essbase will only calculate our new budgets for blocks that have recently been loaded with data. That's definitely not what we want, as some business units will escape with a sensible quota. We definitely can't have that!

The good news is that you don't have to turn off intelligent calculation for the entire database: you can just tell Essbase to ignore it during the calc script with this command:

```
SET UPDATECALC Off;
```

If you want to turn Intelligent Calc on again later in the script (maybe you want a "CALC ALL" command at the end of your script to calculate just the dirty blocks), include the command **SET UPDATECALC ON;** and everything past that point will work "intelligently". We recommend that you include the command to turn intelligent calculation off at the top of every calc script. If there's a case where you actually want to use it, go ahead and remove the line on a case-by-case basis. Leaving it out is courting disaster (and take it from a guy who dated disaster back in high school: you don't want to be courting her).

Calculate Entire Dimensions

As we've already mentioned, there's a simple command that you can include in a calc script that tells Essbase to evaluate all your member formulas and do all of your outline aggregation. While "CALC ALL" is great and powerful, there are times when you only want to calculate specific dimensions. For instance, what would we do if we just wanted to calculate our appliction's Entity dimension? We have a new command for this called "CALC DIM" (short for calculate dimension):

```
CALC DIM (Entity);
```

This line calculates the Entity dimension doing both outline aggregation (such as rolling all the level zero members up into the parent value) and member formulas, if they exist for members in that dimension. If we want to calculate multiple dimensions using this command (say, Entity and Segment), just separate them with commas:

```
CALC DIM (Entity, Segment);
```

Remember how we said that "CALC DIM" not only does aggregation but also member formulas? Well, how many member formulas are there in the Entity and Segment dimensions? That's right - none, so "CALC DIM" is wasting time looking for formulas that you know aren't there. For dimensions that don't have formulas, there's a faster command that only does aggregation:

```
AGG (Entity, Segment);
```

Note!

"AGG" can only be used on sparse dimensions. If you have a dense dimension with no formulas that you only want to aggregate, you cannot use "AGG." You must use the "CALC DIM" command.

Calculate a Subset of Data

While calculating entire dimensions makes you feel very powerful, sometimes you just want to calculate a portion of the database. For instance, let's say you just updated your budgets but you didn't touch actuals. How could you ignore the Actual member? Well it turns out that there's an optional argument to the "CALC ALL" command called "EXCEPT". You use it to calculate everything except specific dimensions (DIM) or members (MBR). If we didn't want to calculate actuals, we'd say:

```
CALC ALL EXCEPT MBR (Actual);
```

It's also possible to list multiple members. Say that we didn't want to calculate Texas and New York (no offense to either state). We'd list the members separated by commas:

```
CALC ALL EXCEPT MBR (TX, NY);
```

If there's an entire dimension you don't want to calculate, replace "MBR" with "DIM":

```
CALC ALL EXCEPT DIM (Measures);
```

While this method may be fun at first, it's not nearly the most powerful method for limiting a calculation to a small portion of the database. Let's say we just loaded starting point budgets for next year for the "MA" member. Now we just want to calculate our accounts dimension for that one member, ignoring the rest of the database. The "CALC ALL EXCEPT..." method from above is really used to do the majority of a database and not just a smidgen, so we need a new command: "FIX" and its sister command "ENDFIX".

If we just want to calculate "MA", we put this in double quotes after the "FIX" as such:

```
FIX ("MA")
        CALC DIM (Account);
ENDFIX
```

Tip!

While the indentation is not necessary, it helps make it easier to see which commands the FIX affects.

"FIX" and "ENDFIX" are called sandwich commands because one command is like the top layer of bread and the other as the bottom with lots of things thrown in between. For instance, we could choose to calculate a few specific accounts:

```
FIX ("MA")
        Op_Income;
        Margin;
ENDFIX
```

It's also possible to list multiple members in a FIX as long as you separate them with commas:

```
FIX ("MA", "NY")
        Op_Income;
        Margin;
ENDFIX
```

Let's say you only loaded budgets to next year for MA and NY sales entities for the home theater audio systems. Here's one way to accomplish that by nesting one "FIX" within another:

```
FIX ("MA", "NY")
        FIX (HTAS)
                Op_Income;
                Margin;
        ENDFIX
ENDFIX
```

Note!

Each "FIX" must conclude with an "ENDFIX". It is not necessary to end a "FIX" or "ENDFIX" statement with a semicolon, but it doesn't hurt anything to use one either.

While this is a valid method, two "FIX"es are not necessary. You can list members from multiple dimensions within one "FIX" command, and this is the traditional way to do it:

```
FIX ("MA", "NY", "HTAS")
        Op_Income;
        Margin;
ENDFIX
```

Tip!   Using "FIX" commands on sparse dimensions will speed up the performance of your calculations, because it limits the number of blocks pulled into memory to just what's listed in the "FIX" statement.

Two new commands were introduced in Essbase 9.3: EXCLUDE / ENDEXCLUDE (you may see these new commands referred to as "Unchanged Cells"). The new commands will calculate everything except what is defined in the EXCLUDE statement. Think of it as the opposite of a FIX / ENDFIX. The following calculation will calculate everything except MA:

```
EXCLUDE ("MA")
Calc Dim (Accounts);
ENDEXCLUDE
```

Point to Another Member

While you're inside a "FIX" command, blocks outside are ignored. What if you want to refer to values from blocks that aren't being retrieved into memory? Surely there must be a way, you cry out of quiet desperation. Stop your incessant bawling, because there is indeed a way. It's called the cross-dimensional operator. Its job is to point to another member in the database and it looks like this:

```
->
```

Note!   There is no "cross-dimensional operator" symbol on your keyboard. You type this in by pressing dash followed by a greater than symbol.

If we wanted to set net revenue for February equal to net revenue for January, we could write a calc script that looks like this:

```
FIX ("Feb")
     Net_Rev = Net_Rev->"Jan";
ENDFIX
```

What exactly is this doing? On the right-side of the equation, we told Essbase to get the value from net revenue for Jan. The left-side of the equation told it to put the result in net revenue, but which net revenue? Well as you see from the "FIX", we told Essbase to only calculate Feb, so it will put the value into net revenue for Feb.

Whenever possible, try to avoid cross-dimensional operators. They're unseemly and slow. For instance, if we had to add another account, we would have to include it within the "FIX":

```
FIX ("Feb")
 Net_Rev = Net_Rev->"Jan";
 Op_Expense = Op_Expense->"Jan";
ENDFIX
```

We could remove the need for the cross-dimensional operator (called "cross-dim" for short) by pivoting the customer and account dimensions. That is, we'll put the account dimension in the "FIX" and the customer dimension inside the "FIX":

```
FIX (Net_Rev, Op_Expense)
  "Feb" = "Jan";
ENDFIX
```

This is much easier to read, and more flexible as well. It's obvious now that we're focusing on two specific accounts and setting one member to be equal to another.

Tip!

If you find yourself repeating a cross-dim to the same member, it might be possible to pivot a dimension as above to remove the need for the cross-dim.

It is also possible to string cross-dims together to point to more and more specific intersections in the database.

Clear Data

Have you ever had one of those days when everything was going wrong and you just wanted to wipe out the entire day and start over? Fortunately, it's much easier to do this in Essbase than it is in reality. If we wanted to clear all of the data in our cube, we'd need the following little calc script:

```
SET UpdateCalc Off;
CLEARBLOCK All;
```

The first line (as no doubt you'll recall from a few pages ago) tells Essbase to operate on all blocks in the database and not just the dirty blocks. The second line tells Essbase to clear all the blocks in the database.

This script will run extremely quickly, and when it's finished, it will certainly appear that your database is empty, but if you look closely, it's not. Look out on your server's hard drive and you'll see that the .PAG file still exists. The reason that "CLEARBLOCK" runs like a paparazzi after Angelina Jolie is that all it does is blank out the index entries: the pointers to the corresponding blocks in the page file. Since it can no longer find the blocks, they might as well be blank.

Tip!

"CLEARBLOCK" will leave your database fragmented. Remember to defragment your database periodically to improve performance (see the Design and Optimize scene for more information on fragmentation).

A powerful way to use "CLEARBLOCK" is within a "FIX" statement. We want to blank out our Sample.Basic budget so that we can try again (our last attempt at the budget was horrendous, let's be honest), so we write this script:

```
FIX (Budget)
        CLEARBLOCK All;
ENDFIX
```

Remember that "CLEARBLOCK" will clear out entire blocks by removing the pointers, but in Sample.Basic, Budget is in the Scenario dimension and Scenario is a dense dimension. Since Budget is in every block in the database, does it remove all the blocks? No, "CLEARBLOCK" is smart enough to only clear out index entries when the entire block is not being "FIX"ed on. In cases where just a portion of a block needs to be cleared, "CLEARBLOCK" will read the blocks into memory, clear out the necessary slices, and write the blocks back out to the page file. As such, "CLEARBLOCK" when used inside a "FIX" on a dense dimension is noticeably slower.

If you want to blank out a specific dense member, there's a simpler way than including a "CLEARBLOCK" inside a "FIX" on that dense member:

```
CLEARDATA Budget;
```

The "CLEARDATA" command allows you to specify a single member (in our case, budget). Do not use this on a sparse member, because the "CLEARBLOCK" command will always be faster. It is also possible to use a cross-dim operator on the right-side of a "CLEARDATA" command. If we wanted to clear out only our sales budget, we could write:

```
CLEARDATA Budget->Sales;
```

If you need to clear out multiple dense members, do not write your script like this:

```
CLEARDATA Actual;
CLEARDATA Budget;
```

This will result in multiple passes through your database since Essbase will not know to clear your data from actual and budget during a single pass. In this case, go back to using the "CLEARBLOCK" command within a "FIX":

```
FIX (Actual, Budget)
     CLEARBLOCK All;
ENDFIX
```

At various times, you'll want to make sure that all of the aggregated blocks in your database are cleared. For instance, if you're about to recalculate all of the totals in your database, it's faster if Essbase doesn't have to read the old totals into memory before writing out the new ones. There is an argument you can use in place of "All" called "Upper":

```
CLEARBLOCK Upper;
```

This command will clear all of the upper-level blocks in your database. As before with the "All" argument, "CLEARBLOCK

Upper" can be used within a "FIX" statement. A related argument is "NonInput":

```
CLEARBLOCK NonInput;
```

This will clear out all the blocks that haven't had data directly input to them. Assuming we're following best practices and only entering data into level-0 blocks, this command will only clear out the upper-level blocks like "CLEARBLOCK Upper".

A new argument was added for the CLEARBLOCK command in Essbase 9.3: "CLEARBLOCK Empty" which removes #Missing blocks from the database. The "CLEARBLOCK Empty" command sets values to #MISSING and if the entire block is empty, Essbase will remove the block. This is helpful if you've run the CREATEBLOCKONEQ in a calc script to create blocks and may have unnecessarily created blocks with no data.

```
CLEARBLOCK Empty;
```

There's one other way to clear data. You can set a member equal to #Missing:

```
Budget = #Missing;
```

While this is valid syntax (and we've even seen a few sub-par consultants use it), it's just weird. Stick to "CLEARBLOCK" or "CLEARDATA".

Copying Data

There are two common ways to copy data. The first is with a simple equation:

```
"Budget"="Actual";
```

This equation copies the Actual data over to the Budget data. Depending on the settings in your database, this method may or may not create blocks. The way to be sure you create all necessary blocks is by using the "DATACOPY" command. It takes two arguments: a member to copy the data from and a member to copy the data to. This command accomplishes the same thing as the line of code above, but with added comfort that there will be no block creation shenanigans:

```
DATACOPY "Actual" TO
        "Budget";
```

Both of these methods can be used within a FIX command. Do not use multiple "DATACOPY" commands on dense members:

```
DATACOPY Jan TO Feb;
DATACOPY Feb TO Mar;
```

In the case of Sample.Basic, this calc script will actually cause two passes through the database since Time is a dense dimension. In this case, the first method of setting one member equal to another would be better.

Tip!

To oversimplify, use the equation method on dense members and the "DATACOPY" method on sparse members.

IF and Its Other Brother, ENDIF

You learned earlier how easy it is to use the "IF...ENDIF" sandwich commands (technically, they're functions, but since they don't start with @, we like to think of them as commands) inside of a member formula. As a refresher, let's say we wanted to check and see if revenues were less than expenses. If so, let's fire everybody (i.e., set headcount equal to zero). Here's what this would look like if you made it the member formula for "Headcount" in the outline:

```
IF (Revenue < Expense)
      Headcount = 0;
ENDIF
```

Now since this is attached to the Headcount member, it's technically not necessary to specify "Headcount =" on the third line. As a matter of policy, we don't tend to include it, because if the "Headcount" member gets renamed, the member formula reference to it will *not* rename. As such, we'd write the member formula like this:

```
IF (Revenue < Expense)
      0;
ENDIF
```

Now, if you just type this into a calc script and verify it, you'll get the following message:

"Error: 1012061 The CALC command [IF] can only be used within a CALC Member Block"

First of all, note that the error message calls "IF" a command, so we were right all along about it not being a real function, on-line documentation be damned. To translate the error message into semi-English, "IF" can only be used in a member formula.

"Uh, oh," you say, "but I want to do IFs in a calc script. Is now the time for ritual suicide?"

While it may indeed be, don't do it over this, because there's a simple work-around: create a temporary member formula within your calc script that contains the needed "IF". You do this by specifying the member that you want to assign the temporary formula and then include the formula in parentheses. For example:

```
Headcount
      (
      IF (Revenue < Expense)
            0;
      ENDIF
      )
```

Notice "Headcount" at the top and the parentheses surrounding the "IF...ENDIF". Voila! The calc script will now validate and run successfully.

FUNCTIONS

Everything we've done up to this point has been focused around using the calculation commands. There are also at least 135 functions that let you do most of the interesting things that Microsoft Excel functions can do (like absolute values, statistical deviations, and internal rate of return calculations) and many things that Excel functions cannot (like return the parent value of the current member in a hierarchy and allocate values down across a hierarchy).

Note! These are the very same functions that you used when creating member formulas. With very few exceptions, all of the functions can be used both in member formulas and calc scripts.

To make it easier to find the functions in the on-line help, Hyperion segmented the functions into several nebulous categories. Some of the categories are easily understood (like "Boolean"). Some, like the mysterious "Miscellaneous" category, are not.

Boolean

Boolean functions return True or False (actually, they return a 1 for True and a 0 for False). Boolean functions are generally used inside an "IF" or an "ELSEIF". One of the common boolean functions is "@ISMBR" and it's used to tell if a specific member is being calculated. Let's say that we want to set budgeted sales equal to 123.45:

```
IF (@ISMBR (Budget))
     Sales = 123.45;
ENDIF
```

It's possible to put a cross-dim operator inside the "@ISMBR". All parts of the cross-dim must be true for the entire statement to be true. In this example, the current intersection being calculated must be "NY" and "Budget":

```
IF (@ISMBR (Budget->"NY"))
     Sales = 123.45;
ENDIF
```

It's even possible to list several members in an "@ISMBR" separated by commas. For instance, if we only want to set NY and MA sales, our script would look like this:

```
IF (@ISMBR ("NY", "MA"))
     Sales = 123.45;
ENDIF
```

At times, you might want to check to see if the current member is in a range of members. For instance, say you want "COGS" to be set to 500 if the month being calculated is between

January and June. To do this, separate the two members (in this case "Jan" and "Jun") with a colon:

```
IF (@ISMBR (Jan:Jun))
    COGS = 500;
ENDIF
```

You might sometimes see "Jan::Jun" with a double-colon between the two members. The single-colon method returns all members from "Jan" to "Jun" that are at the same level. The double-colon method returns all the members from "Jan" to "Jun" that are at the same *generation*. Unless your outline contains ragged hierarchies, the single- and double-colon methods will return the same list. For simplicities sake, we tend to use a single colon.

There are at least fifteen other Boolean functions, some of which are actually helpful (@ISCHILD, @ISGEN, and @ISLEV, among others).

Relationship Functions

Relationship functions are used to look up values at intersections elsewhere in Essbase. Generally, the value being looked up is in the same database, but it doesn't have to be (e.g. the "@XREF" functions that are created by Planning).

One common need is to look at the value at a parent member. For instance, say Penny's application had a stored member named "Product Share" that needed to show each level-0 product's sales as a percentage of its parent's sales:

```
"Product Share" =
    Sales / @PARENTVAL (Segment, Sales);
```

The first argument to the "@PARENTVAL" function is the dimension for which you want to take the value at the parent. If we had a "Market Share" member, we could calculate it like this:

```
"Market Share" =
    Sales / @PARENTVAL (Market, Sales);
```

Mathematical, Statistical, and Forecasting

Mathematical functions perform standard arithmetic type calculations such as absolute value, integer, and factorial. The "@VAR" function used in Sample.Basic to calculate variances is, for no apparent reason, a mathematical function.

While simple statistical functions like maximum and minimum are found in the Mathematical category, advanced statistical functions get their own category: Statistical.

There are also some statistical type functions that have to do with moving sums, averages, minimums, and so on. These functions are found in the Forecasting category along with "@SPLINE" which finds a curve most closely fitting a range of data and "@TREND" which predicts the future (well, kinda). If you're ever curious how "@TREND" comes up with its trend calculations, the programmers at Oracle were kind enough to put the formulas in technical reference documentation. Here's a snippet of the "Algorithm for Triple Exponential Smoothing (TES)." Sing along if you know the melody:

@TREND

Back to main @TREND topic.

Algorithm for Triple Exponential Smoothing (TES)

$Ylist$ $\qquad y_1, y_2, \ldots, y_K$

$Xlist$ $\qquad x_1, x_2, \ldots, x_K$

TES with period T (if T is not given, it is assumed to be $T = 1$)

$\qquad x_1, x_2, \ldots, x_K, \qquad y_1, y_2 \ldots, y_K$ are input to TES, x is forecast value

$$a_i = (1-c)^{x_{i+1}-x_i} \qquad d_i = (1-d)^{x_{i+1}-x_i} \qquad e_i = (1-e)^{x_{i+1}-x_i}$$

Note: When $Xlist$ is missing, the exponents disappear.

Default $\qquad c = .2$
$\qquad\qquad d = .05$
$\qquad\qquad e = .1$

Step 1,

$$S_1 = y_1$$
$$b_1 = \frac{y_2 - y_1}{x_2 - x_1}$$
$$I_1 = 1$$

Step 2, For $i = 1 \ldots, T - 1$

We'll bet you are wishing you hadn't slept through your statistics class in college right about now.

Member Set

Member Set functions simply return lists of members. These are commonly used in "FIX" commands. Say that we wanted to focus on just aggregating products in the East region. Rather than hard-code all the members in "East," we could use a member set function called "@CHILDREN":

```
FIX (@CHILDREN (East))
     AGG (Product);
ENDFIX
```

Essentially, the "@CHILDREN(East)" portion of the "FIX" is replaced by a series of members before the calc script runs. In essence, the calculation actually performed is this (once the "@CHILDREN" is evaluated):

```
FIX ("New York":"New Hampshire")
     AGG (Product);
ENDFIX
```

Or to put it another way (not using the single-colon range indicator):

```
FIX ("New York", "Massachusetts", "Florida",
    "Connecticut", "New Hampshire")
     AGG (Product);
ENDFIX
```

A common request is to calculate all of the members from a certain member on upwards to the top of the dimension. For instance, let's say you just loaded a value to the great state of Utah (thought we were going to say "the great state of Texas," didn't you?). You want to aggregate this value up through the Market dimension, but you don't want to aggregate the entire dimension (since nothing else has changed). Use the "@ANCESTORS" function on a line by itself:

```
@ANCESTORS (Utah);
```

Remembering that member set functions essentially return lists of members, the script is exactly the same as this request:

```
Utah;
West;
Market;
```

Note!

If a member set function returns any dynamic calc or dynamic calc and store members, they will not be evaluated

What if you wanted to calculate just the regions in the Market dimension? You could use the "@CHILDREN" function on a line by itself:

```
@CHILDREN (Market);
```

Range and Financial

Range functions (sometimes called "Financial" functions just to be contrary) operate on a range of members. The most commonly used range function is "@PRIOR" which looks to earlier members in the outline and "@NEXT" which looks to later members in the outline. Both of these functions assume that you want to look forward and backward through the dimension marked as the "Time" dimension if you do not otherwise specify a range. Many people think of them as time-specific because of this, but they do not have to be.

The member "Opening Inventory" in Sample.Basic uses the "@PRIOR" function to refer to the prior month's "Ending Inventory":

```
IF (NOT @ISMBR(Jan))
      "Opening Inventory" =
                  @PRIOR ("Ending Inventory");
ENDIF;
```

The "IF (NOT ..." is used to make sure that we don't try to look back to the prior period if we are in the month of January (because Sample.Basic only contains one year of data, this wouldn't make any sense).

Allocation

Allocation functions allocate summarized higher level values down to detailed members. This is often used for top-down budgeting or targeted forecasting (when values are often loaded to parent members and then spread downward). There are only two functions. "@ALLOCATE" allocates values down a single dimension and its more impressive counterpart "@MDALLOCATE" which allocates values down multiple dimensions simultaneously.

Try It!

Look up the syntax for "@ALLOCATE" in the on-line help and create a calc script using it. Don't use any of the optional arguments for right now: there are too many to deal with right now what with everything else going on in your life and all.

While the allocation functions are powerful, they're not very efficient at complex allocations. If you find that using these functions is slow, you can generally improve performance by "rolling your own" allocations in the form of a more complicated calc script.

Date & Time

Date & Time functions change dates in the form of strings to numeric dates. This category only has one function in it at the moment, "@TODATE", which makes me wonder why they didn't just put this function in the Miscellaneous category. Somehow, we think the marketing department is involved.

Miscellaneous

Miscellaneous is the category for functions that don't have a place elsewhere. The "@TODATE" function should be here, but it's not. Instead, you get the bizarre "@CALCMODE" function which changes the way Essbase calculates a member and three string manipulation functions (@CONCATENATE, @NAME, and @SUBSTRING).

Custom-Defined

Custom-defined functions are whatever you want them to be. It is possible to write your own functions in Java, register them with Essbase using the MaxL "create function" command, and call them from a calc script as if they were part of the native language.

One of the best uses of CDFs (custom-defined functions) is for iterative type calculations (such as the common retail metric "Weeks of Supply") that would take up pages in a calc script but are just a few lines of custom Java code. Other CDFs we've seen include a better implementation of internal rate of return than the "@IRR" function that comes with Essbase and a function that checks a weather database to pull back high and low temperatures.

MORE CALC SCRIPTS

Create Aggall Calc Script

In Essbase Administration Services console, create 2 new calc scripts for each database.

1. Launch the Essbase Administration Services console.
2. Right-click on the Rev database and select Create calculation script:

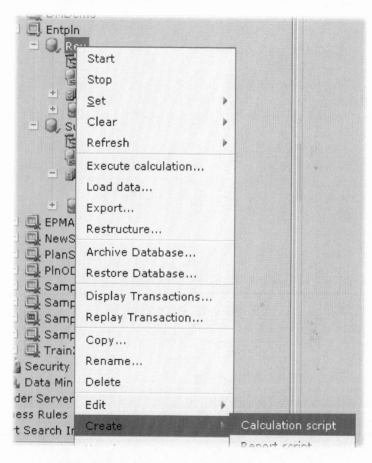

3. The calc script editor will open.
4. Type in the following syntax (or use the Member and Function tools):

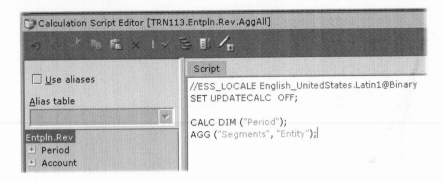

5. Select File >> Save.
6. Name the script AggAll.

Why do we use Calc Dim for Period? Why do we use Agg for other dimensions? Why did we not use Calc Dim or Agg for Period, Segments, Entity? Where are the other dimensions like Version and Scenario?

Agg is faster than calc dim but Agg is only available for Sparse dimensions with no member formulas. So we use Calc Dim for dense dimensions or those dimensions that have member formulas (Account and Period). We use Agg for Entity and Segments– sparse dims with no member formulas. We didn't need to include Account in the Calc Dim statement because all upper levels in this dimension are dynamically calculated. Scenario, Version, and Fiscal Year are sparse dimensions with no requirement for aggregations to upper levels (non-aggregating sparse dimension). Product Manager is an attribute dimension – you do not calculate attribute dimensions in calc scripts as they are dynamically calculated.

Create a similar script for the Sum cube (Hint – you can copy calc scripts from one application to another, which can often speed up the development process):

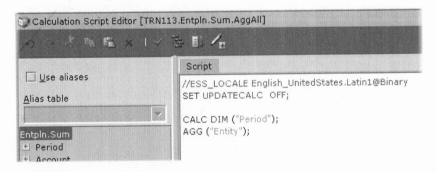

Create Budget Calc Script

1. In Administration Services console, create 1 new calc script for the Sum database that only calculates Budget data:

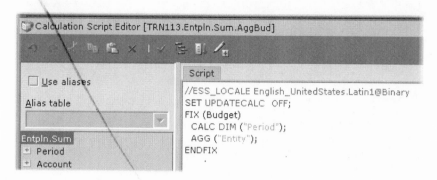

2. Save the script as AggBud.

Why is this calc script helpful?

During the budget cycle, your budget is constantly changing but actuals stay the same. You can speed up your calculations by only calculating the data that needs it assuming no dimensional changes. If you have changed the structure of a dimension - for example, you moved cost centers to new departments in the Entity dimension - you will need to recalculate both budget and actual data (so just remove the Fix statement in the calc script above).

For the Rev cube, Penny's requirements are a bit different for Forecast. While Actual and Budget track revenue at dollars only, users will enter units and price for Forecast, calculating revenue.

1. In the Planning web, create new members, "Metrics" with children "Units" and "Price" in the Dimension editor.
2. The Metrics member should roll directly to Account and have the following settings:

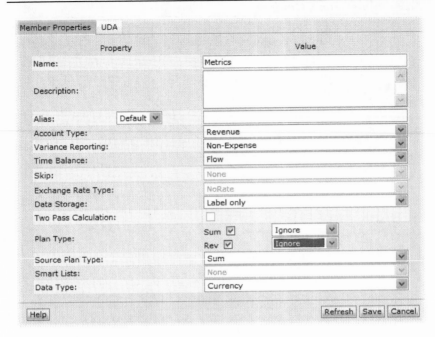

3. The Units member should roll directly to Metrics and have the following settings:

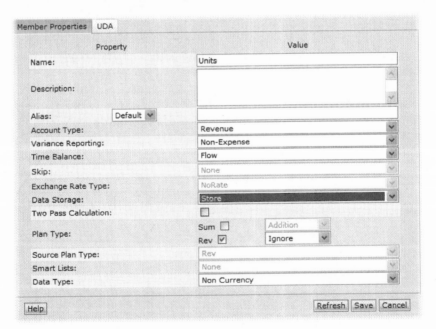

4. The Price member should roll directly to Metrics and have the following settings:

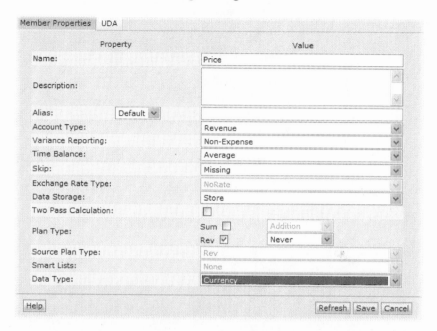

5. After the new metrics have been added, refresh to Essbase (Administration >> Manage Database).
6. In Essbase Administration Services Console, create one new calc script for the Rev database that calculates Forecast data only and performs the sales calculation – Units * Price:

```
SET UPDATECALC OFF;

FIX (Forecast)
    FIX(@LEVMBRS (Segments, 0), @LEVMBRS (Entity,
        0), @LEVMBRS (Period, 0))
        "411100" = "Units"*"Price";
    ENDFIX

    CALC DIM (Period);
    AGG (Entity, Segments);
ENDFIX
```

7. Validate and save the RevFcst calc script.

Execute the Calc Script

You've already run one calc script. Let's now run our new calc scripts.

1. In the Essbase Administration Services console, right-click on the Entpln.Rev AggAll calc script.
2. Click Execute.
3. Check the Message pane to ensure the calc ran successfully (we'll create some forms shortly so you can see the loaded and calculated data sets).
4. In the Administration Services console, right-click on the Sum AggAll calc script.
5. Click Execute.
6. Check the Message pane to ensure the calc ran successfully:

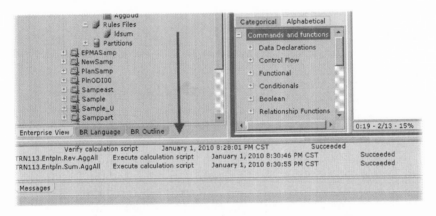

EXPORTING SLICES OF DATA IN A CALC SCRIPT

Data Export Commands

Starting in Essbase 9.3, a new calc script command can be used to export slices of data from Essbase cubes. It is extremely fast and if you use the binary form of the export, it is faster than a traditional Essbase database export. This feature will be helpful when you want to export final budgets to load into other reporting Essbase databases or other sources.

The new command, "DATAEXPORT", leverages the calc engine as a native function and is faster than report scripts and JEXPORT. You simply use the new command in a calc script and embed within a Fix statement to define the data slice for export. Output formats include delimited text files or a relational database table. There are a number of set commands that define information for the export like:

- SET DATAEXPORT DECIMAL <n>
- SET DATAEXPORTCOLFORMAT "ON" OR "OFF"
- SET DATAEXPORTCOLHEADER <DIMENSION NAME>
- SET DATAEXPORTLEVEL "ALL" OR "LEVEL"- OR "INPUT"

Review the example export script below that exports expense data for the HSP_InputValue, Local and NoSegment members to a text file. Period is defined as the headers:

```
Script

//ESS_LOCALE English_UnitedStates.Latin1@Binary
Set UpdateCalc off;
SET DATAEXPORTOPTIONS
    {
    DataExportPrecision 2;
    DataExportLevel "LEVEL0";
    DataExportColFormat On;
    DataExportColHeader "Period";
    DataExportDynamicCalc Off;
    };

FIX( "HSP_InputValue", "Local", "NoSegment", @IDESCENDANTS ("500000") )
DATAEXPORT "File" "," "C:\ExpenseDataFile.txt" ;
ENDFIX
```

The resulting file looks like:

	A	B	C	D	E	F	G	H	I	J	K	L	M	N
1									BegBalanc	Jan	Feb	Mar	Q1	Apr
2	HSP_Inpu	FY09	E01_0	NoSegme	Local	Plan	Working	501111	#MI	390,000	240,000	120,000	750,000	130
3	HSP_Inpu	FY09	E01_0	NoSegme	Local	Plan	Working	501130	#MI	23,000	14,000	6,200	44,000	8
4	HSP_Inpu	FY09	E01_0	NoSegme	Local	Plan	Working	501140	#MI	54,000	34,000	15,000	100,000	20
5	HSP_Inpu	FY09	E01_0	NoSegme	Local	Plan	Working	501240	#MI	70,000	43,000	20,000	130,000	24
6	HSP_Inpu	FY09	E01_0	NoSegme	Local	Plan	Working	501250	#MI	33,000	33,000	33,000	99,000	33
7	HSP_Inpu	FY09	E01_0	NoSegme	Local	Plan	Working	502100	#MI	19,000	11,000	5,900	36,000	
8	HSP_Inpu	FY09	E01_0	NoSegme	Local	Plan	Working	502200	#MI	4,300	2,600	1,500	8,400	
9	HSP_Inpu	FY09	E01_0	NoSegme	Local	Plan	Working	503100	#MI	22,000	13,000	7,600	43,000	6
10	HSP_Inpu	FY09	E01_0	NoSegme	Local	Plan	Working	503200	#MI	28,000	17,000	10,000	55,000	
11	HSP_Inpu	FY09	E01_0	NoSegme	Local	Plan	Working	504100	#MI	30,000	18,000	10,000	59,000	9
12	HSP_Inpu	FY09	E01_0	NoSegme	Local	Plan	Working	504200	#MI	22,000	13,000	7,600	43,000	6
13	HSP_Inpu	FY09	E01_0	NoSegme	Local	Plan	Working	504300	#MI	30,000	19,000	9,100	58,000	10
14	HSP_Inpu	FY09	E01_0	NoSegme	Local	Plan	Working	505100	#MI	100,000	63,000	34,000	200,000	32
15	HSP_Inpu	FY09	E01_0	NoSegme	Local	Plan	Working	505200	#MI	140,000	88,000	40,000	270,000	50
16	HSP_Inpu	FY09	E01_0	NoSegme	Local	Plan	Working	506110	#MI	35,000	21,000	12,000	68,000	10
17	HSP_Inpu	FY09	E01_0	NoSegme	Local	Plan	Working	506120	#MI	78,000	47,000	25,000	150,000	2
18	HSP_Inpu	FY09	E01_0	NoSegme	Local	Plan	Working	506210	#MI	470,000	300,000	150,000	910,000	160
19	HSP_Inpu	FY09	E01_0	NoSegme	Local	Plan	Working	506220	#MI	160,000	99,000	50,000	310,000	53
20	HSP_Inpu	FY09	E01_0	NoSegme	Local	Plan	Working	506311	#MI	96,000	61,000	25,000	180,000	36

Note!   The C:\ is the C drive on the Essbase server (not your PC).

You can also export directly to a table in your data warehouse. The syntax for that option would be:

```
SET DATAEXPORTRELATION "DSN"
DATAEXPORT "DSN" "[dsn_name]" "[table_name]"
    "[user_name]" "[password]";
```

You need to create the relational table beforehand with the appropriate columns. If you want to share this data set with another Essbase cube, you can use load rules to load the exported data set into the target cube.

Binary Calc Export / Import Commands

One other new option for exporting data is the Binary Export/Import calc command. This option moves or copies out data blocks in a compressed encrypted format to a text file. This is a fast backup method and also allows you to embed the commands in fix statements so that you can easily export out slices of data. Binary export/import ignores fixes on dense members (it copies entire blocks – intersection of sparse dimensions). You can also use the import command to import in the export text files. The exported file can only be imported into a database with the same dimensionality. The syntax for binary export / import is as follows:

```
DATAEXPORT "BINFILE" "[file_name]";
DATAIMPORTBIN "[file_name]";
```

WHERE DO WE GO FROM HERE?

Learning everything there is to know about calc scripts would take several years, we're fairly certain. We are considering writing a book that focuses entirely on calc scripts. We are sure we could fill at least 400 pages with non-stop, wall-to-wall, hot, steamy, calc action. Until then we'll point you in the right place for further information: the Essbase Technical Reference. The Technical Reference has a bounty of detailed, look-up information:

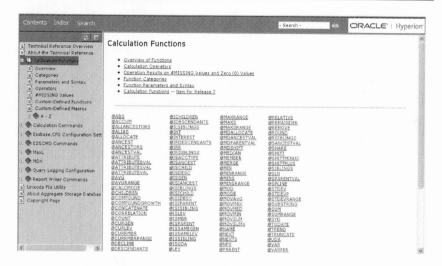

The "Calculation Functions" section contains details on all of the @Functions. The "Calculation Commands" section is where you go to find information on all of the commands that can be used in a calc script that don't start with an @ symbol. Several of the calculation functions contain examples showing you how to use them. While they're not in depth, they're plentiful, so maybe that makes up for it.

How Long?

For our final question of the calc script scene: the million dollar question. How long will the calc script take to run? Many, many factors will impact calculation time including the number of members in each of the dimensions, the block size, the amount of data loaded, the complexity of the calculation logic, and more. Plan time to test calc scripts and don't forget to review the design and optimize scene at the end of the book.

Just when you thought you were through with the calculation portion of Planning, the next musical scenes take you on a journey to further place calculation capabilities in the hands of users during the Planning process: Business Rules and Calculation Manager.

Scene 8:
Business Rules

The basement room was dark and stifling. A single light swayed overhead as Dr. Dementor sat at his work bench, fiddling and banging on his new and improved deathray. "Those tricky consultants won't defeat me this time," he mumbled over and over again. "While they may have been able to implement System 9 in just a week, there's no way they're making it through any new projects if they're dead... or worse."

His evil laugh echoed in the silence. Wah-hah-hah-hah...

Meanwhile back at Penny's desk, she shrugged off an unexpected chill. "Translator, please tell me more about Business Rules."

WHAT IS A BUSINESS RULE?

While calc scripts will run and execute against Planning databases, they are mostly run in after hours processes to aggregate entire databases or perform logic on the entire database set. But what if Eddie wants to aggregate only a small portion of the data? For example, Eddie updates the budget for IT Salary expense, cutting the budget by $500 (Penny gulps. That's the amount of her salary – in 1950). He would like to re-aggregate the IT department to see the overall impact to total expenses. Running our AggAll calc script would aggregate everything and could take minutes instead of seconds (possibly even hours instead of minutes for really big applications). One (really bad) alternative would be to create a different calc script for each entity. No, that would take forever to create and maintain. Thankfully Planning applications, in addition to calc scripts, can also use Business Rules to calculate Planning data which offers a solution to Eddie's IT calculation requirement.

Business Rules under the covers runs the same logic and syntax as Essbase calc scripts and is built to calculate Planning data; however, we use a different interface to create Business Rules. Business Rules are created using Essbase Administration Services (EAS) for 9.3x Planning applications while Calculation Manager for 11x Planning applications. (Technically you could still use EAS Business Rules in version 11 for Classic applications. Once you upgrade you can begin the process to move Business Rules from EAS to Calculation Manager).

Note! If you are on version 9.3.1, read this chapter. If you are version 11 and still use Business Rules in EAS, read this chapter. If you are on version 11 and use (will use) Calculation Manager, skip this chapter and read Scene 9: Calculation Manager.

So you will take all of the calc script knowledge that you gained in the previous chapter and apply in this chapter and the next. We will walk through some basic examples to help get you started.

Classic Planning gives the administrator two options when creating and maintaining business rules in Administration Services. Rules can be managed through the Business Rules Graphical Designer or as an "enhanced calc script".

GRAPHICAL DESIGNER

The Business Rules Graphical Designer allows you to create global or local variables, macros, sequences, assign access privileges, perform syntax validations, and launch business rules. The Graphical Designer has four actions and eight formula options (listed below):

- Aggregate action - Aggregation Template in Calc Manager
- Copy Data action - Copy Template in Calc Manager
- Clear Data action - Clear Data Template in Calc Manager when combined with the Create Block Action
- Create Block action
- Pro-Rata Ratio formula - Allocation Simple Template in Calc Manager
- Distribution Factor formula
- Even-Split formula
- Increase-Decrease formula
- Units-Rates formula - Amount-Rate-Unit Template in Calc Manager
- Combined formula
- Custom formula
- Variable formula

Consideration: The Graphical Designer in EAS Business Rules doesn't generate the most efficient syntax. In order to tune the logic, you have to switch to Business Rules mode or enhanced calc script mode. And then you can't go back to the Graphical Designer. Since that is the case, we recommend using Business Rules mode of Administrative Services.

Administrators with the proper Shared Services provisioning will see the Business Rules menu in EAS after log-in. Business Rules contain the following menus:

- My Project: Assign rules to a project for easier grouping and maintenance.
- Repository View: Maintain rules, sequences, macros, and global variables.
- Administration: Maintain properties, locations, and clusters.

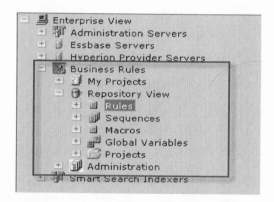

Now that you know where to go to create Business Rules, let's walk through the steps to create a business rule that Eddie can run from Planning to recalculate a specific department.

Note!

Business Rule syntax is the same as an Essbase Calculation Script but different validation logic is used.

CREATE VARIABLES

Now, let's assume you want to pass the Entity member (department) from the Planning data form to this business rule. We could prompt the user but to save him some clicks, we'll tell Planning to use the members on the form. In both cases you have to first create a variable to represent the dimension. You can create a global variable which can be used by other rules or a local variable which is used only in the current business rule. Local variables are defined on the Variables tab.

In the screenshot below, the ScenVar variable is a run time prompt usage type and Prompt String set to "Enter Scenario":

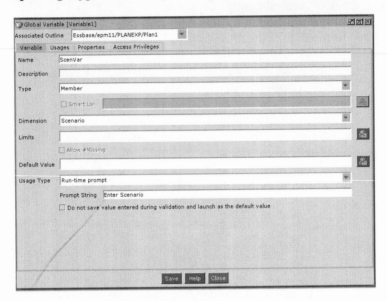

The Usages tab shows all the Business Rules where variables are used. The Properties tab provides high-level information about the variable including a last update date and time. The Access Privileges tab is where you can grant access to this variable. A planner must have access to both the Business Rule and any associated variables.

1. In Administration Services, create new global variables for Fiscal Year and Entity.
2. Right-click on Global Variables and select New Variable:

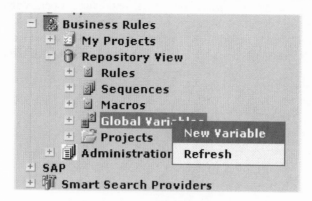

3. Select an outline (our example uses an application called trainxx.Sum) to associate an outline and its dimensions and members to the business rule (you may need to browse to select).

4. Enter the following information to create the FY_VAR:

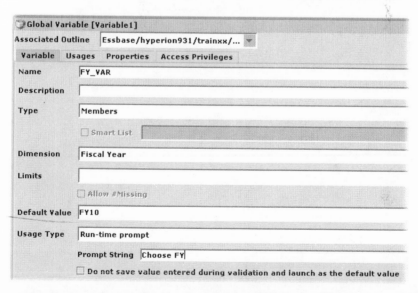

The options for Type of Variable are: Member (individual member), Members (member range), Dimension, String (text), Integer, Real (real number), Percentage, String as Number (text string from Planning), Date as Number (date string from Planning). For our example, we'll set the Type of Variable to Member since we want only one dimension member passed from the Planning web client. We'll also choose Entity for the Dimension (this field is required if member or members is selected for the type of variable). Limits do just what the name says and limit the values a planner can select. Next, select the desired Usage of: Use by Value (static value), Saved Selection (same value for all instances of this variable in the rule), or RTP (run-time-prompt prompts the planner for the value or pass the value set in the form).

5. Click Save.
6. Click Close.
7. Right-click on Global Variables and select New Variable.
8. Select an outline; this example chooses trainxx.Sum (you may need to browse to select).
9. Enter the following information to create the ENTITY_VAR:

Global Variable [Variable2]

Associated Outline: Essbase/hyperion931/trainxx/...

Variable | Usages | Properties | Access Privileges

Name: ENTITY_VAR
Description:
Type: Members
☐ Smart List
Dimension: Entity
Limits:
☐ Allow #Missing
Default Value:
Usage Type: Run-time prompt
Prompt String: Choose Entity
☐ Do not save value entered during validation and launch as the default value

10. Click Save.
11. Click Close.

CREATE A BUSINESS RULE (ENHANCED CALC SCRIPT)

1. In Administration Services, create a new Business rule by right-clicking on Rules.
2. Select New Rule:

3. The new rule will display in graphical mode:

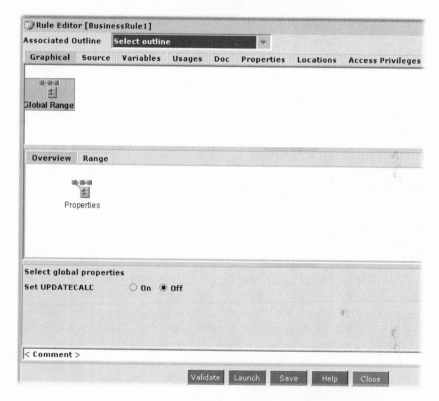

A new, blank Business Rule appears with several tabs. The Graphical tab is where you maintain the rule using graphical mode. We will create a rule using enhanced calc script mode on the source tab.

4. Click on the Source tab within the business rule.
5. Start to type in the source tab and click Yes when prompted (remember we mentioned that once you switch to enhanced calc script mode, there is no going back):

6. Type the following into the Source tab:

> **Rule Editor [Aggregate My Entity]**
>
> **Associated Outline** | **Essbase/hyperion931/trainx**
>
> Graphical | **Source** | **Variables** | **Usages** | **Doc**
>
> SET UPDATECALC OFF;
>
> FIX([FY_VAR], "Budget", "Draft", "Jan":"Dec")
>
>   @IANCESTORS([ENTITY_VAR]);
>
> ENDFIX|

```
SET UPDATECALC OFF;

FIX([FY_VAR], "Budget", "Draft", "Jan":"Dec")
  @IANCESTORS([ENTITY_VAR]);
ENDFIX
```

Notice above that we inserted in the variables by typing them directly into the enhanced calc script (we know the exact member name). Another way to insert variables is to highlight the member within the Business Rule, right-click and choose Insert Variable, and then choose the correct Variable from the list.

7. Select outline to associate the outline.
8. Select trainxx.SUM:

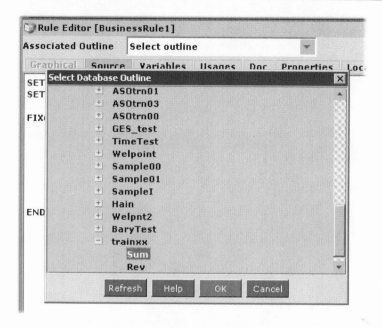

9. Click on the Variables tab and make sure the links to the Global Variables are working:

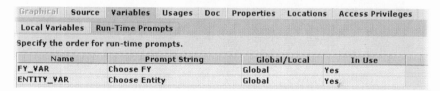

Graphical	Source	Variables	Usages	Doc	Properties	Locations	Access Privileges

Local Variables	Run-Time Prompts

Specify the order for run-time prompts.

Name	Prompt String	Global/Local	In Use
FY_VAR	Choose FY	Global	Yes
ENTITY_VAR	Choose Entity	Global	Yes

Note!

A variable can also be used for the Version and Scenario dimensions using the same steps as described above.

Next you need to add the locations for the Business Rule. By selecting an Essbase database as a location, we are saying "this rule can run on this database". You may create business rules that can run on more than one database.

10. Select the Locations tab.
11. Click Add.
12. Choose the trainxx.Sum outline:

12. Click OK.
13. Click Add.
14. Choose the Planning>>trainxx>>Sum outline:

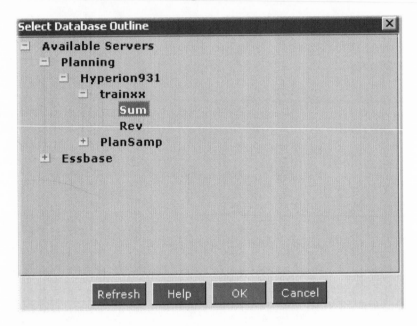

15. Click OK.

Our final step (and one often missed) is to assign security for the Business Rule. Should someone have launch access or modify access?

16. Select the Access Privileges tab.
17. Click Add.
18. Select your id (or PlanSampUsers group if available) and move to the selected area:

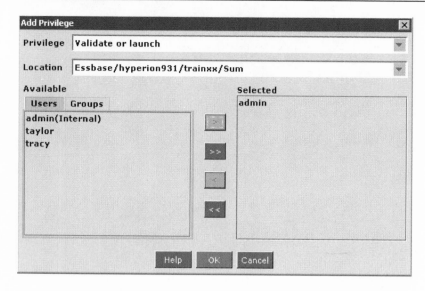

19. Click OK.
20. Click Save to save the business rule.
21. Enter name and description (Aggregate My Entity).
22. Click Validate.
23. You must enter a valid member name for the prompt to validate. Type in East or use member selection to choose East:

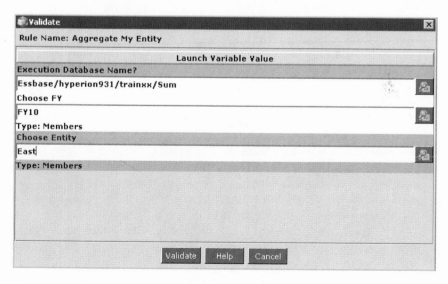

24. Click Validate and look for this message:

25. If you receive an error, click on Get Details and make sure the syntax is correct.
26. Close the business rule.

Once the business rule is complete, you are ready to run.

RUN A BUSINESS RULE

1. Log into the Planning application (back to the web, yeah!).
2. Select Tools>>Launch Business Rules:

3. Select Aggregate My Entity from the Business Rules List.
4. Click Launch.

CREATE A MACRO

Now, let's review the process to create a macro; the example below uses a macro to define the standard SET information at the beginning of a Business Rule. A Macro can be used in any rule needing the same syntax. The obviously benefit is that maintenance is in one Macro instead of multiple Business Rules. A Macro can be used for any syntax within a Business Rule.

To create a macro, right-click on Macro menu and choose New Macro. Copy and paste the SET syntax into the Macro and add access on the Access Privileges tab.

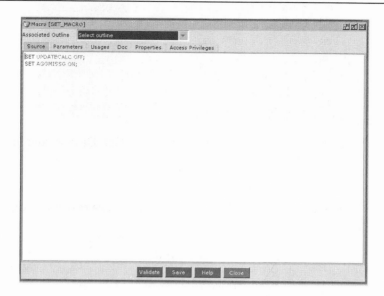

Note!
A macro has to pass validation on its own so be sure to validate the syntax.

Now, to insert the Set_Macro into the Business Rule, right-click and select Insert Macro, choosing the correct Macro from the list. The rule should now look like this:

```
%SET_MACRO()

Fix([FYVar], Final, Budget)
      Agg Entity;
EndFix
```

CREATE A SEQUENCE

A Sequence runs multiple Business Rules in a specific order. Sequences can run multiple Business Rules that use different locations (server, application, or database information).

To create a sequence, right-click on the Sequence menu and choose New Sequence. Next, choose the Add option on the right-hand side of the Sequence tab to add Business Rules to the Sequence.

Use the Move Up or Move Down options to change the order the Business Rules will execute:

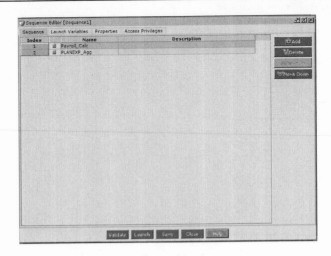

The Launch Variables tab displays all the variables used in the Sequence and allows you to set a location for each rule. The Index on the Launch Variables tab corresponds to the Index on the Sequence tab. The print screen below shows four variables in a sample Payroll_Calc Business Rule and one Variable in an aggregation Business Rule. Notice the option to Merge Launch Variables which combines the variables used in all Business Rules into one Variable. The example below would combine the Execution Database Name and the ScenVar (Enter Scenario).

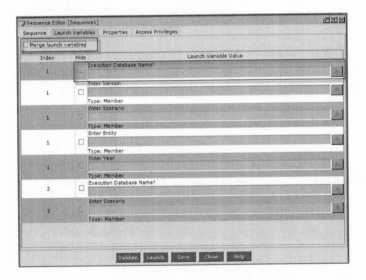

You should set access on the Access Privileges tab just as you did for Business Rules. Only users with access to the Sequence, Business Rules, Variables, and associated Macros will be able to execute the Sequence.

The newly created Business Rules or Sequences can be added to your forms or menus just as described in the previous pages of this book.

We will leave you with one other piece of important information related to Business Rules. The Planning Application Owner is the user who will appear in the Application log as running all Business Rules and Sequences. A great resource for troubleshooting issues related to Business Rules is the HBRLaunch.log which provides additional information such as who kicked off the Business Rule and what variable information was provided.

Now that you know how to build rules the "old way", let's tackle the "new way" in the Calculation Manager.

Scene 9:
Calculation Manager

INTRO TO CALC MANAGER

In version 11, a new way to create and manage Business Rules was introduced: the Calculation Manager. You can create Business Rules for FM and Planning and Essbase in one central place with Calculation Manager. You can design a rule in a graphical environment, toggle to a script ("enhanced calc") view, and back to the graphical display, a feature not available in Essbase Administration Services Business Rules.

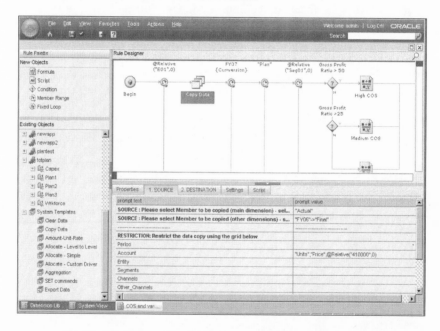

You will take all of the calc script knowledge that you gained in the Calc Scripts chapter and apply it in this chapter. We will walk through some basic examples to help get you started.

In Calculation Manager you design rules in a graphical environment that supports calculation ranges, conditions, scripts, loops, displays the calculation flow in a graphical way, provides predefined templates for standard calculations, allows custom templates definition, and supports the design and use of variables and Run time prompts. You can copy or share rules across Planning applications as well as share component across rules. Objects are organized in the calculation library by objects or in a tree structure.

You can deploy rules for launch in the EPMA applications in Planning 11.1.1 and deploy rules for Classic and Essbase BSO applications in 11.1.1.3. Business Rules and rule sets are run from the Planning web client or Smart View client.

One of the compelling features of Calculation Manager is that you can go back and forth between graphical and script language, something you cannot do in EAS Business Rules.

Let's look a little bit more closely at Calculation Manager features and then we'll create some Business Rules for our Entpln application.

Reusable Formula Components

Reusable formula components are defined once and then used across multiple scripts. As changes are required, you make the change once and it flows through automatically. This can save you big time on development and maintenance. For example, you have a set of logic that calculates fringe expenses for budgets. This same logic is used in the budget startpoint Business Rule as well as the Daily Business Rule. You create the logic in a reusable component that is referenced in both Business Rules. If an update is required, the reusable component is changed once (instead of multiple times).

Templates

Calculation Manager provides out-of-the-box predefined standard calculation templates related to Planning. Supported templates include Clear Data, Copy Data, Set Commands, Amount=Rate * Unit, Aggregate, and Allocations. The Allocations templates support single dimension allocation (simple), custom driver, or multi level (allocate a level down to another level). Custom templates that you create are also supported.

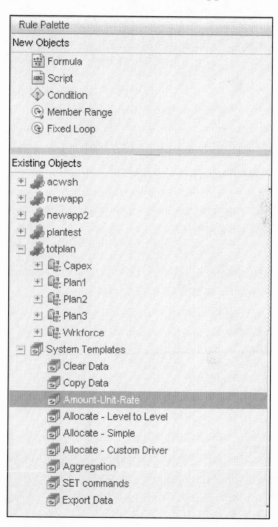

Rule Sets

Rule sets group and sequence selected Business Rules. This allows you to componentize logic for use in multiple calculation scenarios. For example, you may have a Budget Start Point set of logic that creates data based on a series of business rules (e.g Sales is calculated based on last years actuals with a 10% increase, salary expenses are calculated based on metrics entered by users). Each set of logic could be its own rule that could be run independently. You could then create a rule set that grouped those rules to be run once; all together. Be careful though that you aren't unnecessarily passing through the database multiple times.

Variables

Calculation Manager supports both run time prompts and substitution variables. Variables allow business rules to be dynamic. No hard coding in Business Rules (e.g., specifically defining a year "2010" or month "Jan" into a business rule)! The correct syntax to identify each variable is as follows:

```
{} run time prompt
[] substitution variable
```

Now that we've covered some of the components of Calculation Manager, let's create a Business Rule. Penny wants to allow Eddie to aggregate the budget from a Planning data form, because that's surely the way to eternal love. To do so, she'll use her calc script knowledge to focus the calculation for just what she needs.

CREATE A RULE

Create a Rule

1. From within the Workspace, select Navigate >> Administer >> Calculation Manager:

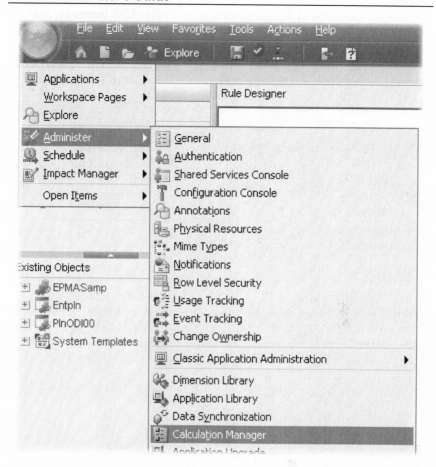

The Calculation Manager will display in System View (you can alternatively view objects in a list view). Notice that rules and rule components will be grouped by Consolidation (Financial Management), Planning and Essbase in the System View:

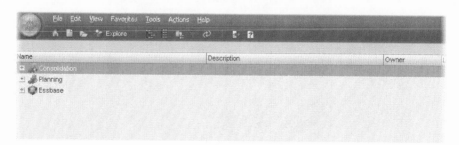

2. Select File >> New >> Rule.

3. Enter the following information for the Business Rule:
    a. Name: AggBud
    b. Application Type: Planning
    c. Application:Entpln
    d. Plan Type: Sum

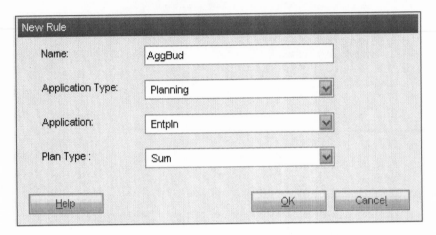

4. Click OK.
The Graphical Rules designer will display:

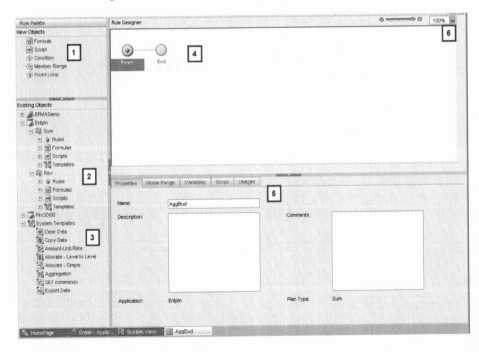

You will create a new Business Rule with the following sections:

- (1) Rules Palette New Objects – Drag and drop objects including formulas, scripts, conditions, member ranges and fixed loops into the Rules Designer
- (2) Rules Palette Existing Objects - Drag and drop objects that have been previously created in Planning applications including existing formulas, scripts, conditions, member ranges and fixed loops into the Rules Designer
- (3) Rules Palette System Templates - Drag and drop System Template objects into the Rules Designer
- (4) Rules Designer Flow Diagram – Displays the rule components in a graphical flow diagram
- (5) Rules Designer Information – Displays and allows updates of rule component properties and parameters. The available tabs may change depending on the component selected in the Rules Designer Flow Diagram.

5. Select the Begin Node.

The Properties tab includes the name, description, comments, application and plan type information:

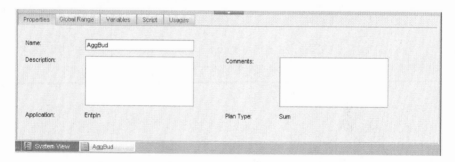

The Global Range is where you define specific member "fixes" that are applicable to the entire business rule:

[Properties | Global Range | Variables | Script | Usages]

Is Exclude   ☐

Use Predefined Selection   [▼]   Member Selector [ ]

Dimension	Select Value
Period	
Account	
Entity	
Version	
Scenario	

[System View] [AggBud]

To select members in all dimensions with one click, choose
(1) Member Selector. To select members dimension by dimension,
place your cursor in the Select Value text box (2) for the desired
dimension.

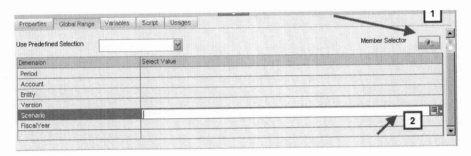

Either way gets you to the same point: selecting members
for the global "fix" of the Business Rule.

6.   Select the Member Select icon:

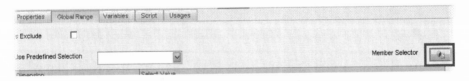

7.   The Member Selector window will launch.
8.   Select Scenario from the dimension drop down:

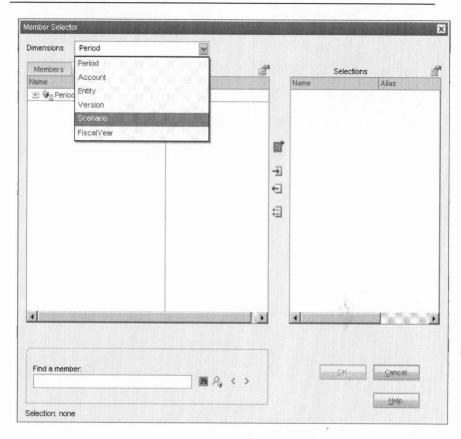

9.   Click + to expand Scenario and select Budget:

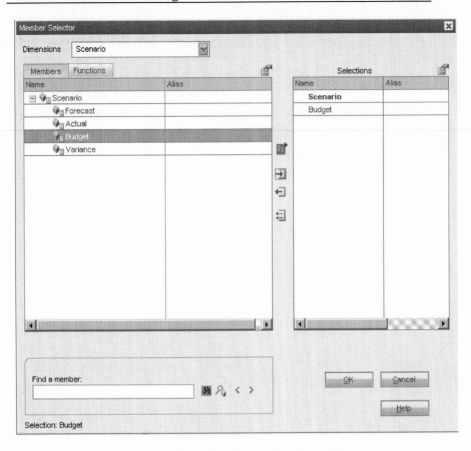

10. Select Version from the dimension drop down.
11. Select Sandbox and Final:

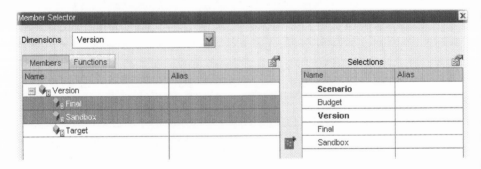

12. Click OK. The values are added:

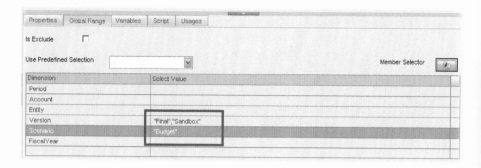

13. Under Fiscal Year, type in "&BY" so the rule will fix on the substitution variable BY (budget year).

14. Click on the Script tab to view the generated logic:

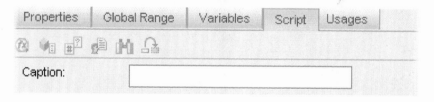

```
0001  FIX ("Final","Sandbox","Budget",&BY)
```

15. Click back to the Properties tab.
16. Select Set commands under System templates in the Existing Objects panel and drag it to the Rules Designer:

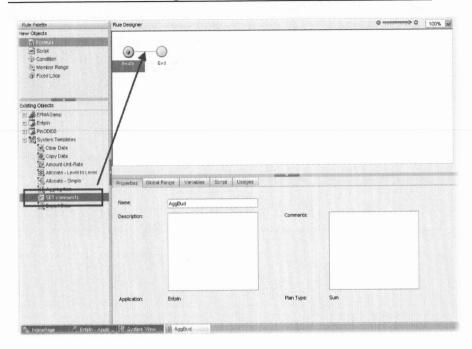

17. If you are on version 11.1.1.3 or later, the Set Commands wizard will display.
18. Step 1 includes set commands related to Data Volume:

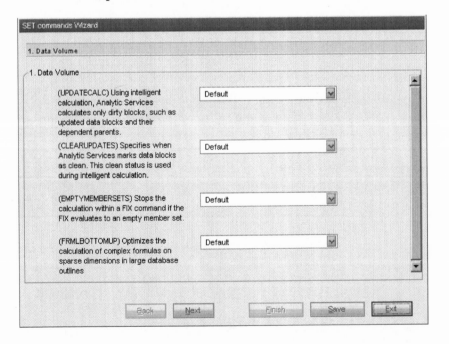

19. Set UPDATECALC to Calculate All Data Blocks (Off) and leave Defaults for remainder of Data Volume SET commands.
20. Click Next.
21. Step 2 includes SET commands for Data Handling. Review the other possible SET commands but leave the selection as Default.
22. Step 3 includes SET commands for Memory Usage. Review the other possible SET commands but leave the selection as Default.
23. Step 4 includes SET commands for Threading. Review the other possible SET commands but leave the selection as Default.

Note – only in rare cases do you want to turn on CALCPARALLEL in Business Rules run by end users.

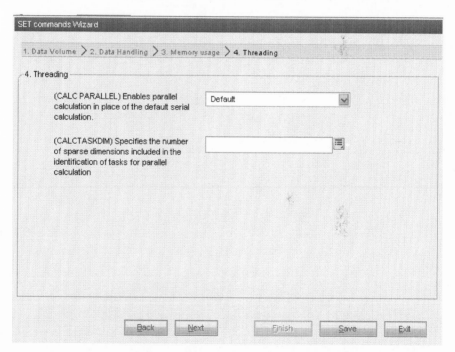

24. Step 5 includes SET commands for Logging. Review the other possible SET commands but leave the selection as Default.
25. Click Save.
26. Click Finish.

The SET Commands component is added to the business rule. Note that you can view the details of those settings in an explanatory fashion below the Rules Designer when the component is selected:

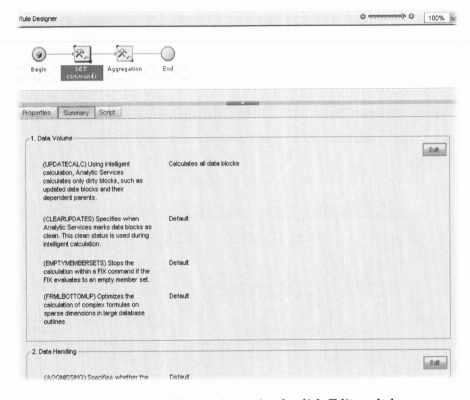

27. To edit any of the settings, simply click Edit and change the value.
28. Click on the Script tab to view the generated syntax.

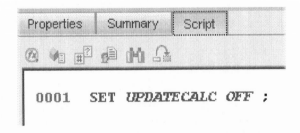

29. Under System Templates in the Rules Palette, select the Aggregation template and drag it to the step after SET commands.

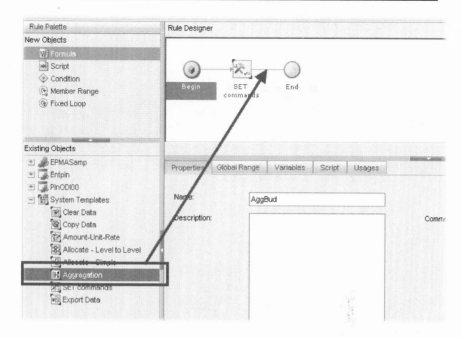

30. If you are on version 11.1.1.3 and higher, the Aggregation wizard will display:

31. Click Next here as there is no Point of view for our aggregation.
32. Select Period as the dense dimension to aggregate (no need to aggregate account because all members are dynamically calculated):

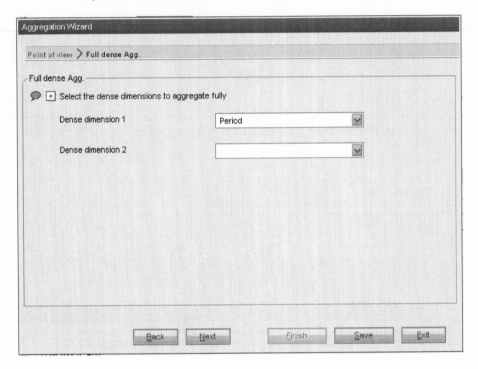

33. Click Next.
34. Select Entity as the sparse dimension to aggregate:

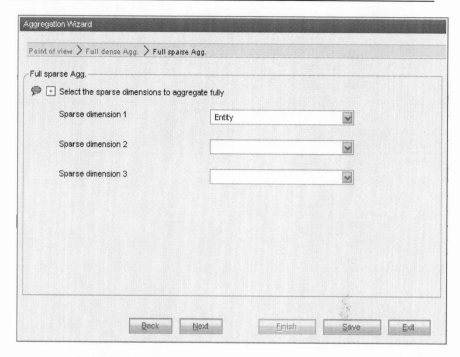

35. Click Next.
36. If any partial aggregations on dense members were required, you would define this information here. In our rule, we do not have that requirement:

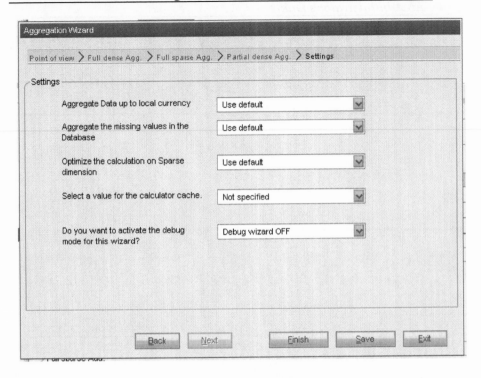

37. Click Next.
38. If any partial aggregations on sparse members were required, you would define this information here. In our rule, we do not have that requirement.
39. Click Next.
40. If any changes to SET commands are required for this specific aggregation component, you could define them here. We want to continue to use the SET commands defined in the global range.
41. Click Finish.
42. The rule component is added:

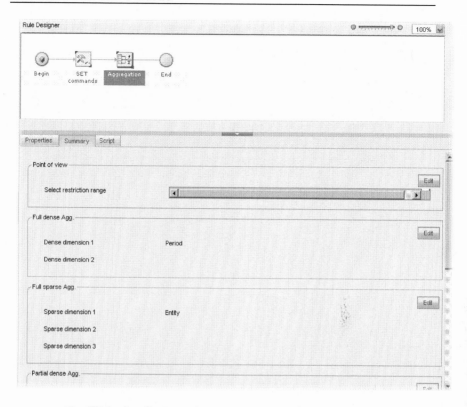

43. Click the Script tab to view the generated syntax:

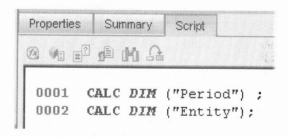

44. Select the Begin Node. Select the Script tab to view the entire script:

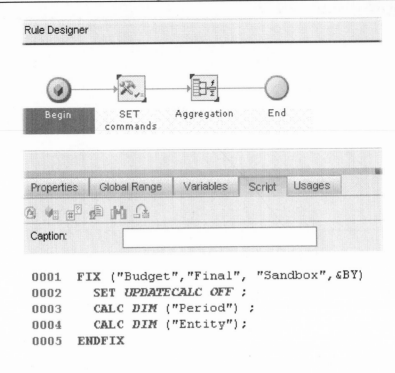

```
0001   FIX ("Budget","Final", "Sandbox",&BY)
0002     SET UPDATECALC OFF ;
0003     CALC DIM ("Period") ;
0004     CALC DIM ("Entity");
0005   ENDFIX
```

45. Select File >> Save.
46. Select the Green check icon to validate.

Update Business Rule Generated Script

The next set of steps is for the more advanced administrators who want to muck around with the syntax that is generated by Calculation Manager System templates. Read along but wait to perform these steps until you are comfortable with calc script language.

It is possible to update the Calculation Manager generated scripts. You can toggle back and forth between the graphical and "script" modes of Calculation Manager.

To edit a Business Rule in script mode,

1. Select Edit >> Script.

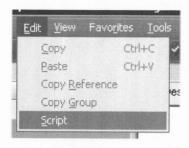

The Script view will display:

```
/*GLOBALRANGE*/
FIX (/*DIM:Scenario*/"Budget",/*DIM:Version*/"Final", "Sandbox",&BY)
   /*ID:-5*/
/*NAME:SET commands*/
/*CAPTION:*/
/*REF_ID:-6*/
/*STARTTEMPLATE*/
   /*
<template_prompts><template_prompt isPrompt="true" name="UPDATECALC" type="Restricted List"
   SET UPDATECALC OFF ;
   /*ENDTEMPLATE*/
   /*ID:-6*/
/*NAME:Aggregation*/
/*CAPTION:Aggregation*/
/*REF_ID:-7*/
/*STARTTEMPLATE*/
   /*
<template_prompts><template_slice_prompt isPrompt="true" name="Restriction" type="Member Ra
   CALC DIM ("Period") ;
   CALC DIM ("Entity");
   /*ENDTEMPLATE*/
ENDFIX
```

You'll see the auto-generated script syntax along with a number of system generated comments. From this interface, you can directly type and update the syntax. Be careful changing the green comments and performing significant moves across the script. The Graphical View may be impacted.

However if you want to change the code generated by a template, you will have to remove the comments related to the component in order to make the changes. For example, if you want to change the Calc Dim statement to Agg for Entity, you have to remove the <template> comment before and after the CALC DIM statements.

2. Find the line of code that says:

```
CALC DIM ("Entity");
```

3. Change it to:

```
AGG ("Entity");
```

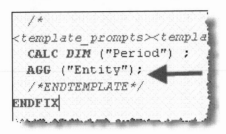

4. Find the line of code that begins */*<template_prompts>* just before CALC DIM ("Period").
5. Delete the entire comment.
6. Find the line of code that begins */*ENDTEMPLATE*/* just before AGG ("Entity").
7. Delete the entire comment.

You need to delete these comments so the Calculation Manager won't try to apply template logic. Trust us. If you are going to manipulate and change script, the comments created by template wizards are something to watch out for.

8. Save and validate the business rule:

9. Select Edit >> Graphical to switch back to Graphical Mode.

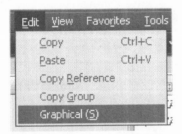

Notice the icon for the component is changed from a system template icon to a script icon.

10. Add a new caption called AggSum:

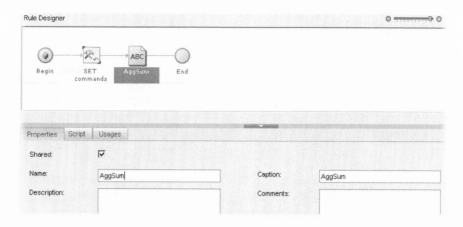

11. Select File >> Save to save the Business Rule.
12. Click Actions >> Validate to validate the Business Rule.

Calculation Manager will perform a check of the logic within the Business Rule and notify you of any issues. Most all calc script syntax will validate within the Calculation Manager but we have found a few instances where a valid calc script may not validate in Calculation Manager.

Deploy a Business Rule

Once the Business Rule has been validated, you must deploy the Business Rule to make it available in Planning.

To make this rule available in Planning,
1. Select Actions>>Deploy:

From this menu you can either Deploy or Quick Deploy. Both options will deploy the rule with the same result; the Quick Deploy takes fewer steps but is only available in the Rules Designer.
2. Select Actions >> Quick Deploy.

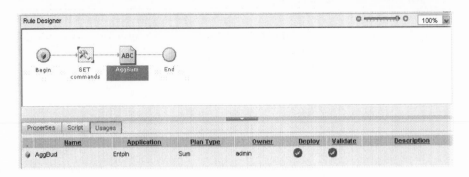

If you navigate back to the Planning application, you'll find your newly deployed business rules along with the calc scripts (as the administrator, you see everything). You have just created a business rule that is exactly like the calc script we created a few scenes back:

Would you ever want to do this in real life? No. You would create this logic in one place or the other.

Now what you really might want to do is create a business rule to just roll up a specific entity specified by the user or even better the entity that is used on the data form.

Let's do that now using a run time prompt variable.

CREATE A VARIABLE

Penny created the Business Rule to calculate the budget scenario for the entire database. However, a better Business Rule would focus on the entity in the data form, only recalculating budget for the entity that changed. She doesn't want to create a different business rule for each entity, so she decides to create a single business rule and use a variable to pass in the selected entity.

1. Select Navigate >> Administer >> Calculation Manager
if necessary or just make sure you select the System
View tab of Calculation Manager.

To create a variable,
2. Select Tools>>Variables:

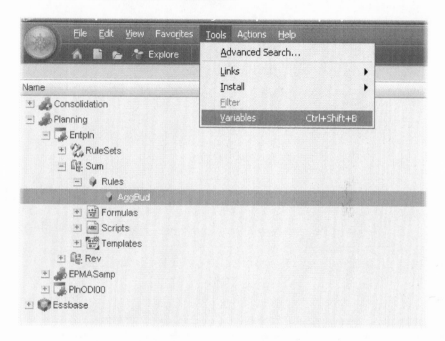

The Variable Designer will display:

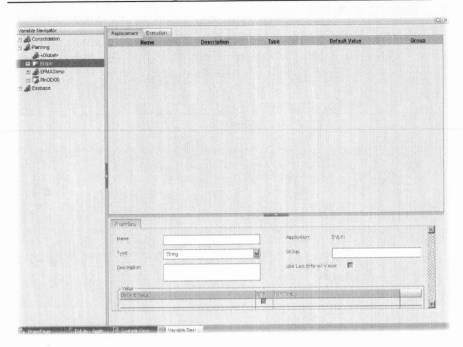

3. Within the Variable Navigator, right-click on Entpln and select New:

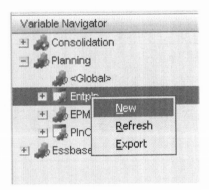

The New Variable window will display.
4. Type in the name "EntityVar".
5. Choose Member as the Type.
6. Select the Entity dimension in the Value table.
7. Check the RTP option and type in "Select Entity" as the RTP Text:

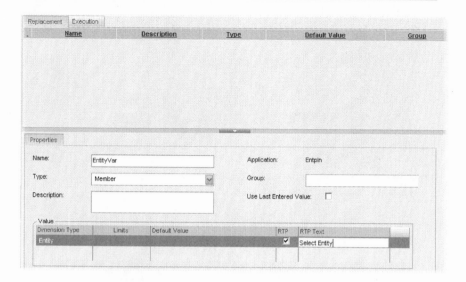

8. Click Save.

In order to validate the variable (and business rules), you need to select a default value.

9. Set a default value for EntityVar.

Repeat the steps creating the ScenarioVar.

10. Type in the name "ScenarioVar".
11. Choose Members as the Type.
12. Select the Scenario dimension in the Value table.
13. Check the RTP option and type in "Select Scenario" as the RTP Text.
14. Repeat the steps creating the following variables:
   a. VersionVar

b. FiscalYearVar

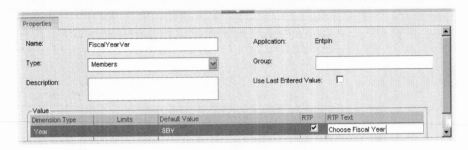

Note that once you have saved a variable, you can manage it from the Variable Designer, deleting, copying, and saving as the variable from the right-click menu:

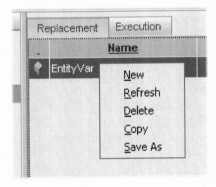

15. Go back to the System View of the Rules Designer.
16. Select Rules.
17. Right-click and select New:

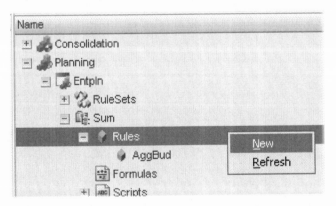

18. Set the following Global Range members (VersionVar, ScenarioVar, and FiscalYearVar) using Member Selector:

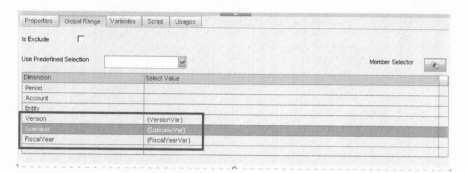

19. From the new objects palette, select and insert the set commands (UPDATE CALC OFF) component into the Business Rule:

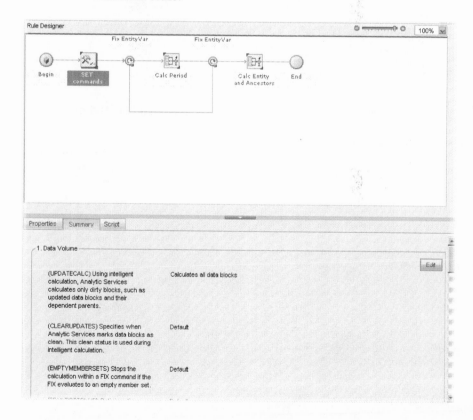

20. Insert a Member Range component.
21. Select @IANCESTORS({EntityVar}) as the Member Range for the Entity dimension:

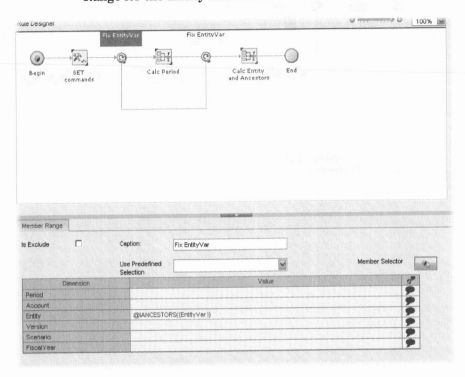

22. Add a caption to the component "FixEntityVar".
23. Insert Aggregation System template into the Business Rule within the FixEntityVar Member Range component.
24. Follow the wizard, choosing to calculate the full dense dimension Period:

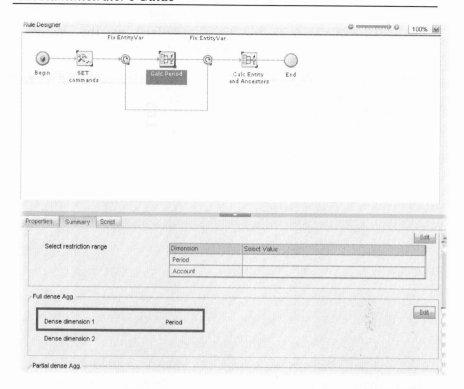

25. Insert Aggregation template after the FixEntityVar Member Range component.
26. Follow the wizard, choosing to calculate the partial sparse dimension Entity for all ancestors of EntityVar.
27. Add a caption for the component "Calc Entity and Ancestors".
28. Click on the Begin node.
29. Select the script tab to view the generated code:

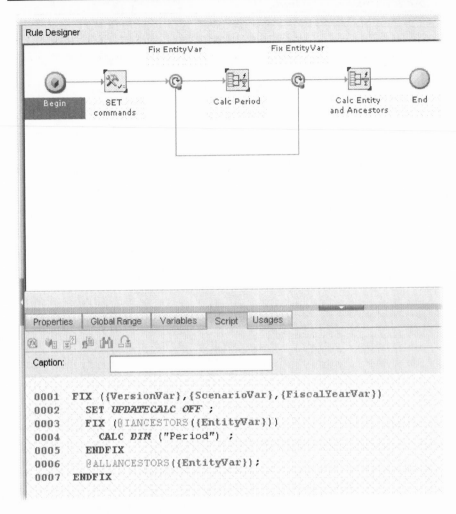

30. Validate and save the Business Rule as "Aggregate Entity on Form".
31. Deploy the Business Rule to Entpln.

Now we are ready to launch the Business Rules.

LAUNCH RULES

To launch Business Rules you must be in the Planning application. You cannot launch from the Calculation Manager.

1. Open the Entpln Planning application.
2. Select Tools >> Business Rules.

The complete listing of Business Rules and calc scripts for which users have access will display. As the administrator, you see everything.

3. You can filter the rules by plan type or by rule type:

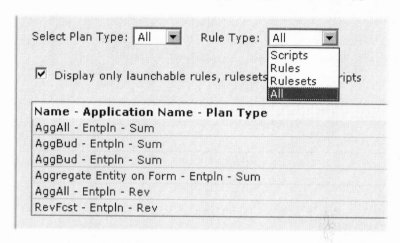

4. Click Launch for the Aggregate Entity on Form – Entpln – Sum Business Rule:

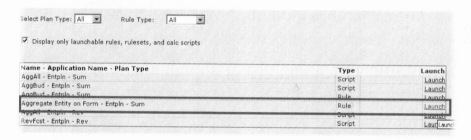

5. The run time prompts will display:

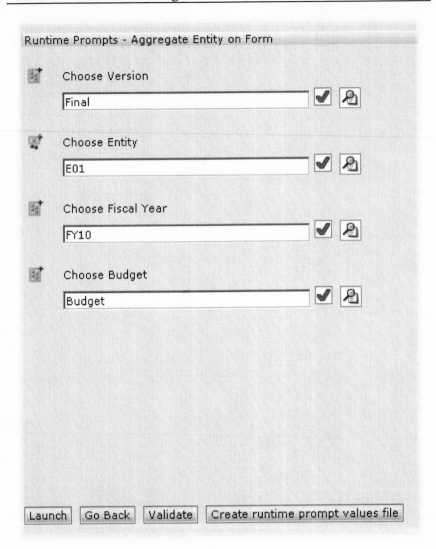

6. Accept the defaults and click Launch.

Remember that you can also launch business rules from a data form.

JOB CONSOLE

The Job Console provides a way to view the status of Business Rules run for Planning. To access the Job Console, select Tools >> Job Console:

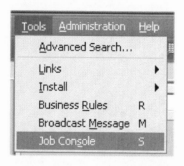

The Job Console will display all recently run Business Rules. You can search and filter console entries by a number of methods including job type, run status, user name or job id:

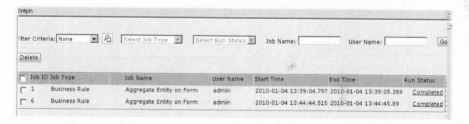

You can also view the status of other Planning tasks like Business Rule, Ruleset (for Calculation Manager), Sequence (for Business Rules), Clear Cell Details, or Copy Data.

This Job Console is different from the EPMA Library console:

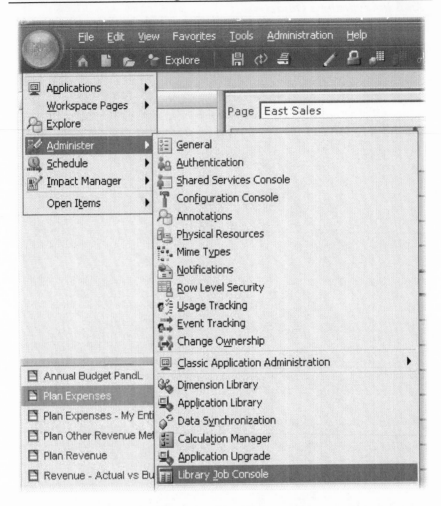

Now that we've covered the basics of Calculation Manager, let's talk best practices. As you design your Business Rules, you want to design business logic efficiently. Try to remove duplicative code used in a number of different Business Rules. Ways to do that include reusable formula components and rules sets. Let's create a reusable formula component now.

Resuable Formula Component

A reusable formula component is a specific set of business rule logic or syntax that can be used across multiple business rules. When an update to the logic is required, you can change the logic in one place and updates flow through automatically.

To create a reusable formula component,
1. Select File >> New >> Formula Component or in the System View of Calculation Manager and right-click on Formulas and click New:

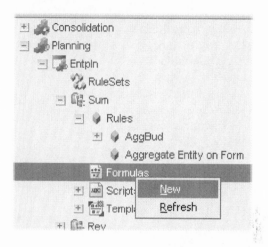

2. Enter the formula name "Calculate Revenue Forecast".
3. Select Planning as Application Type.
4. Select Entpln as Application:
5. Select Rev as Plan Type:

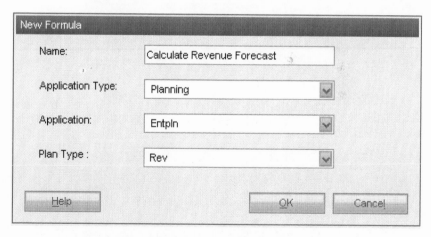

6. Click OK.
7. Enter the formula for calculating revenue "411100" = Units*Price:

8. Save and validate the Formula component.
9. Close the Formula component.

Now let's create a rule that uses the Calculate Revenue Forecast formula component.

1. Select File >> New >> Rule.
2. Enter the name "Calculate Forecast by Entity on Form".
3. Select Planning as Application Type.
4. Select Entpln as Application.
5. Select Rev as Plan Type:

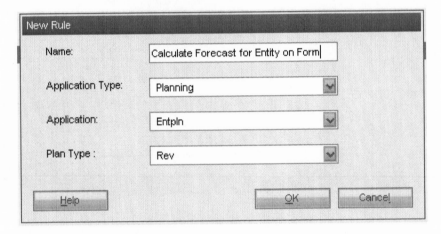

10. Click OK.
11. Set the following members for the Global Range of the Business Rule (VersionVar, Forecast, FiscalYearVar):

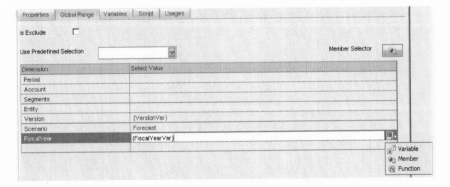

12. Drag a Member Range component into the Flow Diagram.
13. Select EntityVar for the Entity dimension in the Member Range component:

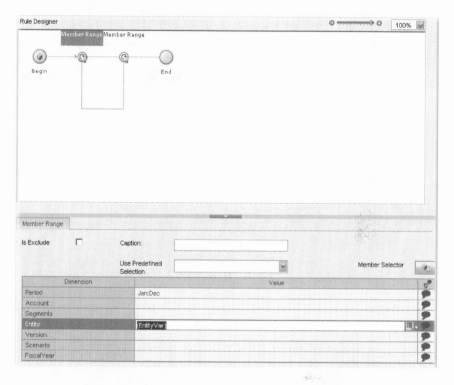

14. Drag another Member Range component into the Business Rule within the EntityVar Member Range component.
15. Set the range for this component to Jan:Dec for Period.
16. Navigate to the Calculate Revenue Forecast component under Existing Objects>>Entpln>>Rev>>Formulas.
17. Drag this component within the Jan:Dec Member Range component:

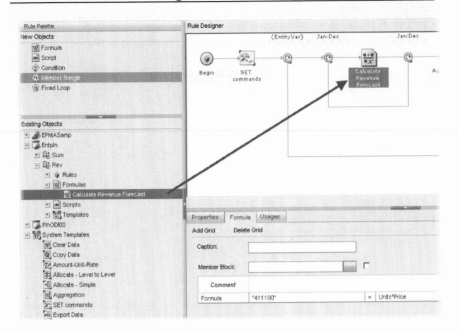

18. Add in an aggregation to rollup the Period dimension for the fixed entity after the Jan:Dec Member Range Component.

19. Add in an aggregation to rollup the Entity and it's ancestors after the EntityVar Member Range Component:

The resulting rule and script should look as follows:

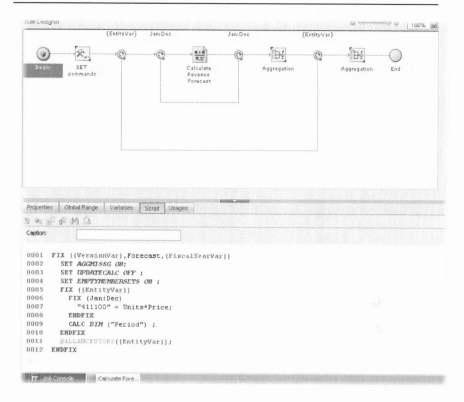

```
0001  FIX ({VersionVar},Forecast,{FiscalYearVar})
0002    SET AGGMISSG ON;
0003    SET UPDATECALC OFF ;
0004    SET EMPTYMEMBERSETS ON ;
0005    FIX ({EntityVar})
0006      FIX (Jan:Dec)
0007        "411100" = Units*Price;
0008      ENDFIX
0009      CALC DIM ("Period") ;
0010    ENDFIX
0011    @ALLANCESTORS({EntityVar});
0012  ENDFIX
```

20. Don't forget to rename captions to help make the flow
    diagram more readable.

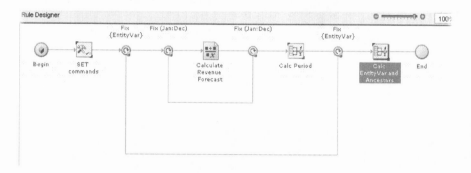

One last "best practices" tool to discuss are rules sets.

Rule Sets

A rule set is a grouping or sequence of business rules that
are run together in a defined order. Grouping componentized

business rules allow for efficient business rule design and rules sets let you combine combinations of rules to achieve a desired requirement.

For example, you have one business rule that performs an allocation that is run on a monthly basis when specific drivers are entered. You have another business rule that calculates the database on a nightly basis. You can create a rule set for the monthly process that runs the allocation rule first and then the calculation business rule (versus including the same nightly calculation logic in the allocation rule).

To create a rule set, select File >> New >> Rules Set or in the System View of Calculation Manager and right-click on RuleSets and click New and follow the remaining steps to select business rules to include in the rule set.

Before we leave the Calculation Manager scene, let's review some of the "managing" aspects.

MANAGE RULES

For any rules, rules sets and other objects, you can perform a number of maintenance actions: Open, Delete, Export, Validate, Deploy, Copy To, Create Short Cut:

You can also "Show Usages", viewing where a rule or component is used throughout the Calculation Manager library.

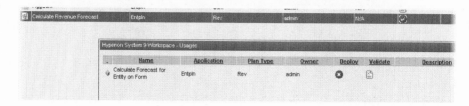

Within Calculation Manager, we've been primarily navigating in the System View. An alternative List View is available that provides filtering and search capabilities for Business Rule objects. Basic filtering options include application, application type, object type, deployment status and validation status:

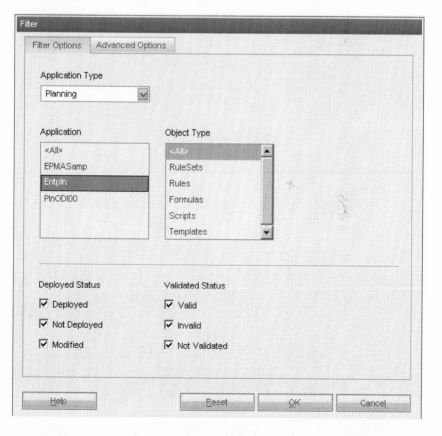

Advanced filtering options include wild card searches and searches by date and author:

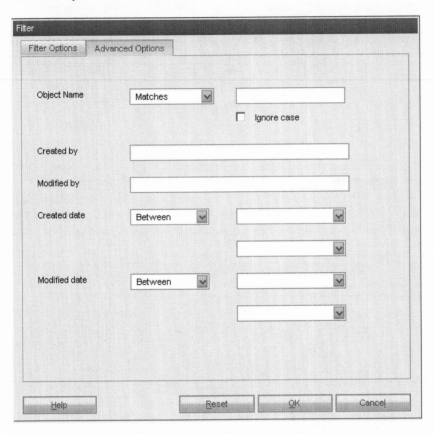

Once filters have been applied, the Business Rules display in list fashion:

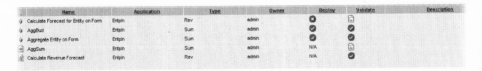

From the List View you can perform a number of actions on the objects (e.g. Validate or Deploy selected Business Rules):

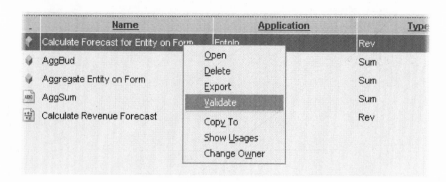

AUTOMATE BUSINESS RULES

You can run Business Rules via the CalcMgrCmdLauncher.cmd for those Business Rules created in Calculation Manager. For more information on how to use this utility, check out the Planning Administration scene, Utilities section.

Meanwhile back at Dr. Dementor's hide out...

"Victory will be mine!" Dr. Dementor shouts, holding up the recently finished – and to be honest, somewhat unimpressive considering it kills people – deathray for all to see. "I will get those consultants... and Penny and Eddie too!"

Scene 10:
Create and Manage Data Forms

Oblivious to the imminent danger from doctor's wielding deathrays, Penny trudges forward with the consultants to create the data forms for end user entry.

DATA FORM BASICS

Data forms are the mechanisms for users to enter plan data. Data forms can be accessed over the web and in Excel via Smart View. If you need to create or manage data forms, you must do this in the Planning Web Client. Select Administration >> Manage Data Forms to manage your data forms.

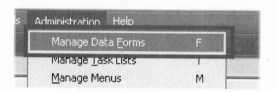

From the Manage Forms section, you can edit, move, or delete data forms folders or data forms by selecting the appropriate button. You can also Search for a particular form.

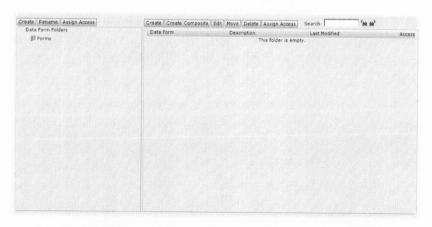

You will define and manage data forms through a series of tabs. After selecting a data form to edit or upon clicking "Create",

the data form definition window will display. The first tab allows
you to define and update data form properties:

- Data form name
- Description
- Source Plan type
- Specify read only
- Data form instructions

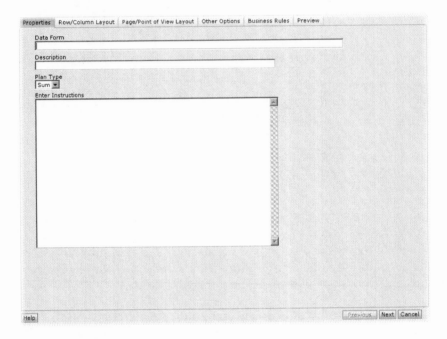

Click Next to move to the Row/Column Layout or choose the
Row/Column Layout tab.

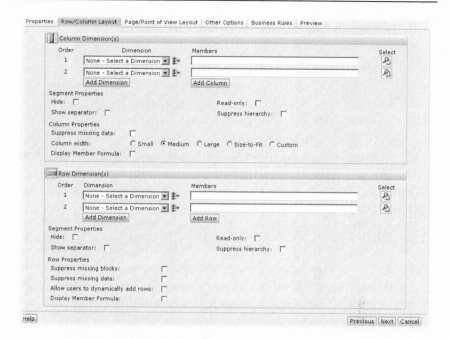

On the Row/Column Layout tab, you must have at least one dimension and member in a row and column. A dimension can exist in one place only – either the row, column, page or point of view.

To define the rows and columns for a data form,

1. Choose the dimension(s) for columns by selecting from the drop down box.
2. Select the dimension members to display.
   a. Manually type in (member names with spaces will require double quotes around the member name)
   b. Or Use Member Selection – Select the Select icon to launch
3. Set column properties.

"Suppress missing data". will suppress any columns that do not have data. Column width allows you to choose the column width displayed:

- Small-Display 7 decimal places on the data form.
- Medium-Display 10 decimal places on the data form.
- Large-Display 13 decimal places on the data form.
- Size-to-Fit-Force all column headings to fit in the displayed space.

- Custom-Display over 13 decimal places on the data form. You can enter a value up to 999.
  4. Choose the dimension(s) for rows by selecting from the drop down box.
  5. Select the dimension members to display.
     a. Manually type in
     b. Or Use Member Selection – Select the Select icon to launch
  6. Set row properties.

"Suppress missing blocks" will suppress entire blocks that do not have data (this can help with performance when suppressing a large number of rows, such as 90% or more; this option can degrade performance if few or no rows are suppressed).

"Suppress missing data" will suppress any rows that do not have data. "Allow users to dynamically add rows" enables users to add rows to data forms in the Planning web client (not available for Smart View in the current version). Watch out for this feature and only use this when necessary. If one user adds a row to a data form, it will be added for all other users. Only Planning Administrators can remove user added rows.

Note! You cannot simultaneously select Suppress Missing Data and Allow Users to Dynamically Add Rows.

If you choose to use Member Selection to define members, click the Select ![icon] icon.

The Member Selection window will display:

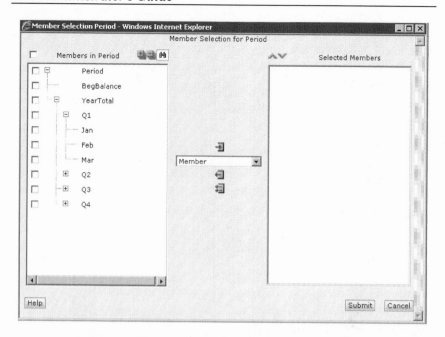

From this window, you can navigate the dimension to select members. Click the binoculars icon to search for members. You can also insert applicable substitution variables. Use the arrow keys to move members between the full dimension list and Selected Members section. Before moving the selected member, choose whether to move the member itself or children of the member or descendants of the member (or other available functions). Click Submit to finalize the member selection.

Segment properties offer more advanced features; we'll come back to segments in just a moment.

Click Next to move to the Page/POV Layout or choose the Page/POV Layout tab.

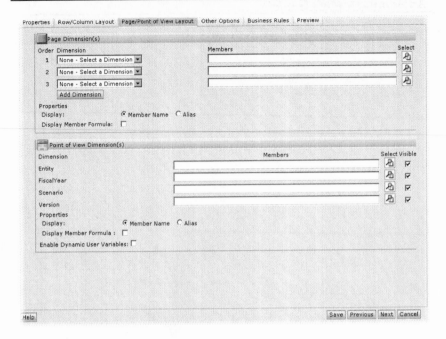

7. Choose the dimension(s) for page by selecting from the drop down box.
8. Select the dimension members to display.
   a. Manually type in
   b. Or Use Member Selection – Select the Select icon to launch
9. Set page properties – Show Member Name or Alias.
10. For the remainder of the dimension in the Point of View, select the dimension members to display.
    a. Manually type in
    b. Or Use Member Selection – Select the Select icon to launch.
11. Set point of view properties.
    a. Member name or alias
    b. Enable use of dynamic user variables

Click Next to move to the Other Options or choose the Other Options tab. You can define the following options for display, functionality and printing:

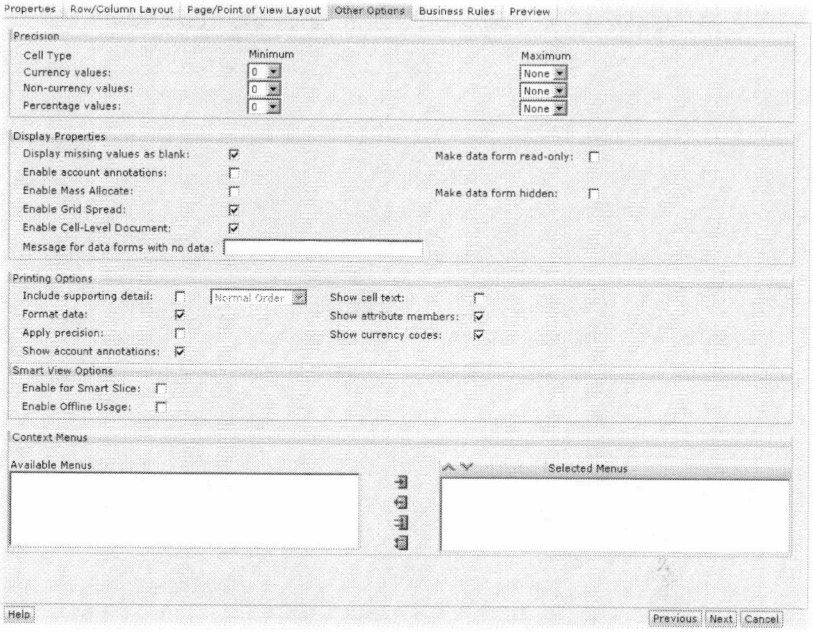

Other options available on this tab include:

- Enable Smart Lists
- Enable Account Annotations
- Enable Mass Allocate
- Enable Grid Spread
- Assign Custom Right-click Menus if available
- Allow multiple currencies per entity – users can choose the currency displayed

We'll address Smart Lists and Right-click Menus in the Extending Planning scene.

To enable account annotations, accounts must be in rows, account, entity, version, and scenario cannot be in the column and version and scenario must be in page or POV. Remember the end user Grid Spread and Mass Allocate functionality? These features are enabled on a form by form basis. The "Allow multiple currencies per entity property" is applicable to multi-currency enabled applications.

Click Next to move to the Business Rules or choose the Business Rules tab.

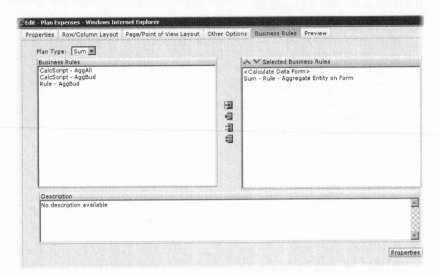

The Calculate Data Form business rule is automatically created for every form. It calculates subtotals for the members on the data form. (Note if every member on you data form is stored or dynamically calculated, you do not have to "Calculate Data Form").

You can also assign custom business rules or calc scripts to a data form, using the arrows to move over the desired business rule to the Selected Business Rules section. For the assigned business rule, you can specify the following:

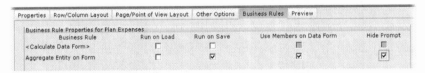

- "Run on Load" runs the business rule when the user opens the data form.
- "Run on Save" runs the business rule when the user clicks the save button on the data form.
- The user may be prompted if runtime prompt is included in the business rule.
- You can select the option, "Use Members on Data Form", to pass the members on the data form through to the runtime prompt and then optionally to "Hide Prompt" which hides the runtime prompt from the user.

For example, Penny created the business rule to calculate the budget for a specific entity. This business rule could run each time the form is saved (Run on Save checked). The entity selection is determined using a run time prompt that is completed by the end user. However, she can check the User Members on Data Form with Hide Prompt options to automate the process for the end user. So instead of the user selecting the entity and clicking the options to run the business rule, the user can simply save the form. Behind the scenes, the business rule runs, pulling the current entity (and other dimension members as necessary) into the run time prompt.

Once the business rules are assigned to the data form, the final step is to review the preview of the data form. The Data Preview tab will show you a layout of the members selected in the data form definition.

Click the Save or Save As button to save the form. If Save As is selected, type in the new data form name.

Pretty easy, right? Let's create some data forms.

CREATE A DATA FORM

Create a Data Form Folder

Data form folders organize the number of data forms that you will create for Planning.

1. In the Planning web client, select Administration >> Manage Data Forms if necessary.
2. Click Create under Form Folders:

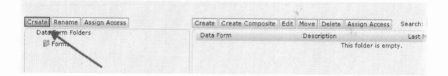

3. Enter the name for the form folder; in our case type in "Annual Budget".

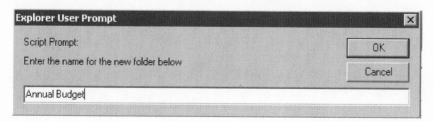

4. Click OK. That's it! Now on to data forms.

Create a Plan Expense Data Form

1. Click the Create button for Data Forms in the Right panel:

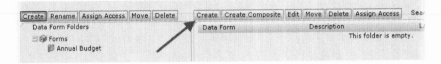

2. Create an Expense data entry form with the following Properties:

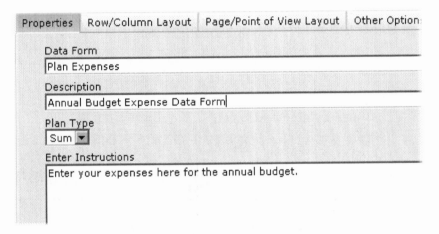

3. Click Next or select the Row/Column Layout.
4. Select Period for Column Dimension 1.
5. Click the Member Selector icon next to the first Column Dimension to select the Period members:

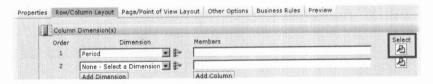

6. Choose Descendants(Inc) of YearTotal:

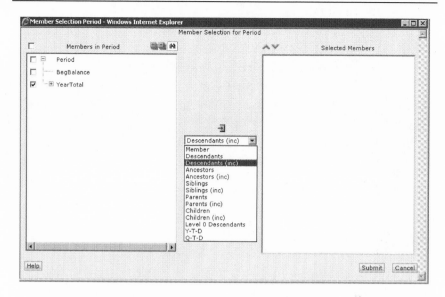

7. Click Submit.

8. Select the Dimension Properties for Column Dimension
    1:

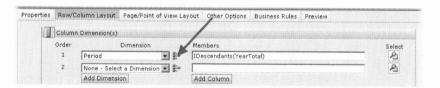

9. Verify Start Expanded is selected:

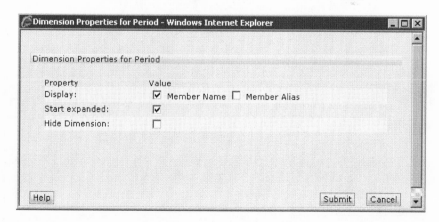

10. Click Submit.
11. Select Account for Row Dimension 1.
12. Click the Member Selector icon next to the first Row Dimension to select the Account members:

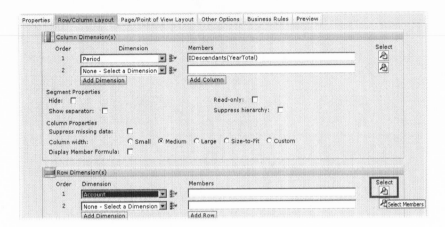

13. Choose Descendants (Inc) 50000.
14. Click Submit:

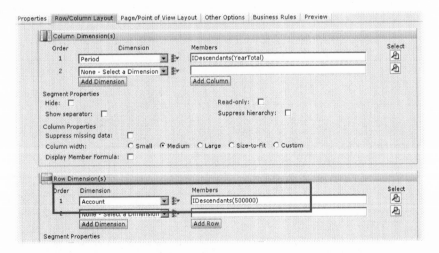

15. Select the Dimension Properties for Row Dimension 1:
16. Select Member Alias (to show the alias on the data form) and Uncheck Start Expanded:

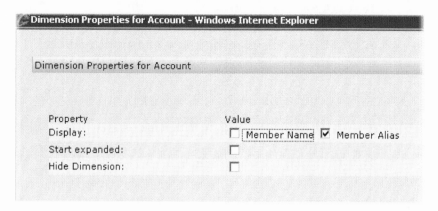

17. Click Submit.
18. Click Next or select the Page/Point of View Layout and enter the following information:
    a. Page Dimension 1: IDescendants(TotalGeography)
    b. Page Dimension 2: Final, Sandbox
    c. Select Alias for display.
    d. FiscalYear: FY10
    e. Scenario: Budget
    f. Uncheck "Visible" so the point of view members do not display for end users.

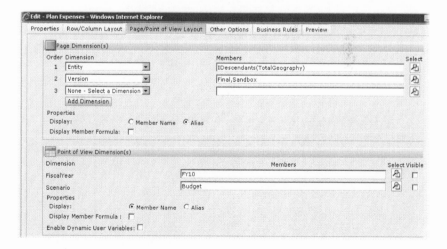

19. Click the Other Options and enter the following
    information (some of these will be default values):
    a. Set minimum and maximum precision to 0
    b. Display missing values as blank
    c. Enable Grid Spread
    d. Enable Cell Level Document
    e. Enable for Smart Slice

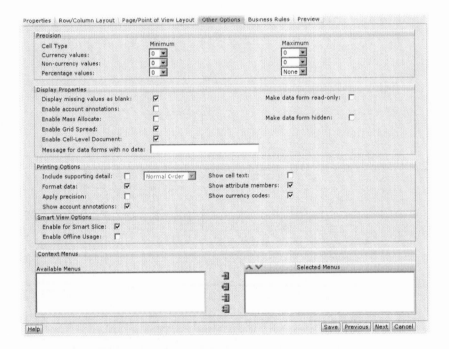

20. Click the Business Rules tab and note the Calculate
    Data Form is already assigned to the data form.
21. Click Save to save the data form.
22. Select View >> View Pane so that it is checked:

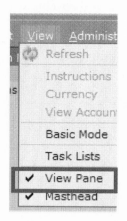

23. From the View Pane, expand the Annual Budget data form folder.
24. Click on the link to the Plan Expenses data form:

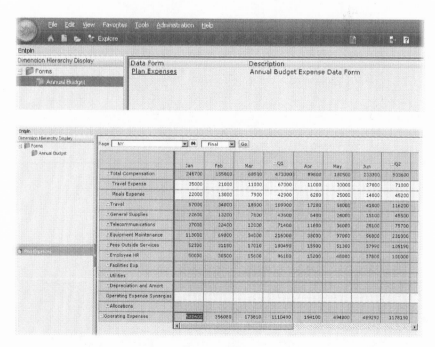

Now let's create the annual budget revenue data form.

1. In the Planning Web client, select Administration >> Manage Data Forms.
2. Select the Annual Plan data form folder.
3. Click the Create button for Data Forms in the Right panel:
4. Create a Revenue data entry form with the following Properties (don't forget to choose Rev as the plan type):

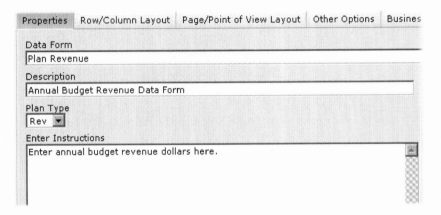

5. Click the Row/Column Layout and enter the following information (type in directly or use Member Selection):

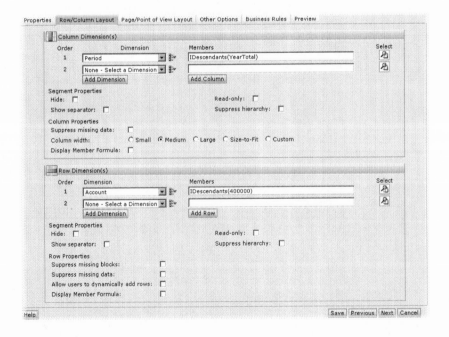

6. Click Next or select the Page/Point of View Layout and enter the following information:

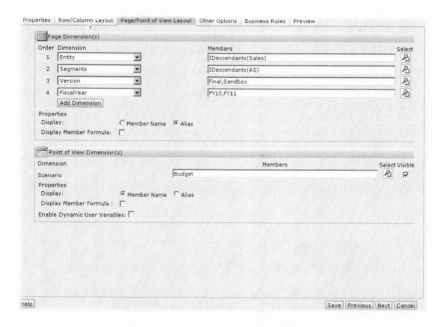

7. Click the Other Options and accept the default settings.
8. Click the Business Rules tab and note the Calculate Data Form is already assigned to the data form.
9. Assign the Aggregate Entity on Form business rule:

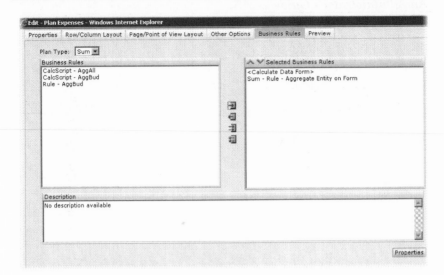

10. Do not choose to Run on Save or Run on Load.

11. Click Save to save the data form.

The revenue planning form is ready to go!

	Jan	Feb	Mar	Q1	Apr	May	Jun	
Operating Revenue	420000	340000	420000	1180000	1200000	360000	340000	190
Revenue Synergies								
IC Revenue								
Gross Revenue	420000	340000	420000	1180000	1200000	360000	340000	190
Sales Returns	-24000	-19000	-23000	-66000	-66000	-20000	-20000	-10
Sales Discounts	-17000	-14000	-16000	-47000	-47000	-14000	-14000	-7
Returns and Allowances	-41000	-33000	-39000	-113000	-113000	-34000	-34000	-18
Net Revenue	379000	307000	381000	1067000	1087000	326000	306000	171
Gross Profit	379000	307000	381000	1067000	1087000	326000	306000	171

Page: MA ▾ Bookshelf Audio Systems ▾ Final ▾ CY ▾ Go

Create a Data Form with Multiple Segments

In this next form we will create a data form that has multiple segments. A segment is a collection of row or columns that may have different properties and/or member selections. For example, you may need to create a data form that displays Actuals from January through the current month and Budget for the remainder of the months (this is called an asymmetric data form). You achieve this through segments:

		Jan	Feb	Mar	Apr	May	Jun	Jul	Aug	Sep	Oct
					Actual					Plan	
Distribution	Gross Revenue	3,001,708	1,876,067	764,998	1,147,498	1,823,246	2,564,566	2,714,692	2,136,029	3,655,201	7,288,061
	Operating Revenue	3,001,708	1,876,067	764,998	1,147,498	1,823,246	2,564,566	2,714,692	2,136,029	3,655,201	7,288,061
	Revenue Synergies										
Government	Gross Revenue										
	Operating Revenue										
	Revenue Synergies										
All Channels	Gross Profit	714,334	446,459	193,185	289,732	393,637	277,192	797,500	670,998	1,209,986	2,287,361

Another use case for segments is creating a data form with specific read and write columns or rows. You can set the following segment properties:

- **Hide** - Hide the segment so it is not displayed on the data form
- **Suppress Hierarchy** - For columns, do not display line breaks
- **Read only** - Create a read-only segment in the data form to allow comparing old, read-only data with new, editable data
- **Show Separator** - Create a bold border before the segment to visually distinguish parts of the data form
- **Apply to All Segments** - Apply these settings to all columns in segments

Penny will create a data form with multiple segments for revenue forecasts:

1. In the Planning Web client, select Administration >> Manage Data Forms.
2. Select the root data form folder.
3. Click the Create button for Data Forms in the Right panel.
4. Create a Forecast Revenue data form with the following Properties (don't forget to choose Rev as the plan type):

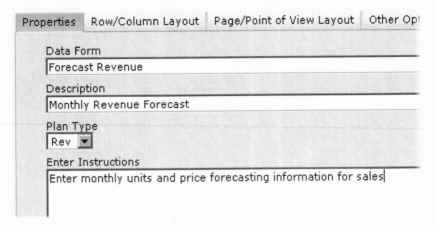

5. Click the Row/Column Layout and enter the following information (type directly in or use Member Selection) for Column Dimension 1:

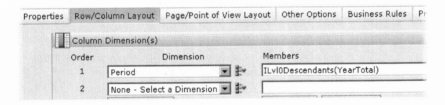

6. Click Add Column.
7. Select the member "YearTotal".
8. Check Read Only.

The CFO wants to force users to focus on monthly units and prices; therefore, this information should not be entered at YearTotal. To accommodate this requirement, we will make this column read only:

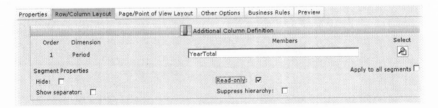

9. Click Submit (Return to Data Form will not save the new row).
10. Select the following members for Row Dimension 1:

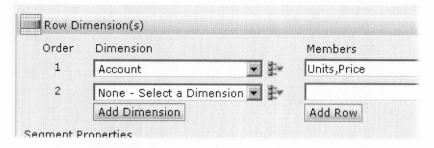

11. Click Add Row.
12. Select the member "411100".
13. Check Read Only ("411100" is calculated by the business rule so we will make this row read only):

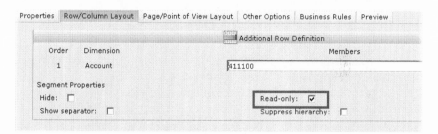

14. Click Submit.

Now that you've added the additional columns, you won't see them on the data form definition. You will see a new button – Edit Columns – that lets you know the form contains an additional column or segment.

15. Click the Page/Point of View Layout and enter the following information:

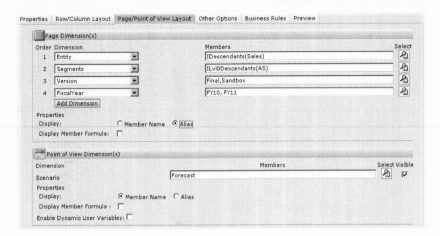

16. Click the Other Options and enter the following information (accept defaults).
17. Click the Business Rules tab and assign the Calculate Revenue Forecast business rule.
18. Once in the selected section, select Calculate Revenue Forecast and select Properties.
19. Choose the business rule property "Run on Save".
20. Click Save.
21. Open the Plan Revenue data form and testing entering data. Is the forecast revenue calculated correctly?

Create an View Only Data Form

Often times in Planning, you will create ready only forms for end users. These forms may contain summary information or other result sets that can be displayed to end users within the Planning application. Penny, for example, creates a Profit and Loss data form so that Eddie can immediately see the impact of an expense or revenue change on margin.

1. In the Planning Web client, Select Administration >> Manage Data Forms.
2. Select the Annual Budget form folder.

3. Click the Create button for Data Forms in the Right panel:
4. Create a form with the following Properties (don't forget to check Make data form read only):

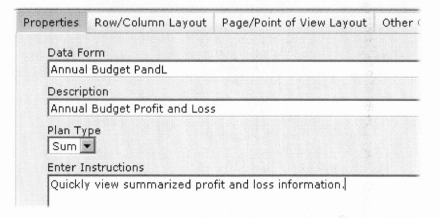

5. Click the Row/Column Layout and enter the following information:

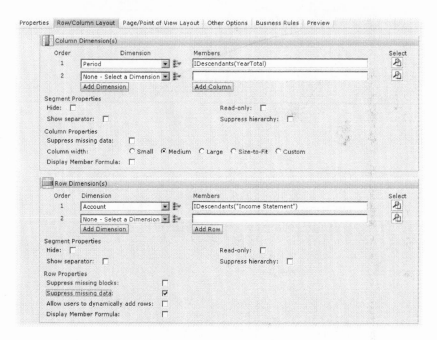

6. Select the Column properties icon for the Period dimension:

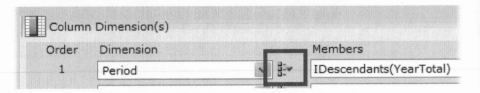

7. Uncheck Start Expanded.
8. Click Submit.
9. Select the Row properties icon for the Account dimension.
10. Uncheck Start Expanded.
11. Click Submit.
12. Click the Page/Point of View Layout and enter the following information:

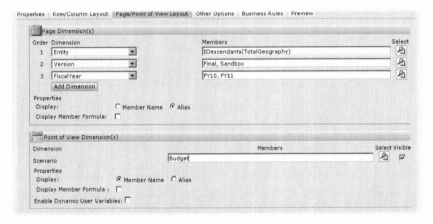

13. Click the Other Options and accept defaults for all options except make sure to check Read Only.
14. Click Save.
15. Open the Plan Summary data form:

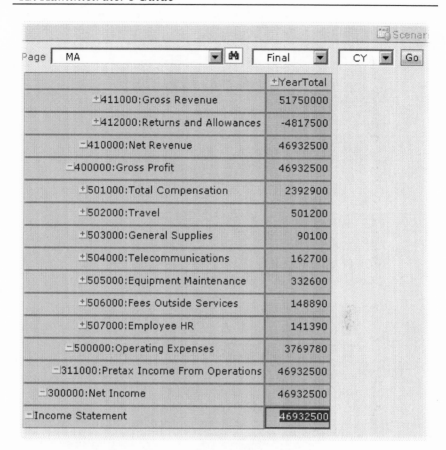

Create an Actual vs. Budget Data Form

Penny has one last data form to create; a summary form that compares actual and budget information. Try creating the following data form on your own.

1. Create the following data form:

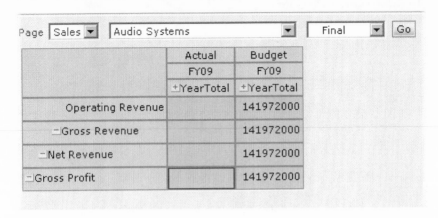

Note!

Don't forget that you can use Attributes as members on a data form as well as substitution variables.

CREATE A COMPOSITE FORM

A composite form is a data form that combines two or more data forms into a single object. Data forms can be from the same or different plan types. You can choose to combine Page and Point of View member selections so that users select a member from a drop down once and both data forms within the composite are updated. When combining data forms, you can choose a horizontal or vertical orientation.

Let us end our data form scene with a bang and create a composite form. Penny has already created a data form to capture revenue forecasts for units and price. Data entered for these metrics will certainly impact the sales returns forecast. First create a data form for sales returns (hint – edit the Forecast Revenue data form and "Save As" the data form as Forecast Sales Returns and make the appropriate row changes to save time).

Check "Make data form hidden" so that users do not see the form:

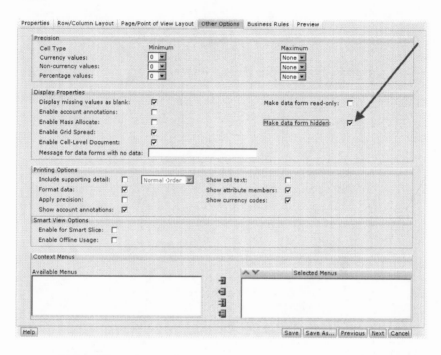

Now our goal is to create a composite with both the Forecast Revenue and Forecast Sales Returns.

1. In the Planning web client, select Administration >> Manage Data Forms.
2. Click Create Composite:

3. Type in the composite form name "Forecast Revenue and Returns":

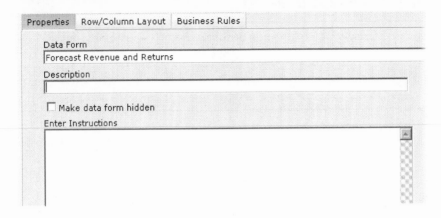

4.   Select Row/Column Layout.
5.   Check the options to Combine POV and Combine Page.
6.   Choose a Rows layout (#2).
7.   Select the forms to combine:

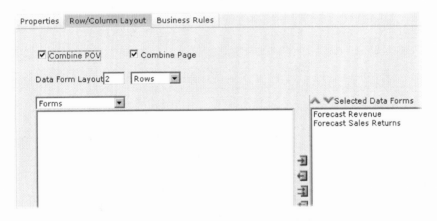

8.   Select Business Rules.

Here you can associate any relevant business rules to the data form. How about we create a business rule to calculate Sales Returns using a sales risk percentage (vs. data entry)?

9.   For now, we won't select any business rules.
10. Click Save.
11. Click OK.

You new composite form is ready for prime time!

	Jan	Feb	Mar	Apr	May	Jun	Jul	Aug	Sep	O
Units										
Price										
Operating Revenue										

Page MA ▼ Bookshelf Audio Systems ▼ Final ▼ FY11 ▼ Go

	Jan	Feb	Mar	Apr	May	Jun	Jul	Aug	Sep	Oct
Sales Returns										

MANAGE DATA FORMS

You are now a data form creating expert. From the same data form administration screens, you can edit, delete, move and assign security for data form folders and data forms.

Create Rename Assign Access   Create Create Composite Edit Move Delete Assign Access   Search:

	Data Form	Description	Last Modified	Access
⊞ 🗐 Forms	Forecast Revenue	Monthly Revenue Forecast	1/1/10 11:44 PM	Write
	Forecast Revenue and Returns		1/1/10 11:56 PM	Write
	Forecast Sales Returns	Monthly Revenue Forecast	1/1/10 11:47 PM	Write

Create a form folder called Forecast under the root directory. Move the Forecast data forms to this folder.

Try It!

Now that Penny has built a few of the initial data forms, she begins to think about how she might need to create a separate data form for each entity. Users can write to their entity but read all entities. That means the entire entity list will show up in their drop down list which will certainly be overwhelming to end users.

Other thoughts race through her mind... And how can users quickly navigate to related data forms and business rules? How can users document Product Status and Product notes, important information collected as part of the sales plan?

Just when she thought she was close, another mound of requirements is heaped onto her never-ending implementation to do list.

But wait, it's a bird. It's a plane. No, it's the consultants with some powerful Planning features to save the day.

Scene 11:
Extend the Planning Application

This musical scene includes some fun songs about how you can make your application more dynamic and more flexible for both administrators and end users. Let's learn about some of the features that will help in the development and maintenance of Planning applications.

USER VARIABLES

User variables act as filters in data forms, enabling planners to focus only on the members they are interested in. In Penny's case, she can create a user variable called "My Entity" and use that variable on the data form member selection. Users set the value for their variable and are ready to plan in a data form tailored for them. Before you can associate a user variable with a data form, you must first create the user variable. Planners cannot open the data form until a value has been specified.

Create a User Variable

1. Select Administration >> Manage Variables.
2. Click Add.
3. Select the Entity dimension.
4. Type in "My Entity":

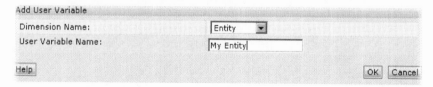

5. Click OK.

Now that the user variable has been created, you can select it in the data form definition.

6. Select Administration >> Manage Data Forms.
7. Navigate to and check the Plan Expenses data form and click Edit.
8. Select the Page/POV Layout tab.
9. Change the entity selection to the new variable (@IDESCENDANTS("&My Entity")):

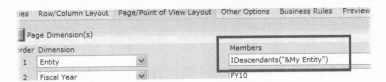

Note you could also simply choose the member or use the other available functions in the member selection. The new user variable is available for selection in the Member Selection window:

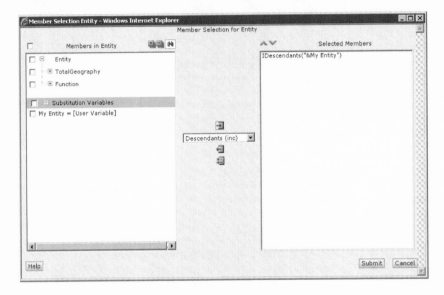

10. Click Save As.
11. Enter a new name for the data form:

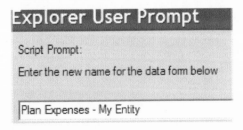

12. Click OK.
13. Click OK.

Now it's in the hands of the end users to set their user variable value.

Set the User Variable Value

Remember this is the step completed by the end user. But follow along so we can test out the data form.

1. Select File>>Preferences.
2. Under Planning preferences, choose the User Variables tab.
3. Select "E01_101_1100" (which is the member name):

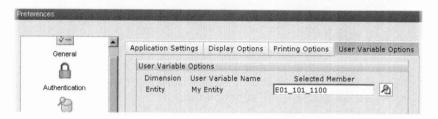

4. Click Save.
5. Open the Plan Expenses – My Entity data form and note the change in page options (the data form page drop down displays "E01_101_1100" a.k.a East Sales and its children):

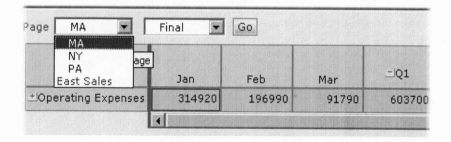

In summary, user variables save the day by making one form seem tailored for their Planning experience.

CUSTOM MENUS

Another handy set of tools that you can add to data forms are right-click menus. These objects provide users a quick way to launch related data forms, business rules, and URLs. They can even jump to workflow from a right-click menu.

Penny decides this is a sure fire way to guide Eddie through the annual budget, placing each step in a helpful right-click menu.

1. In the Planning web client, select Administration >> Manage Menus.
2. Click the Create button.
3. Create a new custom menu called "Annual Budget".

4. Click OK.
5. Select the "Annual Budget" menu and click Edit.

Create the following menu that lists these steps:
   a. Review instructions
   b. Plan revenue
   c. Plan expense
   d. Review P&L
   e. Submit the plan via workflow

6. Click the Add Child / Add Sibling button to enter the menu item:

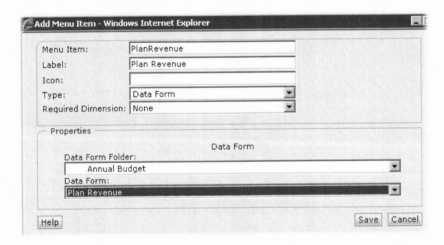

7. Click Save.
8. Click the Add Child / Add Sibling button to enter the menu item:

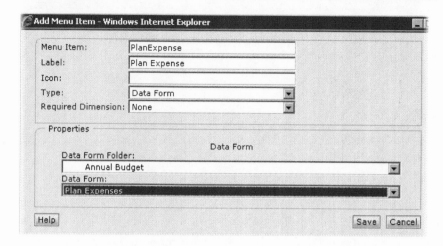

9. Click the Add Child / Add Sibling button to enter the menu item:

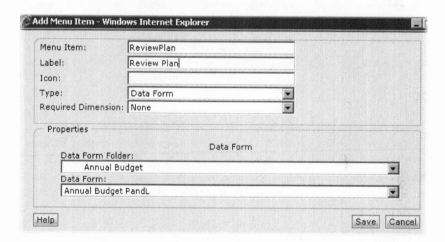

10. Click the Add Child / Add Sibling button to enter the menu item:

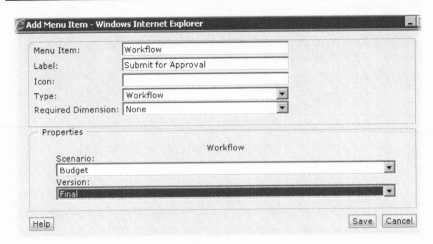

11. Once the following right-click menu items are created, click Save:

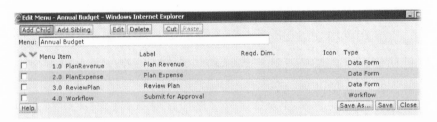

Note while our right-click menu example did not include a business rule, you can certainly include them. To assign a business rule to a right-click menu, select the plan type for which the business rule is available. From Business Rules, select the business rule to launch. From View Type, select how to display runtime prompt pages: Classic View which uses the default Planning view or Streamline View which displays each runtime prompt on a separate line instead of a section.

Optional parameters include:

- Window Title - a title to display instead of Runtime Prompt title
- OK Button Label - the text to display for the OK button
- Cancel Button Label - the text to display for the Cancel button
- Select Launch in a Separate Window - launch the business rule in a separate window than Planning's main window

When choosing workflow as a menu item, you will specify the planning unit to which the user is directed by selecting a scenario and a version.

The right-click menu is complete; now what? You need to add it to the data forms.

12. Click Administration >> Manage Data Forms.
13. Edit the Plan Expense form.
14. Select the Other Options tab. Assign the new "Annual Budget" menu to this form:

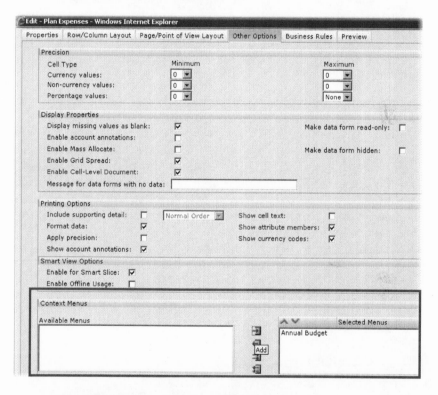

15. Select Save.
16. Open the Plan Expense data form and right-click in the columns or rows section within the form:

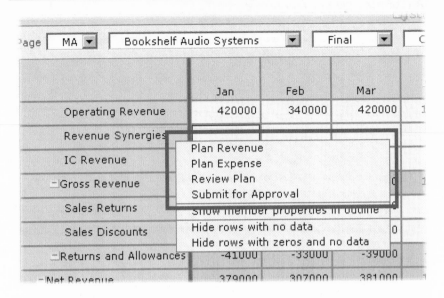

Repeat the above steps to assign the Annual Budget right-click menu to the other annual budget data forms.

Penny is slowly but surely knocking out the additional requirements from the CFO. But what about textual information? Can Planning handle text? Absolutely. Planning provides two ways to collect text information: Smart Lists, controlled text list values defined by the administrator, and text data types for measures, free form text entry for end users.

We'll first review Smart Lists.

SMART LISTS

As noted above, Smart Lists are a way for the administrator to define a controlled list of text values for users to review and input.

	Jan	Feb	Mar	Apr	May	Jun	Jul	Aug	Sep	Oct	Nov
6AS	Active	Active	Active	Active	Active	Active	Active	Active	Active	Active	Active
HTAS											
6B	Active / Discontinued										
PCD											

At a high level the steps to create a Smart List are: define the Smart List, associate the Smart List with members, select dimensions for which Smart Lists are displayed, and turn Smart

Lists on or off in Data Forms. Once you've created a Smart List, you can use its values in member formulas.

Penny needs to create a Smart List to track the product status for all products.

To create a Smart List,

1. Select Administration >> Smart Lists.
2. Click Create.
3. Add the following Smart List properties:

For the Smart List text box, enter a unique name that contains only alphanumeric and underscore characters and no special characters or spaces. This name can be referenced in formula expressions. For Label, enter the text to display when the Smart List is selected; spaces and special characters are allowed in the Label. The Display Order will control how Smart Lists are sorted in the drop-down list: by ID, Name, or Label.

#Missing Drop-Down Label allows you to enter a label to be displayed as an entry in the Smart List whose value is #missing. This value displays as the first selection in the Smart List drop-down, allowing #missing as a valid selection in the data form. When the cell is not in focus, this label displays only if Drop-Down Setting is selected in the next option. Otherwise, #missing or a blank cell is displayed, depending on the Display Missing Values As Blank selection for the data form. #missing labels determine only the display of cells with #missing data; #missing remains the stored value.

The #Missing Data Form Label determines how #missing vales are represented in cells associated with Smart Lists. Options include: Drop-Down Setting which displays the label set in #Missing Drop-Down Label and Data Form Setting which displays #missing or leaves cells blank, depending on the Display Missing Values As Blank selection for the data form. This selection determines what is displayed in the cell when it is not the focus. When the cell is in focus, the Smart List item that is selected from the drop-down is displayed.

The Automatically Generate ID property will automatically generate the numeric ID for each Smart List entry. If you do not select this option, you can customize Smart List ID values.

Once the properties are defined,

4.   Click the Entries tab.
5.   Add the following Smart List entries:

Add Smart Lists - Microsoft Internet Explorer

Properties   Entries   Preview

Add   Delete

ID	Name	Label
1	Active	Active
2	Discontinued	Discontinued

6.   Click Save.
7.   Select Administration >> Dimensions.
8.   Select the Account dimension.
9.   Create an account called Product Status under the Metrics member:

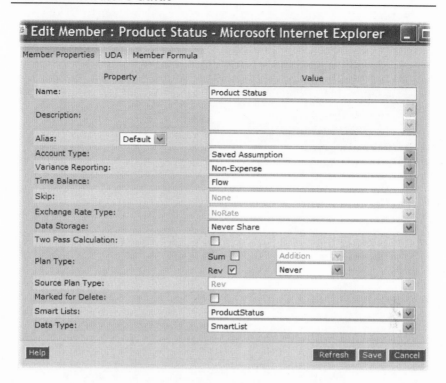

10. Click Save and the new member is added:

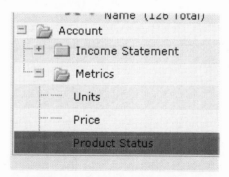

11. Click Evaluation Order.
12. Select the Rev Plan Type and click Go.
13. Move the Account over into the Selected Dimensions section:

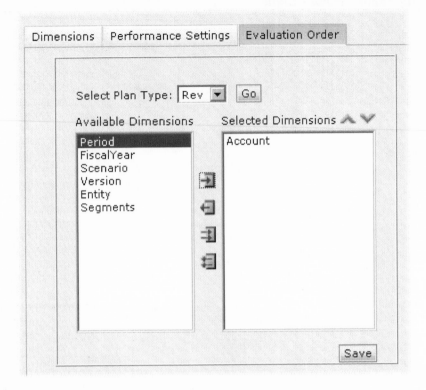

14. Click Save.
15. Create a data form that allows users to enter Product Status:

	Jan	Feb	Mar	Apr	May	Jun	Jul	Aug	Sep	Oct	Nov
BAS	Active	Active	Active	Active	Active	Active	Active	Active	Active	Active	Active
HTAS											
BB	Active / Discontinued										
PCD											

Smart Lists provide controlled text lists for end users. But what about free form entry from users?

TEXT AND DATE MEASURES

Text and Date measures allow free form entry from the end user. Text measures are often seen in capital expenditure applications, allowing users to input equipment model and serial numbers. Date measures can be used for any number of requirements: product intro date, store open date or close date, employee hire date, etc. The trick with text and date measures is they are only available for members of the Accounts dimension.

Penny decides to create a Product Note measure to allow end users to enter a note about the plan for each product. While users could also use cell text to enter comments, she decides that a text measure will work for her requirement.

Create a Text Measure

1. Select Administration >> Dimensions.
2. Create an account called "Product Note" under the Metrics member with a data type of Text:

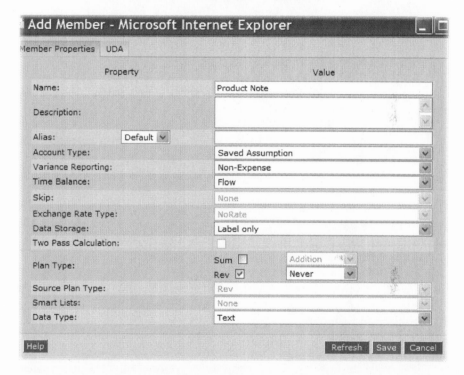

3. Create a data form that allows entry to the new account:

Now regardless of the requirements from the CFO, Penny can build a Smart List or Text measure to meet text requirements for Planning.

SUBSTITUTION VARIABLES

Substitution variables are one of the best tools for Planning and Essbase administrators and report designers who live in a world where the clock advances (which is all of us, to the best of my knowledge). Let's say you have 20 different current month reports across your Planning and Essbase applications. Do you want to modify all 20 reports each month to change the selected month? Do you want to modify all of your calc scripts that calculate current month each month? At year end, things are somewhat slow, so it won't be a problem to update all of your calc scripts and reports to reflect the new year, right? Trust me: you will be busy enough without adding those tasks to your plate.

Substitution variables are variables that serve as a placeholder for specific members. They are defined at the server, application, or database level. Originally, these variables could only be utilized in data forms, load rules, calc scripts and reporting and analysis tools (the Smart View Add-In, Financial Reporting, Web Analysis, and Smart View).

Nowadays, you can use substitution variables in outline formulas, security filters, areas and mapping definitions for partitions, MDX statements, rules file specifications for DSN definitions associated with using the SQL interface, and rules file specifications for dimension/member names in the data load header and in field specification for data load columns.

Common substitution variables include curmth (current month), clsmth (closed month), CY (current year), and PY (prior year). You define the substitution variable name: just remember you are limited to eight characters.

To define a substitution variable,

1. In the Essbase Administration Services Console, under the Essbase Server name, right-click and select Create>>Variable:

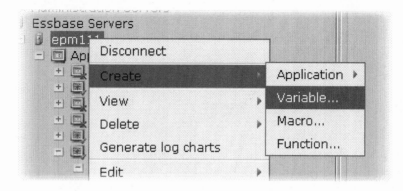

2. Specify the application and database for the substitution variable.

Tip!

Define substitution variables for all applications and all databases when possible. For example, define 'curmo' current month substitution variable once for use in all applications and databases.

3. Specify the variable name.
4. Specify the variable value:

Application	Database	Variable	Value
Click here to add			
Entpln	(all dbs)	Curmo	Feb

Substitution Variables [TRN113]

4. Click OK to save the variable.

Try It!

Eddie needs to build 3 different current month reports to analyze revenue and expense for the budgeting application. Because Eddie should spend time on value added analysis versus time spent updating reports, Penny creates a substitution variable for current month called "curmo" (not to be confused with the long lost brother of that lovable monster Elmo).

Try It!

Create another substitution variable called "BY" for the budget year. Set the year to 2010 to follow along with the book.

To edit variables, right-click on the server and select Edit>>Variables.

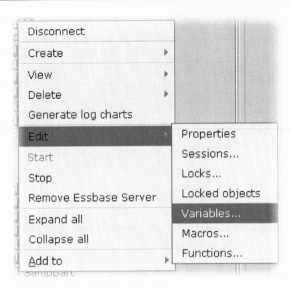

The Substitution variables window will display a listing of all variables for the server. You can update the values for the variables by placing your cursor in the values cell and typing the new value. Click *Set* once you are finished. You can also copy and delete substitution variables from this window.

Application	Database	Variable	Value
Click here to add			
Entpln	(all dbs)	Curmo	Feb
NewSamp	(all dbs)	CurrPrd	Feb
NewSamp	(all dbs)	CurrYr	FY10
NewSamp	(all dbs)	NextYr	FY11
NewSamp	(all dbs)	NextYr1	FY12
NewSamp	(all dbs)	NxtPrd	Mar
NewSamp	(all dbs)	PriorPrd	Jan
NewSamp	(all dbs)	PriorYr	FY09
PlanSamp	(all dbs)	CurrPrd	Feb
PlanSamp	(all dbs)	CurrYr	FY10
PlanSamp	(all dbs)	NextYr	FY11
PlanSamp	(all dbs)	NextYr1	FY12
PlanSamp	(all dbs)	NxtPrd	Mar
PlanSamp	(all dbs)	PriorPrd	Jan
PlanSamp	(all dbs)	PriorYr	FY09

Substitution Variables [TRN113]

Set   Copy   Delete

Refresh   Help   Close

ALTERNATE ALIAS TABLES

Outlines will always have the default alias table to store aliases, but you may have a requirement for different descriptions within your application. For your human capital analysis application, you might need a few more ways to report on a single employee:

- Last_name "," first_name"," title
- First_name last_name
- Employee_id"," last_name"," first_name

In order to meet all of these requirements, you will need to create some new alias tables. Let's create an alternate alias table that will combine product number and name into the alias.

To add additional alias tables,

1. In the Planning web client, click Administration >> Alias Tables.

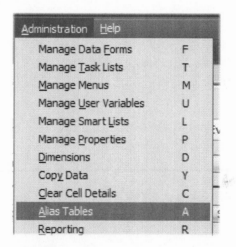

Notice the default alias table already exists. From this menu, you can add, edit, delete and copy alias tables. Copy is helpful when you want to take existing aliases defined in default and copy them to the alternate alias table (instead of re-entering them again). You can also clear the values for the alias tables here.

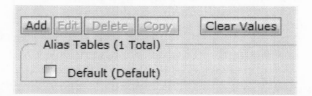

2. Click Add to add a new alias table.
3. Enter the new name for the alias table. Type in "LongNames" for an example alias name:

Script Prompt:	OK
Enter the name for a new Alias Table below	Cancel

LongNames

4. Click OK.

Now that alias table has been added to the application, you can select the new alias table under Edit Member properties.

Member Properties	Attribute Values	UDA	Member Formula

Property	Value
Name:	BAS
Description:	
Alias:	Default / Default / LongNames — Bookshelf Audio Systems
Data Storage:	Never Share
Two Pass Calculation:	☐
Plan Type:	Sum ☐ Addition / Rev ☑ Addition
Marked for Delete:	☐
Smart Lists:	None
Data Type:	Unspecified

Help   Refresh Save

Alternate alias tables can be updated from a file using ODI or the outline load utility.

We've extended our database with text lists, dates, substitution variables, and more. Let's now learn how we can build task lists to guide users in the Planning process.

TASK LISTS

Budgeting and forecasting often require users to perform multiple activities or tasks to complete the process. Task lists in Planning guide users through the planning process, listing the tasks to be completed with instructions and due dates. Administrators and interactive users can create and manage tasks and task lists.

A task list can include the following:

- URL Task—opens a specified URL
- Web Data Form—opens a Web data form
- Business Rule—launches a business rule that you specify
- Workflow—starts the review process with a scenario and version that you specify
- Descriptive—describes an action that users must take

You may want to organize task lists into folders.

To create a task list folder,

1. Select Administration >> Manage Task Lists:

2. In the Task List Folders area, select the folder when the new folder should be created:

3. Click Create to create the folder.
4. Enter the folder name in the dialog box.
5. Click OK.

Once the folder is created, you can move or delete the task list folder using available options in the Task List Folders area.

Penny wants to make the planning process as easy as possible for Eddie so she decides to create a task list to guide him through the forms, business rules and workflow. Follow along to create a task list.

Create a Task List

1. Select Administration >> Task Lists.
2. Click Create in the right panel to create a task list.
3. Type in "Annual Budget".
4. Click OK.

5. Select Annual Budget task list and click Edit.
6. Click Add Child.
7. Enter the first task:

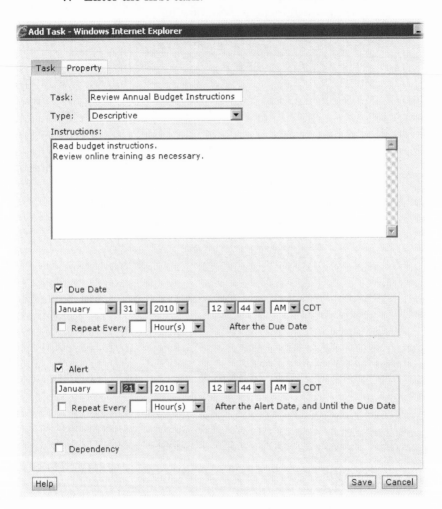

Each task in a task list will have a task name, type, set of instructions, due date, and alert or reminder dates. Alerts will display: Green=on schedule, Yellow=Approaching due date, Red=overdue. If Due Date is checked, you can send emails when a task is not completed by the due date. Optionally, you can select the Dependency check box if the completion of this task is dependent upon completing the primary task.

8. Click Save.

9. Select the first task and click Add Sibling.
10. Enter the second task:

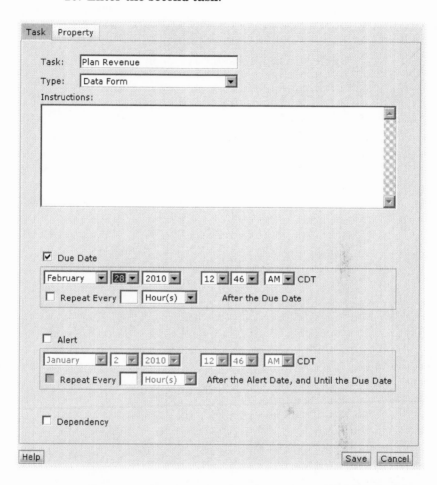

11. Click the Properties tab and select the Plan Revenue data form.

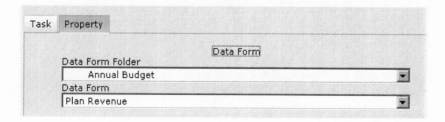

12. Repeat the steps above, creating 3 more tasks:
   a. Plan Expenses (Opens the Plan Expense data form)
   b. Review Plan (Opens the Review Plan data form)
   c. Workflow task (Choose Budget Draft for the properties on the task).
13. The final task list should look as follows:

14. Click Save.

The Task List is ready for planning.

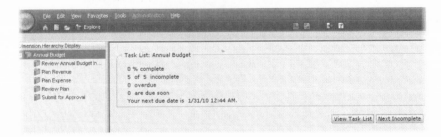

Note you can also "save as" a task list.

Manage a Task List

To manage existing task lists,

1. Select Administration >> Manage Task Lists
2. The Manage Task Lists will display:

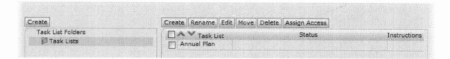

From this screen, you can create, edit, move, or delete task lists and task list folders. This is also where you assign user access for specific task lists.

As an administrator you will want to monitor the status of a specific task list, understanding what steps have been completed and what tasks are outstanding. To view task list status

1. Select View >> Advanced Mode to switch to advanced mode (if you aren't there already).
2. Select View >> Task List and then either the option for Task List, Report or Status:

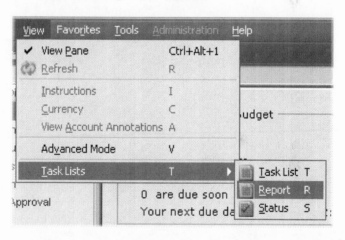

3. From the open dialogue you can view the task list status information:

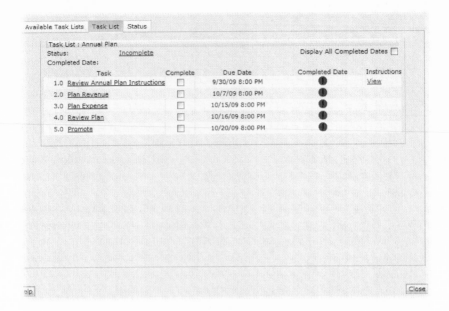

You can also view task list status by user or task list. You can view the Overall Completion %, Overdue Tasks, and Tasks Due Soon. Reports are available in PDF or Excel.

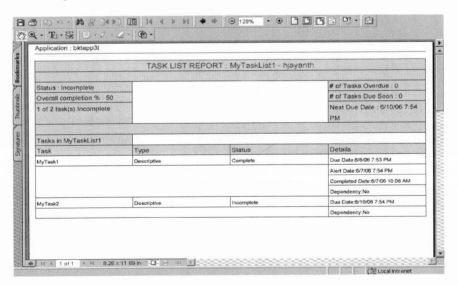

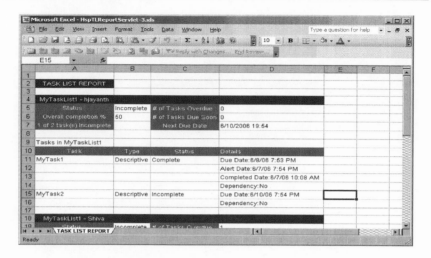

Check out the first scene where we discuss how end users use Task Lists. (We've been on a long journey my friend. Do you remember back when we were learning to enter plan data over the web?)

Now that Penny has extended her application and created a task list for Eddie, we will cover another important topic for Planning applications: Sharing Data.

Scene 12:
Share Data

Penny has a number of existing Essbase reporting databases in addition to her new Planning databases. She will definitely want to share data between the Planning databases, Rev up to Sum. Planning provides built in data sharing mechanisms for plan types within an application with the @XREF function. But she may also need to share data across applications and to other databases and systems. The next inevitable question – how can you share data across Planning applications? A number of ways exist to share data across databases and applications and in this musical scene we'll provide an introduction to most of them.

@XREF FUNCTION

First let's explore @XREF since that has already been added for you in the Sum and Rev databases. In order to transfer data between plan types, Planning creates dynamic XRef's (external reference functions) The source plan type property in members of the Account dimension tells Planning the direction in which the XRef will transfer the data. The picture below shows dynamic XRef's created by Planning:

Intuitively, you can think of the @XREF function as "go get the value from that database". This function retrieves data from a database at a cell level. Planning creates this function in an Account member formula where an account is valid for more than one plan type. Essbase will retrieve data at the specified data intersection into the database. If you make the member a dynamically calculated member, it will retrieve the data when the member called, like a transparent partition. If it's a stored member, it will retrieve that data when the outline is calculated.

The syntax for the @XREF function is

`@XREF(LocationAlias [,MbrList])`

The LocationAlias is a predefined description that references an Essbase server, application, database, username, and password. This saves you from having to save login information inside a calc script or formula that calls @XREF.

MbrList is a list of members to point to when Essbase queries the database mentioned in the Location Alias. This list is similar to the mapping section of a database. The calc engine will first reference all common members in the cell that is currently being accessed. However, if the source has dimensions that do not coincide with the target, the member list will specify which members to use.

For example, consider the following formula:

```
Sales = @XREF(sourceDB, "Total Sales");
```

Remember Planning creates this member formula for you.

Assume that Sales is a measure in the data target database and that Total_Sales is a member in the data source database. This formula will map the Sales member in the target to the Total_Sales member in the source database. When Sales is retrieved, Essbase will actually retrieve the value of Total_Sales in the source database. Note that the source database is the database with the location alias, sourceDB.

Performance Consideration for @XREF

Dynamic XRef's need to calculate all dependencies before transferring the data and this could affect retrieval performance at the target. You might consider replacing them with other data transfer options, such as stored XRefs, replicated partitions, or the Data Export calc script command introduced in version 9.3.

One alternative is to use stored XRef's instead of dynamic XRef's. With stored XRef's, you can use business rules that run on save and execute against the target Plan Type. As a user enters data in the source Plan Type, the XRef pulls that data from the target Plan Type where the user is doing the data submission. Then build forms and business rules that utilize runtime prompts that take the value from the form, focusing the scope of the XRef to only the data on the form.

Writing the XRef formula as sparse equations with the command SET CREATEBLOCKONEQ ON will create the specific block at the target.

```
SET CREATEBLOCKONEQ ON;
FIX([CostCenter], @RELATIVE(NET_SHIPMENTS,0))
                         &Fcst_Yr = @XREF (_sourcecube_
, &Fcst_Yr, [CostCenter] );
ENDFIX
```

If you decide to use partitions or the CALC EXPORT command, use the HSP_NOLINK UDA in accounts that exist in multiple plan types. This will prevent Planning from creating dynamic XREf's automatically.

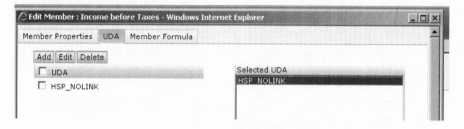

INTRODUCTION TO PARTITIONING

Partitioning has been around for a long, long time, back since the days of good ole Essbase Application Manager (if you don't know what this is, congratulations: you haven't been using Essbase since before dirt was invented). A partition is a definition that connects data between Essbase databases. Depending on the type of partition, data can be shared directly between databases (transparent partition), copied from one database to another (replicated partition), or used as a predefined launching point from one database to another (linked partition):

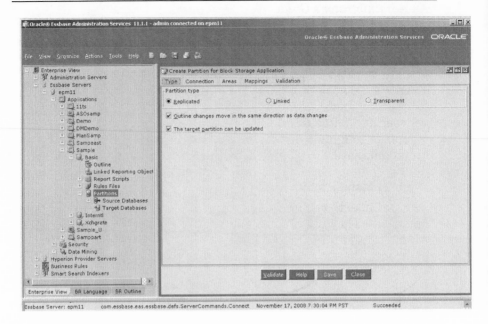

Transparent Partitions

Transparent partitions place a direct link from a target database to a source database. A subsection of the target database is defined and directly linked to the source database. When a user accesses the defined shared section of the target database, data is retrieved directly from the source database. This type of partition allows for real time data to be shared between two databases.

Replicated Partitions

Replicated partitions are similar to transparent partitions. However, instead of the target database containing direct links to the source database, data from the source database is copied into the target database.

Transparent vs. Replicated Partitions

Although transparent partitions allow for real time data, it can be taxing on sensitive networks. Retrievals times can be slower when you are accessing a transparent partition. These days, networks usually have the bandwidth to handle transparent partitions. However, if you have a slow network, you may encounter performance issues with transparent partitions. A replicated partition may not have real time data, but it can be a lot faster for retrievals and easier on your network as data is retrieved directly from the target database. You can schedule your database copies during off peak times and still have the same data between the source and target databases. Replicated partitions tend to be the optimal solution if you have data that doesn't change often and/or you have a slow network.

For both of these types of partitions, the dimensions between the databases do not have to be the same. You can define mappings to handle differences in outlines between the source and target database.

Linked Partitions

Linked partitions do not actually share data across databases. They are predefined links between databases that allow a user to jump from one database to another when drilling into a database. The advantage of using a linked partition is that you are not restricted to the dimensionality of the target database. Data is not physically transferred from one database to another.

Comparing Partitions

Let's now summarize some of the key aspects of partitioning.

Requirement / Restriction	Replicated	Transparent	Linked
Real time data		X	X
Limited Network Traffic	X		X
Limited Disk Space		X	X
Faster calcs	X		
Small database size		X	X
Faster retrievals	X		X
Seamless to the user	X	X	
Connecting databases with different dimensionality			X
Easy Recoverability	X		
Less synchronization			X
Attribute based queries		X	X
Frequent updates and calculations		X	
Update data at the data target		X	X
Contextual Differences			X

Requirement / Restriction	Replicated	Transparent	Linked
Batch updates and simple aggregations	X		

ASO vs. BSO Partition Considerations

The following chart assumes version 11.1.1. ASO as the target of a partition is not supported in 9.3.1.

Target	Source	Replicated	Transparent	Linked
BSO	BSO	Y	Y	Y
BSO	ASO	N	Y	Y
ASO	ASO	N	Y	Y
ASO	BSO	Y	Y	Y

Partitions can be created in the Administration Services Console using the Partitioning Wizard or in MaxL. Below is a quick glimpse of the Partitioning Manager where we are defining the sections of the source and target databases to connect:

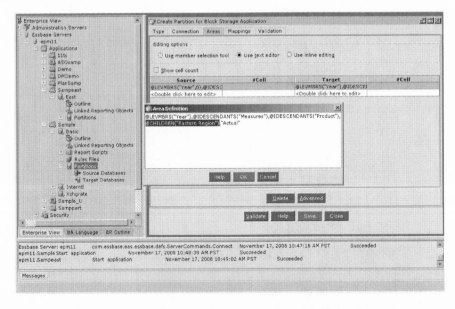

Notice we can use functions to define the sections of the database (e.g. level-0 members of the Year dimension, descendants of Measures, descendants of Product, and children of Eastern Region in the Market dimension are selected in the example above).

A number of tools in the Partitioning Wizard help us create valid partitions like member selection and "Show cell count".

In summary, let's compare these two options and weigh the advantages and disadvantages of each.

@XREF vs. Partitions

When you design the database, considerations must be made to determine whether or not to use @XREFs or partitions. If you only want to share a few members, @XREFs are the best choice. @XREFs work well between databases in the same application since they are sharing the same memory. Partition management is designed to handle data sharing for large groups of members well. However, it is usually more work than it's worth to manage a partition for just a few measures. In this case, it is better to make the few measures calculated with the @XREF formula. Retrieval and calculation performance is another factor. Dynamic @XREFs can be costly especially if those members are used in calculations in the target database. A stored XREF member or replicated partition could address calculation and retrieval issues.

OTHER DATA SHARING ALTERNATIVES

Calc Export Commands/Load Rules

In the calc script scene, we discussed one easy and fast way to extract slices of Essbase block storage data using a calc script command DATAEXPORT. This command allows you to extract data to a text file or relational table from a calc script. Placing this command within Fix statements and If statements allows you to isolate the desired data to be pulled. You can then load the extracted data to a source cube using a load rule. The full process can be automated and scheduled to run as needed. For more information on using the DATAEXPORT command, please revisit the calc script chapter.

Data Synchronization in EPMA

If you are using Oracle Hyperion Enterprise Management Architect, EPMA, to manage your Planning and Financial Management applications, you can also use the Data Synchronization Module. This module allows you to share data between Planning, Financial Management, Essbase (ASO and BSO), Profitability and Cost Management applications from the following sources: Financial Management, Planning, Essbase (BSO), Profitability and Cost Management, flat files, and Interface Tables. Interface tables are tables that are defined in EPMA that access relational databases directly. This allows for changes to flow directly from the relational database into the source application.

There are some caveats to using Data Synchronization. All applications that are used as data sources must be managed by EPMA. If you use a flat file, the format is very specific. The file must be delimited with the final column being the data field. It will not accept fixed length fields. This method is recommended if you are already using EPMA to manage the majority of your applications.

MDX Scripts and Report Scripts

You can run MDX scripts for both ASO and BSO databases to extract data sets from Essbase. Report scripts are also available for block storage databases. Result sets can be written to a text file that is then loaded into a target Essbase database using data load rules files.

JEXPORT Command

The JEXPORT command allows you utilize the flexibility of Java programming language to extract data from databases. You can use JEXPORT to create a Java script that specifically states what section of the database to extract. While this is technically possible, the new calc export commands do essentially the same thing much more quickly.

ETL TOOLS

As most folks on the planet know, Oracle is one of the (if not THE) leading data warehousing solution available. With data warehousing comes ETL tools (data Extraction, Transformation and Load), solutions that help us move data from system A to system B. Up until this point we've focused on data integration between Essbase databases. You may have bigger requirements to integrate data from Essbase to other systems along with other enterprise data integration needs. Oracle provides a number of ETL tools to share data between Essbase and Oracle EPM System tools along with almost any other system. We'll focus on the solutions that work with Essbase here.

ODI – Oracle Data Integrator

Oracle Data Integrator (ODI) is Oracle's current strategic direction for a comprehensive ETL tool (although if you want to be technical about it, ODI is an ELT tool: extraction, load, and transform). Built in adapters exist for Essbase, Planning, Financial Management and most other source transactions systems, allowing you to integrate data across your enterprise. For more information on ODI, please see our appendix.

FDM – Financial Data Quality Management

Where ODI is a true ETL tool, mostly used by the IT types, Financial Data Quality Management (FDM) is an out-of-the-box data transformation and validation tool for the more business oriented individuals. Source-level financial data is fed to consolidation, reporting, planning, and analytical applications, with detailed audit trail and reconciliation capabilities.

HAL – Hyperion Application Link

In the old days of Hyperion, we used Hyperion Application Link (HAL) to build dimensions and share data across Hyperion products. HAL served as an ETL tool but was not as robust as a tool like ODI. HAL is set to be sunset in the future and existing customers should begin to plan for a migration to ODI.

Star Analytics

We'll conclude with one last tip: One strong non-Oracle solution for extracting Essbase data (and Oracle EPM System data) is a product called Star Integration Server by StarAnalytics (http://www.staranalytics.com/).

So which data sharing option is the best? You've learned by now there isn't just one right answer. Depends on a number of factors like what needs to be shared, how often it needs to be refreshed, what the sources are, what the targets are, retrieval and calculation requirements, and more. Make sure you have a clear understanding of the requirements and the best alternatives should begin to stand out.

Unsuspecting Penny is ready for the last Planning application building step: Assigning Security. Little does she know that Dr. Dementor is in route with plans to sabotage the whole implementation with his new deathray just as she is about to finish the application.

Scene 13:
Manage Security

Before we jump into the security and user provisioning details, let's take a step back and introduce you to Shared Services, a core component to the Oracle EPM solution. You will assign security in Shared Services as well as perform other tasks like life cycle management.

INTRODUCTION TO SHARED SERVICES

Shared Services is part of the Foundation Services layer of System 9 and Oracle EPM System 11. Components of Shared Services include:

- User Provisioning
- Enterprise Performance Management Architect (versions 9.3 and later)
- Life Cycle Management (11x)
- Core Services

Core Services is better known as the underlying "plumbing" for Oracle EPM System: session management, authentication and authorization, repository services, and logging and usage.

User provisioning allows you to maintain Oracle EPM System security for all products. Note the one exception is if you use Financial Reporting, Web Analysis, Interactive Reporting, or Production Reporting, you will assign document permissions in the Workspace.

You create a user once, assign the user to groups, assign the user to roles, and assign application access. A common set of roles is available across products. The interface for User Provisioning is called the Shared Services Console in version 11 and the User Management Console in System 9 (it is the same console, they just renamed it in version 11). Beginning in version 11, we use Shared Services for more than just security.

User provisioning provides single sign on access across the Oracle EPM System / Hyperion products (you can even implement single sign on access between external systems). Users can externally authenticate to LDAP, MSAD, NTLM or other third party tools. User provisioning is bundled with OpenLDAP for native Shared Services users and groups.

Two security layers exist in Shared Services. The first is the user authentication layer that validates the user id and password. The authentication can be native or external. The second layer is the product specific authorization that grants the user access to the Hyperion products and applications. Shared Services manages the product specific authorization.

Next we will delve into the capabilities of the Native Directory of Shared Services. The Native Directory manages and maintains the default Shared Services user accounts required for Hyperion products. It is the central repository for all Hyperion provisioning information and stores the relationships between users, groups, and roles. The backend database is OpenLDAP and is easily corrupted, so back up this repository often.

The basic steps to get Shared Services up and running are as follows (see the installation and production documentation for the details):

1. Install and configure Shared Services.
2. Set up external authentication.
3. Install and configure the Oracle EPM System / Hyperion products.
4. Register the products with Shared Services.

LOG INTO THE USER MANAGEMENT CONSOLE

To log into the Shared Services Console, the main interface for Shared Services,

1. Log into the Workspace: http://server:19000/workspace.
2. Select Navigate (steering wheel icon) >> Administer >> Shared Services Console:

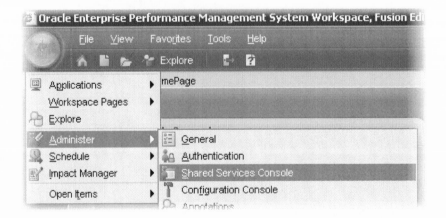

3. The Shared Services Console window will display:

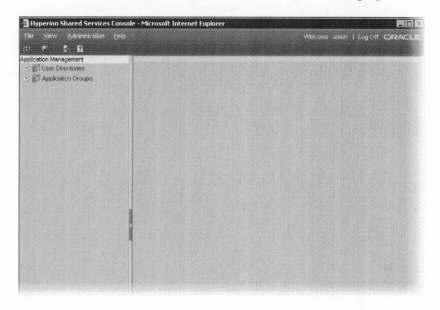

Note! To manage Planning security in Shared Services, your Shared Services administrator must grant you the Provisioning Manager role for the Planning application.

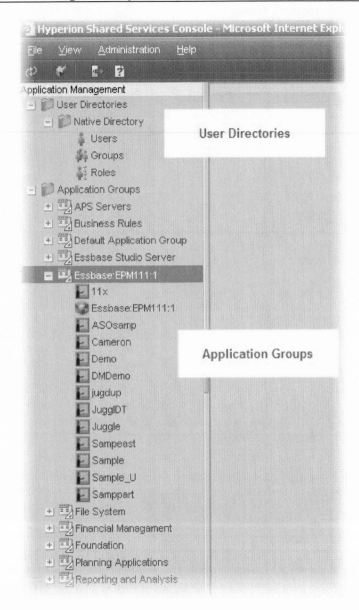

The navigation panel on the left portion of the window controls the main content area. For example, if you select "User Directories", the main content area will allow you to search and display the users. The User Directories section groups native and external directories. The Application Groups section lists all of the products registered with Shared Services (this used to be called Projects in System 9). By default, a separate application group will be created for each Oracle EPM System / Hyperion product that you install and configure through the configuration utility. Your Essbase server(s) will display as *Essbase: servername:1.*

The Planning applications will display under the Planning application group:

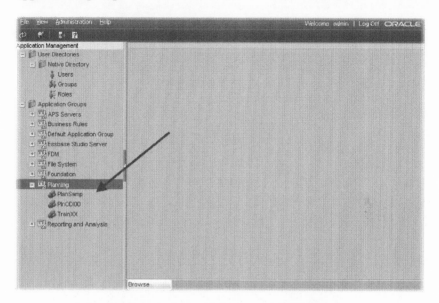

CREATE A NATIVE GROUP

In general, you want to use Group security assignments as much as possible. Groups reduce the overall maintenance for your security application. You define security once and as users come and go, they can be added to and removed from groups. If security requirements change, you update the group security once vs. many times for individual users. Specific to Shared Services, you can use external or native groups which can contain both native users and external users. Native groups that can contain other groups are called nested groups.

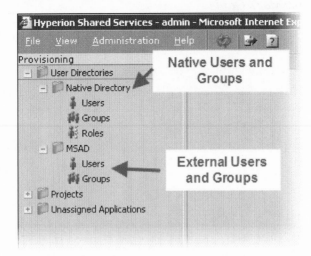

 Note!

Externally authenticated groups cannot be managed with Shared Services. That means you can't modify the users in the group, though you can assign security to the group.

 Tip!

The same group can be used across multiple applications and databases. This is actually a pretty good practice.

Let's walk through an example creating a group for Finance.

1. Within Shared Services, select Groups.
2. Select File >> New
   or
Right-click on Groups and select New:

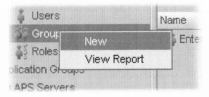

1. The Create Group window displays.
2. Type in the group name and description:

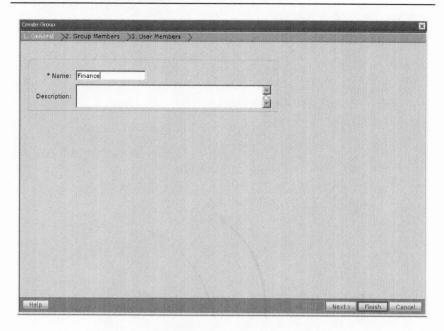

3. Click the Next button to advance to the Group Members tab.

On this tab, you can select desired available groups (either native or external) to assign (nested group security). You can search for specific groups or search for all groups. Next just check the group and use the arrow icons to move into the "assigned" section.

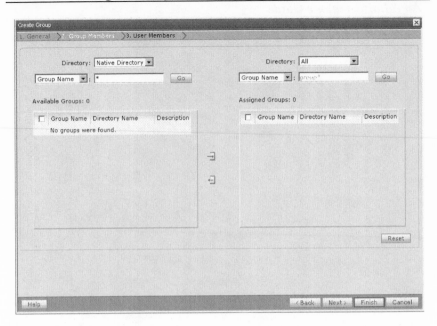

4. For our example, we won't assign any groups to Finance. Click the Next button to advance to the User Members tab.

On the final tab, you select desired available users (either native or external). You have the same search capabilities for specific users as you did for groups. Use the arrow icons to assign the selected users:

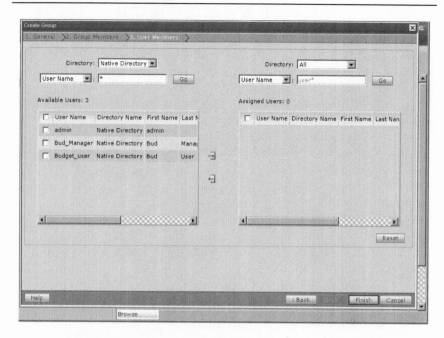

For our example, we don't have any users yet (we need to create the Eddie user id).

5. Click Finish to create the group.

6. Click OK to close the Create Group window:

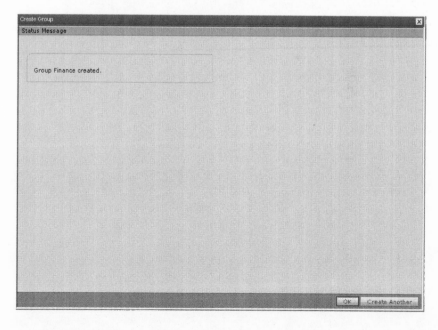

CREATE A NATIVE USER

It is time to set Eddie up as a user. Let's create a new Shared Services native user, 'Eddie' and assign him to the Finance group.

1. Within Shared Services, select File >> New (you should have Groups selected).
   or
   Right-click on Users and select New:

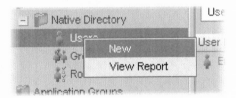

2. The Create User window displays.
3. Type in the user id "eddie", name, password and other information.

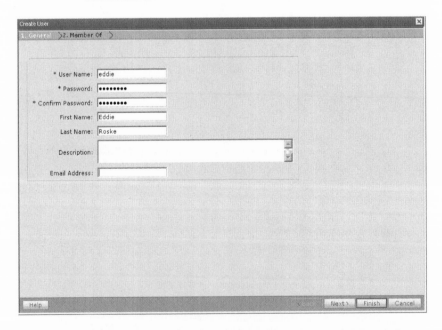

4. Select Next to advance to the Group Membership tab.
5. Click the Go button to list all groups or search for a specific group:

6. Select desired available groups, using the arrow icons to assign the user to specific groups. We'll assign Eddie to the Finance group:

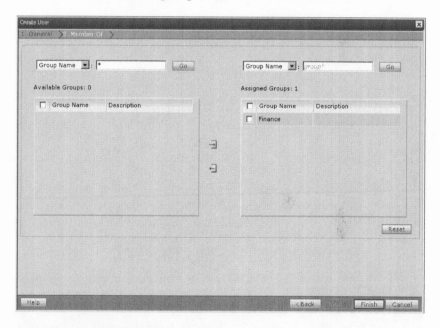

7. Click Finish.

Try It!

Silent Bob will need to input budgets for the North America (E01) entities in the Entpln application. Create a new user "Bob". Create a new "E01" group and assign Silent Bob to this group.

VIEW USERS AND GROUPS

Sometimes it's fun to see a list of users. To view users:

1. Select the Users in the left pane.
2. Search for a specific user or click Search:

A number of search options are available for filtering the user list:

- User Property: First Name, Last Name, User Name, Description, email
- Group
- View: active, inactive or all users

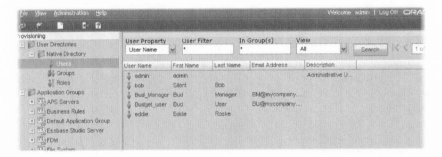

Follow the same steps to view groups. This is not nearly as fun, because groups usually don't have cool names like "Bob" and "Eddie".

PROVISION USERS AND GROUPS

So far we we've created users and groups but we haven't assigned any roles or application access. Next, we'll go through the steps to provision a user. So what exactly are we doing when we provision a user? You are assigning a role for the user; for example, you are giving a user Planner access to an application or Content Publisher role for Reporting and Analysis modules (which means they can create adhoc queries and save them in their personal directories).

The steps to provision a user and group are the same. If you need to provision a group, right-click on the group and select
Note!   Provision. Follow the steps provided below.

To provision a group,

1. Right-click on the group (in our example, right-click on Finance) and select Provision:

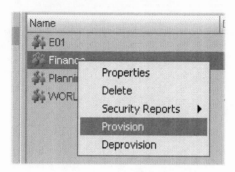

The Available Roles section will display on the left. You should see your Planning server.

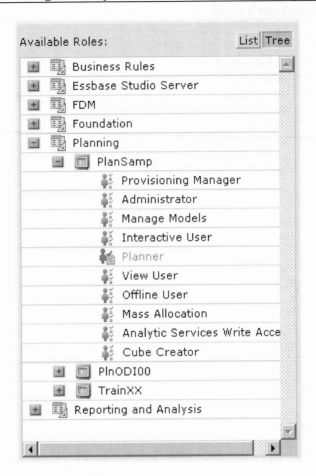

The main Planning roles include Owner, Administrator, Interactive User, Planner, and Viewer. The Planning Administrator can create and manage applications, maintain metadata, initiate and manage the budget process, enter and view data, create and maintain Web-based data forms, and more (pretty much all those tasks you've completed throughout this book).

The Planning Owner has all those same capabilities but can also delete applications.

Interactive users can enter and view data, manage the budget process, and create and maintain data forms.

Planners can input, submit, and view data in the web or in Smart View. They can execute business rules and other processes associated with validating and preparing data for which they have been assigned. They can submit information and data for approval.

Viewers have limited access within Planning to view data.

Other applicable Planning roles include the following:
Provisioning Managers can assign security access for the
application. Manage Models is related to the old Hub component
(this role is not really used). Offline User allows the user to take
Planning forms offline, creating their own personal cubes where
they can run business rules when not connected to the Planning
Server. Mass Allocations allows the users to utilize the Mass
Allocation feature (introduced in 9.3.1). Essbase Write Access
creates Essbase filters so they can send data back to Planning via
the Excel Spreadsheet Add-in.

If you are using Enterprise Performance Architect (EPMA),
you will assign EPMA roles. The Dimension Editor maintains
dimensions in EPMA. The Dimension Viewer views dimensions in
EPMA. The Application Creator creates applications in EPMA.

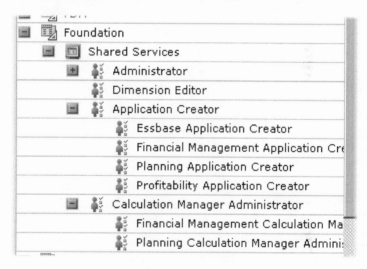

2. Expand the Planning application group server. The list
    of Applications will follow. As you continue to expand
    the hierarchy, the Planning roles will display:

3. Next, choose the desired role and use the arrow icon to move the role over to the Selected Roles section. For our example, choose the Interactive User role:

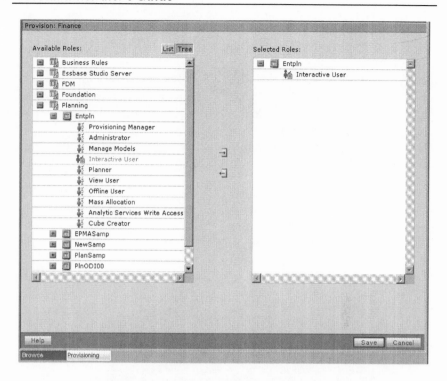

4. Click the Save button to save the role assignments. A
    Provision Summary report will display:

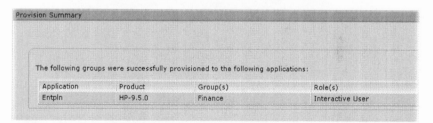

Try It!

If you didn't follow along, provision the Finance group for
the Interactive User role. Next provision the E01 group for
the Planner role.

You're not finished yet. You still need to assign access to
Planning components like dimensions, data forms, business rules,
task lists and more.

We'll jump into more details in the next session but we did want to show you that it is possible to assign security for Planning objects within the Shared Services console.

Assign Planning Security in Shared Services

It is possible to assign application specific access to dimension members, data forms, business rules, and task lists in the Shared Services console.

To assign Planning application security in Shared Services,

1. Navigate to the Application Groups section in the Shared Services Console.
2. Expand the Application Groups section.
3. Right-click on the application and notice you can launch the Dimension editor, Task Lists or Data forms from within Shared Services:

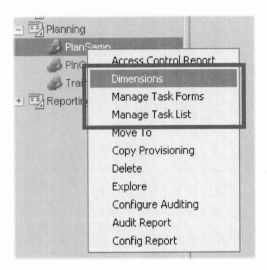

Does anyone see a typo in the menu? Depending on your version, the menu may list "Manage Task Forms" but this really means "Data Forms".

Note in 9.3.1 the menu structure may look slightly different. You may see a menu for Assign Access Control. This will take you to the same place to assign dimension, task list and data form security.

While you can assign object security in Shared Services, most of the time you will use the Planning web client so we will spend our time there.

Before we leave the Shared Services Console, we wanted to highlight one last point. Did you happen to select or double select a Planning application? If you did and you are on version 11, you probably saw the following:

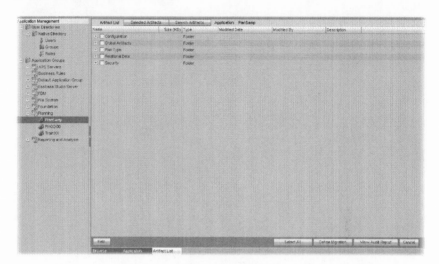

This is the Life Cycle Management interface. For more information, check out the LCM appendix.

ASSIGN PLANNING SECURITY ACCESS

The last part of Planning security is to assign access to all of the components. You will assign member specific security for the Account, Entity, Version, Scenario, and User-Defined Dimensions (if selected). You also need to assign data form folders, data forms, business rule and task list security. Thankfully the steps to do so are the same for all objects. You can perform these steps in the Shared Services Console as noted above or in the Planning web client.

To assign security in the Planning web client, select Administration >> *object for which you need to assign security* (e.g. Dimensions, Manage Data Forms, Manage Task Lists, Business Rules). Next select the desired object (e.g. dimension member Income Statement, data form Plan Revenue, business Rule AggAll or task list Annual Plan) and click Assign Access.

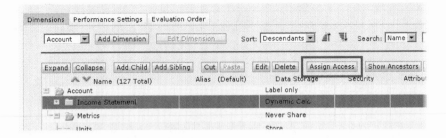

Click the Add Access button to launch the security assignment window.

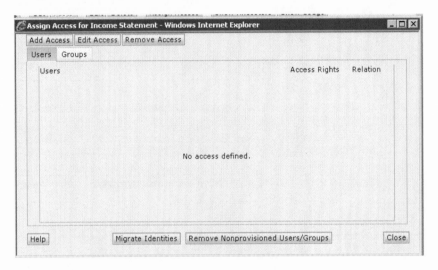

Select the Users or Groups tab. Select the desired User/Group and choose Read, Write or None and choose Member, Children, Children (Inclusive), Descendants, or Descendants (Inclusive):

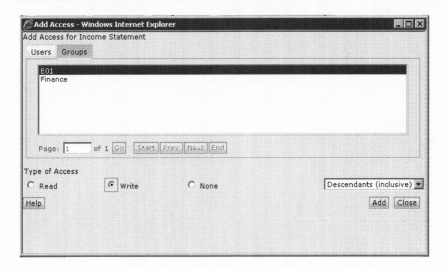

Member security will be assigned for the selected object or in the case of dimensions, member. Children security will be assigned for the children of the member in the dimension but not the member. Children (Inclusive) security will be assigned for the member and its children in the dimension. Descendants and Descendants (Inclusive) are similar to Children / Children (Inclusive) except that all members below the selected member will be assigned access.

Once you've defined the appropriate access, click the Add button and the security will be assigned. To sync the security with Essbase you will need to refresh the database, checking the security option.

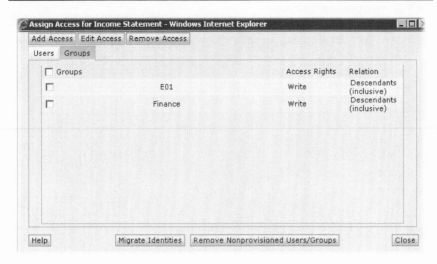

Penny needs to put those steps into action and assign security for the Entpln application.

Assign Security from the Planning Web Client

To assign dimension member security within the Planning web client,

1. Select Administration >> Dimensions.
2. Select the Scenario dimension.
3. Click Actual.
4. Select Assign Access:

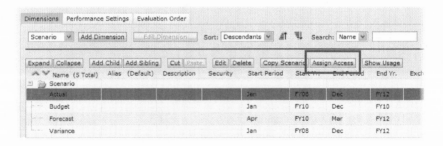

If you need to assign access to a user, select the Users tab. If you need to assign access to a group, select the Groups tab.

5. Select the Groups tab.
6. Click Add Access:

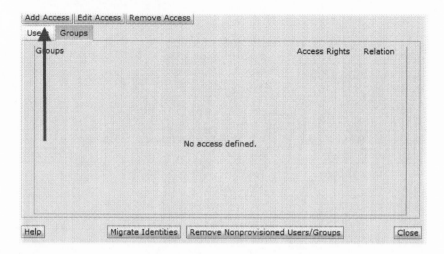

The Add Access window will display the list of available provisioned users and groups. From here you will select the user(s) and/or group(s) and then define their access for the object: read, write or none and Member, Children, Children (Inclusive), Descendants, or Descendants (Inclusive).

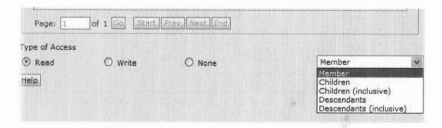

7. Select the Finance group.
8. Select Read.
9. Select Member (Actual has no children or descendants).
10. Click Add.
11. The security should be added. Click Close.

Remember, to assign task list security, select Administration >> Manage Task List to apply task list security using the same steps above. To assign data form folder or data form security, select Administration >> Manage Data Forms. Select the object and click Assign Security. Note security (beginning in version 11.1.1) is inherited from its ancestor data form folders.

Assign the following security for the following objects in Entpln:

Item	Security Access	Group
Account Dimension – IncomeStatement	Write – Descendants Inclusive	Finance, E01
Account Dimension – Metrics	Write – Descendants Inclusive	Finance, E01
Entity Dimension – Total Geography	Write – Descendants Inclusive	Finance
Entity Dimension - Function	Write – Descendants Inclusive	Finance
Entity Dimension – E01	Write – Descendants Inclusive	E01
Scenario – Budget, Forecast	Write – Member	Finance, E01
Scenario - Actual	Read – Member (you already did this one if you followed along with Penny)	Finance, E01
Version – Working, Final, Target, Variance	Write – Member	Finance, E01
TaskList – Annual Budget	Assign	Finance, E01
Forms (main folder)	Read	Finance, E01

Why isn't security assigned by Fiscal Periods or Years? All users have access to all periods and years. You control write access for periods by defining the Start Yr., Start Period, End Yr. and End Period.

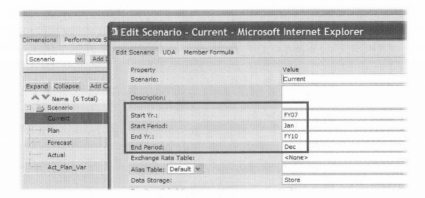

Note! Is it possible to assign cell level security in Planning? Unfortunately no.

If you need to edit or delete security, you will still click the Assign Access button. Click Edit Access or Remove Access instead of selecting Add.

REFRESH SECURITY TO ESSBASE

By now you've been refreshing to Essbase for a while. It is time to check the Security Filters option. The security information you've just assigned is only stored in the relational database. The refresh to Essbase will create security filters required for the Essbase database. Essbase must be in sync with the security information stored in the underlying Planning relational repository. Manage Database is how you sync.

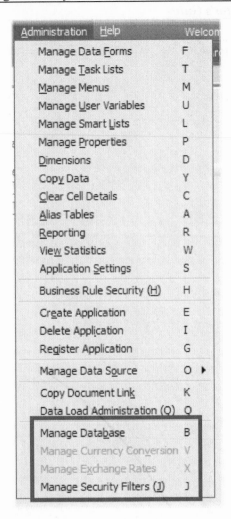

Select Administration >> Manage Database. To refresh security, check Security Filters. You can additionally apply security to Shared Members and validate the limit of security filters (4KB per row).

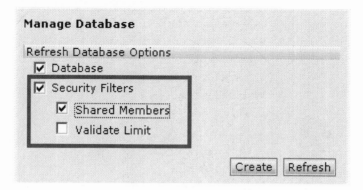

Refresh the security filters for the Entpln application.

Try It!

Refreshing all of security can be a time consuming process. You can update security filters by individual user if desired (versus updating all security filters when they may not have changed). This is helpful when you make a change to one user and don't want update all other users. To update specific security filters select Administration >> Manage Security Filters.

Well, congratulations, Penny. The created application has dimensions, data, business rules, data forms, and finally, security. The plan is ready for budgeting! It's definitely time to call Eddie.

Penny gulps. This is it. She picks up the phone and dials Eddie's extension...

MANAGE ORACLE HYPERION PLANNING

Scene 14:
Planning Under the Covers

Penny places the phone back on the receiver and begins talking to herself in a way that makes her coworkers question her sanity: "I can't do it. I need to be fully prepared. What if Eddie has an issue during the budgeting process? I need to be able to fully manage and administer Planning. What do I need to know to successfully manage Planning?"

To become an all knowing, all seeing Planning administrator, you have to understand some of the more complex aspects of Planning and Essbase. So let's pull back the covers and take a look.

RELATIONAL REPOSITORY

Planning stores most of its metadata in an underlying relational repository. Along with a DBA, it can be helpful to understand the tables and information. The utilities provide supported ways to add or update data in these tables. The key to the Planning tables is the HSP_Object, the main listing of all objects in Planning. HSP_OBJECT_TYPE is the reference table for items in HSP_OBJECT table.

Note you will be unsupported by Oracle if you change data in the tables directly.

ESSBASE BSO DIRECTORY STRUCTURE

Planning stores all of its data in Essbase so we will tackle the Essbase directory structure. The Essbase directory structure contains folders and files created when you install the program. In the 11x version, Essbase uses a system variable called ESSBASEPATH for this directory structure. Older versions of Essbase used a system variable called ARBORPATH which you still see hanging around in 11x. These environment variables are %ESSBASEPATH% and %ARBORPATH% in Windows and $ESSBASEPATH and $ARBORPATH in UNIX. Because both variables are the same, we will refer to it generically as "arborpath" (we love you Arbor Software, may you rest in pieces).

- arborpath\bin stores Essbase executables, the Essbase.cfg configuration file, the Essbase.sec security definition file, and the Essbase.bak backup security file.
- arborpath\app stores server-based applications (more on this shortly).
- arborpath\client stores any client based files and applications.
- arborpath\docs stores online documentation.
- arborpath\locale contains the character-set files necessary for multi-language use.

Need To Know – Essbase Executables

Helpful
Info

Stored in *arborpath*\bin
- Essbase.exe – Essbase server agent process
- Esssvr.exe – application process
- Essmsh.exe – MaxL shell
- Esscmd.exe – Esscmd command line interface

Stored in *eas*\Server\bin
- Starteas.exe – start the Administration Server executable
- Admincon.exe – Administration Services Console application

The *arborpath*\app directory contains all of the application files. An application will contain databases. For block storage databases, you may have up to three databases (more if you are using Planning and the Workforce Planning or Capital Expenditure modules). Each database will contain one outline file. Other objects like calc scripts in BSO databases and rules files can be stored at the application or database level.

Let's take a look at the directory structure for Sample.Basic:

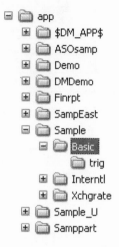

Tip!

You can store rules files, calc scripts, and report scripts at the application OR database level. If you have a calc script that will be run against one or more databases, store this script at the application level once instead of stored multiple times at the database level.

CALCULATE THE BLOCK SIZE

We've already learned the basics about the Essbase block structure in the calc script scene. Blocks are composed of dense members. In the case below, Measures, Time and Scenario are dense dimensions. The dense members, like Jan at Profit at Actual, make up the cells within the block.

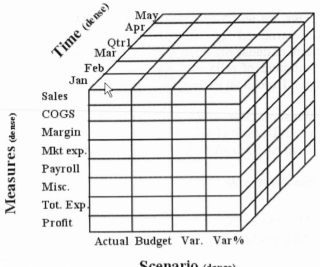

Scenario (dense)

A unique block is created for each intersection of the sparse members. Product and Market are sparse dimensions in the example below. A block is created for Cola at New York, for Cola at Florida, for Cola at East, and so forth.

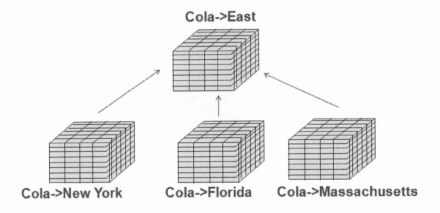

So what else is there to know? And why do you care? Oh, if only we could go back to the innocence of a new Planning administrator. Everything seemed so simple – dimensions, hierarchies, and spreadsheets. Understanding these components helps us more effectively tune and optimize our Planning databases. Let's start digging.

First, we will learn how to calculate block size. Data block size is determined by the amount of data in a particular combination of dense dimensions. Data block size is $8n$ bytes, where n is the number of cells that exist for that combination of dense dimensions. Here is an example:

Measures (Dense): 40 stored members
Time (Dense): 17 stored members
Scenario (Dense): 2 stored members

Block size = 40 * 17 * 2 * 8 = 10880 bytes or 11 KB

Note! Use the number of stored members when calculating block size, not the total number of members.

Despite what the Essbase Database Administrator's Guide says, we recommend a block size of about 8 KB in 32 bit Essbase. Larger block sizes will hurt parallel calculations (which is what most of your calculations will be these days). Too small block sizes may result in an increased index file size. This forces Essbase to write and retrieve the index from disk, slowing calculations When in doubt, err on the side of smaller. That is, 1 KB is better than 40 KB. Unless you're using 64-bit Essbase (in which case 1+ MB block sizes are not abnormal), avoid blocks larger than 40 KB and strongly avoid blocks larger than 100 KB.

Tip! As with anything Essbase, these guidelines are not definitive and are just a starting point. Hence, the term "guideline". We have implemented applications that violated the block size guideline and still realized fast performance.

Let's calculate the block size for our Entpln.Sum database. We have two dense dimensions right now: Account and Period. The period dimension has 19 stored members and the account dimension has 77 stored members:

Database Properties: [TRN113.Entpln.Sum]				

Database: **TRN113.Entpln.Sum**   Status: **Loaded**

General Dimensions Statistics Caches Transactions Storage Currency Modifications

Number of dimensions 6

Dimension	Type	Members in Dimension	Members Stored
Period	Dense	21	19
Account	Dense	123	77
Entity	Sparse	150	120
Version	Sparse	4	4
Scenario	Sparse	5	4
FiscalYear	Sparse	6	6

So the block size for the Sum plan type is $17*19*8 = 11{,}704$ bytes or 11 KB.

Calculate the block size for the Entpln.Rev plan type.

Try It!

Oh, we forgot to mention that Essbase also calculates the block size for you. Select the database and right-click. Select Edit >> Properties. Select the Statistics tab:

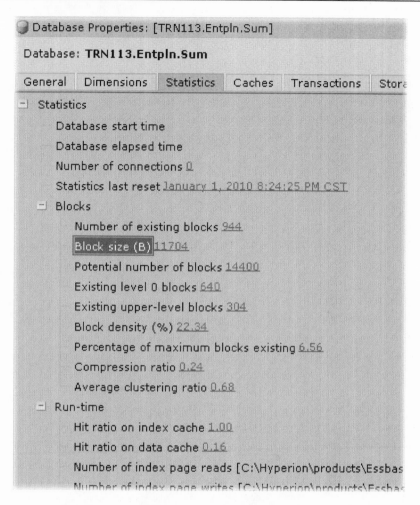

So why did we teach you how to calculate block size? One, it is important to understand the concept of what members make up a block. Getting the block size to a reasonable size is important in tuning. You can reduce block size by making more members dynamic and changing a dense dimension to sparse. Two, you may want to use this calculation when you are performing an initial design to figure out your starting point dense and sparse dimensions.

CALCULATE THE NUMBER OF BLOCKS

So now we know the size of the data blocks. But how many blocks could we possibly have? A block is created for each unique intersection of stored sparse members. So to calculate the total possible blocks, multiply the number for stored members for each sparse dimension. The sparse dimension member counts for Entpln.Sum are:

Database Properties: [TRN113.Entpln.Sum]			
Database: **TRN113.Entpln.Sum**		Status: **Loaded**	

General Dimensions Statistics Caches Transactions Storage Currency Modifications

Number of dimensions 6

Dimension	Type	Members in Dimension	Members Stored
Period	Dense	21	19
Account	Dense	123	77
Entity	Sparse	150	120
Version	Sparse	4	4
Scenario	Sparse	5	4
FiscalYear	Sparse	6	6

Number of Possible Blocks = 120*4*4*6 = 14400

This time we will mention up front that Essbase also calculates the total possible blocks for you. Select the database and right-click. Select Edit >> Properties. Select the Statistics tab again:

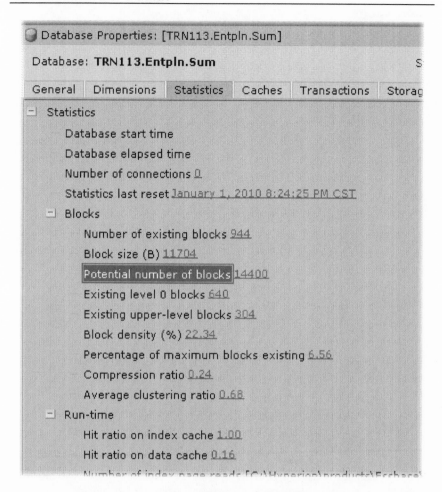

When you see this number for a production database, you may get really scared. This number will probably be really big, sometimes into the quadrillions. But remember, we've tagged these dimensions sparse for a reason. The likelihood that data exists for every single combination is very, very rare. So we recommend you understand this concept but don't worry about it any further (don't you just love it when the teacher teaches you something that you won't ever really use?). In certain cases, really large potential block counts (in excess of 100 trillion) can cause inefficient calcs, so watch out if you see this occurring.

The more helpful statistic is the number of existing blocks. Make sure you have loaded and calculated the database before you check this statistic. Go back to the Statistics tab under Database Properties:

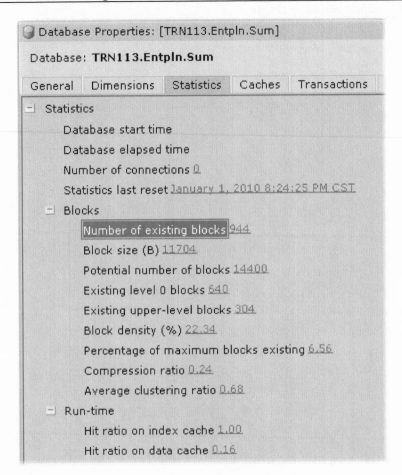

While you are there, note that Essbase also tracks the number of existing level-zero blocks and upper level blocks.

INDEX AND PAGE FILES

The index file is a file that contains pointers to all of the different blocks in the database. The index file is named ess*n*.ind and is stored in your database directory (n starts with 00001 and increments by 1 every time the file size reaches 2 GB). Essbase uses this file to locate the blocks that are requested during Essbase operations.

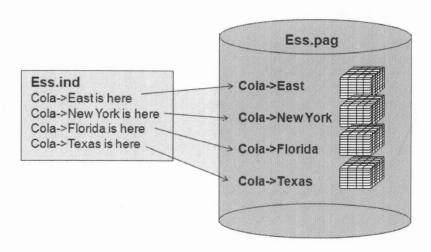

Data is stored in page files, named ess*n*.pag and stored in the database directory (also starting with 00001 and incrementing every 2 GB). These files are stored in the database directory. Essbase uses both the index and page files when performing operations on data blocks.

Try It!

Find the index and page files for the Entpln Sum plan type. Let's open the page files and take a look at the data. WAIT! We caught you again. This was another trick "Try It!" Do not open the page or index files. Ever. Always leave these files alone (unless you are backing them up). You cannot view data via the page files or a list of sparse blocks in the index file. If you open these files, not only will you see quite a bit of mumbo jumbo, you will probably corrupt your application and database. Don't say we didn't warn you.

Memory (index and data caches) can be set aside to help performance during operations. The index cache stores a portion or all of the index in memory for quicker access. The data cache stores a portion of the data blocks in memory for quicker access. We'll show you how to define these memory caches in the Design and Optimize scene.

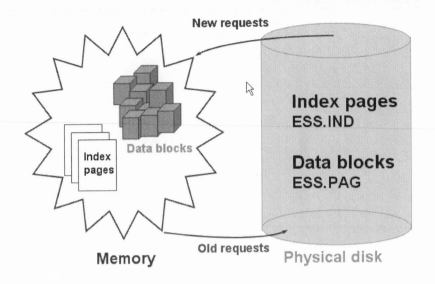

Did you know that interRel Consulting provides free concierge service for every paying client? Just kidding. We wanted to make sure you were still awake and paying attention through this valuable but dry and slightly boring section (OK, really boring section).

RESTRUCTURING FOR ESSBASE

Restructuring of your Planning databases takes place after the outline changes, like when you add new, edit, and delete members and dimensions. Any and every change forces Essbase to restructure the database, so think of it as "re-saving" the database. This can be a time consuming process depending on the type of restructure and database size.

A full restructure, the most time consuming type of restructure, will take place when an outline is updated with the movement, deletion, or addition of a member from a dense dimension. This will reorganize every data block in the page file and regenerate the index. A re-calculation will also be required.

A sparse restructure is a much faster type of restructure and takes place when you move, delete, or add a member from a sparse dimension. This type of restructure regenerates the index file but does not restructure the data blocks.

An outline restructure is the last type of restructure and will take place when you make a change that impacts the outline only, like changing an alias or member formula. This restructure will not regenerate the index file or restructure the data blocks, so is very quick indeed.

Note!

Each action you perform on Planning dimensions will cause some type of restructure. For a full list of the actions and what type of restructure will occur, see the Essbase Database Administrator's Guide and search for a table called "How Actions Affect Databases and Restructuring".

If your restructuring times are too long and impacting your users, consider the following tuning tips:

- If you change a dimension frequently, make it sparse.
- Use incremental restructuring to control when Essbase performs a required database restructuring.
- Push dense dimension changes to a nightly process where a longer batch window is acceptable.

While Penny is moving and grooving in the more technical aspects of Planning (this can be fun stuff for the IT oriented), you may be ready to jump ship. Don't put on your swimsuit just yet, the Translator is about to break out in song for Planning Administration.

Scene 15:
Planning Administration

Just as Mr. Anachronism is about to sing a fun ditty on workflow in Planning, the lights dim and a spotlight forms on him. His eyes glaze over and his body is suddenly rigid. As if seeing something far off, he mumbles, "I'm seeing something in the future; big trouble for Eddie..." and begins to describe the dire premonition.

MANAGE WORKFLOW

Just as Eddie is about to realize his happy ending, Dr. Dementor, the super villain with the deathray, appears from nowhere.

"I, Dr. Dementor, will see to it that those highly priced but deservedly so consultants and those HR policy violating employees, Eddie and Penny, will never be able to approve the budget in time. The first step in making sure that their company went bankrupt was killing Jack with that large motorized vehicle. Then I tried to sabotage their System 9 implementation but that superhero, Aquaman, foiled my plan. Now I will put the rest of my deliciously evil, deliberately vague plan into action to stop the budget approval! Bahahaha!"

"Eddie, what are we going to do?" Penny cries in an 'empowered female' sort of way.

"Don't worry, Penny. Just tell me how to use Planning workflow process management and we'll get this plan approved," Eddie says with determination. "After everything we've been through, we *can* get the budget approved, even if Dr. Dementor kills us with his deathray."

Eddie's commitment to finishing the budget even at the expense of his own life calms Penny, distracting her from the deathray pointed right at her chest. "OK, Eddie. Let's promote this plan through the Oracle Hyperion Planning process management component."

Introduction to Workflow

Workflow is the process management procedure for reviewing and approving budgets and is performed through the web client (as of version 11.1.1).

The budget administrator begins the review process by starting a planning unit. A planning unit is the combination of entity, scenario and version. It's used in the review and approval of plans. The Start action changes the state of the planning unit to First Pass, which is the beginning state of the review process. During the First Pass state, the budget administrator may choose to exclude some or all of the entities from the workflow process.

When the planning unit is ready to undergo the formal review process, any user (with read or write access) may promote a planning unit from First Pass to Under Review and take ownership of the planning unit. Once ownership is assigned, only the current owner or the Planning administrator can modify data or perform an action on a planning unit. This maintains the integrity of the data and the values entered by each user.

"So the CFO can't change my budget without my knowledge?" Eddie asks incredulously. The CFO always sneaks changes into the plan and then holds Eddie accountable for the new and not improved numbers for which he had no input.

"That's right, Eddie. Just for you, I assigned Read access for the CFO so any changes must go through you," Penny smiles.

"I love you so much right now," Eddie says oblivious to any threats of imminent death.

"Umm... I'm about to kill you with my deathray," reminds Dr. Dementor.

Once the planning unit is in an Under Review state, it may undergo several iterations of promotions, sign offs, and rejections before it is finally approved. Once a planning unit is approved, the Planning administrator becomes the owner of the planning unit.

 Note! A planning unit may also skip a number of process states. For example, a budget administrator may approve a started planning unit from any state and change it to an Approved state.

The process above discusses workflow by base level entities but workflow can be managed at a higher level with parent entities as well.

Workflow States and Actions

There are six process states available:

Not Started. The initial state of all planning units. The budget administrator initiates the review process using the Start action.

First Pass. The first state for planning units selected to go through the budgeting process. There is no owner of a planning unit during First Pass. Any user with data access can enter data and promote the planning unit during the First Pass state.

Under Review. This state occurs when a Promote action is taken on a planning unit and signifies that a planning unit is being reviewed by someone in the organization. Only the current owner or the budget administrator can modify data or perform an action on a planning unit that is in the Under Review state.

Signed Off. This state occurs when a Sign Off action is taken on a planning unit. Only the current owner or the budget administrator can modify data or perform an action on a planning unit that is in a Signed Off state. Ownership does not change when a planning unit is signed off.

Not Signed Off. This state occurs when a Reject action is taken on a planning unit. Only the current owner or the budget administrator can modify data or perform an action on a planning unit that is in a Not Signed Off state.

Approved. This state occurs when an Approve action is taken on a planning unit. After a planning unit is approved, the budget administrator becomes the owner of the planning unit. Only the budget administrator can modify data or perform an action on a planning unit that is in an Approved state. Once all the planning units are approved, the budgeting cycle is complete.

Note!

In all states except the Not Started state, all users with read access can view data, view the process state, view the history, and read and enter new annotations.

There are four workflow actions:

Promote. Take this action when you are ready for another user to review the planning unit. This action assigns ownership of a planning unit the first time, and thereafter transfers ownership of a planning unit from one reviewer to another. Promote causes an implicit sign-off by the current owner and changes the state of the planning unit to Under Review.

Sign Off. This action indicates you are signing off on a planning unit. Sign Off does not transfer ownership of the planning unit, but changes the state of the planning unit to Signed Off.

Reject. This action indicates you are not satisfied with the planning unit, and typically requires the previous owner or the originator to create another iteration. By default, Reject reverts ownership of the planning unit back to the previous owner.

However, you may also select the next owner of the planning unit. A Reject action changes the state of the planning unit to Not Signed Off.

Approve. This action indicates you approve the planning unit. Approve changes the state of the planning unit to Approved. A planning unit can be approved from any state except Not Started. However, only an administrator can approve from a Not Signed Off or First Pass state. Approving a planning unit causes an implicit sign-off by the reviewer.

 Typically, a planning unit is approved only once. An administrator can, however, reject a previously approved **Note!** planning unit.

Now that we've covered workflow from a conceptual standpoint, let's start reviewing and promoting the plan before Dr. Dementor kills everyone..

Check the Status of a Planning Unit

To check a planning unit's status:

1.   Select File >> Workflow >> Manage Process:

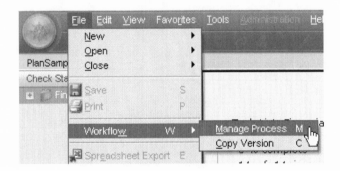

2.   From the Scenario drop-down list, select a Scenario (for our example, we'll choose "Plan").
3.   From the Version drop-down list, select a Version (for our example, we'll choose "Working"):

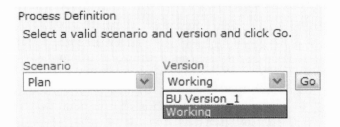

4. Click Go and the list of entities for the scenario and version for which you have access will display with their status and current owner:

Process Definition
Select a valid scenario and version and click Go.

Scenario	Version		
Plan ▾	Working ▾	Go	

Entity	Process Status	Current Owner	Action
E01_0	First Pass	Not Available	Details
E01_101_1110	First Pass	Not Available	Details
E01_101_1120	First Pass	Not Available	Details
E01_101_1130	First Pass	Not Available	Details
E01_101_1100	First Pass	Not Available	Details
E01_101_1210	First Pass	Not Available	Details
E01_101_1220	First Pass	Not Available	Details
E01_101_1230	First Pass	Not Available	Details
E01_101_1200	First Pass	Not Available	Details
E01_101_1310	First Pass	Not Available	Details
E01_101_1320	First Pass	Not Available	Details
E01_101_1300	First Pass	Not Available	Details
E01_101_1410	First Pass	Not Available	Details
E01_101_1420	First Pass	Not Available	Details
E01_101_1400	First Pass	Not Available	Details
E01_101_1000	First Pass	Not Available	Details
E01_101_2110	First Pass	Not Available	Details
E01_101_2120	First Pass	Not Available	Details
E01_101_2130	First Pass	Not Available	Details

If you have a long list of entities, you can Ctrl+F to search for a particular entity.

To view the details of the planning unit status,

5. Click Details link in the Action column for a planning unit.

Historic information is displayed for process status, owner, actions taken, and the date and times of status change.

Take Ownership of a Planning Unit

At the beginning of the plan process, the Planning Administrator will start all or specific Planning units for workflow. For a user to take ownership of the planning unit, they must promote it to themselves. This will prevent other users with write access from changing plan data. (Some of these steps will seem a bit familiar).

1. Select File >> Workflow >> Manage Process:

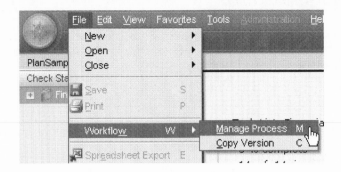

2. From the Scenario drop-down list, select a Scenario (for our example, we'll choose "Plan").

3. From the Version drop-down list, select a Version (for our example, we'll choose "Working"):

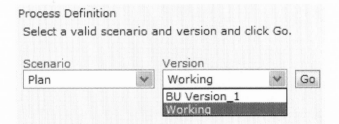

4. Click Go and the list of entities for the scenario and version for which you have access will display:

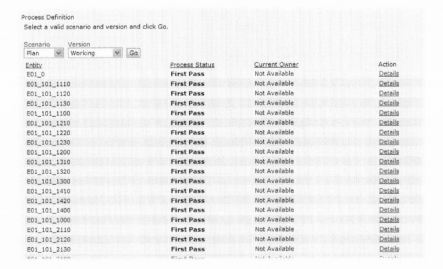

The entities listed above for Plan and Working are in a state of First Pass with no current owner. You see the full list of entities for which you have either read or write access. Notice that upper level entities are shown as well as level zero entities.

Note! Your workflow view may look a bit different if other users have been testing workflow in the Planning sample application.

Also notice that by default the member names are displayed. Let's change the view to display the aliases instead.

5. Select File >> Preferences from the Workspace menu.
6. Select Planning and the Planning preferences will display.
7. Under Workflow Options, change the drop-down box next to Show Planning Units as Aliases to "Yes":

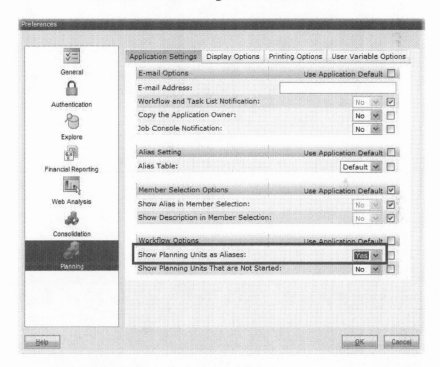

8. Click OK.

To refresh the list, we have to go back through the steps completed earlier.

9. Select File >> Workflow >> Manage Process.

10. From the Scenario drop-down list, select *Plan*.
11. From the Version drop-down list, select Working.
12. Click Go and the aliases for the entities should display:

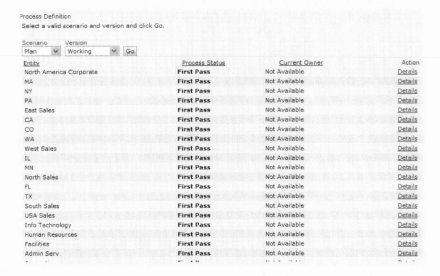

13. Click Details under the Action column for the Entity "MA" (if MA is owned by another user in your application, choose an entity with a current owner of "Not Available"). The following window will display:

14. Click Change Status.
15. From the Select Action drop-down list, select an action - Promote.
16. From the Select Next Owner drop-down list, select your Planning ID (brubble, in the example below):

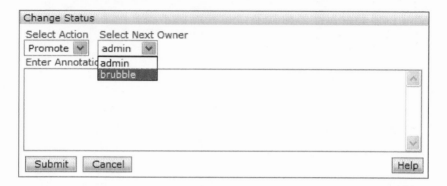

17. Optional: In the Enter Annotation text box, enter any comments:

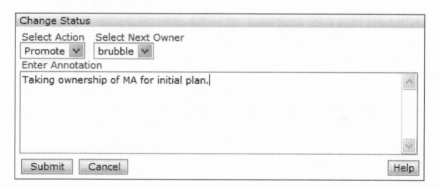

18. Click Submit.

The planning unit status is changed from First Pass to Under Review and the owner is now you (in our example brubble). You can also view the last action, date of that action and the new annotation just posted:

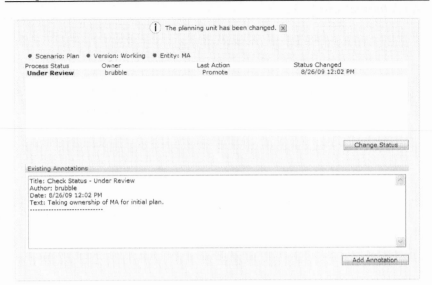

19. Click *Done* to return to the main workflow screen where you now see the planning unit MA->Plan->Working is owned by brubble (or you) and it is Under Review:

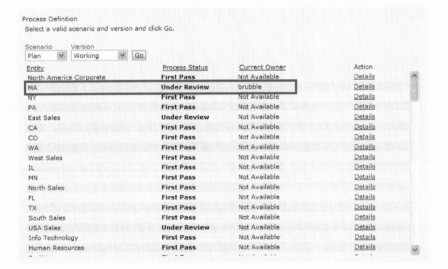

Note! Taking ownership of a planning unit is really just changing the status.

Change the Status of a Planning Unit

Changing the status of a planning unit allows you to select an action for that planning unit, such as Promote, Sign Off, Reject or Approve, as well the ability to select the next owner. As an extra option you can also enter annotations while changing the status.

To change the status of a planning unit,
1. Select File >> Workflow >> Manage Process.
2. From the Scenario drop-down list, select a Scenario (Plan).
3. From the Version drop-down list, select a Version (Working).
4. Click Go.
5. Click Details under the Action column for the Entity MA.
6. Click Change Status.
7. From the Select Action drop-down list, you can select an action – Promote, Sign Off, Reject or Approve:

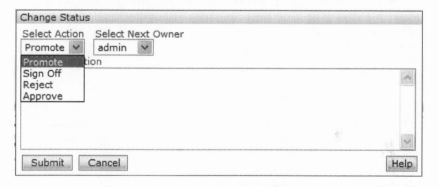

8. For our example, choose Sign Off.
9. From the Select Next Owner drop-down list, select the next owner of the planning unit. For this example, choose your Planning ID:
10. If you have any comments, type them into the Enter Annotation box:

11. Click Submit.
12. Click Done:

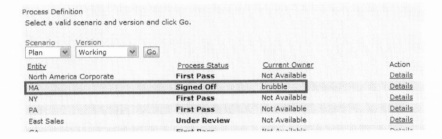

If you change the status of a parent entity (e.g. East Sales), all its children change too (MA, NY, PA), unless they were excluded during the First Pass state or already approved.

Copy Versions

Copy Version is a feature within workflow that allows end users to copy data for a planning unit from one version to another. For example, a user is budgeting in the Working version. Once the version has been approved, they should copy all of the data from Working to Final version. Copy versions functionality will copy data as well as Account Annotations, Cell Text and Supporting Detail if desired.

To access the Copy Version feature:

1. Click File >> Workflow >> Copy Version.

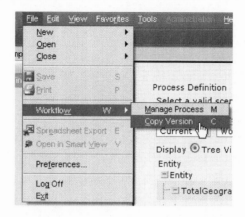

2. Select the Scenario, the source Version, and the target Version. For our example, choose:
   a. Scenario: Plan
   b. Source Version: Working
   c. Target Version: BU_Version1

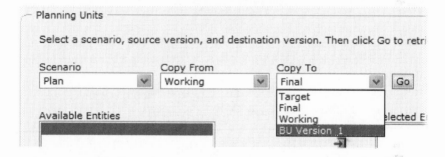

3. Click Go.

After you click "Go" you will see a list of Available Entities. Select the entities whose data you want to copy from the Available Entities box, and transfer them over to the Selected Entities section.

4. Select Entity E01_101_1120 and move to the Selected Entities section.

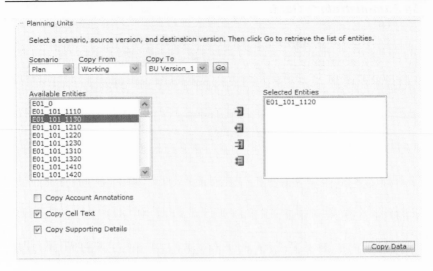

You might also see the following warning at the top of the screen to take note of if you copy to Target:

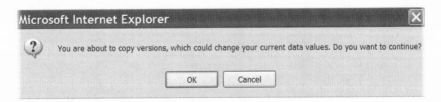

Once you have selected your entities you can choose if you want to copy the Account Annotations, Cell Text and Supporting detail.

5. Check Copy Cell Text and Copy Support Details.
6. Finally, click Copy Data.
7. Click OK if you are prompted with the following message:

Microsoft Internet Explorer

(?) You are about to copy versions, which could change your current data values. Do you want to continue?

[OK] [Cancel]

Look for the following successful message:

(i) The version has been successfully copied. ⊠

Once data has been copied from a version, you will need to run Business Rules to aggregate data to upper levels or perform other calculation logic.

Annotate the Plan

Annotations let you add or view comments about the data in a planning unit (combination of Scenario, Entity, and Version) that has been started.

To view or add an annotation, you simply follow the steps we reviewed earlier, skipping the Change Status portion of the planning unit Details screen.

1. Click File > > Workflow >> Manage Process button.
2. Select the desired Scenario and Version.
3. Click Go.
4. Click Details under the Action column for the entity for which you want to add a planning unit.

From this screen you can view all of the annotations sorted chronically for the planning unit.

To add an annotation,

5. Click Add Annotations.
6. Enter a title in the Enter Title text box.
7. Enter your comments (up to 1500 characters) in the Enter Annotation text box:

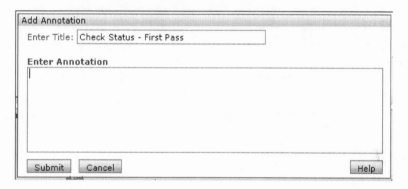

8. Click Submit.

The Translator's premonition fades as Dr. Dementor raises his deathray at Penny and Eddie and prepares to fire (mostly out of boredom). Mr. Anachronism shakes his head, instantly alert. "That's all there is," Mr. Anachronism says weakly.

"What do you mean 'that's all there is'?!?" Penny desperately cries (but again, in a 'female empowerment' sort of way, not in a 'women are weak and need men to save them' sort of way).

Mr. Anachronism shrugs. "I don't see anything else. But I'm sure it is nothing to worry about. On to more topics for administering Planning applications."

APPLICATION SETTINGS

Planning provides a number of settings that can be defined by application: current application defaults, display settings, and advanced settings. For each application, you can enable certain application defaults like enable email notification (users receive an email when they become the new owner of a planning unit), copy the owner (application owner receives a copy of all email notifications), default alias table, whether to show alias and/or description for member selection, whether to show Planning unit aliases in Workflow and show Planning units that have not been started.

Display settings can also be defined under application settings. Options include specify number formatting, retain page and POV selections, enable warnings for large forms and more. Follow along with us as we set application settings for our Entpln.

In the Advanced system settings, you specify the email server and administrator email address, task list date format, and Shared Services registration information. You can choose to show the full user name instead of id for Workflow. An important setting that you will definitely use is Application Maintenance mode. You can define when users or other administrators can access the application. For example, if you want to take the system down for maintenance, you can turn off access for end users.

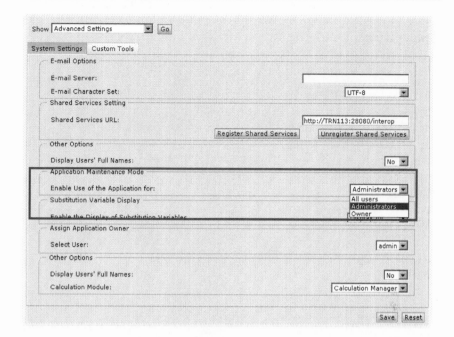

Advanced System Settings is also where you can change the application owner.

Under Advanced Settings >> Custom Tools, you can add customized links to your Planning application by user type (Basic, Interactive, or Administrator). Users access the links by selecting Tools >> Links.

To hit home some of the application settings, let's set the application settings for Entpln

1. Select Administration >> Application Settings.
2. Select Current Application Defaults and click Go.
3. Review all of the available Current Application Defaults - Application Settings.
4. On the Application Settings tab, change the following options:
   a. Show Alias in Member Selection – Yes.
   b. Show Planning Units as Aliases – Yes:

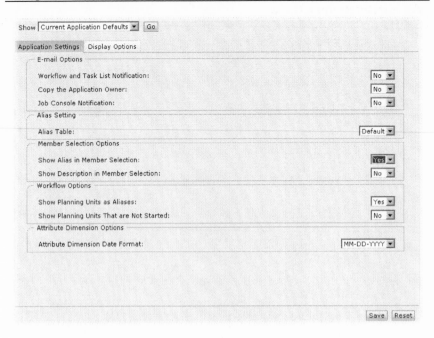

5. On the Display options tab, change the following options:
   a. Allow Search When Number of Pages Exceeds: 5
   b. Indentation of Members on Page: Indent based on Hierarchy.
   c. Set Warn if data form larger than cells specified: 7500

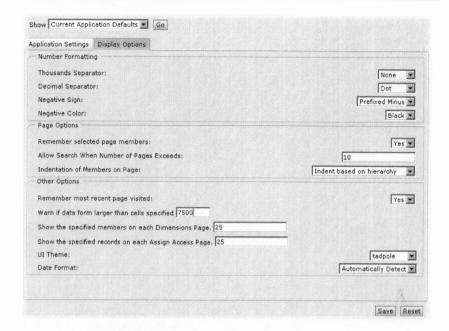

6. Click Save.
7. Select Advanced Settings and click Go.
8. Review all of the available options.
9. On the System Settings tab, set Enable Use for Application for Administrator (helpful when you want to keep users out of Planning):

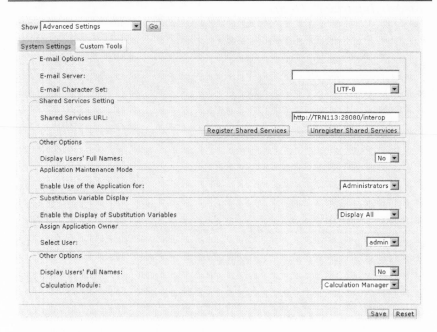

10. On the Custom Tools tab, add a link to interRel's website – www.interrel.com – for interactive users to view:

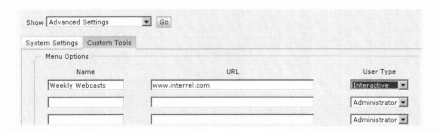

Now make sure to communicate to users that they can choose to accept application defaults or set their own preferences.

1. Select File >> Preferences.
2. Select Planning preferences.
3. For Application Settings, check all of the boxes to use Application Defaults (users can choose to use the application defaults or set their own preferences):

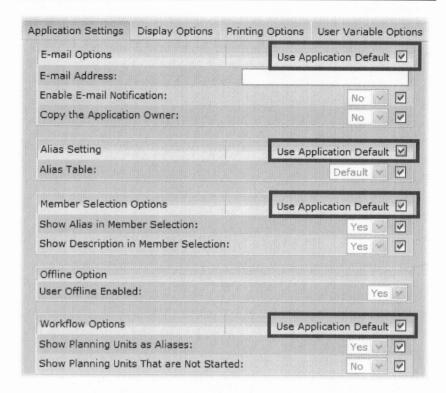

4. For Display Options tab, check all of the boxes to use Application Defaults.
5. Open the Plan Revenue – All Years data form and note the changes.

MANAGE PROPERTIES

A number of Planning properties exist. Select Administration >> Manage Properties to tune settings for the Planning application. The properties are saved in the HSPSYS_PROPERTIES system database table. In earlier versions, you updated this information in a file on the server manually.

Property Name	Property Value
EDIT_DIM_ENABLED	true
ENABLE_FOR_OFFLINE	true
JDBC_MAX_CONNECTIONS	10
JDBC_MIN_CONNECTIONS	1
OLAP_MAX_CONNECTIONS	10
OLAP_MIN_CONNECTIONS	1
SUPPORTING_DETAIL_CACHE_SIZE	20
SYNC_USER_ON_LOGON	true

Application Properties   System Properties

Add

Save Reset

VIEW STATISTICS

As an administrator, you can view the names of users logged on to the Planning application as well as the last time a user has accessed the Planning application. You can also tell how much available supporting detail cache exists (if this is 100%, then you may want to increase this cache setting).

To view statistics,

1. Select Administration >> View Statistics:

Administration Help	
Manage Data Forms	F
Manage Task Lists	T
Manage Menus	M
Manage User Variables	U
Manage Smart Lists	L
Manage Properties	P
Dimensions	D
Copy Data	Y
Clear Cell Details	C
Alias Tables	A
Reporting	R
View Statistics	W

The stats will display:

Application:	Entpln
Users:	1
Supporting Detail Detection Cache Usage: 0%	

| User Name | Time since last access (hh:mm:ss) |
| admin | 00:00:00 |

COPY DATA

Another handy admin feature is the copy data feature. Planning administrators can copy the entire plan from one year to another or from a specific intersection to another. For example, the Planning Administrator may be ready to copy revenue data to the final version while expenses are still in draft versions. The Copy Data feature copies all relational data, including supporting detail, account annotations, and cell text, from one dimensional intersection to another dimensional intersection. The settings that you select in the Copy Data page are preserved for the current session only. Members and dimensions that you copy must be present in the selected plan types and data must be copied into cells that can accept data.

Note!   You cannot copy planning unit annotations.

Note!   Calculations must be run after using the Copy Data feature.

To copy data,
1. Select Administration >> Copy Data.

In the following example, you need to copy all expense data for North America for all periods for next year's Budget from Sandbox to Final.

2. Set the following options to do so including cell text and supporting detail:

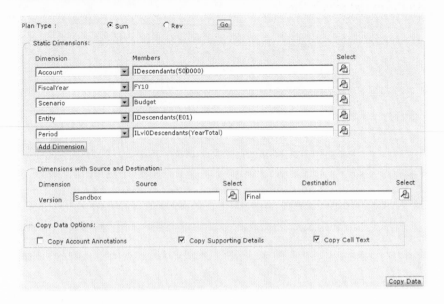

3. Click Copy Data.

Just as you've done in the other member selection windows, you can use functions and variables to identify members. You can type directly into the text box if you know the exact member name or use the member selection icon.

CLEAR CELL DETAILS

You may at times want to clear cell details for a dimensional intersection like supporting detail or cell text. In version 9.3.1, you have to go to the backend tables to do this. In version 11, you have the Clear Cell Details feature in the Planning web client.

To clear cell details,

1. Select Administration >> Clear Cell Details:

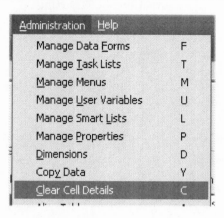

2. Select the plan type, dimensions, members and clear
    options:

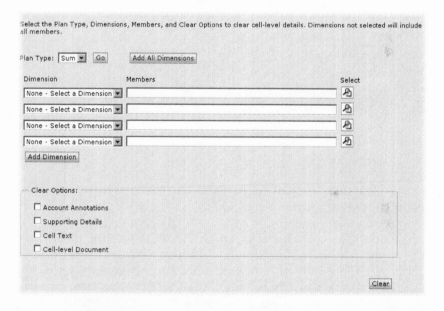

3. Click Clear.

REPORTING

Planning provides standard administration reports
available for data forms and planning unit annotations. They also
included audit tracking features under Reporting (for some strange
reason) even though no audit reports are actually available.

To run Planning reports,

1. Click Administration >> Reporting.
2. Create a Form Definition report by selecting one or more data forms on the Data Forms tab.
3. Move the selected data forms into the Selected Data Forms section.
4. Optionally check Include Member Selection List and Business Rules:

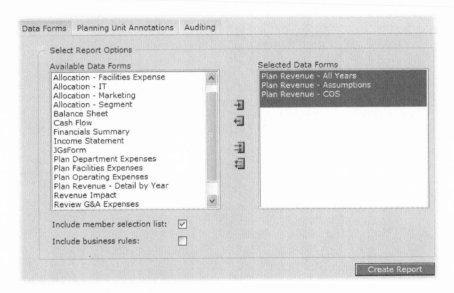

5. Click Create Report.

This is a helpful documentation tool for form definitions. Planning unit annotations reports follow similar steps.

Next lets discuss auditing, a Planning feature that tracks the who, when, and what of Planning actions. There is a performance consideration so only track those items you need. For example, if you only have 1 or 2 administrators that manage Planning, don't worry about tracking the administrative tasks. Focus on tracking those actions of end users like data changes, business rules and copy version.

Audit details capture the following information:

- Data Form: Expenses 04
- Group: Marketing
- User SBakey
- Time Posted 12/12/2005 9:17

- Action Add
- Property Currency
- Old value Default
- New value USD

You should archive off audit tables periodically. You must use SQL to access backend table. To clear the audit tables you will run a SQL delete statement similar to the following:

```
DELETE FROM HSP_AUDIT_RECORDS
```

To view audit records, sorted by the time they were posted will as expected require SQL:

```
SELECT * FROM HSP_AUDIT_RECORDS ORDER BY TIME_POSTED
```

Our last Planning administration topic is an important one: the Planning utilities. These utilities can save you hours in development and administration so definitely read this section.

PLANNING UTILITIES

The Hyperion Planning utilities can be found in the HYPERION_HOME\products\Planning\bin folder. The picture below shows the Planning\bin folder and all the utilities available in version 11.1.1.1 (note a few of these are not available in 9.3.1). In this section we will review and show you examples of each utility.

We will start with PasswordEncryption.cmd as the output password file can be used by the other utilities. PasswordEncryption.cmd and OutlineLoad.cmd were introduced in version 11.1.1. Planning utilities need to be run on the server where Planning is installed, they can be executed from the command line or from batch files that can be scheduled using third party scheduling tools.

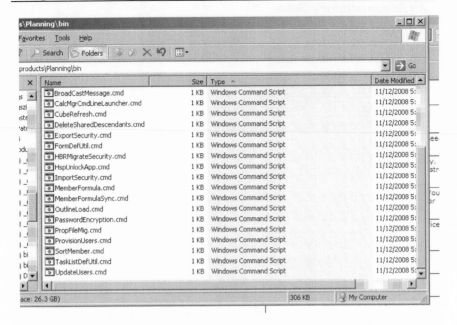

PasswordEncryption.cmd

The Password Encryption utility, introduced in version 11.1.1, creates files that store an encrypted password for use by other Planning utilities. Each file may contain only one password. You choose the location and the name of each file when running the utility. Once you create a password file, you can run other utilities from the command line or from batch files with the option "[-f:passwordFile]" as a parameter instead of typing the password.

This utility is normally located in the HYPERION_HOME\Products\Planning\bin folder with the other Planning utilities.

In order to create a password encryption file with the Password Encryption utility in a Windows environment, use: PasswordEncryption.cmd with the name and path of the password File; In a UNIX environment use: PasswordEncryption.sh with the name and path of the password File, you will be prompted to enter the password to encrypt.

Open the command line, go to the Planning bin folder, enter PasswordEncryption.cmd with the name and path of the password File, and enter the password to encrypt.

Try It!

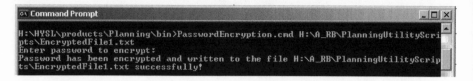

You will see a notification that your password has been encrypted and stored in the location you indicated:

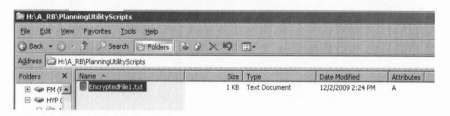

Go to the specified folder location and you will see the file:

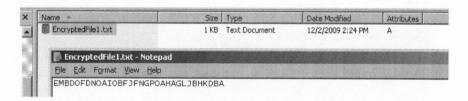

Open the file:

Name	Size	Type	Date Modified	Attributes
Encryp... Open	1 KB	Text Document	12/2/2009 2:24 PM	A

You will see the password is stored in the file in encrypted form:

Name	Size	Type	Date Modified	Attributes
EncryptedFile1.txt	1 KB	Text Document	12/2/2009 2:24 PM	A

EncryptedFile1.txt - Notepad
File Edit Format View Help
EMBDOFDNOAIOBFJFNGPOAHAGLJBHKDBA

This password file can be used as a first parameter in the utilities that are explained in the remainder of the utilities section.

BroadCastMessage.cmd

You can use the Broadcast Message utility to send text messages to all Planning users who are logged into the application at the time the message is sent. With broadcast messaging you can ask folks to log out of the system or communicate upcoming maintenance; the text message only appears in Planning and can be up to 127 characters. The utility is an alternative to sending broadcast messages using the Planning Web Client. Using the web client, messages go to users of the application from which you are sending; using the utility you can specify the application and schedule messages using a third party scheduler.

The syntax and parameters are:

```
Broadcastmessage.cmd -f:passwordfile  server_name,
application_name, username, message
```

Try It! Open the command line, go to the Planning\Bin folder, and enter: BroadcastMessage.cmd -f: the name and path of the password File [space] *server name*, Entpln, *youruserid*, "Eddie – Dr. Dementor is right behind you". Do not use a comma between the password file and the server name and the server name for this utility needs to be "localhost".

All planning users connected to the specified application receive the following message:

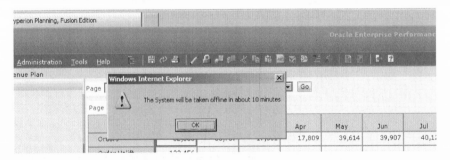

Tip!

You can execute the Planning utilities from a batch file. For example, you can create a batch file to send a broadcast message to your Planning users and schedule it using a third party tool to execute 10 minutes before the application is taken offline for maintenance.

Try It!

Create a new text document, change the file extension from "txt" to "bat", edit the file and add: the path to the utility: `HYPERION_HOME\Planning\Bin folder\BroadcastMessage.cmd -f:` the name and path of the password File [space] server name, application name, user, "I'm about to kick you out of the system for the midday process."

You can now execute the batch file with a double click or schedule it using a third party tool.

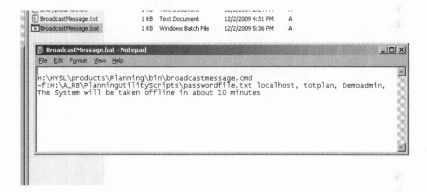

ExportSecurity.cmd

With the Export Security utility you can export access permissions to a Planning security file SecFile.txt. It can export security for selected groups or selected users or all groups and users in the planning application. It can export security for members, data forms, data form folders, task lists, Calculation Manager business rules, Calculation Manager business rules folders. By exporting a security file you can then import access permissions into other applications using the Import Security utility that is explained in the following section of this scene. The syntax and parameters are:

```
ExportSecurity.cmd [-f:passwordFile]
/A=appname,/U=username,
```

```
[/S=searchCriteria|/S_USER=user|/S_GROUP=group],
[/S_MEMBER=memberName|/S_MEMBER_ID=memberName
|/S_MEMBER_D=memberName|/S_MEMBER_IC=memberName|/S_M
EMBER_C=memberName],[/DELIM=delim] ,
[/DEBUG=true|false],[/TO_FILE=fileName],[/HELP=Y]
The mandatory parameters are:
/A=appname,/U=username. If a password file is setup
it can be used as an option. Just as with the other
utilities, if a password file is set up, it can be
used as the first parameter,
```

If you specify only the mandatory parameters, the utility will export access to all artifacts for all users and groups in the application. You can't export access permissions to task lists for administrators but you can manually add those records into the file for future importing.

Optional parameters are:

/S	Search criteria (search for a user or group)
/S_USER	user (specify a user)
/S_GROUP	group (specify a group)
/S_MEMBER	member name (specify a member)
/S_MEMBER_ID	member name (specify a member and its descendants)
/S_MEMBER_D	member name (specify a member's descendants)
/S_MEMBER_IC	member name (specify a member and its children)
/S_MEMBER_C	member name (specify a member's descendants)
/DELIM	delimit (specify a delimiter)
/DEBUG	true/false
/TO_FILE	(specify the path to the SecFile.txt (
/HELP	Y

Try It! In this example we are going to export all security from a Planning application. Open the command prompt, go to the Planning\Bin directory, and execute the ExportSecurity.cmd utility with the mandatory parameters as shown below.

```
Command Prompt                                                         _ □ ×
H:\HYSL\products\Planning\bin>\H:\HYSL\products\Planning\bin\ExportSecurity.cmd
-f:H:\A_RB\PlanningUtilityScripts\passwordfile.txt /A=totplan, /U=Planadmin_
```

The Output SecFile.txt looks like:

```
secfile.txt - Notepad                                                  _ □ ×
File Edit Format View Help
Planner,Depreciation Summary,READ,MEMBER,SL_FORM
Planner,11 Balance Sheet,READWRITE,MEMBER,SL_FORM
Henry,E01_101_1110,READWRITE,MEMBER
Henry,Sales Manager,READ,MEMBER,SL_TASKLIST
Frank,TotalGeography,READ,@IDESCENDANTS
Frank,Var %,READ,MEMBER
Planner,Plan,READWRITE,MEMBER
Planner,Target,READ,MEMBER
Planner,Final,READWRITE,@ICHILDREN
Planner,working,READWRITE,MEMBER
Planner,Forecast,READWRITE,MEMBER
Planner,Actual,READ,MEMBER
Planner,CashFlow,READ,@IDESCENDANTS
Planner,BalanceSheet,READ,@IDESCENDANTS
Planner,IncomeStatement,READWRITE,@DESCENDANTS
Planner,515000,READ,@IDESCENDANTS
Planner,511000,READ,@IDESCENDANTS
Planner,511100,READWRITE,MEMBER
Planner,506560,NONE,MEMBER
Planner,506321,READ,MEMBER
Planner,506311,READ,MEMBER
Planner,400000,READ,@IDESCENDANTS
Planner,Statistics,READWRITE,@DESCENDANTS
Planner,COSRate,READ,MEMBER
Planner,01 Facilities Allocation,READWRITE,MEMBER,SL_FORM
Planner,02 IT Allocation,READWRITE,MEMBER,SL_FORM
Planner,03 Marketing Allocation,READWRITE,MEMBER,SL_FORM
Planner,02 Product Revenue,READWRITE,MEMBER,SL_FORM
```

The exported SecFile.txt includes fields for: user or group, member name in the application, access permissions, relationship funtion. Artifacts are, SL_FORM, SL_COMPOSITE, SL_TASKLIST, SL_CALCRULE, SL_FORMFOLDER and SL_CALCFOLDER

ImportSecurity.cmd

The Import Security utility loads access permissions for users and groups from a text file. The utility imports security for these items: members, data forms, data form folders, task lists, Calculation Manager Business Rules, Calculation Manager Business Rules folders. Permissions are overwritten for existing members while all other existing permissions are not. You can clear existing access permissions with SL_CLEARALL parameter. All users, groups and objects must be defined in the application before running the Import utility.

The text file must be named "SecFile.txt" and must be placed in the HYPERION_HOME\Planning\Bin folder. You can use the SecFile.txt extracted with the Export Security utility to update security across applications or you can manually create the SecFile.txt file. Available delimiters for the secfile.txt include comma, tab, semi-colon, pipe, colon, and space. Comma is default delimiter.

After running the utility, verify results in importsecurity.log. You can improve import security performance by disabling the display of full names of users; this change is made in the Planning Web client under advanced system settings.

The syntax and parameters are:

```
ImportSecurity.cmd [-f:passwordFile] appname,
username, [delimiter], [RUN_SILENT], [SL_CLEARALL]
```

An example would be:

```
ImportSecurity.cmd "entbud,admin,SL_TAB,1"
```

Try
It!

Create a simple security file (the name must be SecFile.txt) and import it using the utility.

Open the command line, go to the Planing\Bin folder and enter this:

You should receive a success notification:

Look at the ImportSecuritylog.txt located in the Planning\bin folder. All rows should have loaded successfully.

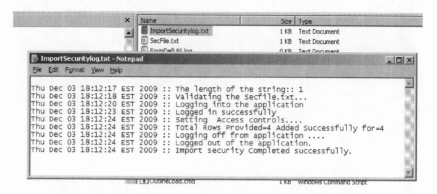

ProvisionUsers.cmd

The Provision Users utility synchronizes Planning users, groups and roles in Shared Services with a Planning application and with Essbase. It is an alternative to refreshing security filters from the Planning Web client.

The syntax and parameters are:

```
ProvisionUsers [-f:passwordFile] /ADMIN:adminName
/A:appName [/U:user1[;user2;user3]]
```

Mandatory parameters:	
/ADMIN	adminName
/A	appName
Optional parameters:	
[-f:passwordFile]	If the password file is set up, use as first parameter
/U:	Specifies the users to sync
/R:n	Specifies the interval in minutes for the sync to run (no argument runs the sync once)

Try It!

Open the command line and enter the mandatory parameters as shown below.

```
Command Prompt                                              _ □ x
H:\HYSL\products\Planning\bin>ProvisionUsers.cmd -f:H:\A_RB\PlanningUtilityScrip
ts\passwordfile.txt /ADMIN:Planadmin /A:TotPlan_
```

If you don't get a success message, you can look at the log in the Planning\Bin folder the log is called UserProvisionSync.Log. If you execute the utility from a batch file, the log will go to the same folder as the batch file:

```
Select Command Prompt                                       _ □ x
H:\HYSL\products\Planning\bin>ProvisionUsers.cmd -f:H:\A_RB\PlanningUtilityScrip
ts\passwordfile.txt /ADMIN:Planadmin /A:TotPlan
H:\HYSL\common\config\9.5.0.0\product\planning\9.5.0.0\planning_1.xml
displayName = Planning
componentTypes =

priority = 50
version = 9.5.0.0
build = 1
location = H:\HYSL\products\Planning
taskSequence =

task =

Fri Dec 04 12:07:11 EST 2009 :: [Fri Dec 04 12:07:11 EST 2009] Starting synchron
ization.
using Java property for Hyperion Home H:\HYSL
Setting Arbor path to: H:\HYSL\common\EssbaseRTC\9.5.0.0
Fri Dec 04 12:07:14 EST 2009 :: [Fri Dec 04 12:07:14 EST 2009] TotPlan: Synchron
izing all users with user provisioning.

H:\HYSL\products\Planning\bin>_
```

Other examples:

`ProvisionUsers /ADMIN:admin /A:Entpln` syncs all users for Entpln application.

`ProvisionUsers /ADMIN:admin /A:entpln /U:eddie /R:60` syncs user eddie in entpln every 60 minutes.

UpdateUsers.cmd

The Update Users utility is used with the UpdateNativeDir Shared Services utility to synchronize identities between Planning and Shared services. Update Users must be run after running the UpdateNativeDir Shared Services utility. Users and groups can lose their assigned access when their identities (SIDs) change, and the only way to prevent this is to synchronize identities between Planning and Shared services. Synchronization is required when the authentication provider is changed, users and groups are moved in an external provider, or when migrating an application from one environment to another with different Shared Services instances.

The two utilities need to run in a specific order. First, run the UpdateNativeDir utility to update user and group identities in Shared Services. This utility and its documentation are in the HYPERION_HOME/Common/Utilities/SyncOpenLDAPUtility directory. Second, run the UpdateUsers.cmd to update SIDs in Planning with the changes in Shared Services. The server needs to be local host. Check results in UpdateUsers.log in the bin directory.

The syntax and parameters are:

```
updateusers.cmd [-f:passwordFile] serverName
adminName applicationName
```

Try
It!

Open the command line and enter the mandatory parameters as shown below:

You should receive a completion message:

To view details, look at the UpdateUsers.log in the bin directory.

UserMigrUtil.cmd

This utility was used to delete the underscore users when you were migrating from Planning 3.5 or 4x .

HspUnlockApp.cmd

Use this utility when a Planning application becomes locked. This utility clears the HSP_Lock table. It must be run from the Planning server.

The syntax and parameters are:

```
HspUnlockApp.cmd[-f:passwordFile] servername
username appname
```

Open the command line and unlock the app.

Try It!

```
H:\HYSL\products\Planning\bin>HspUnlockApp.cmd -f:H:\A_RB\PlanningUtilityScripts
\passwordfile.txt localhost Planadmin TotPlan
```

You should get a confirmation message:

```
taskSequence =

task =

*******H:\HYSL\common\config\9.5.0.0\registry.properties
using Java property for Hyperion Home H:\HYSL
Setting Arbor path to: H:\HYSL\common\EssbaseRTC\9.5.0.0
d<ISO8601> INFO main com.hyperion.audit.client.runtime.AuditRuntime - Entering A
udit Client http://demodrive.oracle.com:28080/interop/Audit
d<ISO8601> INFO main com.hyperion.audit.client.runtime.AuditRuntime - Initializi
ng Manager for the serverhttp://demodrive.oracle.com:28080/interop/Audit
d<ISO8601> INFO main com.hyperion.audit.client.manager.AuditContext - Creating N
ew Audit Client Instance .... http://demodrive.oracle.com:28080/interop/Audit
d<ISO8601> INFO main com.hyperion.audit.client.runtime.AuditRuntime - Audit Clie
nt has been created for the server http://demodrive.oracle.com:28080/interop/Aud
it
The application has been successfully unlocked
d<ISO8601> INFO Thread-15 com.hyperion.audit.client.runtime.AuditRuntime - Writi
ng Audit Records for migrated Artifacts ...
d<ISO8601> INFO Thread-15 com.hyperion.audit.client.runtime.AuditRuntime - Store
d Audited Data Successfully !!!
Usage:    HspUnlockApp.cmd
          HspUnlockApp.cmd   [-f:passwordFile] servername username appname
Example: HspUnlockApp.cmd   localhost xyz app1
H:\HYSL\products\Planning\bin>
```

FormDefUtil.cmd

You can use the Form Definition utility to move data forms between Planning applications. It exports or imports form definitions to and from XML files. You can import or export one by one or you can use the –all parameter that allows you to import or export all the forms. When you export forms, the xml files go to the directory from which you execute the utility, by default the bin directory. You can copy the utility to another directory, if you want to export the files to that directory. You can execute the export from a batch file and the xml will go to the same folder as the batch file. Exporting/importing forms does not export/import assigned access.

The syntax and parameters are:

```
formdefutil [-
f:passwordFile]import|exportfilename|formname|-all
server name user name application
```

Try It!

In this example we are going to export all forms from a Planning application. Let's create a batch file with the parameters below to execute the utility. The folder where we save and execute the batch file will be the destination of the exported .XML files.

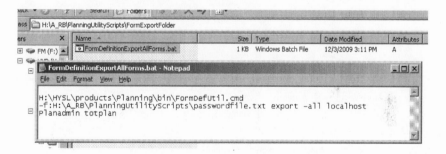

If the file executes successfully, you will see all the expected .XML files in the same folder and an empty log file. Take a look at the log, if not all the expected forms are exported:

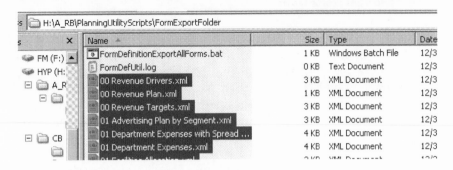

To import all forms, you can use the same batch file changing the parameter from "export" to "import":

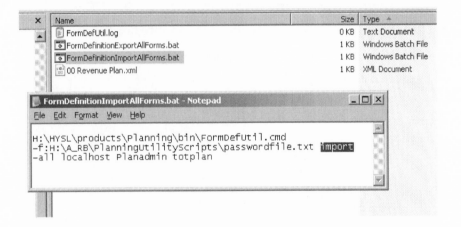

Tip!

If you want to import or export a selected form or a selected list of forms, you can leave only those forms (delete or move the rest) in the folder from which you run the utility, and use the –all parameter in the script. This is a lot easier than typing the name and the location for each form you want to import or export.

If you are exporting or importing a form that already in the target, the process will stop at that point and prompt you if you want to overwrite it:

Respond "yes" and hit enter to continue and replace the existing form, or respond "no" and hit enter to stop the process.

To import a form definition from a specific location:

```
FormDefUtil.cmd import
c:\Hyperion\products\Planning\bin\form1.xml
localhost admin entbud
```

To export a form definition:

```
FormDefUtil.cmd export Form1 localhost admin entbud
```

Check out results in FormDefUtil.log.

CubeRefresh.cmd

Use the Cube Refresh utility to refresh the Planning Application via the command line or from a batch file that can be scheduled using a third party tool. It refreshes Planning metadata and security filters to Essbase application via command line, pushing all Planning web client changes to the Essbase databases. Take the same cautions when refreshing the application using this utility as you do when refreshing through the web client (e.g., you don't delete members that have data and the Essbase outlines are not locked). Like other utilities, this one needs to run on the Planning server.

The syntax and parameters are:

```
CubeRefresh.cmd [-f:passwordFile]
/A:application_name /U:user_name [/C|/R] /D
[/F[S|V]][/RMIPORT:rmi_port] [/L] [/DEBUG]
```

[-f:passwordFile]	If the password file is set up, use as first parameter

/C	Creates the database outline
/R	Refreshes the database outline
/D	Specify the database during create or refresh
/F	Refreshes all security filters
/FS	Generate shared member security filters
/FV	Validate security filters but don't save
/FSV	Validate the shared member security filters
/RMIPORT	Specify an RMI port number if is different than default
/-L	Default option (connecting to an app server locally or remote)
/L	Create or refresh without connecting to the application server
/DEBUG	Specify detailed error messages

For example if you want to refresh the outline and security filters, type the following:

```
CubeRefresh.cmd -f:passwordFile /A:entbud /U:eddie
/R /D /FS
```

Try It!

Open the command line and refresh the cube, outline and security changes will be refreshed with the options below:

Look for the following confirmation message:

DeleteSharedDescendants.cmd

Use this utility to delete shared members that are descendants of a given member. When running this utility you might see "java.rmi" or "port already in use" errors but they do not affect the functionality of the utility. Make sure the Manage Database task is not open. To view results, check out the following logs in the bin directory: DeleteSharedDescendants.log for status, and DeleteSharedDescendantsExceptions.log for errors.

The syntax and parameters are:

```
DeleteSharedDescendants [-f:passwordFile] servername
username application "member name"
```

For example, if you wanted to delete the descendants under member Southwest region, you would type:

```
DeleteSharedDescendants -f:passwordFile epm111server
eddie entbud "Southwest Region"
```

Try
It!

Let's open the command line and delete shared members under a specific member.

```
H:\HYSL\products\Planning\bin>DeleteSharedDescendants.cmd -f:H:\A_RB\PlanningUti
lityScripts\passwordfile.txt localhost Planadmin TotPlan "Ratios"
```

Look for a a confirmation message. If there were no shared members under the specified member, the utility lets you know:

```
Command Prompt                                                     _ □ ×
H:\HYSL\products\Planning\bin>DeleteSharedDescendants.cmd -f:H:\A_RB\PlanningUti
lityScripts\passwordfile.txt localhost Planadmin TotPlan "Ratios"
[INFO] RegistryLogger - REGISTRY LOG INITIALIZED
[INFO] RegistryLogger - REGISTRY LOG INITIALIZED
H:\HYSL\common\config\9.5.0.0\product\planning\9.5.0.0\planning_1.xml
displayName = Planning
componentTypes =

priority = 50
version = 9.5.0.0
build = 1
location = H:\HYSL\products\Planning
taskSequence =

task =

using Java property for Hyperion Home H:\HYSL
Setting Arbor path to: H:\HYSL\common\EssbaseRTC\9.5.0.0
d<ISO8601> INFO main com.hyperion.audit.client.runtime.AuditRuntime - Entering A
udit Client http://demodrive.oracle.com:28080/interop/Audit
d<ISO8601> INFO main com.hyperion.audit.client.runtime.AuditRuntime - Initializi
ng Manager for the serverhttp://demodrive.oracle.com:28080/interop/Audit
d<ISO8601> INFO main com.hyperion.audit.client.manager.AuditContext - Creating N
ew Audit Client Instance .... http://demodrive.oracle.com:28080/interop/Audit
d<ISO8601> INFO main com.hyperion.audit.client.runtime.AuditRuntime - Audit Clie
nt has been created for the server http://demodrive.oracle.com:28080/interop/Aud
it
No shared descendants of Ratios were found.
d<ISO8601> INFO Thread-15 com.hyperion.audit.client.runtime.AuditRuntime - Writi
ng Audit Records for migrated Artifacts ...
d<ISO8601> INFO Thread-15 com.hyperion.audit.client.runtime.AuditRuntime - Store
d Audited Data Successfully !!!

H:\HYSL\products\Planning\bin>
```

MemberFormulaSync.cmd

You can use this utility to push the member formulas in the Planning application to Essbase.

The syntax is:

```
MemberFormulaSync /A:appname
```

Try It!

Let's open the command line and push the member formulas in the Planning app to Essbase.

```
Command Prompt                                                     _ □ ×
H:\HYSL\products\Planning\bin>MemberFormulaSync /A:TotPlan_
```

You don't get any message when it completes the refresh:

```
Command Prompt                                                     _ □ ×
H:\HYSL\products\Planning\bin>MemberFormulaSync /A:TotPlan

H:\HYSL\products\Planning\bin>_
```

So look at the log file:

Outline Load Utility

The Outline Load utility was introduced to Planning in version 11.1.1 and you can use it to load metadata and data. If you've been following along with Penny, you used this utility to build Entity and Account members. You loaded .CSV metadata files in parent-child format directly into Planning. This utility can be used to maintain the following dimensions and outline components: Account, Period, Year, Scenario, Version, Currency, Entity, user-defined dimensions, attributes, UDAs and exchange rates. You can also load .CSV data files. If loading data, you have to set the DIRECT_DATA_LOAD and DATA_LOAD_FILE_PATH system variables. You have to create a load file for each dimension to update or for each data set to load. The utility can load data for Smart Lists, Dates and Text Lists (though it cannot import Smart Lists).

The syntax and parameters are:

```
OutlineLoad [-f:passwordFile][/S:server]
/A:application /U:userName [/
M] [/I:inputFileName/D[U]:loadDimensionName|/
DA:attributeDimensionName:baseDimensionName] [/TR]
[/N] [[/R] [/U]] [/
C] [/F] [/K] [/X:exceptionFileName] [L:logFileName]
[/?]
```

Here is a sample.CSV metadata file for the Accounts dimension. If you ever loaded metadata into Planning using HAL, you will find this file very similar to a file you upload with HAL. Fields can be in any order, but headers are case sensitive:

	A	B	C	D	E	F	G	H
1	Parent	Accounts	Alias: Default	Data Storage	Plan Type (Plan1)	Aggregation (Plan1)	Plan Type (Wrkforce)	Aggregation (Wrkforce)
2	Accounts	Ratios		Label Only	1 ~		0	
3	Ratios	GROSS_MARGIN%	Gross Margin %	Store	1 ~		0	
4	Ratios	EBITDA%	EBITDA %	Store	1 ~		0	
5								

Try It!

We will load the above sample .CSV metadata file into planning to add 3 members to the accounts dimension. Create a .CSV file with the same rows and columns as the sample file above. Open the command line, go to the Planning\Bin folder and enter the script below. We recommend you create a batch file and execute the utility from there. You can create a batch file for each dimension by doing a simple "Save As" and changing parameters as needed

Execute this batch file with the OutlineLoad.cmd script to update the accounts dimension, or do the same thing using from the command line:

Now let's take a look at the log:

According to the log, my three members were added successfully. Now let's take a look at the Account dimension in the

Planning web client and you will see the 3 members were successfully loaded:

For a complete list of all the properties and values by dimension go to the Hyperion Planning Administrators guide (available online) and check out the section called Working with the Outline Load Utility.

Let's review an example of using the Outline Load Utility to load data. Log on to the Hyperion Planning Web client, go to Administration, go to Manage properties, and select the System Variables tab:

Property Name	Property Value
	ⓘ Properties have been saved to the system database. The changes will take ☒
	effect when the Application Server is restarted.

Application Properties   System Properties

Add

Property Name	Property Value
DATA_LOAD_FILE_PATH	C:\HyperionWorkFiles\OutlineLoad\PlanSamp.txt
DIRECT_DATA_LOAD	False
SECURITY_PROVIDER	CSS
SMART_VIEW_DISPLAY_WARNING	yes
SMART_VIEW_FORCE_INSTALL	no
SMART_VIEW_INSTALL_FILES_DIR	C:\Hyperion\products\Planning\bin\SmartView
SMARTVIEW_COMPRESSION_THRESHOLD	-1

When DIRECT_DATA_LOAD is set to True or empty, the utility loads data directly into Essbase. For this option to work the Planning and Essbase outlines must be in synch. When DIRECT_DATA_LOAD is set to false, the utility generates a .TXT data file and a .RUL file that can be used on demand.

Example: load data into the salary account for all employees. Salary account is the driver account. Employees are the load dimension:

```
Employee,Salary,Point-of-View,Data Load Cube Name
Emp1,50000,"Local,entity1,Current,Ver1,FY08,BegBalance",Plan1
Emp2,30000,"Local,entity1,Current,Ver1,FY08,BegBalance",Plan1
Emp3,55000,"Local,entity1,Current,Ver1,FY08,BegBalance",Plan1
Emp4,73000,"Local,entity1,Current,Ver1,FY08,BegBalance",Plan1
```

SortMember.cmd

You can use the Sort Member utility for sorting dimension members that are children or descendants of a specified member in Planning, similar to the sort order functionality of the Planning Web client. Period, Year and currency dimension members cannot be sorted with this utility.

Syntax:

```
SortMember [-f:passwordFile] servername username
application member children|descendants
ascend|descend
```

Let's sort the children of Ratios in ascending order.

Try It!

This is the order of the children of "Ratios" before running the utility:

Open the command line and sort the children of "Ratios" in ascending order:

You should receive a completion message:

The result shows new sorted children of Ratios:

TaskListDefUtil.cmd

You can use the Task List definition utility to move task lists between applications. You can export or import task list definitions to or from XML files, and similar to the form definition utility, it allows you to export/import task lists one by one or all at the same time by using the –all parameter.

The syntax and parameters are:

```
TaskListDefUtil [-f:passwordFile]
import|exportFILE_NAME|TASK_LIST_NAME|-all
SERVER_NAME USER_NAME APPLICATION
```

Try It!

In this example we are going to export all task lists from a Planning application using the –all function. You could create a batch file with the parameters below to execute the utility. The folder where we save and execute the batch file will be the destination of the exported .XML files.

You will receive a completion line for each exported task list:

By default the XML files go to the Planning\Bin folder:

Tip!

If you want to import/export specific task lists, you can leave only the ones to move in the folder from which you run the utility as a batch, and use the –all parameter in the script. This is a lot easier than typing the name and the location for each form you want to import/export.

Look at the TaskListDefUtil.log file for errors. An empty log file means all task lists were imported/exported successfully.

CalcMgrCmdLineLauncher.cmd

With the Calc Manager Command Launcher utility you can launch business rules or rules sets created with the Calculation Manager. It can run for a business rule or ruleset but not both. The errors are displayed on console or written to the Calc Manager log file. A runtime prompts file is required when the business rule or rule set contains one or more run time prompts. The Validate option checks the command syntax for the utility, not the business rule or rule set syntax.

The syntax and parameters are:

```
CalcMgrCmdLineLauncher.cmd [-f:passwordFile]
/A:appname /U:username /D:database [/R:business rule
name | /S:business ruleset name] /F:runtime prompts
file [/validate]
```

If the business rule contains runtime prompts, you must create a file containing the runtime prompt values. There are two ways: specify the name of the runtime prompt values file that you generated on the RunTimesPrompt page, or create a runtime prompt ASCII file. In the runtime prompt file, list each runtime prompt and its value in separate lines. Separate name and value with "::". For example: MarketRTP:: East. You can save the file in the Planning\bin directory or specify full path when running the utility.

In this example we are going to execute a Business Rule using the utility.

Try It!

Create a run-time-prompt file. You can put it in the Planning\Bin folder or specify the location as a parameter in the utility:

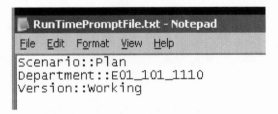

Open the command line and specify all the parameters, the business rule will take the prompts from the file:

```
Command Prompt                                                    _ □ ×
H:\HYSL\products\Planning\bin>CalcMgrCmdLineLauncher.cmd -f:H:\A_RB\PlanningUtil
ityScripts\passwordfile.txt /A:TotPlan /U:PlanAdmin /D:capex /R:RollupAssets /F:
RunTimePromptFile.txt
```

You should receive a completion message:

```
n         Values entered for run-time prompts:     [Variable]       Scenario:"Plan"[
Variable]            Department:"E01_101_1110"[Variable]    Version:"Working"
d<ISO8601> INFO Thread-16 calcmgr.launch - Date/Time Started:     2009/12/04:14:31
:44.807 EST    Server/Application/Database:      localhost/TotPlan/capex Business
 Rule Name:    RollupAssets   By Planning user:      PlanAdmin     Values e
ntered for run-time prompts:     [Variable]     Scenario:"Plan"[Variable]
Department:"E01_101_1110"[Variable]    Version:"Working"

 cpp setActive : 02009-12-04 14:31:45.103 INFO Thread-16 calcmgr.launch - Date/T
ime Ended:     2009/12/04:14:31:45.103 EST    Server/Application/Database:
localhost/TotPlan/capex Business Rule Name:    RollupAssets   By Planning user
:      PlanAdmin.
d<ISO8601> INFO Thread-16 calcmgr.launch - Date/Time Ended:     2009/12/04:14:31
:45.103 EST    Server/Application/Database:      localhost/TotPlan/capex Business
 Rule Name:    RollupAssets   By Planning user:      PlanAdmin.
d<ISO8601> INFO Thread-15 com.hyperion.audit.client.runtime.AuditRuntime - Writi
ng Audit Records for migrated Artifacts ...
d<ISO8601> INFO Thread-15 com.hyperion.audit.client.runtime.AuditRuntime - Store
d Audited Data Successfully !!!
H:\HYSL\products\Planning\bin>
```

Export/Import Utility

The last utility we will cover is not actually a Planning utility but you can use it to help maintain security for the users and groups used by Planning.

The CSS Import/Export Utility is a command-line utility that enables you to export, import, and validate user provisioning data in the native Open LDAP directory. This utility is part of Shared Services (not Planning). You can use the utility to create, modify, and delete users, groups, and roles that originate from the native user directory bundled with Shared Services, and you can modify relationship data for users/groups stored externally. You can export data from ALL directories, but you can import data to the NATIVE directory only, the utility lets you validate the import file for errors prior to import.

You can find the utility and its documentation in the Shared Services Server under Hyperion_Home\common\utilities\CSSImportExportUtility. All the components of the utility, including the documentation, are contained in a zip file called cssimportexport.zip. Install the utility by extracting the content of the zip file into folder where the user running the utility has read, write and execute access. The zip file extraction creates the importexport directory that contains all required files the documentation file is called impexp.pdf. In the extracted directory you will find the properties file, sample.CSV and .XML export files, and three batch scripts: CSSExport, CSSImport and CSSValidate. Before starting the import export operations, back up the native directory to an LDAP data file, ensure Shared Services is running, and prepare the importexport.properties file.

Just when Penny thought she was through with administration topics, SuperManager jumps in with the next topic near and dear to all Planning administrators' hearts: Essbase Administration.

Scene 16:
Essbase Administration

Because Planning sits on top of Essbase, you are not just a Planning administrator. You are an Essbase administrator. So let's jump into some Essbase specific items (for lots of Essbase detail, check out the sister guide to this book, Look Smarter Than You Are with Essbase: An Administrator's Guide).

ADMINISTRATION SERVICES

You should be familiar with Administration Services by now (also known as *Essbase* Administration Services – EAS – or *Analytic* Administration Services – AAS – depending on your version). Administration Services is a central administration tool for managing and maintaining all of Essbase.

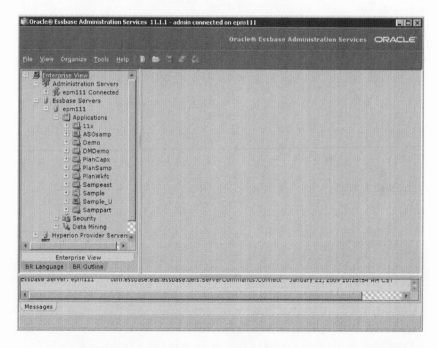

In the case of Planning you won't be making any changes to the outline in EAS. You should only make changes in the Planning web client (or EPMA if using EPMA).

Administration Services consists of a client console (Administration Services Console). This is the graphical interface that Essbase administrators and designers use to build and manage Essbase applications. The Administration Services Console talks to a middle-tier application server (the "Administration Server").

The Administration Server is something that no one will see once it's working correctly. The Administration Server serves as a centralized management point as it communicates directly with multiple Essbase servers and allows multiple administrators to focus their work in a single shared environment.

Administration Server communicates directly with Essbase servers. One Administration Server can talk to multiple Essbase servers. All Administration Services components are J2EE-compliant. J2EE stands for Java 2 Enterprise Edition, which in English-speak means that they're java-based. For those who believe a picture is worth a thousand words, here's a diagram to illustrate all those tiers:

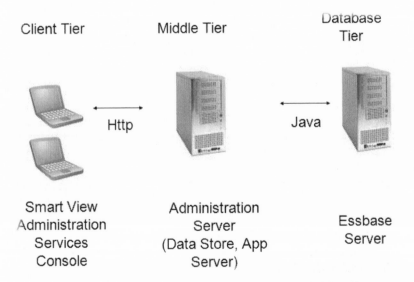

Client Tier	Middle Tier	Database Tier
Http		Java
Smart View Administration Services Console	Administration Server (Data Store, App Server)	Essbase Server

In the console, you can view and manage all Administration servers installed in your environment. In most cases, you have one Administration Server that manages all of your Essbase servers including development and production:

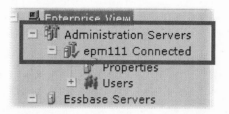

To view and manage all of the Essbase servers installed in your environment, expand the *Essbase Servers* section of the Enterprise View:

One of the big benefits of Administration Services is that you can manage development, QA, test, and production environments in one window. Copying objects across Essbase servers (even if they are different platforms like Unix and Windows) becomes child's play in Administration Services.

An Essbase administrator once deleted a production application, thinking he was connected to the development Essbase server. This same administrator also copied an unfinished development application from the development Essbase server to the production server, mixing up the 'to' and 'from' server during the copy. If you don't want to get fired, make sure you know which server you are connected to before you start performing potentially serious actions.

Navigate in Administration Services

There are three main ways to perform actions in the Administration Services console:

1. Menu items:

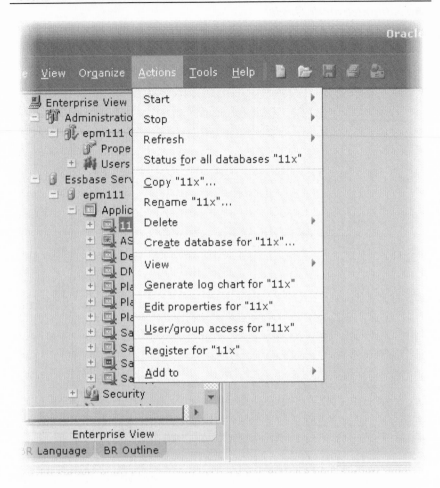

2. Icons:

3. Right-click:

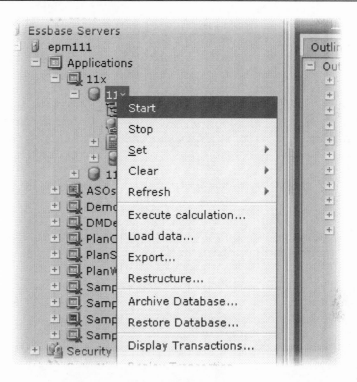

We personally prefer right-clicking since it's an easy way not to have to remember which actions are available for a specific item. Right-click on an object in the Enterprise View (the pane on the left) and you'll see all the relevant actions available to you.

Generally, when you open an item on the left (in the View pane), it will open in the pane to the right. There is another important pane in Administration Services: Messages. This section is found (unless you went to the *View* menu and turned it off) in the lower part of your window. Messages about whether actions are successful or not will be posted here:

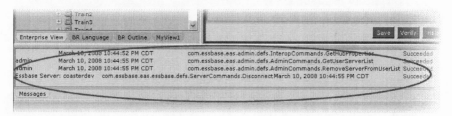

Administration Services may not send up a big, flashy error message so be mindful of the information communicated in this section. Although messages will almost always be displayed here, the messages displayed here will almost always be highly summarized, and in computer-speak.

Stare at the messages a while and at least you'll be able to tell if the message is informational or it's a major error. For example, if a message was displayed saying "It's currently sunny with a chance of rain late in the day," this would be informational. If the message "Fatal error occurred: self-destruct sequence initiated" appears, stare at it for a nanosecond and then run.

Note!

You are very unlikely to see a "self-destruct" message.

What Can You Do in Administration Services for Planning applications?

Helpful
Info

- View the database outline.
- Create data load rules.
- Create calculation scripts.
- Partition databases.
- Review log reports and database / server information.
- Manage Essbase servers.

ESSBASE.CFG

The Essbase.cfg file is the main configuration file for Essbase, and it is simply a text file stored in the arborpath\bin directory. Administrators may add or change parameters and values in this file to customize Essbase functionality. Most of these settings apply to the entire Essbase Server. Essbase reads the configuration file at startup of the Essbase Agent and every time an Application is loaded. Be aware of the potential requirement to restart the system or an application when you are making changes to this file.

In this file you can define settings that control TCP/IP ports and connections, define how detailed you would like your log files, specify cache settings for performance improvements, define query governors for the server or specific application, and much more highly technical gobbledygook. Here is a sample Essbase.cfg file:

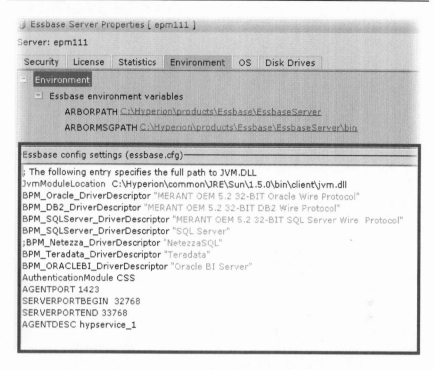

For a full listing of the Essbase.cfg settings, see the Technical Reference provided by Hyperion.

To update the Essbase.cfg,

1. In the Administration Services console, right-click on the Essbase server and select Edit >> Properties.
2. Choose the Environment tab.
3. Update the parameters by typing directly in the Essbase.cfg.
4. Restart the Essbase server for settings to take effect.

The "old school" way to update the Essbase.cfg settings is as follows:

1. Edit the file in text format with any text editor, such as Windows Notepad.
2. Enter each setting on a separate line in the file. You do not need to end each line with a semicolon.
3. Make sure the file is named essbase.cfg,
4. Save the file in the arborpath \ bin directory.
5. Restart the Essbase Server or the Essbase Application after changing the configuration file.

```
essbase.cfg - Notepad
File  Edit  Format  View  Help
; The following entry specifies the full path to JVM.DLL
;  JvmModuleLocation   C:\Hyperion\common\JRE\Sun\1.4.2\bin\client\jvm.dll
;This statement loads the essldap.dll as a valid authentication module
;AuthenticationModule LDAP essldap.dll x;
EssbaseLicenseServer C:\Install
AnalyticServerId 1
UPDATECALC FALSE
CALCCACHEHIGH  150000000
CALCCACHEDEFAULT 50000000
CALCCACHELOW  20000000
CALCNOTICEHIGH 20
CALCNOTICEDEFAULT 10
CALCNOTICELOW 5|
```

View the settings defined in your Essbase.cfg file.

Try It!

ESSBASE.SEC

The Essbase.sec stores information about users, groups, passwords for native security, and privileges on applications and databases. It also stores many application and database properties. This isn't a file you can open and read but it is critical to your Essbase server. It lives next door to essbase.exe in the arborpath\bin neighborhood.

Each time that you successfully start the Essbase Server, a backup copy of the security file is created (named essbase.bak). You can restore from the last successful backup by copying essbase.bak to essbase.sec. If you have a corrupt application, you often times will need to recover from the security file backup as well as recreate the application from scratch.

Find the Essbase.sec file on your server and take a look at the security settings assigned. WAIT! This was a trick "Try It!" *Do not* open the Essbase.sec. You don't ever open up this file and read it. To view security, go to the Security section in Administration Services.

Try It!

Since Essbase 9.3, you can export the Essbase.sec into a readable file. In Administration Services, right-click on Security and select "Export security file":

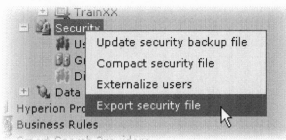

You can also use MaxL statement export security. The MaxL syntax is as follows:

```
EXPORT SECURITY_FILE to DATA_FILE file_name;
```

The resulting file will be available:

```
exp_sec.txt - Notepad

File  Edit  Format  View  Help
Essbase security file dump:        Fri Feb 29 11:32:27 2008
Company:                           interRel
Registered Username:               admin
Essbase installation date:         Wednesday, November 28, 2007 1:45:21 PM
Essbase Location:                  CoasterDev.interrel.com:1423
EAS Location:                      CoasterDev.interrel.com:10080
MyOlapEnabled:                     DISABLED
All HSS identity migrated:         Yes
Encoding:                          UTF8
Product Version:                   9.3.1
Security File Version:             22.0
Number of Ports:                   65535
Named User license. 65535 user server
Maximum Possible Planning Users:   65535
Maximum Connection allowed per user/port:65535
Security:                          ENABLED
Default Access Level:              None
Logins:                            ENABLED
Auto-Logout time (seconds):        3600
Auto-Logout check interval:        300
Currency:                          ENABLED
SQL:                               ENABLED
Aggregate Storage (ASO):               ENABLED
Spreadsheet Macros:                ENABLED
Read Only Spreadsheet:             DISABLED
Read Only Spreadsheet Macros:      DISABLED
64-bit port:                       ENABLED
Spreadsheet Addin:                 ENABLED
Reports:                           DISABLED
Busines Rules:                     ENABLED
EDS (High Concurrency):            ENABLED
Crystal:                           ENABLED
Limited SKU Appman:                DISABLED
Limited SKU Spreadsheet:           DISABLED
Single-User Essbase:               DISABLED
Development Server Option:         DISABLED
Block Storage (BSO):               ENABLED
MultiCube:                         ENABLED
Hyperion Integration Server Option: ENABLED
EssbaseObjects:                    ENABLED
Visual Explorer:                   ENABLED
Triggers:                          ENABLED
DataMining:                        ENABLED
SAPBW:                             ENABLED
```

If you scroll down through the file, you will notice stored user information as well as database information.

```
exp_sec.txt - Notepad
File Edit Format View Help
                        APP: usfsNEW  ; Manage
                        DB:  usfsNEW  ; APP: usfsNEW  ; Manage
                        DB:  usfsNEW2 ; APP: usfsNEW  ; Manage

     ldejohn                    User
          Default Access:         Administrator
          HSS Identity:          msad://OBJECTGUID=\24\3a\94\ec\6f\d4\17\41\8c\ea\de\5a\20\2d\81\d7?USER
          HSS Identity Migrated: Yes
          Last Login:            Monday, February 25, 2008 3:51:29 PM
          Password Expires on:   NOT SET
          User Locked out:       FALSE
          Change Password on next Login:FALSE

                        APP: Coaster1 ; Manage
                        DB:  Demo     ; APP: Coaster1 ; Manage
                        DB:  ver1     ; APP: Coaster1 ; Manage
                        DB:  ver2     ; APP: Coaster1 ; Manage
                        DB:  ver0     ; APP: Coaster1 ; Manage
                        DB:  CoasStor ; APP: Coaster1 ; Manage
                        DB:  Backup   ; APP: Coaster1 ; Manage
                        DB:  Coaster  ; APP: Coaster1 ; Manage
                        DB:  BackStor ; APP: Coaster1 ; Manage
                        APP: Bery     ; Manage
                        DB:  AFE      ; APP: Bery    ; Manage
                        DB:  FinAD    ; APP: Bery    ; Manage
                        DB:  FinPE    ; APP: Bery    ; Manage
                        DB:  Prod     ; APP: Bery    ; Manage

**** Applications:
       Demo             Created by:           ???
          Default Access:        None
          Connects:              TRUE
          Commands:              TRUE
          Updates:               TRUE
          Security:              TRUE
          Loadable:              TRUE
          Autoload:              FALSE
          Lock Timeout:          3600
          Data Storage Type:     Multidiminsional Data Storage
          LRO File size Limit:   NOT SET
          Application Type:      NONUNICODE
          Application Locale Description:English_UnitedStates.Latin1@Binary
                  tion Type    ESSBASE
```

VIEW THE SERVER LOG FILE

You are going to have to troubleshoot at some point. Really? Errors? Issues with Planning? Yes, yes, and yes. The Essbase Server log file is one of your first starting points when investigating an issue (because Planning stores all of its data in Essbase, Essbase could likely be the problem). The server log file is stored in the main Essbase folder as ESSBASE.log. This log file captures all server activity, including user logins, application level activities, and database activities. We can see that Eddie, the end user, logged in at 7am on Tuesday. We can see that Trixie renamed an application at 10am (glad we're paying the big bucks for those hardworking users).

You can view this log file through Administration Services. Select the Essbase server from the Enterprise View panel in Administration Services. Right-click and select View >> Log:

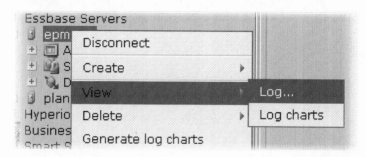

Choose Starting Date and enter the desired start date in most cases. Your log files will get really big and if you open the entire log file, be prepared to wait.

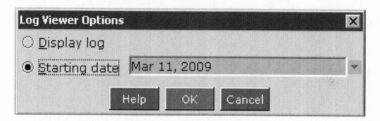

Have you ever tried to read text in a foreign language? Just a little confusing, right? Well, prepare yourself for a similar experience with the Essbase server log files:

Wed Mar 11 11:41:16 2009]Local/ESSBASE0///Info(1051283)
Retrieving License Information Please Wait...

Wed Mar 11 11:41:16 2009]Local/ESSBASE0///Info(1051286)
License information retrieved.

Wed Mar 11 11:41:36 2009]Local/ESSBASE0///Info(1051199)
Single Sign-On Initialization Succeeded !

Wed Mar 11 11:41:36 2009]Local/ESSBASE0///Info(1051232)

Using English_UnitedStates.Latin1@Binary as the Essbase Locale

Wed Mar 11 11:42:04 2009]Local/ESSBASE0///Info(1051134)
External Authentication Module: [Single Sign-On] enabled

Wed Mar 11 11:42:04 2009]Local/ESSBASE0///Info(1051051)
Essbase Server - started

Wed Mar 11 22:01:40 2009]Local/ESSBASE0///Info(1051164)
Received login request from [100.100.100.25]

Wed Mar 11 22:01:42 2009]Local/ESSBASE0///Info(1051187)
Logging in user [admin] from [100.100.100.25]

1:2 - 1/1308 - 0%

Refresh   Help   Close

Actually, interpreting the log files isn't that bad. We'll give you a brief translation course on some of the common messages. Here are some example Startup Messages that you will see in the Essbase.log. We see the Sample application is loaded and started, and then the database Basic is loaded.

```
[Tue Nov 06 07:54:16
    2006]Local/ESSBASE0///Info(1051061)
    Application Sample loaded - connection
    established
[Tue Nov 06 07:54:16
    2006]Local/ESSBASE0///Info(1054027)
    Application [Sample] started with process id
    [1300]
[Tue Nov 06 07:54:18
    2006]Local/ESSBASE0///Info(1054014) Database
    Basic loaded
```

Here is an error message captured in the log file when user admin tried to rename an application. He received an error message stating that an application already existed with the name 'Testing'.

```
[Tue Nov 06 08:00:04
    2006]Local/ESSBASE0///Info(1051001) Received
    client request: Rename Application (from user
    admin)
[Tue Nov 06 08:00:04
    2006]Local/ESSBASE0///Error(1051031)
    Application Testing already exists
[Tue Nov 06 08:00:04
    2006]Local/ESSBASE0///Warning(1051003) Error
    1051031 processing request [Rename
    Application] - disconnecting
```

Here is an example of the messages you will see when you stop the Sample application and shutdown the Essbase server.

```
[Tue Nov 06 08:00:46
    2006]Local/ESSBASE0///Info(1054005) Shutting
    down application Sample
[Tue Nov 06 08:00:52
    2006]Local/ESSBASE0///Info(1051052) Hyperion
    Essbase Analytic Server - finished
```

Congratulations! You now speak Essbase-log-ish (like Elvish except that you might actually put this on your resume).

Periodically archive off the Essbase.log file. Smaller log files can help with performance. In 11.1.1.1, Oracle moved the Essbase.log location to hyperion\logs\essbase and app logs to hyperion\logs\essbase\app\.

Tip!

Take a look at your Essbase.log file. Look for instances where applications are started and users have logged into the server. Find them?

Try It!

VIEW ESSBASE SERVER PROPERTIES

Within Administration Services you can view Essbase server level properties like username and password management settings, version information, server statistics, and OS/CPU and Memory information.

Within Administration Services, right-click on the Essbase server. Select Edit >> Properties. Select the Security tab:

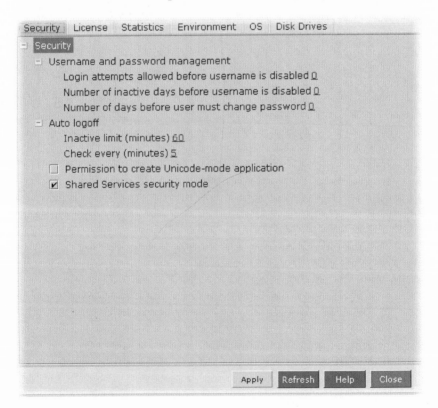

Let's say we decide to set "Login attempts allowed before username disabled" to 3 and set "Number of inactive days before username disabled" to 365. If a user enters an invalid password, after three tries, the username is disabled. If a user hasn't logged into the server in a year, their username is disabled (don't waste those precious, costly Essbase licenses).

Select the License tab. This used to provide pretty important information back when Hyperion was still an independent company. Want to see what version you've installed, what additional components are installed, and when the license expires? Beginning in Essbase 9.3.1, all of the additional components are installed with Essbase (no additional licensing required):

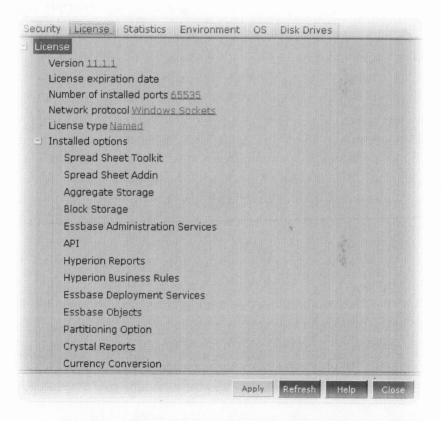

On the remaining tabs, you can view server statistics, environment information, and other hardware related information.

What is the inactive limit on your server? What version of Essbase are you running? Check out these settings and more for the Essbase server.

Try It!

VIEW SERVER SESSIONS

You can view current activity for the server: Who's connected? For how long? And more importantly, what are they doing? It is fun to be Big Brother. For example, you receive a call from a user complaining that performance has slowed significantly on the Essbase server. You check out the current sessions and see that Trixie kicked off an application copy that has brought the system to its knees.

To view Sessions, right-click on the Essbase server and select Edit >> Sessions in the Enterprise View panel:

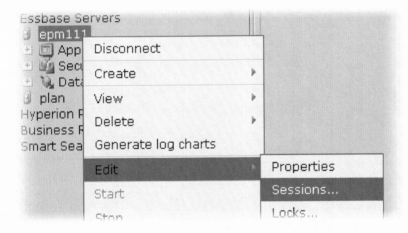

From the Sessions module, you can log off and kill users from their sessions. Why would you want to kill someone? No matter how much of a pacifist you may be, you will want to kill someone in your Essbase world.

You will definitely receive this call at some point. "I just accidentally drilled down to Dimbottom on the Product dimension which has 10,000 products. Now my computer is frozen." What is the resolution to this problem? View sessions and log off or kill this particular user. Killing may be a bit drastic but sometimes it's required. Don't worry – killing a user in Essbase is quite legal.

To log off or kill, select the desired option from the dropdown at the top of the Sessions window:

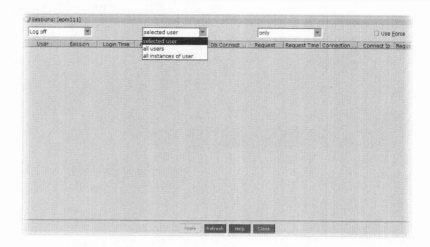

Select User, All Users or All Instances of User. Select On Server, On selected Application, or On selected Database (the available options here depend on your two previous selections). Select Use Force (if necessary).

So we have some flexibility with logging off or killing. In our request above, we may only have to kill the user for a specific database. You may need to log all users off of a particular application just before the monthly load and calc takes place. You may need to log all users off of a server before nightly backups run.

As an almighty Essbase administrator, see what the minions in your domain are doing right now. View the current sessions for your Essbase server.

Try It!

SERVER DATA LOCKS

Essbase will lock cells when they are being updated whether it is through Essbase Add-In lock and send, data load, or calculation. Once the update is complete, the lock is released. Occasionally locks are not released. You select Essbase >> Lock in the Essbase Add-In and then Excel crashes. You may want to periodically check for data locks or you may get a call from a user saying that Essbase won't accept their data changes.

To view data locks, right-click on the Essbase server and select Edit >> Locks:

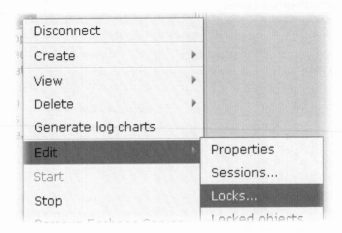

From the Locks window, you can view locks by application, database, and user. You can unlock locks by selecting Unlock (very tricky, we know).

LOCKED OBJECTS

Similar to data locks, you can also have locks on Essbase objects. Remember how you are prompted with the following message each time you edit an object:

Most of the time we say "Yes" because we don't want anyone else to change the object while we are viewing or editing it. Once we save our changes and close the object, the object lock is released. But what happens if your computer freezes and causes you to reboot while you had the act.rul data load rule open? You weren't able to successfully close the rules file within Administration Services so the lock remains on the rules file.

You can unlock the rules file in the Locked Objects window. To view locked objects, right-click on the Essbase server and select Edit >> Locked Objects:

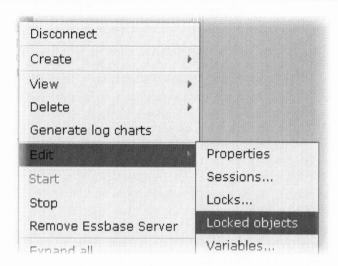

From the Locked Objects window, you can view locked objects by application, database, and user. You can unlock locked objects by selecting Unlock:

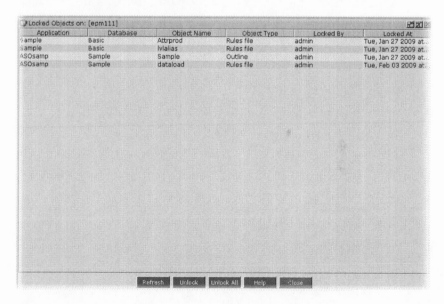

See if you have any data locks or locked objects on your Essbase server.

Try It!

VIEW AND EDIT APPLICATION PROPERTIES

The application properties and statistics tabs provide some helpful options to administrators. Remember, this is where we set the default minimum security for an application. You may want to enable "Allow Users to Start Application" for rarely used applications. This way the application and database won't take up precious memory if it is not being used. When the application is needed, it will start when the user tries to connect via Smart View or other reporting tool. This will, however, add a bit more initial response time for the user. Alternatively, if you have a highly used application, you can check "Start application when Analytic Server starts" because you know this application will need to be started and you can save some time for the first user to connect.

To view and edit application properties,
1. Select the application.
2. Right-click and select Edit Properties.
3. The Application properties window will display:

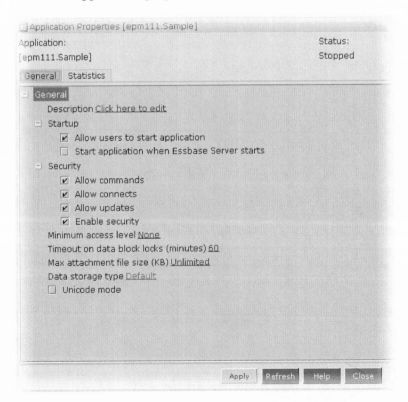

VIEW APPLICATION LOG FILE

The Application log file displays all activity for an application and its databases. There is a different application log file for each application. The log file name is the *application_name.log* and is stored in the application App file. This file tracks activity for the specific application, including the "who" and "when" of an operation and any errors of operations. For example, we can see Trixie ran a calc script on Monday at 12 p.m. We can see that Eddie performed a series of retrievals on Tuesday at 1 p.m. (more Big Brother capabilities).

You can view this log file through Administration Services. Right-click on the application and select View >> Log:

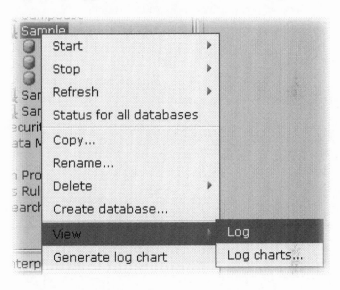

When prompted, choose the Starting Date option and enter the desired date (your log files will get really big and if you open the entire log file, be prepared to wait).

The application log file will display:

Let's learn more Essbase-log-ish. Here are some example Startup Messages that you will see in the application log file. Essbase writes information about the dimensions and members in the outline, such as the dimension sizes and dynamic calculation information, to the application log.

```
[Tue Nov 06 08:47:14
     2006]Local/Sample///Info(1002035) Starting
     Essbase Server - Application [Sample]
[Tue Nov 06 08:47:15
     2006]Local/Sample///Info(1200480) Loaded and
     initialized JVM module
[Tue Nov 06 08:47:15
     2006]Local/Sample///Info(1019008) Reading
     Application Definition For [Sample]
[Tue Nov 06 08:47:15
     2006]Local/Sample///Info(1019009) Reading
     Database Definition For [Basic]
[Tue Nov 06 08:47:15
     2006]Local/Sample///Info(1019021) Reading
     Database Mapping For [Sample]
[Tue Nov 06 08:47:15
     2006]Local/Sample///Info(1019010) Writing
     Application Definition For [Sample]
[Tue Nov 06 08:47:15
     2006]Local/Sample///Info(1019011) Writing
     Database Definition For [Basic]
[Tue Nov 06 08:47:15
     2006]Local/Sample///Info(1019022) Writing
     Database Mapping For [Sample]
[Tue Nov 06 08:47:15
     2006]Local/Sample///Info(1013202) Waiting for
     Login Requests
[Tue Nov 06 08:47:15
     2006]Local/Sample///Info(1013205) Received
     Command [Load Database]
[Tue Nov 06 08:47:15
     2006]Local/Sample///Info(1019018) Writing
     Parameters For Database [Basic]
[Tue Nov 06 08:47:15
     2006]Local/Sample///Info(1019017) Reading
     Parameters For Database [Basic
```

Essbase also writes information about the outlines for each
database to the application log.

```
[Tue Nov 06 08:47:15
     2006]Local/Sample///Info(1019012) Reading
     Outline For Database [Basic]
[Tue Nov 06 08:47:15
     2006]Local/Sample///Info(1007043) Declared
```

```
          Dimension Sizes = [20 17 23 25 5 3 5 3 15 8 6
          ]
[Tue Nov 06 08:47:15
          2006]Local/Sample///Info(1007042) Actual
          Dimension Sizes = [20 14 20 25 4 3 5 3 15 8 5
          ]
[Tue Nov 06 08:47:15
          2006]Local/Sample///Info(1007125) The number
          of Dynamic Calc Non-Store Members = [8 6 0 0 2
          ]
[Tue Nov 06 08:47:15
          2006]Local/Sample///Info(1007126) The number
          of Dynamic Calc Store Members = [0 0 0 0 0 ]
```

Here is an example of an error message in an application log file. The user Admin tried to load data to the Sample.Basic but the data file contained the member '500-10' which does not exist in the outline. We are told that zero records were loaded (the rules file was most likely set to abort on error).

```
[Tue Nov 06 08:49:52
          2001]Local/Sample///Info(1013210) User [admin]
          set active on database [Basic]
[Tue Nov 06 08:49:52 2001]
          Local/Sample/Basic/admin/Info(1013091)
          Received Command [DataLoad] from user [admin]
[Tue Nov 06 08:49:52 2001]
          Local/Sample/Basic/admin/Info(1003040)
          Parallel dataload enabled: [1] block prepare
          threads, [1] block write threads.
[Tue Nov 06 08:49:52 2001]
          Local/Sample/Basic/admin/Error(1003000)
          Unknown Item [500-10] in Data Load, [0]
          Records Completed
[Tue Nov 06 08:49:52 2001]
          Local/Sample/Basic/admin/Warning(1003035) No
          data values modified by load of this data file
[Tue Nov 06 08:49:52 2001]
          Local/Sample/Basic/admin/Info(1003024) Data
          Load Elapsed Time : [0.11] seconds
[Tue Nov 06 08:49:52 2001]
          Local/Sample/Basic/admin/Info(1019018) Writing
          Parameters For Database [Basic]
```

Try It!

Take a look at the Entpln.Sum application log file. What date and time did we load data most recently? How long did the default calculation take place?

Managing Log Files

We recommend you archive log files on a periodic basis (depending on the level of activity on an application). These files can become quite large and could slow performance. Application log files should be stored in Logs in your Oracle EPM / Hyperion install folder (e.g. hyperion\logs\essbase\app\). Within Administration Services, after you've made a backup of the file, you can clear the file.

View Log Charts

Starting in version 7, Essbase added log charts, which help you review and understand Essbase activity much better than those easy-to-read log files (by "easy-to-read," we mean "easier to read than Edward's handwriting"). With log charts, Essbase-log-ish is no longer required.

To view the log file in chart format, select the application in Administration Services. Right-click and select View >> Log Chart:

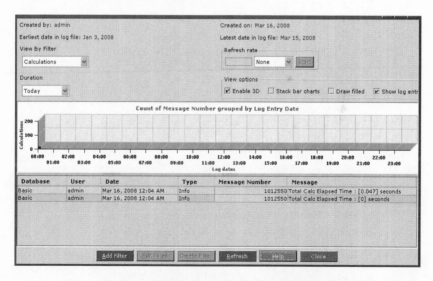

You can filter Log charts by predefined filters: errors, warnings, calculations, data loads, and spreadsheet queries:

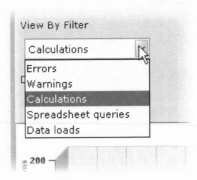

OTHER APPLICATION TASKS

Via Administration Services, several other actions for applications are available. Select an application in the Enterprise View panel and right-click. These are the other actions you can perform on applications. While you can copy, rename, and delete Essbase applications from Administration Services, you will NEVER do this for your Planning applications:

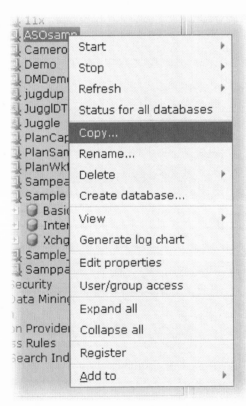

When you copy an application, all objects will be copied within Essbase including the outline, rules files, report scripts, calc scripts, and data. During the copy process, users are prohibited from accessing both the 'from' and the 'to' applications. You can copy across servers if desired.

VIEW AND EDIT DATABASE PROPERTIES

Get to know your database properties! You can define startup options and default access privileges for databases just as you can applications. Database properties will vary depending on the database type (ASO versus BSO) and remember Planning databases are BSO, so we'll focus there.

To view and edit database properties,

1. Select the database.
2. Right-click and select Edit >> Properties.

BSO Database Properties

Important information is displayed for BSO databases including dimension dense / sparse settings, member counts, and other helpful ratios and statistics. You can manage commit settings, cache settings, data storage volumes, and much more via database properties.

Database level settings like startup options and data retrieval buffers are defined on the General tab:

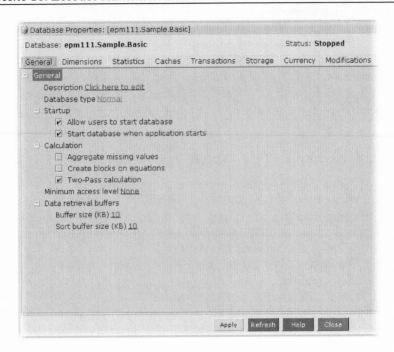

The Dimensions tab presents the dimensions in a helpful table, labeling dense and sparse settings and giving you a count of all members and stored members:

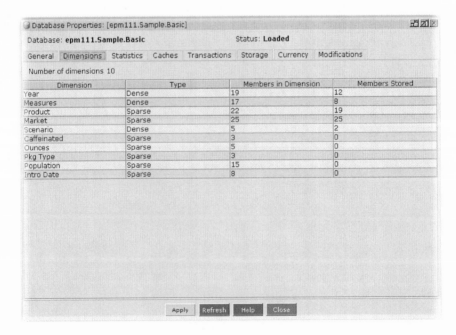

BSO statistics like cache hit ratios and block size are available on the Statistics tab:

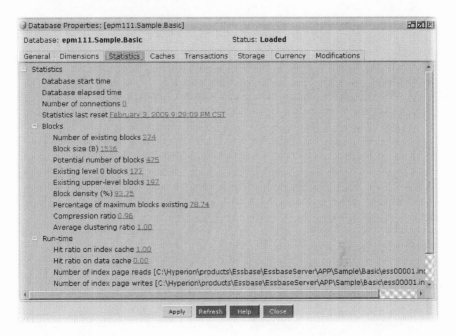

Cache settings are defined on the Caches Tab:

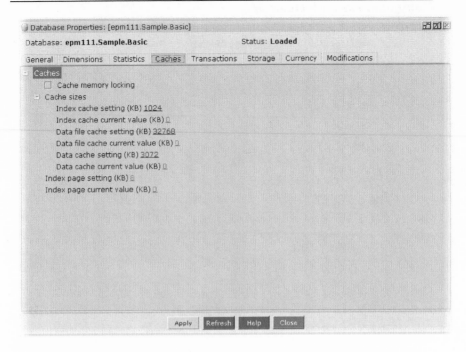

Commit settings are defined on the Transactions Tab:

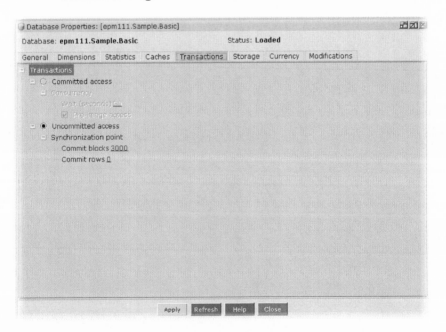

BSO compression and index and data file volumes are specified on the Storage Tab:

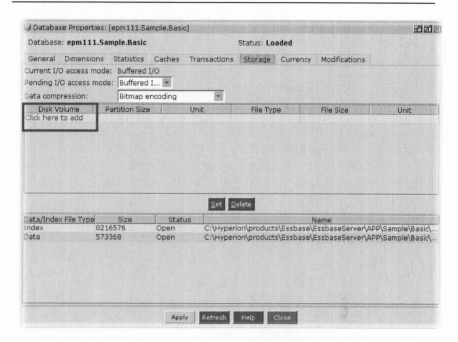

The Modifications tab lists any recent updates to the database:

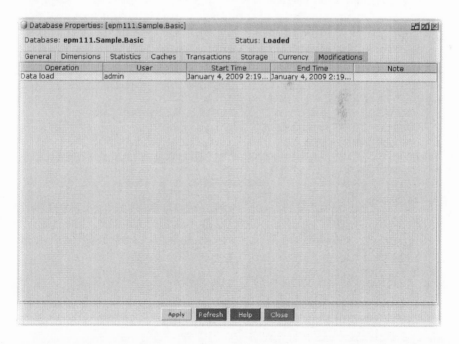

We've covered some of the key topics in Essbase administration. For full blown Essbase, please refer to Look Smarter Than You Are with Essbase. We'll next turn our attention to an introduction of automation in Essbase.

AUTOMATE ESSBASE WITH MAXL

You've learned how to load and calculate data and maintain Essbase via the Administration Services Console. However, you certainly don't want to perform all of these tasks manually every day. Essbase of course has a scripting alternative to automate almost any Essbase task. MaxL is the scripting language for Essbase and is installed with every instance of the Essbase server, on all operating systems. These are some of the more common actions that MaxL is used for:

- Loading a database
- Building a dimension
- Altering a substitution variable
- Viewing database statistics

Having a good knowledge of MaxL is absolutely essential to the smooth running of your Essbase environment. In addition to daily database updates and administration, developers can also automate repetitive tasks in order to speed up testing cycles, a trick that can save much stress when under tight deadlines.

Let us review some examples. This statement will load data from a SQL database. You don't have to specify the ODBC data source name as that is contained within the load rule itself (named sql_load).

```
IMPORT DATABASE Sample.Basic DATA
 CONNECT AS dbadmin IDENTIFIED BY dbpasswd
 USING SERVER RULES_FILE 'sql_load'
 ON ERROR WRITE TO
    'c:\\hyperion\\MaxL_logs\\load.sample_basic.er
    r';
```

Of course, MaxL can run a calc script that you've already saved (in this example, the calc script named "Allocate" is executed). There are two ways to do this (both of these commands have the exact same result):

```
EXECUTE CALCULATION 'Sample.Basic.Allocate';

EXECUTE CALCULATION 'Allocate' ON Sample.Basic;
```

For more information on MaxL scripting, check out the Essbase Technical Reference. Also note there is a handy utility that can help you convert any existing Esscmd scripts to MaxL.

Thankfully you now have the tools to manage the day to day administration tasks for Planning and Essbase. But we can't forget one of the most important action items for you as an administrator – backups!

Scene 17:
Backups and Recovery

This will probably never happen to you. Well, maybe. Actually, this will probably happen more than once in your Essbase career. An Essbase database will crash just before close and you need to get the data back. Fast. Because the CFO is standing over your shoulder saying "Where are my reports?" At first you think, "Can I book my Southwest flight without him seeing"? (Wanna getaway? Eddie who?) But then you remember that you have a proven, tested backup and recovery plan and process. You are not like the girl or guy who spills beer over all of the fans at the basketball game. We can't stress how important it is to back up your applications. Listen to us – this is *really* important.

BACKUP / RESTORE FOR BSO

Version 11x introduces new backup and restore functionality for block storage option databases. This new Backup and Restore feature backs up and restores all the necessary files for a BSO database (previously you had to manually perform this process). During the backup process, the database is placed in read-only mode and files are archived to the specified location. When a restore is launched, the database is locked while the files are restored from the archive folder. The backup and restore feature is available in the Administration Services Console and MaxL.

Note!

Because Planning creates block storage option databases, you can use the backup and restore feature on Planning databases.

In the example below, we will archive a database called "11x".

To back up a BSO database,

1. In the Administration Services Console, right-click on the database and select Archive Database:

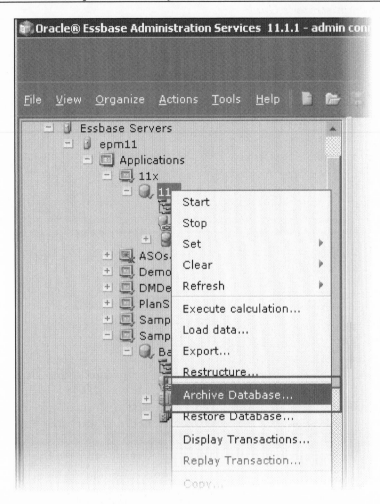

2. Provide a name for the archive:

3. Optionally, select Force archive and/or Archive in the background. Force archive will replace any archives that exist with the same name.
4. Click *OK*.

5. A file will be created in the essbasepath\app directory:

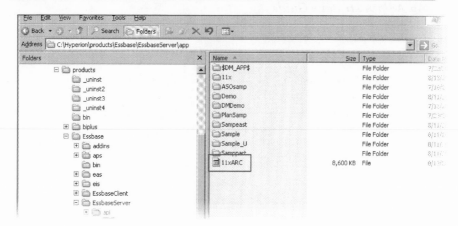

Then use your third party back up tools to backup the archive files created by Essbase.

So now when the Essbase server goes down or a database crashes and the CFO is breathing down your neck, rest assured you have a good backup file. So how do you get it back up? Fast.

To restore a database,
1. If necessary, place the archive files in the Essbase\app folder.
2. Right-click on the database and select Stop to stop the database.
3. Right-click on the database and select Restore Database.

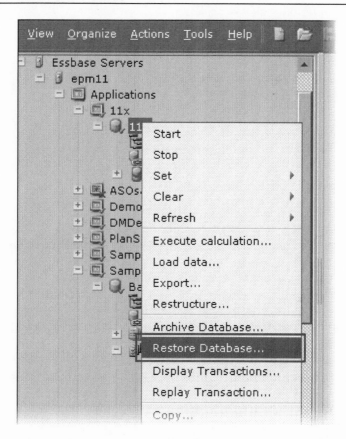

4. Choose the restore file from the drop down box:

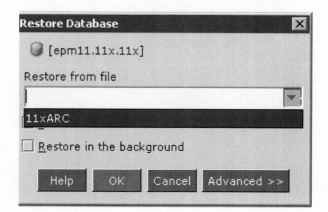

5. Optionally choose to Force Restore and/or to Restore in the background.
6. Click *OK*.

Ta-da! Like magic, the database is restored (along with some of the CFO's facial color).

Archive the Entpln application.

Try It!

TRANSACTION LOGGING / REPLAY

Another new feature that goes along with backup and restore is the transaction logging and replay capability. Essbase can now track operations in the database like data loads, calculations, and data submissions from Smart View or the Excel Add-in.

Because the events are tracked, the administrator can display and replay those transactions. The administrator can choose to replay all transactions from a certain point or she can pick and choose the transactions to replay.

The real power comes with using backup and restore along with transaction logging / play back to restore a database to a previous state. This will probably never happen... wait, actually this could definitely happen. Your budgeting and planning database crashes just after lunch and plans are due at the end of the day. You backup on a nightly basis so you could restore from last night's backup. However, your chances of getting the plan data changes from the morning were pretty slim. Now in Essbase 11, you can use transaction replay to get those data changes back, restoring the BSO database fully with minimal data loss (picture Essbase as a superhero with a big "S" emblazoned across its chest).

The replay for data loads uses a reference or pointer to the data source file (not the actual file). If the underlying data file changes, the new data will be loaded to the database.

Tip!

First you have to enable transaction logging for the desired database (by default, transaction logging is not enabled). To turn on transaction logging, update the essbase.cfg with the following setting.

```
TransactionLogLocation AppName DbName LogLocation
Native Enable
```

For example:

```
TransactionLogLocation Sample Basic
c:\hyperion\trlog native enable
```

In this example, we'll enable transaction logging for our 11x database.

1. In the Administration Services console, right-click on the Essbase server and select Edit >> Properties.
2. Choose the Environment tab.
3. Update the TransactionLogLocation parameter in the Essbase.cfg by typing:

```
TransactionLogLocation 11x 11x c:\hyperion\TRLog
NATIVE ENABLE
```

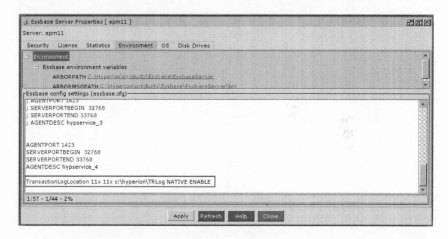

4. Click Apply.
5. Restart the Essbase server.
6. Create the directory and folder if necessary (we created a TRLog folder in the Hyperion directory to store the transaction log files). The name must match exactly or the application won't start.
7. Right-click on the application and select Start.

8. Right-click on the database and select Start.
9. Right-click on the database and select Display Transactions:

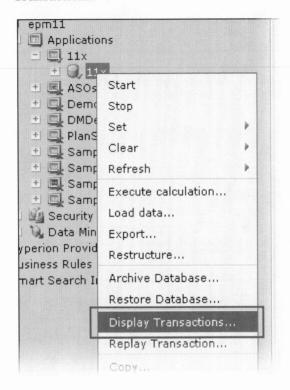

10. Display transactions based on one of the following options:
    *   Last replay time
    *   Since a specific date and time

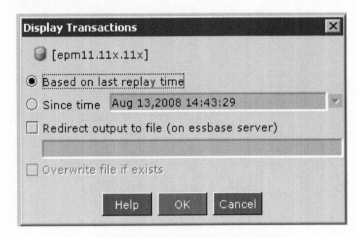

11. Check the Redirect output to a file if desired (and optionally overwrite the file if it exists).
12. The Transaction List displays:

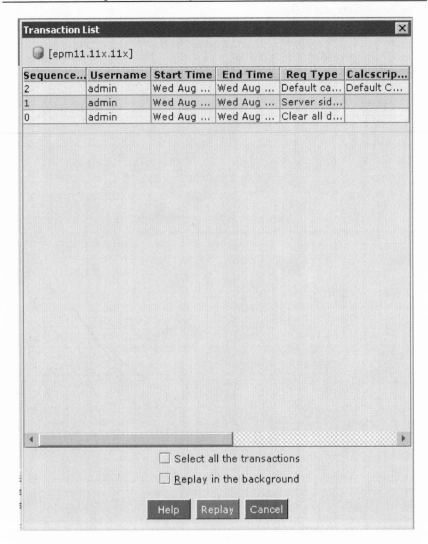

The following columns are shown: Sequence, username, start time, end time, action (or req type), Calcscript name, dataload file, dataload file type, rules file, rules file location, and sql or ftp file user name. (For you existing admins, admit it – you are saying "Wow, this is really cool. What took so long?")

So what transactions have taken place for the 11x database? If we adjusted the columns you would see that first (Sequence 0) all data was cleared by the user *admin* Wednesday, August 1, 2008, beginning at 8:01 am and ending at 8:02 am. Next (Sequence 1) we see that user *admin* loaded data using the calcdat.txt Wednesday, August 1, 2008, beginning at 8:05 am and ending at 8:06 am. And finally (Sequence 2), we see the default calc script was run by admin on Wednesday, August 1, 2008, beginning at 8:07 am and ending at 8:08 am.

To replay a single transaction, select the desired transaction and click Replay.

13. Select 0 and select the Replay button (to clear all of the data).

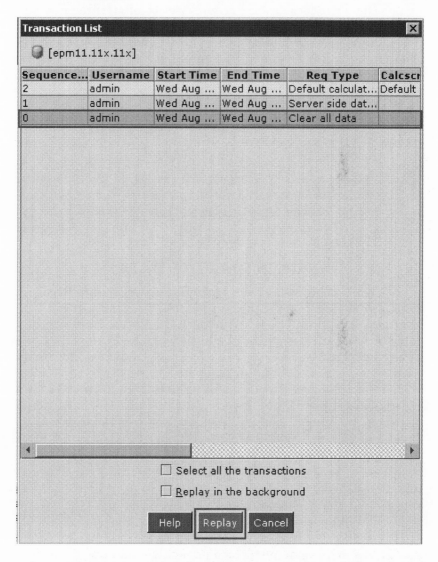

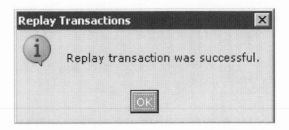

Optionally, you can choose to select all transactions and have them replay in the background.

So back to our midday budget crisis... because you turned on transaction logging for the budget database, you can easily recover last night's archive file, restoring the database. You can replay all transactions that have taken place since the backup, returning the plan data to its original state just before the crash. We think we see a budget increase for a certain Planning Administrator salary because of the quick recovery.

Enable transaction logging for the Entpln Sum database. Enter some expense data via the data forms and run a calc script for Sum. Test viewing and replaying transactions.

Try It!

EXPORTING THE DATA

The second method for backups is data exports. Exporting will copy data to a text file that you specify. You can export all data, level zero data, or input-level data for BSO databases and level zero data for ASO databases. The thing with exports is that they only export data. Essbase objects like outline files, rules files, etc. are not included so you will need to use file system backups for those items.

So if we have to do a file system backup anyway, why export? Use exports when you want to transfer data across platforms, when you want to back up only a certain portion of the data (level 0 blocks), or when you want to create an exported file in text format, rather than binary format. If you have a copy of the outline and data export, this can be a quick way to recover a corrupted database.

To perform a data export,
1. Select the database.
2. Right-click and select Export or Select Actions >> Export "dbname":

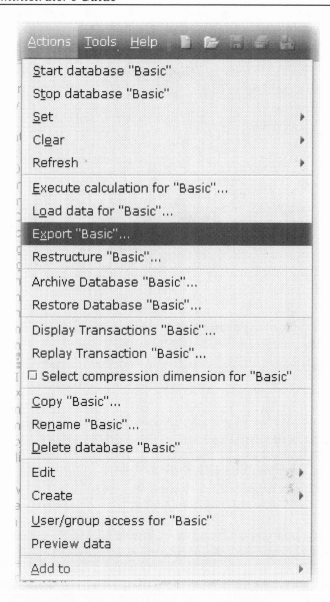

3. Specify the name for the exported data file.
4. Choose the export option:
   - BSO - All data, Level 0 blocks, or Input blocks
   - ASO – Level 0 blocks
5. Choose either column or non-column format.

Column format often facilitates loads to relational databases or other systems. Non-column format is faster for loading or reloading to the Essbase database. Column format exports are not available for ASO.

    6. Select "Execute in the background" in most cases:

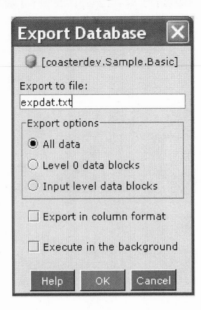

    The export file is by default placed in the \arborpath\essbase\app directory.

    To reload an exported file, you will follow the same steps to load any data file though you won't need a rules file.

1. Right-click on the database and select Load Data.
2. Select Find Data File and navigate to the exported data file.
3. Specify the error file location and name.
4. Click OK to load the data.

    If you are reloading a level zero export or input level export file for a BSO database, the database must be recalculated.

Don't forget about the binary data export commands; these are other good options for exporting data sets for backup purposes.

Tip!

BACKUPS IN 9.3.1

In the olden days of backups, before we had the 11x backup and restore feature, we had to walk to school every day in the snow with no shoes and prepare the Essbase server and applications for file system backup ourselves . To do this,

1. Place database in read-only ("archive") mode. Using MaxL, type "`alter database begin archive`".
2. Perform backup using third-party backup utility, backing up the entire Essbase directory or specific files.
3. Return database to read-write mode. Using MaxL, type "`alter database end archive`".

BEGINARCHIVE commits any modified data to disk, switches the database to read-only mode, reopens the database files in shared, read-only mode and creates a file containing a list of files that need to be backed up. By default, the file is called archive.lst and is stored in the *ARBORPATH*\app\appname\dbname directory. ENDARCHIVE switches the database back to read-write mode.

It is important to back up all .ind and .pag files related to a database because a single database can have multiple .ind and .pag files. These files could be placed on different volumes so make sure you are backing up everything.

These are the key BSO files to back up (these are captured for us in the 11x Backup feature):

ess*n*.ind	*ARBORPATH*\app*appname**dbname*
ess*n*.pag	*ARBORPATH*\app*appname**dbname*
dbname.esm	*ARBORPATH*\app*appname**dbname*
dbname.tct	*ARBORPATH*\app*appname**dbname*
dbname.ind	*ARBORPATH*\app*appname**dbname*
dbname.app	*ARBORPATH*\app
dbname.db	*ARBORPATH*\app*appname**dbname*
x.lro	*ARBORPATH*\app*appname**dbname*
dbname.otl	*ARBORPATH*\app*appname**dbname*
Database object files (.otl, .csc, .rul)	*ARBORPATH*\app*appname**dbname*

Just as we did for an ASO database, to restore files from a backup,

1. Stop the application and databases.
2. Replace the files on disk with the corresponding files from the backup.

Do not move, copy, modify, or delete any of the following files: essn.ind, essn.pag, dbname.ind, dbname.esm, and dbname.tct. Doing so may result in data corruption.

CRITICAL PIECES TO BACKUP

Don't forget to backup the following files along with your Essbase application and database files:

essbase.sec	*ARBORPATH*\\bin
essbase.bak	*ARBORPATH*\\bin
essbase.cfg	*ARBORPATH*\\bin

Don't forget to backup the underlying relational repository for Planning on a frequent basis. You will also want to back up the Shared Services underlying relational repository and all Shared Services files on the Shared Services server.

Finally a last piece of advice: Regularly test your backup and recovery process. We know some of the smartest Essbase administrators who thought their backup process was working correctly but found out otherwise at the most critical time. Trust us. When you get that 2 a.m. I-need-my-data-where-is-it-and-how-could-you-be-asleep-when-the-sky-is-falling call from your panicked boss, you can calmly say "I'll have the database up shortly Mr. CFO." No need for panic and mayhem.

Scene 18:
Design & Optimize

There is so much to be said about designing and tuning Planning and Essbase, we could write another full book (Look Smarter Than You Are: Tuning Faster than the Speed of Light). For an introduction, this scene will review some of the design best practices and optimization steps that you can take for your Planning applications.

DESIGN FOR PLANNING

The Case for Multiple Applications

First we'll cover one of the most important questions: Should you create multiple applications or a single application with multiple plan types? Several requirements drive the number of Planning applications that are necessary for your budgeting and forecasting process. These requirements include: business purpose, user audience, user location, security, dimensionality, down time, and hardware and software limitations. A single application results in less overall overhead and maintenance when compared to a multiple application solution. For example, having one application simplifies the maintenance of master data, because you only need to update it in one place. One application can also be considered if the system does not have to be highly available to users in different time zones. A single application will always be easier to maintain. But that isn't always feasible.

Some planning and reporting requirements will dictate multiple Planning applications. A good example would be a global company that requires the Planning application to be available during business hours to all users around the world. In this case you could divide the system into separate regional Planning applications and create a global view of the business in a separate Planning or even Essbase ASO reporting database. Because Planning data forms are attached to applications and plan types, you can use the form definition utility to export and import form definitions across multiple applications. If the calculation requirements are similar in all applications, the same business rules can be shared across applications them via multiple locations. Other Essbase objects like substitution variables can be used for all the applications on the server. If you opt for a global ASO reporting database option, it can be updated via BSO-to-ASO replicated partitioning (available in version 11.1.1).

Think about the user experience interacting with separate applications. Users can simultaneously open several Planning applications, or the same application multiple times, and navigate among them by clicking their names on the tabs at the bottom of the EPM Workspace window. There is no need for end users to log out and log back in thanks to the EPM Workspace. The same way, users can also open Financial Reporting objects that connect to Essbase or other data sources without having to leave the current Workspace session.

The Case for Multiple Plan Types

Utilizing multiple plan types in applications allow for planning different subject areas in a single application. Because entity, account, and custom dimensions and members are plan type specific, you can avoid inter-dimensional irrelevance for end users. Implementing multiple plan types may improve the overall performance of the Planning application by reducing the database size; it also gives you more flexibility with parallel calculations and other processes, more efficiently utilizing server resources. Calculations will execute faster when focused on specific areas and data sets; you can also aggregate each plan type separately.

Let's analyze the standard dimensions that come with Hyperion Planning. Within a Planning application, plan types share the exact same Time Period, Year, Scenario and Version dimensions. Each plan type can have different Entity and Account dimension members. For these dimensions you can select specific members and assign them to plan types. User defined dimensions such as Product, Operating Area and Employee can also be assigned to selected plan types, but Planning requires that the assigned plan types get all the members in the custom dimension.

The picture below shows member properties for a custom dimension. You can assign the entire dimension to selected plan types, but you cannot assign selected members to different plan types.

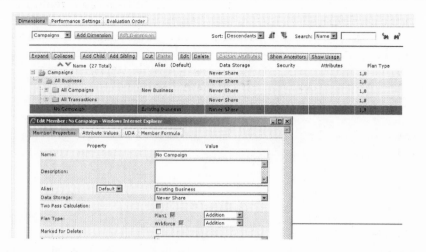

A common way to define plan types within a Planning application is based on the chart of accounts each. Each plan type only includes the custom dimensions that are relevant to each separate group of accounts. Within a Planning application you can create up to 5 Plan types. A common example of a Planning application divided based on the chart of accounts could include separate plan types for Capex, Workforce, Revenue and Financial Statements. In this example, the Revenue plan type can include a Customer and a Product Dimension that are not needed in the other plan types; Employee or Job Grade dimensions are only relevant to Workforce only; Projects and Asset Class dimensions are only needed in the Capex plan type. Each plan type uses different sections of the chart of accounts. If we talk about dataflow using the same example, the Capex plan type have detailed driver accounts to calculate depreciation expense, once the depreciation expense is calculated in Capex, it can be transferred to the P&L depreciation account in the financials plan type. Because Planning data forms are attached to a plan type and separate forms are normally created by the different groups of accounts, separating plan types and forms based on the Account dimension minimizes the number of data forms that need to be created and maintained.

The picture below shows the member property window for a member of the account dimension. For accounts, you can assign individual members to different plan types.

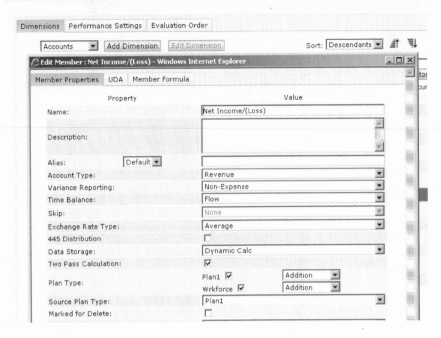

The picture below shows a property window for a member of the Entity dimension, where you can assign individual members to different plan types:

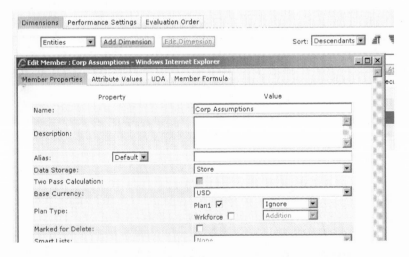

One additional consideration is that security applied to a dimension member will follow in all plan types. For example, if you assign the user "Bob" read access to the West region, he will have read access in all plan types. To address this, you can apply security by other dimensions in the specific plan types but every once in a while, you run into a "sticking" point that may prompt you to create a separate application or create different dimensionality and rollups to address how security is applied.

So in summary, there isn't one right answer to the design question: should you implement multiple applications vs. a single application with multiple plan types?

Minimize the number of dimensions

The general rule for the number of dimensions in a Planning plan type (a.k.a block storage database) is 5-9 dimensions. Make every one of them count! You will want to avoid dimensions that do not offer descriptive data points. This will help reduce complexity and size of database. Remember that adding a dimension increases the size and complexity of a database *exponentially*, not arithmetically.

Avoid Repetition in Dimensions

Repeating members may indicate a need to split dimensions, thereby reducing redundancy. In the example below, we repeat FTE, Average Hourly Rate (AHR), and Expense dollars for every payroll account. A better design would be to split the metrics from the Accounts dimension.

Before: 1 Dimension (Payroll):

```
⊟ Payroll (+)
   ⊟ 50001 (+)
       50001_FTE (+)
       50001_AHR (+)
       50001_Exp (+)
   ⊟ 50002 (+)
       50002_FTE (+)
       50002_AHR (+)
       50002_Exp (+)
   ⊟ 50003 (+)
       50003_FTE (+)
       50003_AHR (+)
       50003_Exp (+)
```

After: 2 Dimensions (Payroll and Metric):

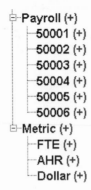

Although this rule might seem to contradict the first tip in this section about minimizing the number of dimensions, this one is really about making sure you have the *right* number of dimensions given a specified analytical requirement. Repeating members can become awkward for end-users and causes a potential maintenance nightmare for administrators. However in the example above, if only 6 accounts are repeated, a single dimension with the repeated members will result in a much smaller database. If a large number of members are repeated, consider this "split the dimension" design practice.

Avoid Inter-dimensional Irrelevance

This occurs when many members of a dimension are irrelevant across other dimensions. For example, Product and Customer dimensions will probably not be needed in a Human Resources headcount analysis database. Another example would be an Asset Category dimension placed in a sales analysis application.

The important point here is not to try to meet everyone's requirements into a single database. Split databases into meaningful analytical domains with common dimensions wherever possible.

Consistent Reporting and Planning Terminology

For consistency and ease of use, it is important to keep dimensionality between your Planning applications and your reporting applications the same. Hyperion Planning requires the following:

- Separate Fiscal Year dimension
- Separate Time Periods dimension
- Scenario dimension (used for members like Actual, Budget, and Forecast)

- Version dimension (used for members like Working, Final, What-if, Sandbox)

If at all possible, keep the dimension names consistent across your Planning and your reporting applications. For example, don't name a dimension in your reporting application "Version" and then put members like "Actual" or "Budget". This will only confuse your end users.

Use Substitution Variables

Substitution variables are global placeholders for values that change regularly, such as Current Month, Current Yr. You just need to update the value in one place, and all objects using the substitution variable will take the new value. Substitution variables can be used in most Planning and Essbase items including: Data forms, member formulas, business rules, Essbase load rules and reports. The picture below shows a web form definition set to use substitution variables for the year dimension.

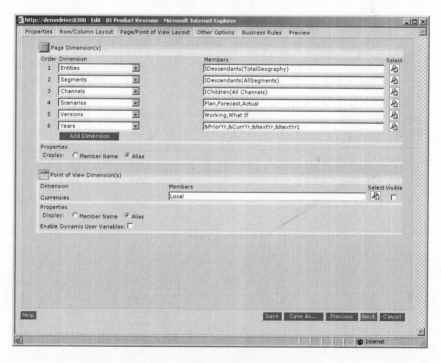

When a user opens the form, the form will take the values from the substitution variable.

		Feb	Mar	Apr	May	Jun	Jul	Aug
Units	74	4,359	1,778	2,666	4,236	5,958	5,899	4,17
Price	73	73	73	73	73	73	74	7
Sales Return %	5.9%	5.9%	5.8%	5.8%	6.1%	6.9%	7.0%	6.0
Sales Allowance %	4.2%	4.2%	4.1%	4.1%	4.3%	4.9%	5.0%	4.0
Operating Revenue	506,312	316,445	129,036	193,554	307,535	432,577	438,532	310,07
Sales Returns	(29,786)	(18,617)	(7,447)	(11,170)	(18,617)	(29,786)	(30,697)	(18,60
Sales Discounts	(21,143)	(13,214)	(5,286)	(7,929)	(13,214)	(21,143)	(21,927)	(12,40
Returns and Allowances	(50,930)	(31,831)	(12,732)	(19,099)	(31,831)	(50,930)	(52,624)	(31,00
Net Revenue	455,383	284,614	116,303	174,455	275,705	381,648	385,908	279,06
Operating COS	273,853	171,158	68,463	102,695	171,158	273,853	253,952	179,56
Gross Profit	181,530	113,456	47,840	71,760	104,546	107,795	131,956	99,50

Page controls: MA | Bookshelf Audio System | Distribution | Forecast
Working | Current Year
Dropdown: Prior Year / Current Year / Next Year / Next Year + 1

Substitution Variables are set in Essbase. And the value of each substitution value is retrieved by Planning every 5 minutes, but you can change the update frequency in the Planning properties file HspJSHome.properties, the property is SUBST_VAR_CACHE_LIFETIME. You can create and assign substitution variable values in Essbase Administration Services or via MaxL automation scripts.

When selecting substitution variables in a Planning data form definition, make sure the variable matches the dimension you are trying to set. In the picture below, you can see that the member selection window for the Year dimension also shows substitution variables for the period dimension. If you select a Period substitution variable, the form will error out.

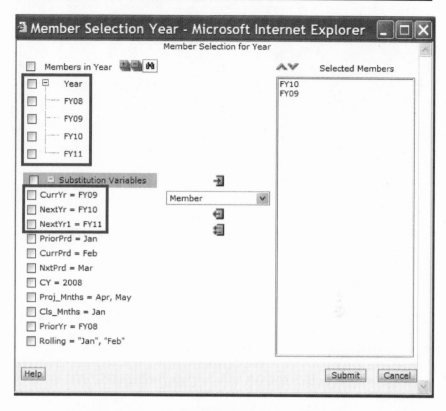

Create Dynamic Forms with Member Functions

It is highly recommended to use member selection functions when creating forms or any other Planning and Essbase object that allows you to use them. Point the member functions to high-level members that are not going to change frequently. As the outline changes, your data forms are automatically updated.

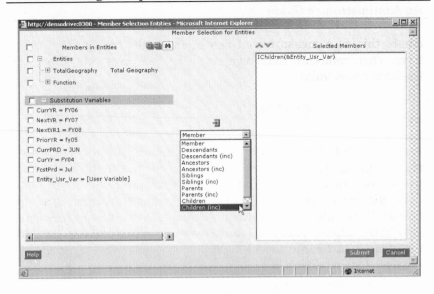

Create Dynamic Business Rules

Use runtime prompts when creating Business Rules to dramatically reduce the number of redundant rules in the system. With runtime prompts you can create a business rule once and then use runtime prompts to filter the logic for user selected members.

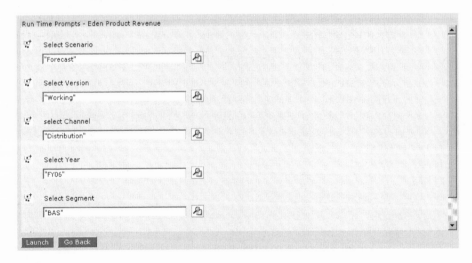

Never hard code "numbers" within the business rule. If business rule logic calculates plan as last year's actual with a 30% increase, do not hardcode ".3" into the business rule. What if the increase % changes? The user can't make the change. The Planning administrator must make the change. The design best practice is to create this as a measure that can be entered by users via a data form. Then reference that measure in the business rule instead of the hard coded value.

OPTIMIZE PLANNING

Disclaimer: **There isn't simply one right answer when it comes to optimization and tuning.** Some of the tuning guidelines can contradict other tuning guidelines. Optimizing can have different perspectives: are you tuning for calculations or retrievals or both? In some databases these tuning tips will have significant impact and in other databases they won't. Make sure you test, test, test. Did we say that tuning wasn't an exact science? One further warning - most of the information in this scene assumes 32-bit Essbase and Planning.

Factors in Tuning Planning Applications

Tuning for Planning applications has different considerations than reporting only Essbase databases. In a Planning environment, data is loaded to the cubes in several ways. Data can be loaded into Essbase in batch processes (using data loads, replicated partitions, etc.). Calc scripts are executed to allocate and aggregate the data in offline batch processes. End-user data, however, is input online to the cube via the Planning interfaces and is calculated by Business Rules. During peak time, data is continuously and concurrently being moved between caches and disk to accommodate query requests, database updates from the data forms, and end-user business rule executions. Needless to say it is a very busy processing environment. So keep this in mind as you tune your Planning applications.

Faster Data Forms

When designing Planning forms, keep in mind that smaller forms will always perform better. The memory usage on the client machine is found to be fairly static when the form size ranges from 200 cells to 5,000 cells. Split a large single data form into multiple smaller data forms with fewer rows and columns. The impact on a data form's performance relates to its grid size. The grid size doubles if a data form uses multiple currencies so design multi-currency enabled forms carefully.

The Suppress Missing Data option can help you improve the time it takes a user to open a form by suppressing the rows with no data. The Suppress Missing Blocks option can help you improve performance for sparse retrievals when large sets of sparse members are on the row section of the form (this setting is also available in Financial Reporting version 11.1.1). Use caution when enabling this setting as it can degrade performance if few or no rows are suppressed. Also note you cannot display attributes in data forms when this setting is enabled. Test data forms before and after using this setting to determine if performance is improved. Both options are defined on the Row tab of the data form definition.

Another important recommendation to improve performance of data forms is to place dense dimensions in the rows and columns sections of the data form definition. An example of this would be placing the dense Accounts dimension in the rows and dense Period dimension in the columns section of the data form with all remaining sparse dimensions in the Page and POV sections. This design will bring back a single block in the data form. If you place one or more sparse dimensions in the rows or columns, multiple blocks are returned and processed by the data form.

Design fewer dimensions

Analyze your requirements very carefully and try to design applications with only the dimensions that are required for Planning. Fewer dimensions generate smaller databases resulting in better performance, and less complexity for end users to find their data. Don't try to build an Actuals reporting system in your Planning application. Create an ASO reporting database to perform Actuals and Variance reporting and analysis and then take advantage of the BSO-to-ASO replicated partitions to share plan data to the reporting database. You can store more years and more detail in the ASO database for reporting purposes. In Planning, only store the historical data that is needed as part of the Planning process.

Take advantage of Smart Lists as possible replacements for attribute and stored dimensions. The sample below illustrates how you can classify a product by level of risk using a Smart List instead of using an attribute or a stored dimension.

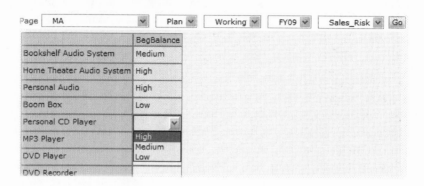

Use Calc on Save / Calc on Load only when necessary

You can attach the Calculate Data Form business rule or custom business rules to data forms. The Calculate Data form rules are automatically created for every form and it calculate plan data for the members on the data form. Custom Business Rules can be added to forms and set to "Run on Save" and "Run on Load". These options run the business rule when the user clicks the Save button on the data form or when the user opens the form.

While this is a powerful feature, to the end user it looks as if the data form is taking a long time to open or save. Only use this features when needed. If your data form requires no additional calculation (possibly all members on the data form are dynamic), do not enable Calculate Data Form or other custom business rules. Add any business rules to a right-click menu or task list so the end user understands the rule may take a few seconds or minutes to execute. If you use this feature, communicate to end users the expected form save and/or open times.

Focus Business Rules

Focus Business Rule logic on only those members that need to be calculated. E.g. if you need to roll up a specific section of the entity dimension, don't aggregate the entire Entity dimension. Use a runtime prompt to focus the calculation on the desired member(s).

Members available to users for runtime prompts are limited by security and specific limitations that can be established when creating the runtime prompt. You can prompt for single or multiple members, numeric value, Smart List value, or text value.

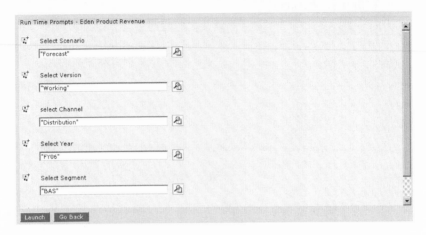

Make upper members Dynamic in dense dimensions

Consider setting the storage property to Dynamic on all upper-level members in your dense dimensions. This reduces the size of the data block and eliminates the need to execute business rules when saving data.

Let's assume the Periods and Accounts dimensions are dense, upper level members are set to "Dynamic Calc" and most data forms have Periods on the columns and Accounts on the rows. When users enter data into these forms or refresh the forms, all totals will be dynamically calculated without running any business rule. In the example below, "Total Orders" is an upper level account that is dynamically calculated. The form does not need to execute business rules to display the "Total Orders" result.

Order Rate		Store
⊟ 📄 Total Orders		Dynamic Calc
Orders		Store
Order Uplift		Store

	Jan	Feb	Mar
Orders	52,330	33,737	17,6C
Order Uplift	123,456	20	
−Total Orders	175,786	33,757	17,6C
Average Sales Price			
Sales Revenue			

Page [CA ▼] 🔍 [Distribution ▼] [Plan ▼] [F

Page [Working ▼] [Go]

Aggressive Use Dynamic Calc Member Tags

We discussed the benefits of using dynamic calcs (which result in smaller block size). However, an aggressive use of the dynamic calc tag can create a large difference between the size of the block in the dynamic calculator cache and the size of the block in the data cache. If you use a large number of Dynamic Calc tags, you will probably need to tune the Dynamic Calculator cache.

Also watch out for business rules and calc scripts that reference or require dynamically calculated members. Do not do this. Ever.

Tune the Index Cache

The index cache is a reserved set of memory that is used to store all or a portion of the index file for quick access. You want to try and place as much of the index file into memory as possible to help with performance.

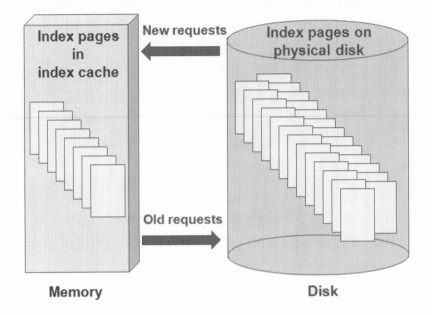

Here is a guideline for setting the index cache:

Set the index cache equal to the combined size of all ess*n*.ind files, if possible. If you can't do that, then size the index cache as large as possible. Do not set this cache size higher than the total index size, as no performance improvement will be realized and you'll be consuming memory that other processes might need to use. It is possible for the index to be too large: Essbase will spend more time looking in the index cache than it would use by giving up and reading from the hard drive. In other words, if your index is 1,750 GB, don't set your index cache to 1,750 GB.

Here's an example: the index size for Sample.Basic is 8024 KB. We have enough memory on the server, so we will increase the index cache to 8024 KB.

To set the index cache, select the database, right-click and select Edit >> Properties. Select the Caches tab:

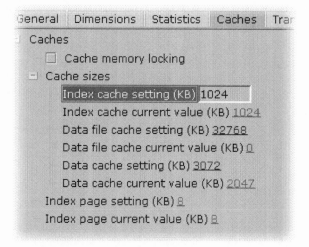

Enter the new index cache value.

Tune the Data Cache

The data cache is the memory set aside to hold data blocks. You'll want to place as many blocks in memory as possible, but with the caveat that too much places a management burden on the system and can hurt overall performance.

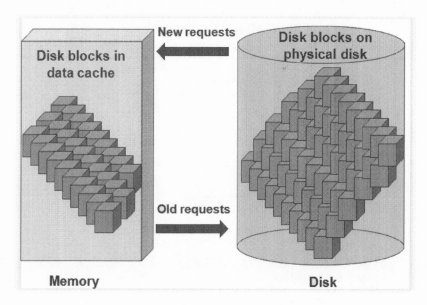

A guideline for setting the data cache is to set it to 0.125 times the combined size of all ess*n*.pag files with a minimum value of about 307,200 KB (the default is only a miserly 3 Mb, and we're forcing back another diatribe on stupid defaults that never get increased). Consider increasing this value even further if you have a high number of concurrent users and they're complaining about retrieval times during peak times. Another time to further increase the Data Cache is when you have calculation scripts that contain functions that operate across sparse ranges and the functions require all members of a range to be in memory; for example, when using @RANK and @RANGE.

Here's an example of the recommended initial setting: the page size for your database is 3 GB. We have more than enough memory on the server, so we will increase the data cache to .125 * 3072000KB or 384,000 KB which equals about 300 MB.

To set the data cache, select the database, right-click and select Edit >> Properties. Select the Caches tab:

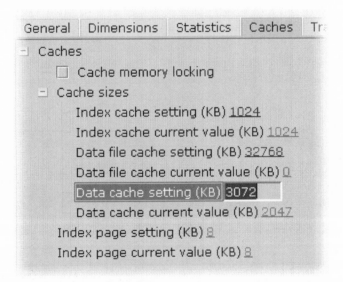

Enter the new data cache value.

The priority for cache tuning is as follows:
1. Index Cache
2. Data File Cache (when using Direct I/O which shouldn't be 99% of the time)
3. Data Cache

The new cache settings will not take effect until the database is restarted.

Cache hit ratios will tell you how well your caches are being utilized. The ratio will tell you the percentage of time that a requested piece of information is available in the cache. As a general rule, the higher the ratio, the better. The goal for the index cache ratio should be close to 1. The goal for the data cache ratio should be 1, but values as low as 0.3 are acceptable. Why so low for data cache ratio? Your page files are a lot bigger than the index file. The chances that you can fit all of the page files or data into memory is pretty slim to impossible.

To view the cache ratios, right-click on the database and select Edit >> Properties. Select the Statistics tab to view hit ratios:

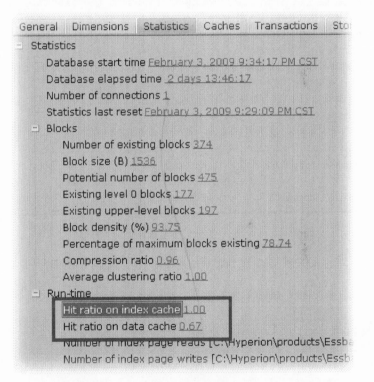

Dimension Order within the Outline

Here is another tuning tip related to the order of dimensions within an outline. Dimension ordering within outlines is critical to your overall Essbase performance. You will want to test different iterations of dimension orders to determine the optimal structure.

Historically, outlines were ordered from largest dense to smallest dense and then smallest sparse to largest sparse (sometimes called the "hourglass" format). This works well when parallel calculation is not utilized. Since Essbase 6.5, though, everyone is using parallel calculation, so an improved method for ordering the dimensions was created.

First a few definitions:

Dense dimensions are the dimensions that define the internal structure of the data block. They should reside at the top of the outline.

Aggregating Sparse dimensions are dimensions that will be calculated to create new parent values. These dimensions should reside directly below the last Dense dimension in the outline. Placing these dimensions as the first Sparse dimensions positions them to be the first dimensions included in the calculator cache. This gives them an ideal location within the database for optimized calculation performance.

Non-Aggregating Sparse dimensions are dimensions that organize the data into logical slices. Examples include Scenario, Year or Version. It is not crucial for these dimensions to be included in the calculator cache because their members are typically isolated in FIX statements.

With this in mind, try the following guidelines to create an optimal outline order (sometimes called a "dress form" or an "hourglass on a stick"):

1. Time (assuming it's a dense dimension)
2. Largest Dense Dimensions
3. Smallest Dense Dimensions
4. Smallest Aggregating Sparse Dimensions
5. Largest Aggregating Sparse Dimensions
6. Non-aggregating Sparse Dimensions

Example – An Employee Analysis Database:

Dimension	Type-Stored Member Count	Density After Calc	Density After Load	Data Points Created
Time Periods	D – 21	85%	85%	-
Accounts	D – 94	3 %	2%	-
Scenarios	AS – 9	22%	11%	199

Dimension	Type-Stored Member Count	Density After Calc	Density After Load	Data Points Created
Job Code	AS – 1,524	.56%	.23%	853
Organization	AS – 2,304	.34%	.09%	783
Versions	NAS – 7	19%	19%	-
Years	NAS – 7	14%	14%	-

D=Dense, AS=Aggregating Sparse, NAS=Non-Aggregating Sparse

Outlines can be ordered based on dimension stored member count or on dimension density. Ordering by stored member count is the easy option but may not be as accurate as ordering by dimension density. In the example above, the optimized outline should follow this order (assuming we order the outline based on dimension density and our other rule, Time first and then Accounts):

Original Dimension Order (Typical Hourglass)	Optimized Dimension Order (Modified Hourglass)
Accounts (D)	Time Periods (D)
Time Periods (D)	Accounts (D)
Years	Job Code (AS)
Versions	Organization (AS)
Scenarios	Years (NAS)
Job Code	Versions (NAS)
Organization	Scenarios (NAS)
Employee Status (Attr Dim)	Employee Status (Attr Dim)
Fund Group (Attr Dim)	Fund Group (Attr Dim)

Optimize Calculations and Business Rules

Many folks ask "Why does my calc script take 5 hours?" or "How can I get my calc time down?" Changing a number of the database and outline settings can significantly impact your calculation time. These settings are discussed in other sections of the book, but here are a few more tips.

Calculate only those dimensions requiring calculation. For example, do you need to rollup Scenario (Actual + Budget)? If all of the upper level members in your Accounts dimension are dynamic, do you need to calculate Accounts? Nope. By utilizing a lean and mean "CALC DIM" or "AGG" with only the dimensions that need it, you'll shave valuable time from your calc scripts.

"AGG" and "CALC DIM" are not the same. "AGG" is faster for straight aggregation of sparse dimensions with no member formulas so use this when you can. There are some cases where a sparse dimension with 7+ levels may CALC DIM faster than it AGGs, but this is rare.

In general, use "Fix" on Sparse dimensions and use "If" on Dense dimensions if you're going to be doing different logic on different members from the same dimension. If you need to do a bunch of logic against a set of members of a dimension (dense or sparse) and you don't need to do *different* logic against different members of that dimension, always use a FIX.

Other last general calculation optimization tips: simplify the calculation if possible by using unary calcs instead of member formulas and member formulas instead of logic within a calc script. Take advantage of built-in Essbase functionality like Dynamic Time Series whenever possible.

Optimize Retrievals

You *can* speed up data retrievals by increasing the value of two retrieval-specific buffer settings. These buffers hold extracted row data cells before they are evaluated or sorted. If the buffer is too small, retrieval times can increase with the constant emptying and re-filling of the buffer. If the buffer is too large, retrieval times can increase when too much memory is used as concurrent users perform queries. The default buffer is set to 10KB for 32-bit platforms and 20 KB for 64-bit. As a rule, don't exceed 100KB for either buffer.

To set the retrieval buffers,

1. Right-click on the Database and select Edit Properties.
2. Go to the General tab and set the retrieval buffers:

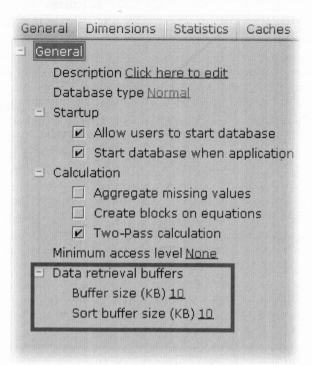

Fragmentation

Fragmentation can be a potentially crippling side-effect of frequently updated databases. Let's assume that we have a very simple block with only eight cells:

100	#Missing	#Missing	#Missing
#Missing	#Missing	#Missing	#Missing

Any one of Essbase's compression methods would work well for this example, but let's assume Run-Length Encoding is used and is able to compress the data storage component to 32 bytes (8 Bytes for the 100 and 24 Bytes to compress all the #Missing values together). Then, a user writes some budget data to this block:

100	150	200	#Missing
#Missing	#Missing	#Missing	#Missing

This block will now require 48 Bytes to store (8 Bytes for each number, and 24 Bytes for the #Missing values). Fragmentation happens because Essbase can't fit 48 Bytes back into the original 32 Byte location and it is written to the end of the file. The original block still remains in the file, but there is no corresponding pointer in the index file so it is lost forever but still taking up space. Actually, it's not quite forever. Essbase tracks empty space in the database directory in a .esm file.

Now that you understand fragmentation, an alarm should be going off for all budgeting application administrators – Ding, Ding! Budgeting not only involves frequent updates, but also calc scripts that expand block size. Fragmentation also runs rampant when data load rules aren't sorted properly and blocks are written to the .pag file, then updated later in the load and re-written to a new block location.

To eliminate fragmentation, you can export the data from the database to a file, clear all data from the database and reload from the export file (see the Backup and Recovery scene). This workaround (and various other unseemly workarounds like adding "dummy members" to dense dimensions) was the only method to defragment an Essbase cube until recently. Newer versions of Essbase MaxL support a command called `alter database [database name] force restructure` which removes all fragmentation from the database.

Penny's head is buried in her arms on the desk, fast asleep, a pile of drool forming under her chin. The Translator gently taps Penny on the shoulder, waking her.

Penny sits up, a bit groggy.

"Penny, that's it. We've covered all of the Administrator topics. Granted you slept through the last scene but that's why you have this book. You can come back and review this information when you need it," The Translator says.

"It's time to call Eddie," says SuperManager. That wakes Penny up.

"I don't know if I can."

"Sure you can," says Aquaman.

"We're here for you," says Mr. Anachronism.

(Lights dim. Disco ball and wild colored lights start up. Spotlight goes on The Consultants. EVERYONE including BAND dons wild disco wigs and puts on bling and sings the reprisal set to I Believe in Miracles.)

I BELIEVE THAT PENNY, CAN WIN OVER EDDIE!
(LIKE CONSULTANTS DO)

BUT I THINK TO DO IT, PENNY WILL NEED,
HYPERION PLANNING!

YOU'RE GOING TO HELP EDDIE.
IT'S SO GREAT THAT HE NEEDS YOU.
IT'S GREAT THAT HE NEEDS YOU SO BADLY.
BECAUSE BY NEXT WEEK, HE'LL HAVE FALLEN
BACK IN LOVE MADLY.

YESTERDAY, YOU WERE A PATHETIC IT GEEK
NOW YOU'VE GOT A WEEK TO SINK OR SWIM, NO
PRESSURE YOU SEE, CAUSE
I BELIEVE IN PENNY, SHE CAN DO, ANYTHING
(ANYTHING IT'S TRUE)
I BELIEVE IN PENNY, AND ORACLE HYPERION
PLANNING...

"OK," Penny says and picks up the phone.

EPILOGUE

You can plan on the web, plan in Excel, approve plans, and set preferences. We've reached the end of our computer book / musical. To find out whether our heroine lives happily ever after, you'll have to read the "sequel": Look Smarter Than You are with Planning: An End User's Guide.

Really, we're going to end the book with a cliffhanger? OK, if you can make it through the end of the appendix, we'll provide some spoilers for our musical finale.

Appendix A:
Prepare for Book Exercises

This book uses the Planning Sample application that is delivered with Oracle Hyperion Planning in the beginning of this book. In order for you to follow along with the exercises in this book, you will have to set up a few things. Don't shoot the messenger (or write a bad book review). We wish we could deliver an easy-to-use built in example for you but it just isn't possible with the current version of the software. While there are a number of steps below, this is still the easiest and fastest way to set up a sample application for learning.

SET UP PLANNING SAMPLE

1. Create a Planning Sample application and load the sample data following the instructions in the Planning Administrator's Guide – see last section on Sample application
   (http://download.oracle.com/docs/cd/E12825_01/epm.111/hp_admin/frameset.htm?launch.html).
13. Create a group in Shared Services called *PlanSampEndUsers*.
14. Provision the *PlanSampEndUsers* group for:
    a. *Planner* access for the Planning Sample application
    b. Reporting and Analysis – *Content Publisher*
    c. Optionally *Mass Allocate* role (if you want users to use this feature); know that Mass Allocate creates and launches Business Rules behind the scenes so only assign if end users really need it

15. Assign the following security for the PlanSampEndUsers:

Item	Security Access
Account Dimension – Statistics, Income	Write – Descendants Inclusive
Account Dimension – IncomeStatement	Write – Descendants Inclusive
Account Dimension – BalanceSheet	Write – Descendants Inclusive
Account Dimension – CashFlow	Write – Descendants Inclusive
Account Dimension – Ratios	Write – Descendants Inclusive
Entity Dimension – Total Geography	Write – Descendants Inclusive
Entity Dimension - Function	Write – Descendants Inclusive
Scenario – Current, Plan, Forecast	Write – Member
Scenario - Actual	Read – Member
Version – Working, Final, Target, Variance	Write – Member
Version –Variance	Read – Member
TaskList – Financial Plan	Assign
Forms (main folder)	Read

16. Start the Planning units for Plan Scenario, Working Version:

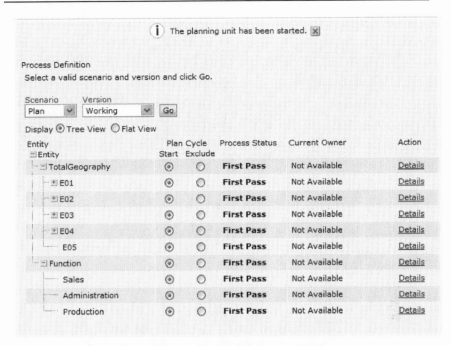

UPDATE FORM SETTINGS

17. Check *Enable Account Annotations* for the Plan Operating Expenses data form.
18. Optional: Check *Allow Add Rows* to the Plan Operating Expenses data form (if you want users to learn and use this feature).

Enable Plan Department Expenses Data Form to *Attach Cell Level Documents* (new 11x feature).

19. Go to the Administration menu and select *Manage Data Forms*.
20. Expand Forms and select the Expenses group. Select the *Plan Department Expenses* form and click *Edit*:

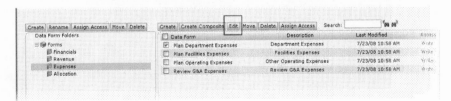

21. Go to the Other Options tab and check box for *Enable Cell-level Document*. Click *Save*.

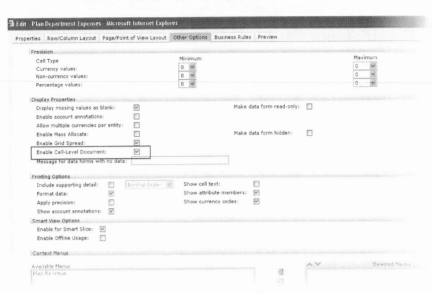

Enable Income Statement Data Form to Display Member Formulas (new 11x feature)

22. From the Administration menu in Planning, go to *Manage Data Forms,* and select *Financials>>Income Statement*.

23. Go to the Row/Column Layout tab and enable Display Member Formula options for the Row Dimension.

24. Click *Save*.

Note: This option is available for Column Dimensions, as well.

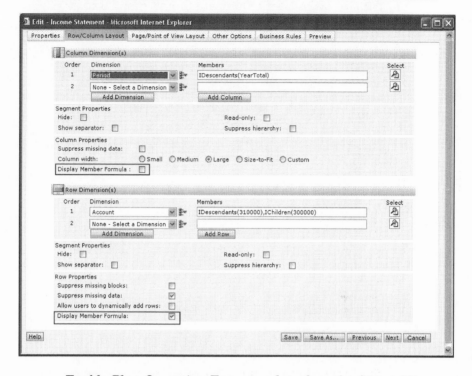

Enable Plan Operating Expenses data form for Smart Slice (new 11x feature).

25. Go to the Administration menu and select *Manage Data Forms*.

26. Expand Forms and select the Expenses group. Select the *Plan Operating Expenses* form and click *Edit*:

27. Go to the Other Options tab and check box for *Enable for Smart Slice*.

28. Click *Save*.

29. Create a Smart Slice following the steps listed in Scene
    4 – Smart Slices in a Data Form.

Provide Information to End Users

Provide the following information to your end users if they
need access to the Planning Sample application

- URL for EPM Workspace
- Optional: URL for Planning Web client (if using Planning
  web client directly)
- User ID and Password
- For Smart View, Server Name
- For Smart View, APS URL for Provider Services.
- Planning version

What's Missing?

The Planning Sample application has some great examples
of data forms, dimensions and other components to help illustrate
Planning's capabilities. However, there are a few things missing:

- Smart Lists
- Text and Date type measures

- Attribute dimensions
- Business Rules
- Enabled forms for the following features:
  - Mass Allocate
  - View member formulas
  - Account annotations
  - Add rows, attach documents
  - Smart Slices
  - Offline Planning

If you would like to train end users on these features, you'll need to build in these components yourself (some of which we've done above).

MY PLANNING APPLICATION

This book covers the Planning Sample application. As part of the training for your end users, they will need to know about the specifics of the Planning applications that you have created for them. You have probably provided some training and/or information on your specific applications and processes. If not, complete the a matrix similar to the one provided below to help your end users better understand your specific Planning environment. Planning administrators, use this matrix as a tool to help train your own users. Couple the matrix and this book and you have some folks who are ready to plan.

Application Overview	*Define the Planning application name and purpose*
Plan Types	*Name the Plan Types and provide a general description*
Planning Timeframe	*Define the planning process timeframe*
Audience/End Users	*Define the users of the application*
Data Sources	*List the data sources that feed the Planning application*
Dimensions in Each Plan Type	*List the dimensions for each Plan Type*
Smart Lists	*List the Smart Lists*
User Variables	*List the user variables they will need to set*
Task Lists	*List task lists, their purpose, audience, and steps*
Data Form	*List data form folders, their purpose, audience*

Folders	
Data Forms	*List data forms, their purpose, audience, assigned Business Rules, enabled for grid spread, enabled for Mass Allocate, enabled for adhoc analysis, assigned right-click menus*
Right-Click Menus	*List right-click menus, their purpose, audience, and steps*
Independent Business Rules	*List any standalone Business Rules that exist, purpose, run-time prompts and who will use them*

Appendix B:
Introduction to EPMA

As you begin to rollout Oracle EPM / Hyperion, the number of applications required to meet performance management needs is likely to grow. With a growing environment, you encounter many challenges in developing and maintaining a number of different dimensions and data sets across applications. The result is duplicate efforts and higher development and maintenance costs which are never a good thing.

Does your dimension maintenance process look like the following?

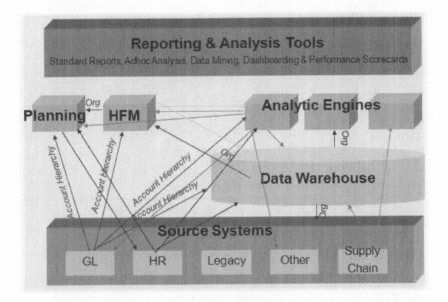

For example, the Accounts dimension is sourced from the GL system and shared with the data warehouse, Essbase, Planning and Financial Management. The Organization dimension is sourced and maintained in the data warehouse to all Hyperion applications. Other dimensions may be maintained in Essbase or other applications, resulting in a hodge-podge of dimension maintenance processes.

Enterprise Performance Architect is a solution that can address some of these concerns and issues. Enterprise Performance

Management Architect (EPMA) provides a single interface to build, deploy, and manage all financial applications for Planning, Financial Management, Essbase and Profitability and Cost Management. EPMA uses a visual interface to manage, link, and synchronize applications for Hyperion administrators.

EPMA contains the following components:

- Dimensions Library – one place to create and maintain dimensions across Hyperion applications
- Applications Library – one place to manage Hyperion applications
- Data Synchronization View – synchronize data across Hyperion applications
- Application Upgrade – upgrade Planning and FM applications from previous releases
- Job Console – view a summary of Dimension Library and Application activities like imports, deployments and data synchronizations

The basic architecture for EPMA contains a number of underlying EPMA services and a backend relational repository.

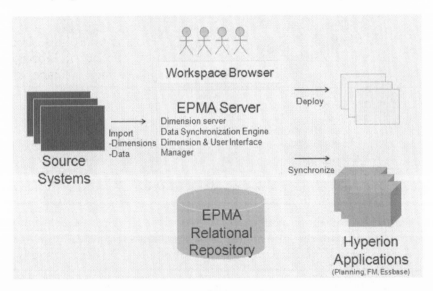

Do you have to use Enterprise Performance Management Architect? No. You can continue to use Planning "Classic" if desired.

 If you are on version 9.3.1, stop reading now. Revisit EPMA when you upgrade to version 11. EPMA was

Note!   introduced in version 9.3 and while you can get it to work, it will be a long, painful, buggy process. Version 11 addressed a number of different items that make the deployment process a much smoother sailing effort.

The content in this appendix is based on 11.1.1.

Note!

At a very high level, the process is as follows: Dimensions are imported into or manually created in EPMA via the Workspace browser and then grouped together to create EPMA applications. The EPMA application is deployed to the specific solution like Planning, Essbase or Financial Management. The easiest way to learn EPMA is to create an EPMA deployed application, so let us jump head first into your first EPMA application.

Access EPMA

Test question: Where do you access EPMA? This should be an easy one. The Workspace, of course. You get to practically everything via the Workspace.

1. Log into the Workspace.
2. Select Navigate icon >> Administer and then the desired EPMA module: Dimension Library, Application Library, Data Synchronization, Calculation Manager, Application Upgrade, and Job Console.
3. To get started, we'll select Dimension Library.

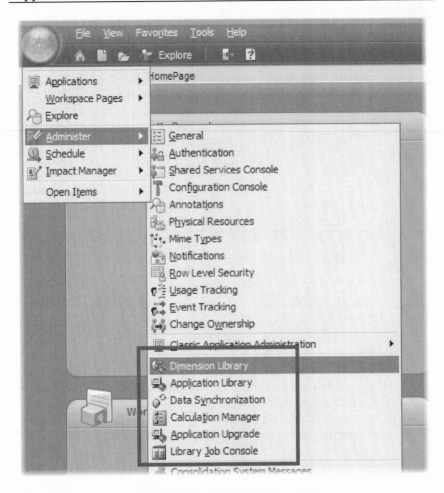

DIMENSION LIBRARY

The Dimension Library will open and may or may not have dimensions listed in your environment (this depends on if others have created dimensions):

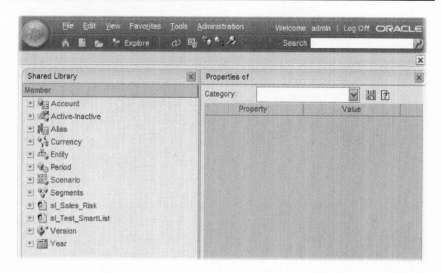

The EPMA Dimension Library provides one place to create and maintain dimensions across Oracle EPM / Hyperion applications. You can maintain the hierarchies for the dimensions as well as global and application specific properties. Dimensions can be used in multiple applications. For EPMA deployed applications, you will maintain dimensions here and not in the web clients for Planning and Financial Management. You can still view dimensions in the Classic applications but you can't change them.

Within the Dimension Library you can have two types of dimensions: shared dimensions and local dimensions. Shared dimensions are dimensions that can be used by multiple applications. Local dimensions are detached, independent dimensions that exist in only one application. Dimensions can be switched from shared to local and local to shared as well synchronized in applications.

Create a Dimension

To create a dimension in the Dimension Library,

1. Select File>> New>>Dimension:

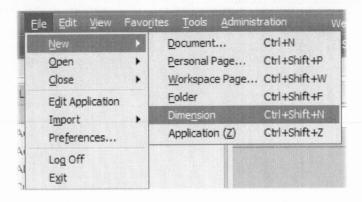

2. Type in the dimension name and description.
3. Select the dimension type. To follow along choose Generic:

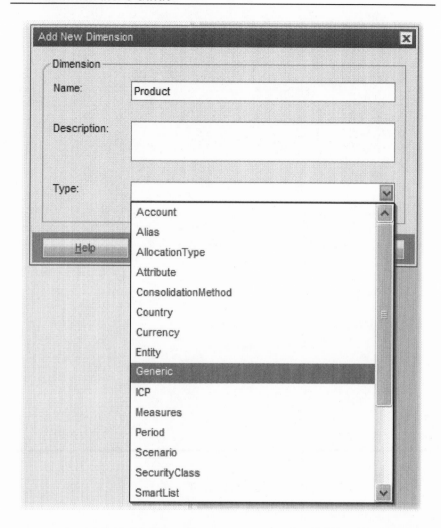

A number of dimension types exist for EPMA dimensions and not all of those types are applicable to Planning. For example, Financial Management will use dimension types like Security Class or Consolidation Method.

The dimension types that you could possibly use in Planning include:

- Account
- Alias
- Attribute
- Country
- Currency

- Entity
- Generic
- Period
- Scenario
- Smart List
- Time
- UDA
- Version
- Year

By selecting the dimension type, the appropriate properties will be created (e.g. Time Balance properties only apply to Accounts dimensions). These dimension types and elements are covered throughout the main content of the book so we're going to assume that you know and understand these concepts.

    4. Click OK.

The Product dimension is created in the Shared Library:

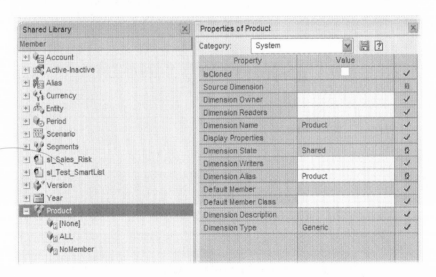

Now all you need to do is create the members and hierarchies.

    5. Right-click on Product and select Create Member >> As Child:

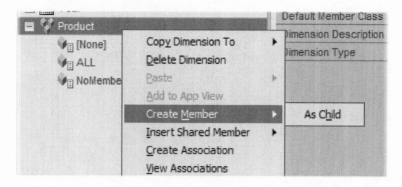

6. Type in the member name "Colas":

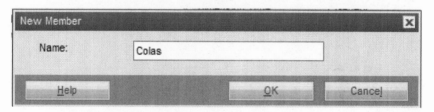

7. Click OK.
8. Repeat the same Create Member steps to build the following hierarchy under Product:

9. Select the member "Colas".
10. From the property drop down box, select Planning:

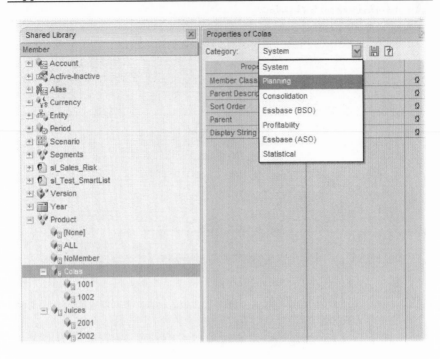

11. The Planning properties will display:

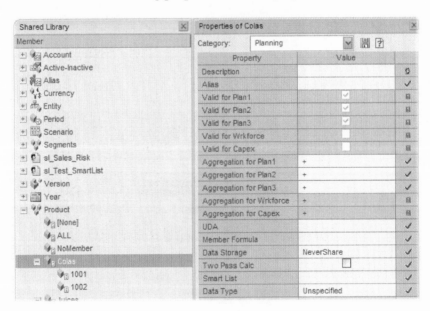

Notice the plan type options are grayed out. This is because those are application specific properties. You can define an alias, consolidation tag, UDA, data storage and other Planning properties.

12. Change the Data Storage property from NeverShare to StoreData.

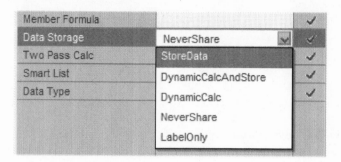

The Data Storage property is changed to yellow to highlight that a change has been made but not saved.

13. Click the Save icon:

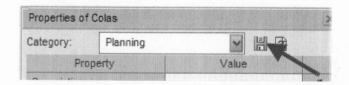

14. Click in the Alias text box and select the ellipses icon to define an alias:

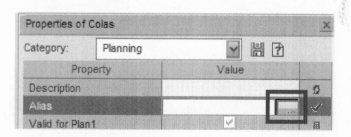

Did you get an error message?

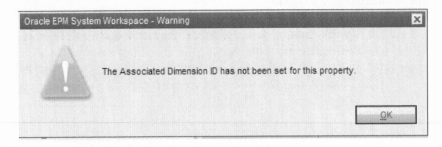

Create an Associated Dimension

Dimension associations are used in EPMA to relate dimensions within the Shared Library and applications. A dimension association is created for all properties where the property value refers to a member of another dimension.

The alias property requires an associated dimension. So your steps are to: 1) create an alias dimension and 2) associate it with the Product dimension. Once you pull the Product dimension or any other dimension with dimensions associations into an application, you must activate the dimension associations.

1. Select File >> New >> Dimension.
2. Type in "Aliases" for the dimension name and choose Alias as the dimension type:

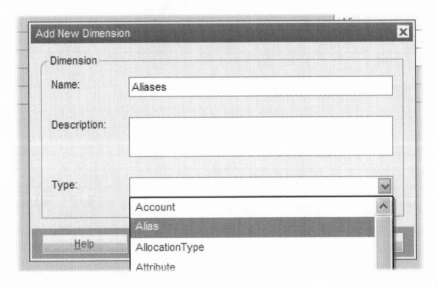

3. Click OK.
4. The Aliases dimension is created in the Dimension Library.

5. Right-click on the Product dimension and select Create
    Association:

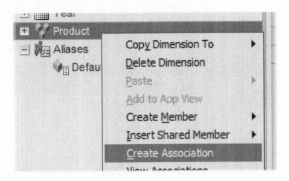

6. Select Existing Property.
7. Choose the property Alias.
8. Choose the dimension Aliases (the new Aliases
    dimension you just created):

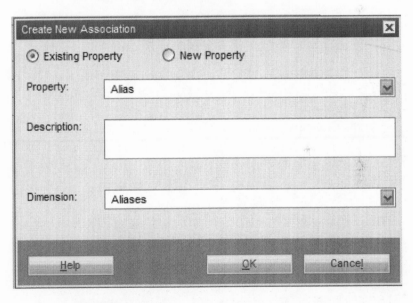

9. Click OK.
10. Navigate back to the "Colas" member and its Planning
    properties.
11. Click in the Alias text box and select the ellipses icon to
    define an alias.
12. Enter an alias in the default text box:

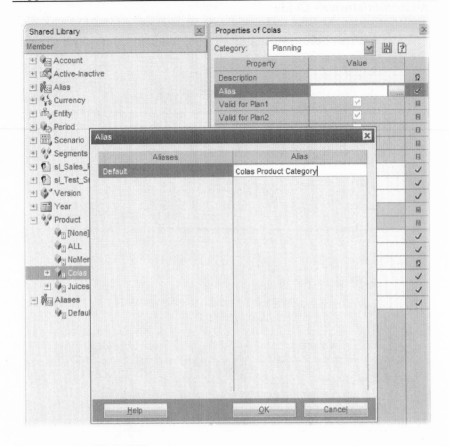

13. Click OK.

The alias is added though you can't see it in the property window:

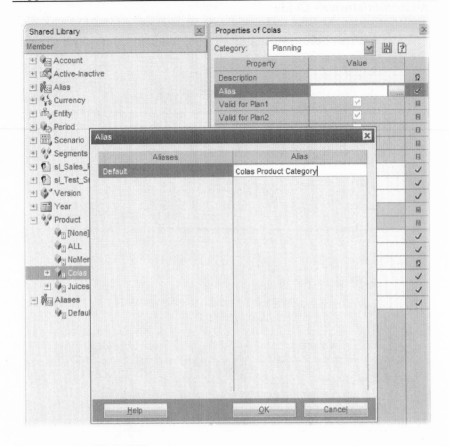

14. Click the Save icon to save the alias.

You can perform the following actions on dimensions within the EPMA Dimension Library:

- Copy local dimensions to the Shared Library
- Copy dimensions to an application
- Delete dimensions
- Create and view associations
- View application membership and deployment status
- Find members and orphan members

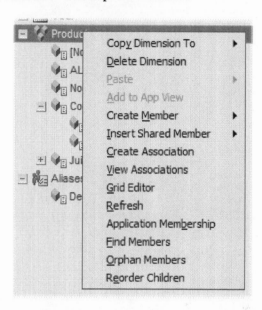

You can perform the following actions on members within the EPMA Dimension Library:

- Cut and copy
- Create members
- Insert shared members
- Remove members
- Delete members
- Rename members
- View application membership (in which applications does the member exist)
- Find members
- Reorder a members children

Import File Format

For most dimensions with a large number of members, you will want to import the dimension (versus manually typing the members into EPMA). You may import the dimension once and then maintain the hierarchy in EPMA going forward or you may run dimension imports on a periodic basis from other sources to keep the hierarchy current.

EPMA supports dimension imports using a specific flat file format or user interface tables. In this appendix, we will cover the flat file method. Within the flat file, five sections are possible:

- Dimensions
- Dimension Associations
- Members
- Hierarchies
- Property Array

Additionally there is a header that must be included:
FILE_FORMAT = ADS
VERSION=1.0

The Dimensions section lists the dimension contained in the import file along with any defined dimension properties:

```
!FILE_FORMAT=ADS
!VERSION=1.0

!Section=Dimensions
'Name|DimensionClass|DimensionAlias|DimDataStorage|DimTwoPassCalc|Plan1Density|P
Active-Inactive|Attribute|Active-Inactive||||||Boolean||||||||||||||
Account|Account|Account|NeverShare||Dense|Dense|Dense||||1|0|0|||Y|N|N|N|N|2|1|1
Currency|Currency|Currency|NeverShare||Sparse|Sparse|Sparse||||2|0|0|||Y|N|N|N|N
Entity|Entity|Entity|NeverShare||Sparse|Sparse|Sparse||||3|0|0|||Y|N|N|N|N|3|7|7
Period|Period|Period|NeverShare||Dense|Dense|Dense||||4|0|0|||Y|N|N|N|N|2|2|2|2|
Scenario|Scenario|Scenario|NeverShare||Sparse|Sparse|Sparse||||5|0|0|||Y|N|N|N|N
Segments|Generic|Segments|StoreData||Sparse|Sparse|Sparse||||6|0|0|||Y|N|N|N|N|4
Version|Version|Version|NeverShare||Sparse|Sparse|Sparse||||7|0|0|||Y|N|N|N|N|8|
Year|Year|Year|NeverShare||Sparse|Sparse|Sparse||||8|0|0|||Y|N|N|N|N|3|3|3|3|3||
sl_Sales_Risk|SmartList|Sales_Risk||||||||||||||||ID|Grid|Y|Sales Risk|
sl_Test_SmartList|SmartList|Test_SmartList||||||||||||||||||||Pick One|NAME|
Alias|Alias|Alias||||||||||||||||||||||||||

!Section=DimensionAssociations
'BaseDimension|Property|TargetDimension
Active-Inactive|Alias|Alias
Account|Alias|Alias
Currency|Alias|Alias
Currency|TriangulationCurrency|Currency
```

The DimensionAssociations section lists the base dimension,
the property to be mapped using an associated dimension, and the
associated dimension itself:

```
Scenario|Scenario|Scenario|NeverShare||Sparse|Sparse|S
Segments|Generic|Segments|StoreData||Sparse|Sparse|Spa
Version|Version|Version|Version|NeverShare||Sparse|Sparse|Spar
Year|Year|Year|NeverShare||Sparse|Sparse|Sparse||||8|0
sl_Sales_Risk|SmartList|Sales_Risk|||||||||||||||
sl_Test_SmartList|SmartList|Test_SmartList|||||||||||
Alias|Alias|Alias|||||||||||||||||||||||

!Section=DimensionAssociations
'BaseDimension|Property|TargetDimension
Active-Inactive|Alias|Alias
Account|Alias|Alias
Currency|Alias|Alias
Currency|TriangulationCurrency|Currency
Entity|Alias|Alias
Entity|Currency|Currency
Period|Alias|Alias
Scenario|Alias|Alias
Scenario|StartPeriod|Period
Scenario|EndPeriod|Period
Scenario|StartYear|Year
Scenario|EndYear|Year
Segments|Alias|Alias
Segments|Active-Inactive|Active-Inactive
Version|Alias|Alias
Year|Alias|Alias

!Hierarchies=Active-Inactive
'Parent|Child|DataStorage|IsPrimary|Alias=Default
#root|True||Y|Active
```

The Hierarchies section defines the hierarchy in parent child format along with any defined properties for the child:

```
!Hierarchies=Active-Inactive
'Parent|Child|DataStorage|IsPrimary|Alias=Default
#root|True| |Y|Active
#root|False| |Y|Inactive

!Hierarchies=Account
'Parent|Child|DataStorage|IsPrimary|MemberValidForPlan1|MemberValidForPlan2|Memb
#root|Statistics|DynamicCalc|Y|Y|N|N| | |~| | | | |NonCurrency|Plan1|SavedAssumption|N
Statistics|CapitalExpenditures|DynamicCalc|Y|Y|N|N| | |~| | | | |NonCurrency|Plan1|Sav
CapitalExpenditures|CapExLand|StoreData|Y|Y|N|N| | |+| | | | |NonCurrency|Plan1|SavedA
CapitalExpenditures|CapExBuildings|StoreData|Y|Y|N|N| | |+| | | |NonCurrency|Plan1|S
CapitalExpenditures|CapExLsholdImprov|StoreData|Y|Y|N|N| | |+| | | |NonCurrency|Plan
CapitalExpenditures|CapExMfgMach|StoreData|Y|Y|N|N| | |+| | | |NonCurrency|Plan1|Sav
CapitalExpenditures|CapExOffFurn|StoreData|Y|Y|N|N| | |+| | | |NonCurrency|Plan1|Sav
CapitalExpenditures|CapExCompEquip|StoreData|Y|Y|N|N| | |+| | | |NonCurrency|Plan1|S
CapitalExpenditures|CapExCompSftwr|StoreData|Y|Y|N|N| | |+| | | |NonCurrency|Plan1|S
CapitalExpenditures|CapExVehicles|StoreData|Y|Y|N|N| | |+| | | |NonCurrency|Plan1|Sa
Statistics|OtherDrivers|DynamicCalc|Y|Y|N|N| | |~| | | |NonCurrency|Plan1|SavedAssum
OtherDrivers|NI|StoreData|Y|Y|N|N| | |~| | | |Currency|Plan1|SavedAssumption|Average
OtherDrivers|EBITDA|StoreData|Y|Y|N|N| | |~| | | |NonCurrency|Plan1|SavedAssumption|
OtherDrivers|InventoryDays|StoreData|Y|Y|N|N| | |~| | | |NonCurrency|Plan1|SavedAssu
OtherDrivers|PayablesDays|StoreData|Y|Y|N|N| | |~| | | |NonCurrency|Plan1|SavedAssum
OtherDrivers|ReceivablesDays|StoreData|Y|Y|N|N| | |~| | | |NonCurrency|Plan1|SavedAs
OtherDrivers|WorkingDays|StoreData|Y|Y|N|N| | |~| | | |NonCurrency|Plan1|SavedAssump
```

Depending on what you need to do, you may not need all sections. If you are creating a new dimension, the Dimension, Dimension Association, and Relationship sections are required. If you are updating a dimension, only the Relationship section is required. The Members and PropArray (alias property) sections are optional.

EPMA File Generator

Creating the import file can be the trickiest part of EPMA. To jump start the process, you can create an EPMA import file from an existing Planning application (or other) using the EPMA File Generator. This utility generates import files from existing applications from existing Planning and Financial Management applications, Financial Management metadata files, existing EPMA applications and even Excel.

To create an EPMA import file from the EPMA File Generator,

1. On the EPMA server, select *Start Programs >> Oracle EPM>>*Foundation Services>>Performance Management Architect>>Start EPMA File Generator. (Your start menu structure may vary).

The EPMA File Generator will launch:

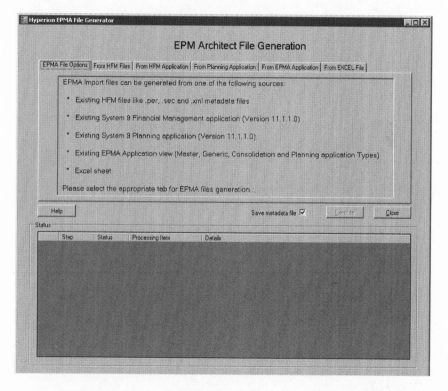

2. Select the From Planning Application tab.
3. Enter the Planning administrator user name and password.
4. Enter the Workspace URL.
5. Enter the Planning Web URL.
6. Enter the Planning application name and application server. To follow along, choose the Planning Sample application (we are using a slightly modified version of the Planning Sample application).

7. Specify the directory where the file should be placed.

8. Optionally add a prefix to all of the dimensions.

For example, the EPMA Dimension Library already contains an Entity dimension. You want to import the Entity dimension from the Planning application that may be different than the one already in EPMA so you'll need to create it as its own dimension. You could add a prefix of "NewSamp" that will be added to the Entity name so that the 2 dimensions can coexist separately. (If you are testing this in a development EPMA environment, consider adding a prefix of your initials so that you won't run into issues with other administrators who have tested this same process.)

9.   Click Execute and the file will generate.

```
 EPMAImport.ads - Notepad
 File  Edit  Format  View  Help
!FILE_FORMAT=ADS
!VERSION=1.0

!Section=Dimensions
 Name|DimensionClass|DimensionAlias|DimDataStorage|DimTwoPassCalc|Plan1Density|Plan2Density|Plan3Density|Wo
Introduction Date|Attribute|Attribute|Introduction Date|||||Date|||||||||||||||||
Active-Inactive Products|Attribute|Active-Inactive Products|||||||||||Boolean|||||||||||||||||||
weight|Attribute|weight||||||Numeric|||||||||||||||||||
Account|Account|Account|NeverShare||Dense|Dense|Dense||||1|0|0||Y|N|N|N|N|2|1|1|2|2|||||
Currency|Currency|Currency|NeverShare||Sparse|Sparse|Sparse|||0|0|0||Y|N|N|N|N|6|6|6|6|6|||||
Entity|Entity|Entity|NeverShare||Sparse|Sparse|Sparse|||0|0|0||Y|N|N|N|N|3|7|7|3|3|||||
Period|Period|Period|NeverShare||Dense|Dense|Dense|||0|0|0||Y|N|N|N|N|2|2|2|2|2|||||
Scenario|Scenario|Scenario|NeverShare||Sparse|Sparse|Sparse|||2|0|0||Y|N|N|N|N|7|4|4|7|7|||||
Segments|Generic|Segments|StoreData||Sparse|Sparse|Sparse|||0|0|0||Y|N|N|N|N|4|8|8|4|4|||||
Version|Version|Version|NeverShare||Sparse|Sparse|Sparse|||4|0|0||Y|N|N|N|N|8|5|5|8|8|||||
Year|Year|Year|NeverShare||Sparse|Sparse|Sparse||||0|0|0||Y|N|N|N|N|3|3|3|3|3|||||
Alias|Alias|Alias|||||||||||||||||||||||||||||

!Section=DimensionAssociations
 BaseDimension|Property|TargetDimension
Introduction Date|Alias|Alias
Active-Inactive Products|Alias|Alias
weight|Alias|Alias
Account|Alias|Alias
Currency|Alias|Alias
Currency|TriangulationCurrency|Currency
Entity|Alias|Alias
Entity|Currency|Currency
Period|Alias|Alias
Scenario|Alias|Alias
Scenario|StartPeriod|Period
Scenario|EndPeriod|Period
Scenario|StartYear|Year
Scenario|EndYear|Year
Segments|Alias|Alias
Segments|Introduction Date|Introduction Date
Segments|Active-Inactive Products|Active-Inactive Products
Segments|weight|weight
Version|Alias|Alias
Year|Alias|Alias

!Hierarchies=Introduction Date
```

Now that we have an EPMA import file ready to go, let's create an import profile.

Create an Import Profile

An import profile tells EPMA how to handle the import file including whether or not to create dimensions, what columns should be mapped to what properties, and how merges should take place.

To create an import profile,

1. Select File >> Import >> Create Profile:

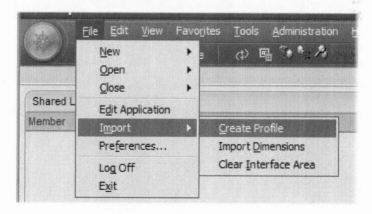

2. Define the Profile Name.

3.   Select the Import Type; in our example choose Flat File:

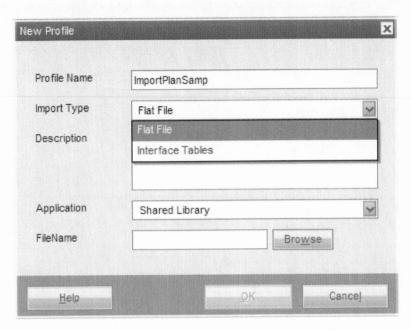

4.   For Application, select Shared Library.

If EPMA applications exist, you can alternatively import metadata directly into an application.

5.   Browse to and select the import file.
6.   Click OK.
7.   Define the appropriate File Properties to match the import file: Column Delimiter, Remove Double Quotes on Strings, Remove White Space, and Suppress Transaction logs:

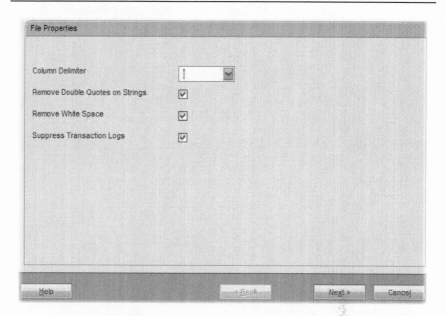

In most cases for imports, you will want to turn off transaction logging.

8. Click Next.
9. Map each dimension in the flat file to a dimension in the Shared Library.
10. Optionally check the option to Create Dimensions for non-mapped dimensions.
11. Optionally click Select All, Merge as Shared.

When you perform an import into the Dimension Library, you control how the dimension data in the flat file should be incorporated with existing dimensions, either Merge as Shared or Replace Mode where only incremental changes are processed.

12. To follow along in our example, set your selections to match the following:

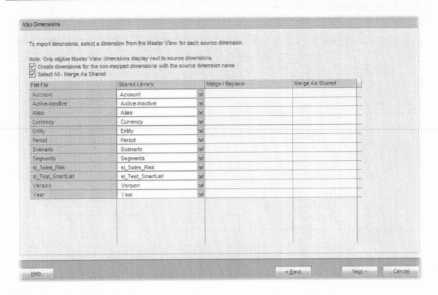

13. Click Next.
14. For each dimension in the import file, map the properties in the file to the properties in the Shared Library.

The Account dimension properties should match as follows:

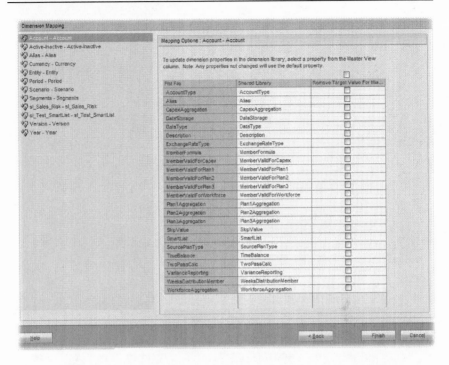

The Entity dimension properties should match as follows:

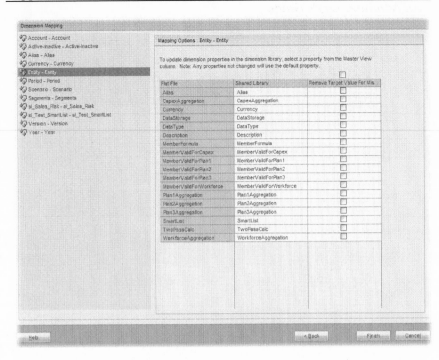

The Period dimension properties should match as follows:

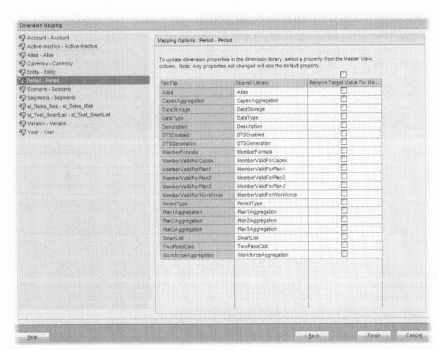

The Scenario dimension properties should match as follows:

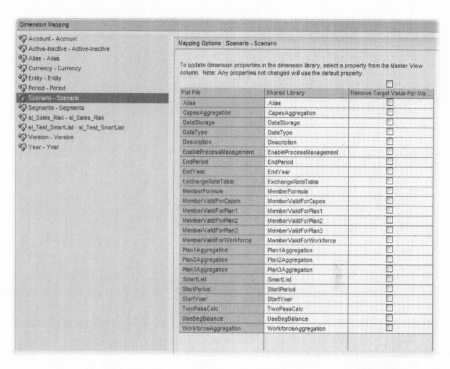

Our modified Planning Sample application contains a Smart List dimension with the following properties (if you are using the 9.3.1 or 11.1.1 Sample application, you will not have a Smart List dimension):

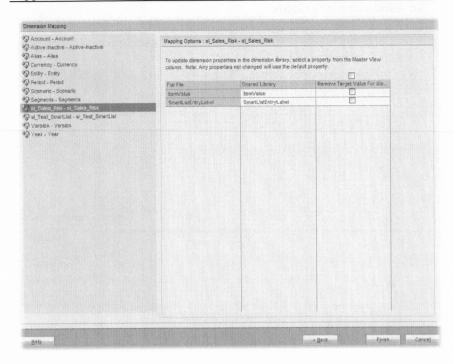

The Version dimension properties should match as follows:

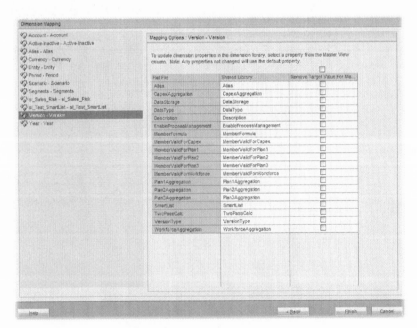

15. Once the properties have been mapped for all dimensions, click Finish.

The import profile will be created and you'll be prompted to execute the profile (a.k.a. run the import process).

16. Click Yes to run the import.

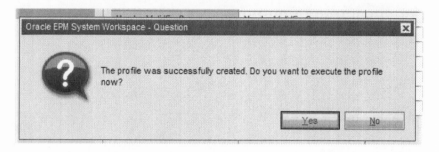

A message will display informing you of the Job ID. If desired, you can click on the link to navigate to the Job Console and view the status. Otherwise click Close.

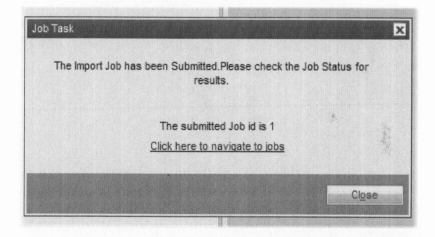

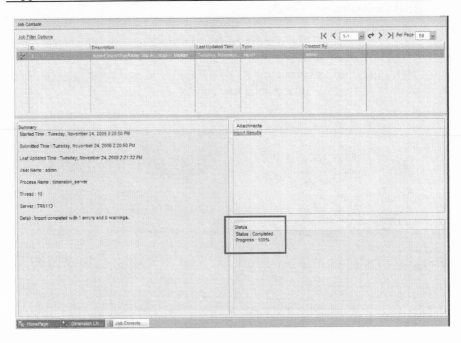

The dimensions should import successfully into the Dimension Library upon completion of the import:

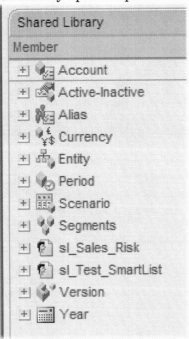

Now that the import profile is created, you can rerun the import process with new data files (as long as the sections and mappings are the same).

To import dimensions with an existing import profile,

1. Select File>>Import>>Import Dimensions:

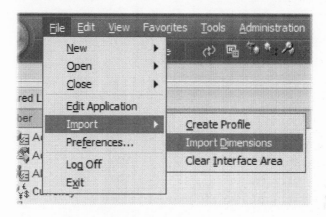

2. Select the Import Profile.
3. Select the Import Type: Flat File or Interface Tables.
4. Browse to the import file.
5. Click Upload.

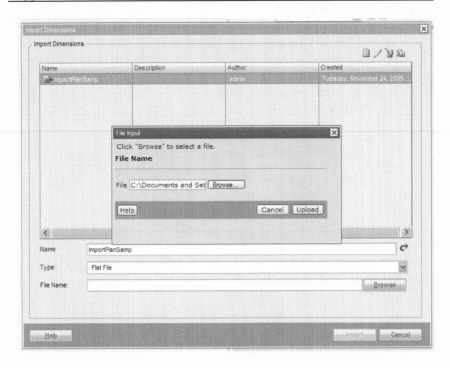

6. Click Import.

Edit Properties

Once you have imported dimensions or created them manually, you are ready to set the properties. EPMA supports the following properties:

- System
- Planning
- Consolidation
- Essbase ASO
- Essbase BSO
- Hyperion Profitability and Cost Management
- Statistical

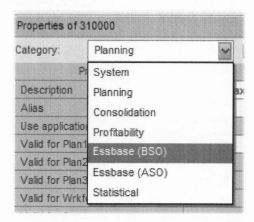

Some of the properties are maintained by EPMA. Others are set to a default but can be overridden by an administrator and some properties are blank, ready to be defined. These are the same properties that you have worked with in the Planning web client:

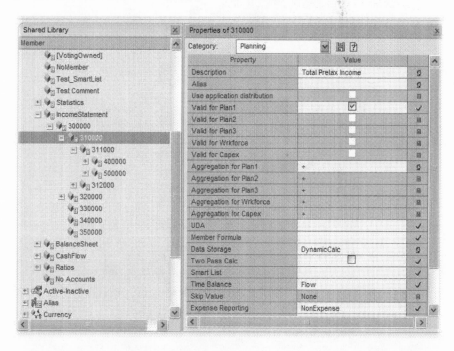

Notice in this Shared Library view, we can only view properties one member at a time. Is there another way to view the properties for multiple members at once?

In the Planning web client, no. In EPMA, yes, with the Grid Spreader option introduced in 11.1.1.

Grid Editor

The Grid Editor is an option within the Dimension Library that allows you to view, manage, and update many members and properties at the same time in a grid display. This is one of the convincing factors for migrating from Classic to EPMA.

To use the Grid Editor,

1. Right-click on the dimension (or member) and select Grid Editor:

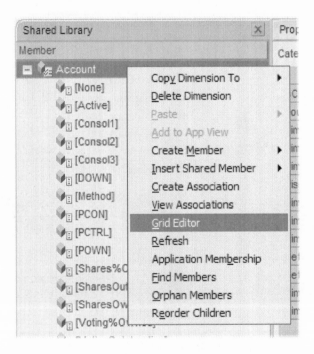

2. Select the desired member or members. In our example, choose IDescendants of NetRevenue.

Note you can use the member selection functions to select a dynamic list of members:

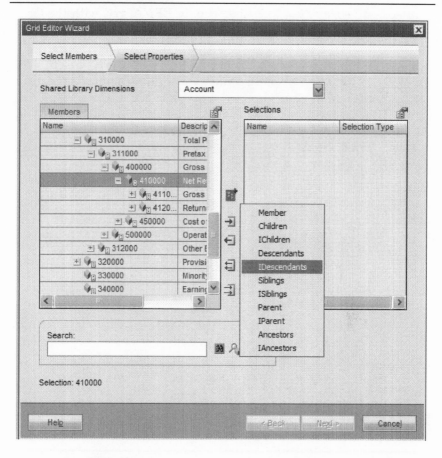

3. Click Next.
4. Select the property (or properties) that you want to display by property category. In our example we chose all of the Planning properties:

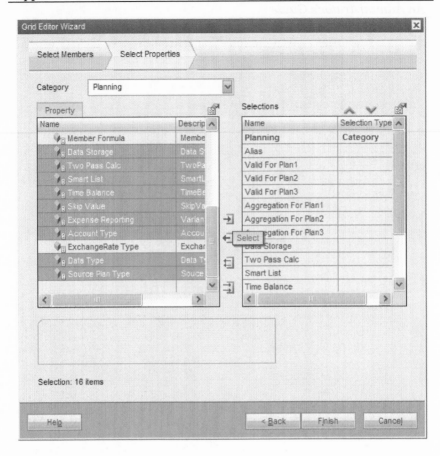

5. Click Finish.

The Grid Editor will display with the selected members and the properties. From this window you can view and update properties. You can add or remove members from the dimension.

Now that we've taken you through the basics of the Dimension Library and created some dimensions, let's create an EPMA application.

APPLICATION LIBRARY

An application in EPMA is a grouping of dimensions (either Shared or Local) that will ultimately be deployed to create an application in Planning or other Hyperion solution. With EPMA's drag and drop interface, the application creation process is simple. Let's create one now.

Create an Application

To create an application,

1. Select File >> New >> Application.

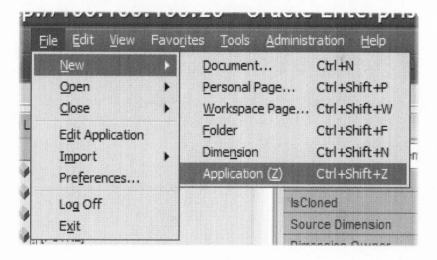

2. Enter the Application Name; for our example, we entered EPMASamp.
3. Select Planning for the Application Type:

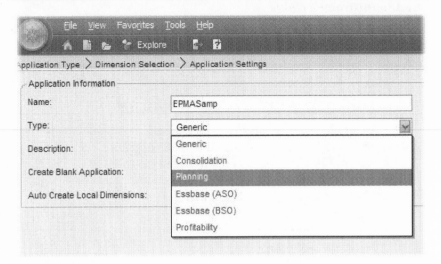

At that point the Planning Application Creation Wizard will display. Define the same application information as you did in Classic: Plan types, Currency and Calendar information.

4. Because we are "recreating" the Planning Sample application and we know the properties are defined correctly for Planning Sample structure, set the information as follows (one plan type named Consol, Yes-Multi-currency, Default currency, 12 months, Jan, Even):

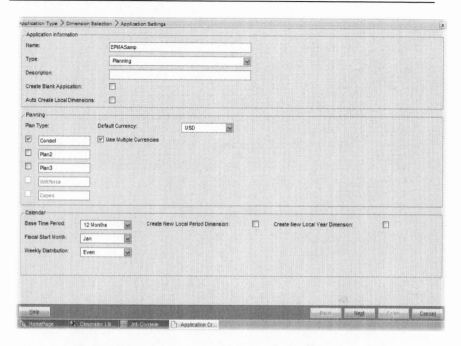

If you wanted, you could have chosen a new local period and year dimension. For our example we will use the shared dimensions in the Dimension Library.

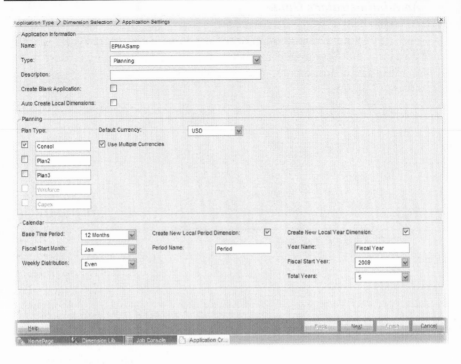

5. Click Next.
6. Select the dimensions to be added to the application:

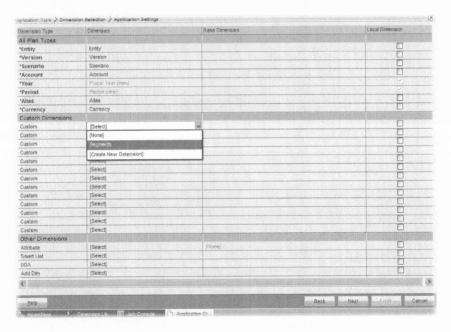

If your Dimension Library contains a single Account, Entity, Version, and Scenario dimension, they will automatically associate. If more than one exists, you can choose the specific dimension for the application.

7. Click Finish once the dimensions are defined. The EPMA application is created:

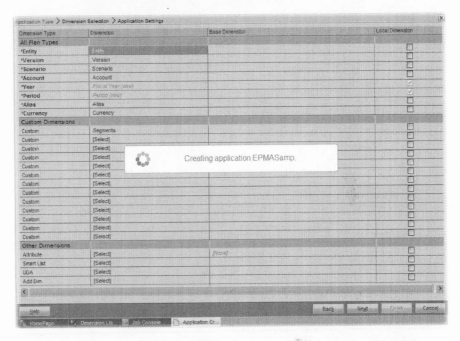

8. The next step in the wizard driven process is to define any application specific settings or properties (those that may vary from the Shared Library):

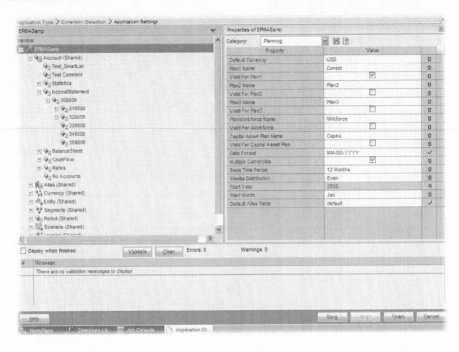

For example, you can right-click on a member and select Exclude to filter the member (and its descendants) for the application.

In this portion of the Application definition, you can also define the outline order of dimensions.

    9. Right-click on the application and select Performance Settings.

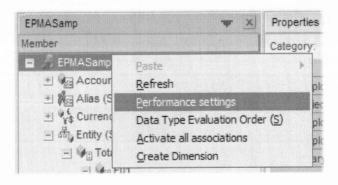

   10. Update the dense and sparse settings and move the order of dimensions to achieve optimal performance in the deployed application.

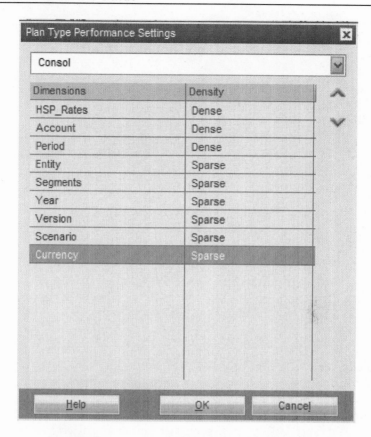

11. Click OK.

You can also set the Data Type evaluation order (important when you define Smart Lists across multiple dimensions).

Remember earlier in this appendix when we created a dimension association we said "Once you pull a dimension with dimensions associations into an application, you must activate the dimension associations." We're at that step now.

12. Right-click on the application and select Activate All Associations.

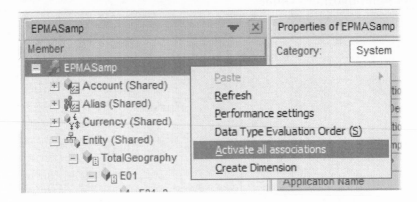

13. Click Finish. (Optionally you can click Deploy when finished but let's hold off with deployment for now.)

Manage Applications in the Application Library

The application has now been created in the Application Library. The Application Library displays all of the applications that have been created within EPMA.

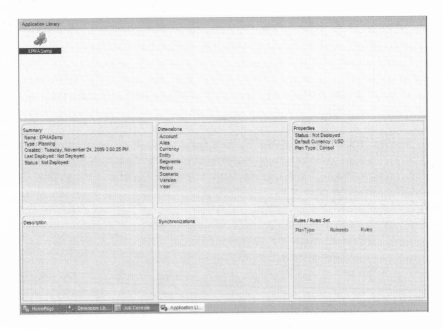

To access the Application Library,

1. Select File >> Administer >> Application Library:

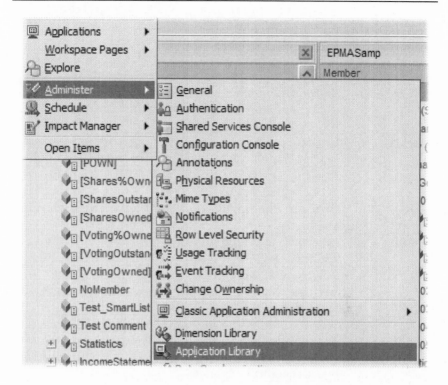

The applications can have the following statuses: Not Deployed means the application has been created, but has not been deployed to an environment and Deployed means application has been created and deployed to an environment.

When an application icon is selected, the summary information that is available for this application is visible. The summary information includes:

- Summary – Name, type, created, deployed, synchronization status
- Description – Application description that was entered when the application was created
- Dimensions – A listing of all dimensions that are available within the application
- Application Properties – Organization by Period, Deployed, Default Currency
- Synchronizations – displays all data synchronizations that contain the application

You can perform a number of actions on EPMA applications.

Edit	Allows the end user to edit the EPMA application
Duplicate	Allows the end user to make a copy of the application's dimensions and hierarchies
Delete	Deletes the application from EPMA and, if previously deployed, from the deployed environment
Open	Allows the application to be opened in the Planning web client and the administrator to begin working within the deployed application
Validate	Validates dimensions and their properties to ensure the application can be deployed correctly
Reregister	Reregisters the application with Hyperion Shared Services
Data Flow	Displays the inputs and outputs related to this application
Synchronize	Allows the creation of data synchronizations for this application
Migrate	Allows the application to be moved from one environment to another (e.g. development to production)
Compare	When an application has been deployed and the library has been updated, the end user can compare the deployed application to the library and accept or reject the library changes.

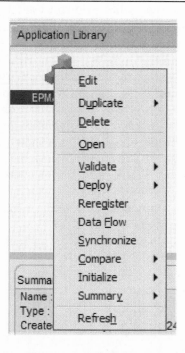

If you edit the application, you can now view dimensions in the Application as well as the Shared Library:

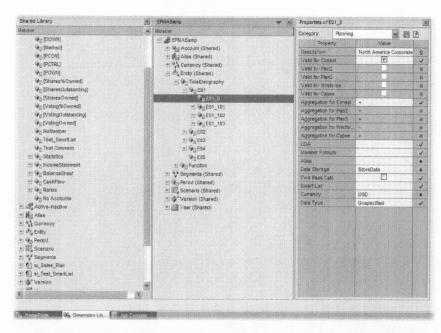

Validate and Deploy the Application

Now that we've created the application, we need to perform a validation to make sure it is deployment ready. (While you think the validation will catch all possible issues, this isn't necessarily the case. You could still encounter errors during deployment.)

Before deploying, the application needs to be validated, issues corrected and then deployed Planning/FM/Essbase. Validation can be executed separately from the right mouse click menu or if not run separately, the validation will be executed as part of the deployment process.

New inversion 11.1.1, you can validate and deploy Calc Manager rules, application metadata or both. A number of issues between validation commands and deploy commands have been resolved in the 11.1.1 release. New validations have been added for the application creation wizard, DTS, Calculation Manager rules, shared members, udas, member formulas, and alternate hierarchies. Validation results are saved in Job Console.

To validate an application,
1. Right-click on the application in the Application Library and click Validate.
2. A job will be submitted and you can view the status in the Job Console.

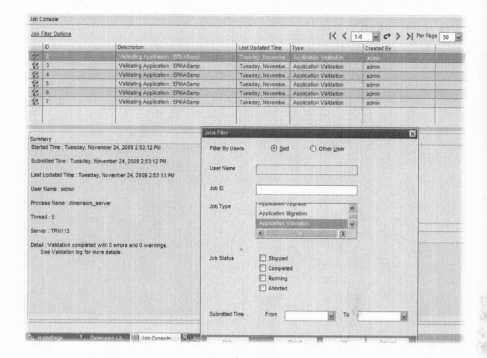

Note!

Did you know you can filter the jobs in the Job Console by user, job ID, job type, job status or submitted time? Click on Job Filter Options to search for a specific job.

Once the application has been validated you are ready to deploy! Deployment is required to push EPMA application information to the target solution. This will actually create the Planning application and the underlying Essbase database (in Classic Administration, this is performed in two steps; in EPMA, just one step). A prerequisite step to deploying a Planning application is creating the underlying relational repository. We assume this has been done in our example.

To deploy an application,
1. Right-click on the application in the Application Library and click Deploy>> Application.

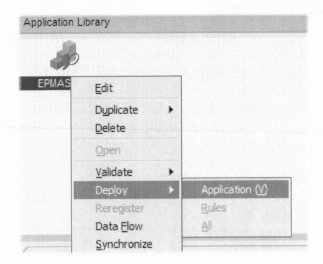

2. Select the Planning Instance, Application Server, and Shared Services project (probably Planning).
3. Select an existing data source or click the New icon to create a new data source (in our example, we click the New icon).
4. Enter the Data Source Name and Description:

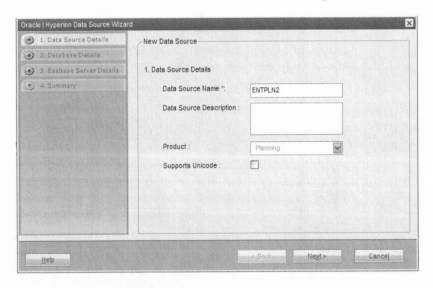

5. Click Next.
6. Enter the relational database information:

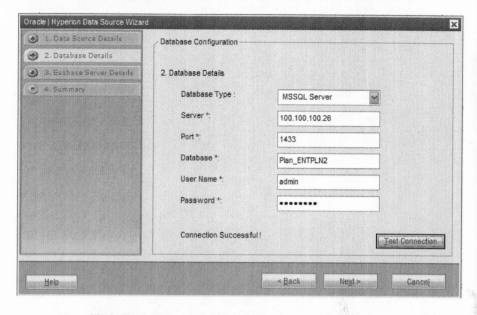

7. Click Test Connection to verify a successful connection.
8. Click Next.
9. Enter the Essbase database information (make sure to use an Essbase supervisor ID):

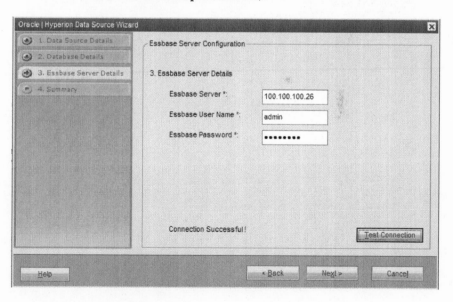

10. Click Test Connection to verify a successful connection.
11. Click Next.

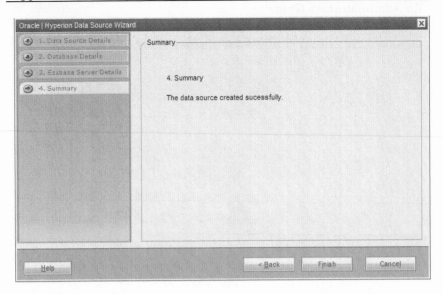

12. Click Finish.
13. Check the option to Create Outline (you will check Create Outline the first time and check Refresh Outline all other times):

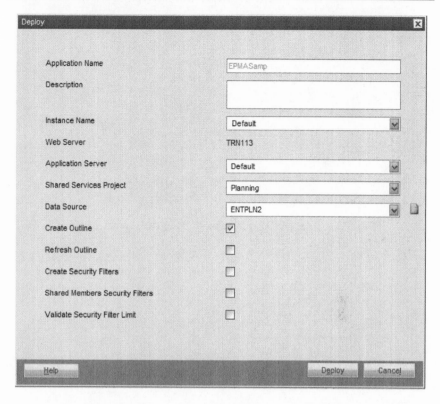

14. Click Deploy.

The deployment process will begin and the job will be submitted to the job console. To view the status, select the link to navigate to jobs.

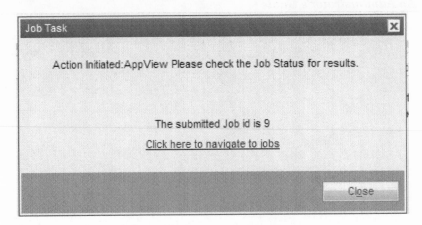

Ideally the job will complete successfully with no errors.

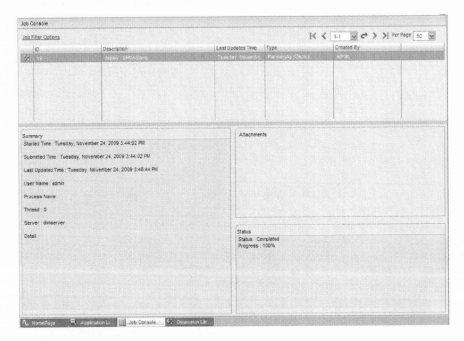

But that is not always the case. Let's look at one example. The following deployment resulted in a number of issues related to member formulas:

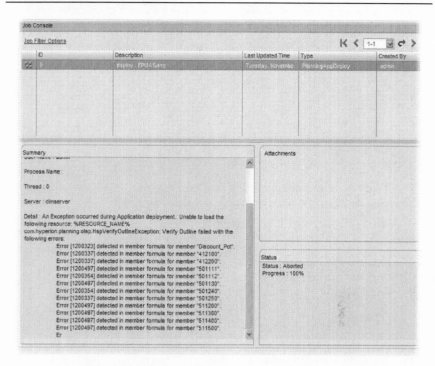

To investigate further, we search for the member in the Dimension Library by right-clicking in the dimension and choosing Find. You can then search by Name or other property:

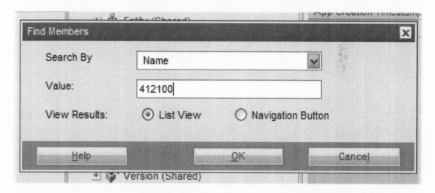

The member is quickly found and now we open the member formula property. Do you see any issues? The double quotes are missing from the members with spaces. How did that happen?

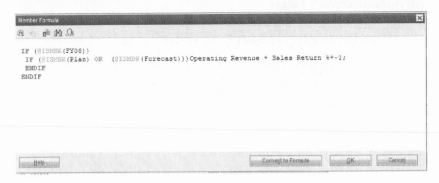

Do you remember back to the beginning of the appendix when we created the import profile? In the Import Profile definition we specified the option to remove double quotes. Be careful checking this option because, as you can see, in some cases you want to keep double quotes.

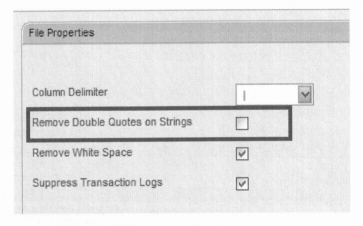

Access an EPMA Deployed Application

The application has now been created and is ready for further development; items like data forms, task lists, and business rules.

To access the application,

1. Select Navigation icon >> Applications >> Planning >> Refresh
2. Select Navigate icon>>Applications >> Planning >> EPMASamp

3. Select Administration >> Dimensions and notice that the dimensions cannot be edited within the Planning web client.

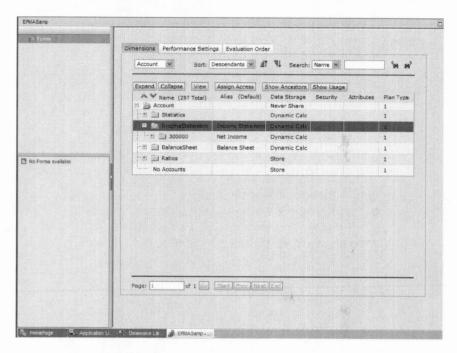

Sync / Redeploy an Application

As you make updates to the dimensions in the Dimension Library, your application will be come out of sync with deployment.

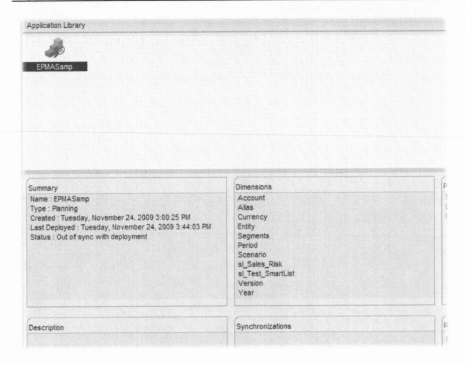

Follow along with our example.
1. Add a new member to the Segment dimension, "SP" for Support services in the Shared Library under Seg02.
2. The new member is also added in the EPMA application:

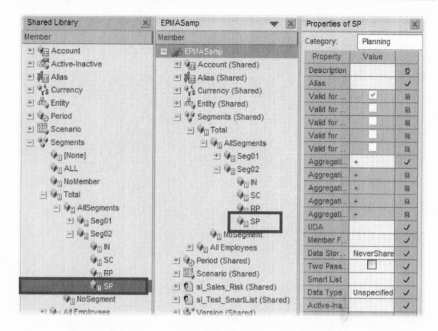

Next we have to redeploy to push this member to Planning and Essbase.

3. In the Application Library, right-click on the application and click Deploy >> Application.

4. Select the option to Refresh the outline.

5. Additionally if you have security filters that require refreshing you could check this option as well:

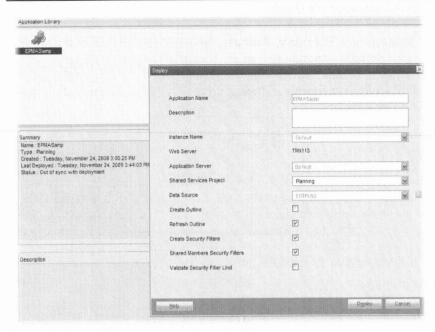

6. Click Deploy. The application and underlying Essbase database should now be in sync.

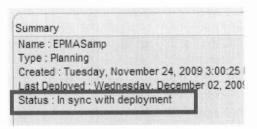

Now that we've covered the basics of dimension and application creation and maintenance, we will conclude this introduction to Enterprise Performance Architect with two last concepts: the data synchronizations and EPMA batch client.

DATA SYNCHRONIZATIONS

Data synchronization in EPMA enables you to synchronize and map data between Hyperion applications, interface tables, and external files. With data synchronizations you can share data from applications in Financial Management, Planning, and Essbase as well as external source flat files and interface tables to Financial

Management, Planning, Essbase, and HPCM applications. Filters and default members are possible when creating data synchronizations. Basic mapping tables are also possible. Note: EPMA data synchronization is not a full blown ETL tool (see Oracle Data Integrator).

BATCH CLIENT

We've been working with EPMA in the Workspace but a command line interface is also available for scripting EPMA tasks. Via the batch client you can perform incremental changes to data objects like applications, dimensions, members, and properties. You can run jobs for imports, deployments and synchronizations. Version 11.1.1.3 introduced several new commands in the batch client to further support automated EPMA tasks.

We've jump started your EPMA process with this appendix. This tool is certainly worth testing if you have a large number of Planning or Financial Management applications.

Appendix C:
Workforce & CapEx Planning

The nice developers at Oracle have put in some additional efforts to help customers quickly and easily plan for your people and capital expenses with add on modules for Workforce (WFP) and Capital Expenditure (Cap Ex). And of course, with an additional price tag.

Are these modules new software? No, in fact they are plain old Planning applications with prebuilt dimensions, calculations, business rules and data forms designed for workforce planning and capital expenditure planning.

Let's look in more detail at each one of these add-on Planning modules.

INTRODUCTION TO WFP

The Workforce Planning module provides out-of-the-box functionality for the most common workforce and workforce-related expense planning activities facing any organization. Built-in components address budget headcount and workforce expenses, forecasts for total compensation, variance analysis and more. WFP assumes planning at the employee level of detail. You can also directly link the WFP plan type to main planning applications for real-time impact analysis.

Workforce planning comes with 121 accounts, 60 member formulas, 8 business rules, 15 data forms, 6 right click menus, and 8 attributes, all customizable for your specific requirements*. Come back to this note* at the end of this appendix.

Let us walk through a typical end user planning experience in WFP.

Employees can manage employee status within workforce planning via a data form or business rule. For example, when an employee takes leave or is terminated, salary and total personnel expense are impacted.

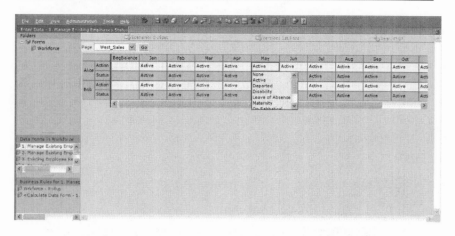

Business rules also help end users transfer employees in and out of departments, moving attribute and expense information to the appropriate organizational unit.

In addition to transfers, users can also plan the departures of employees.

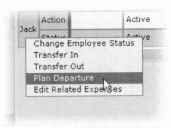

WFP also delivers rules and data forms for processing new hires.

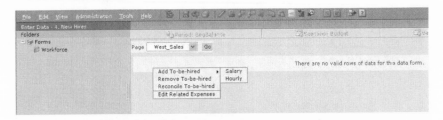

Once an employee is hired, you can reconcile the To-Be-hired information to the new employee.

Employee related expenses are also managed in WFP.

Pretty powerful, right? In summary, workforce planning can be a good solution for your organization to manage and plan for your most important asset, your people.

INTRODUCTION TO CAP EX

Planning for capital expenses isn't an easy thing to do, coping with uncertain projections for unusual activities. The Capital Expenditure module for Hyperion Planning assists you in the management of assets and provides a process for creating capital expense plans for submission and approval. CapEx establishes global assumptions for each asset class and provides driver based calculations. A structure for timing and cost adjustments to capital expenses and functionality for asset transfers across departments are all features of CapEx. Like its cohort WFP, it can easily integrate the capex plan with other Hyperion Planning applications.

End users can set assumptions like the useful life of assets, depreciation methods, depreciation conventions, amortization methods and more.

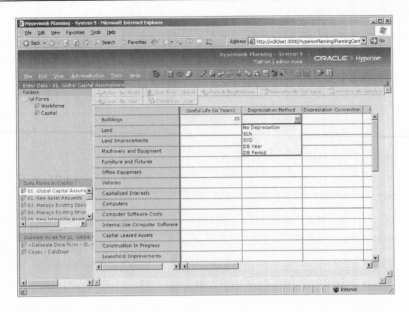

Built-in forms and business rules support the addition of new assets and transfer of existing assets.

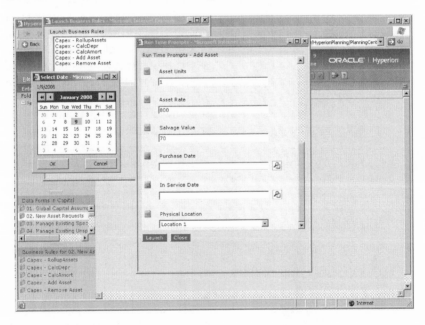

Capex includes tangible and intangible classes like buildings, land / land improvements, machinery and equipment, furniture and fixtures, copyrights, and customer relationships.

Custom asset classes (both tangible and intangible) can be added along with asset class attributes (like useful life and depreciation method).

We've only had time in this appendix to provide a glimpse of WFP and CapEx. For more information, training classes from interRel or Oracle are your best bet for getting into the details. Your friendly Oracle sales rep or partner (nudge, nudge interRel Consulting) can also provide demos and more information.

BENEFITS & CONSIDERATIONS

Before we conclude the appendix, let's re-cap the benefits and considerations for these solutions. The WFP and CapEx modules provide a number of benefits to you: less time to setup, reduction in planning cycle time, increased visibility into drivers, and improved accountability, accuracy and predictability in these plans.

When it comes to development, these modules can help you achieve faster implementation time (hey, everything is already built, right?). But remember the earlier *? If you have a very specific workforce and/or capital expenditure planning process, carefully evaluate whether the WFP and CapEX predefined processes and objects meet your requirements. We've seen about a 50/50 split in our client base where for about 50% of clients, it made more sense to design a custom Planning solution. For the other 50% of clients, the prebuilt modules worked beautifully. While you can customize these modules, depending on the customization, it could actually take longer to customize than developing an application from scratch.

And also note that while a number of objects are already built, you still have steps to complete after initialization (e.g. build the Organization and Employee dimension, integrate with existing account structure, setup and assign security, create reports, and create aggregation calc scripts).

Note!

You can customize anything but edit with care and make to understand the model completely and dependencies between all of the data forms, member formulas and rules.

In summary, the Workforce and Capital Expenditure modules for Oracle Hyperion Planning are great solutions to evaluate for your planning processes.

Appendix D:
Life Cycle Management

By Rob Donahue, interRel Consulting

Life Cycle Management (LCM) is a new set of tools introduced with version 11 of Oracle EPM System that provides a consistent way to migrate applications, a repository, or individual artifacts across environments and operating systems. LCM is part of the Foundation services component of an Oracle EPM implementation.

The LCM tools are designed to facilitate the movement of objects in connected and disconnected environments for development, test & production.

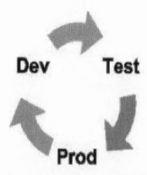

A connected environment is where dev, test, and prod environments are managed by a single Shared Services instance. A disconnected environment is one where each logical environment (dev, test, prod) has its own Shared Services instance. Most user configurations will have disconnected environments.

Let's now review some of the features of the Oracle EPM Life Cycle Management.

Application Groups & File System Group

An application group in Shared Services essentially maps to a product like Essbase or Planning. Previously known as "projects", application groups allow for more simplified management of the applications registered with Shared Services. A new application group called 'File System' is introduced in 11x to support disconnected migrations in LCM.

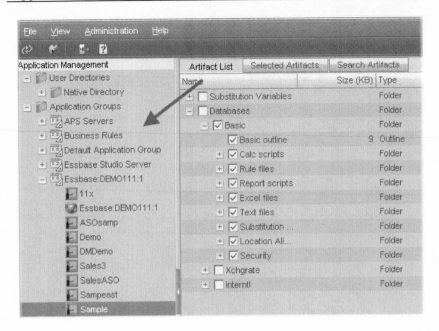

The File System Group references the artifacts that have been selected for migration to the file system as opposed to a target application in the same Shared Services environment. This is what allows for the support of disconnected Shared Services environments and will be used in most situations.

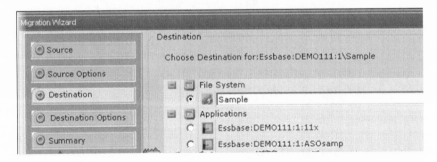

Each migration that is defined to have a file system destination will get a folder created on the Shared Services server that will contain the objects in scope for the migration. Additionally each user gets a named folder to help organize the migrations. The default location on the file system is <HYPERION_HOME>/common/import_export/<USER_NAME>.

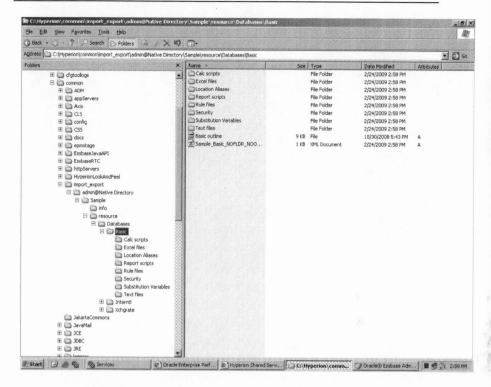

Application Artifacts

The Life Cycle Management tools can be used to manage a variety of artifacts from the different Oracle EPM applications. The supported applications & artifacts are currently:

- Essbase
    - Substitution Variables
    - Rule Files
    - Calculation Scripts
    - Report Scripts
    - Excel Files
    - Location Aliases
    - Security Filters

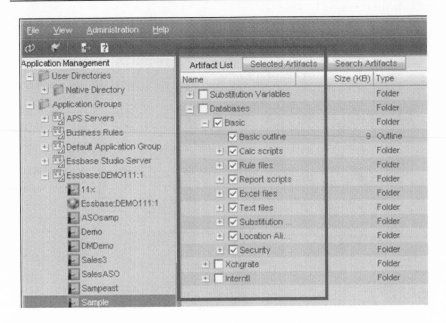

- Financial Management
  - Security
  - Dimension
  - Phased Submission
  - Rules
  - Documents
  - Forms
  - InterCompany
  - Journals
  - Member Lists
- Planning
  - Configuration
  - Relational Data
  - Global Artifacts
  - Plan Types
  - Security
- Reporting & Analysis
  - Financial Reporting
  - Interactive Reporting
  - Production Reporting
  - Web Analysis
- EPMA / Calc Manager
  - Application Metadata
  - Shared Dimensions
  - Dimension Access

- o Data Synchronization
- Profitability Management
  - o Driver definitions
  - o Stage definitions
  - o POV definitions
  - o Driver selections
  - o Assignments
  - o Application preferences
  - o Assignment Rules
  - o Assignment Rule selections
- Performance Scorecard
  - o Administrative Options
  - o Objects
- Shared Services (users & task flows)
  - o Native Directory (Security)
  - o Task flows

Migration Wizard

A migration is defined in the Shared Services Console utilizing the Migration Wizard. This wizard guides the user through the steps required to define an artifact migration. To migrate,

1. Select Source Artifacts
2. Define any Source Options
3. Select Destination – Either a specified folder for the file system or an application in the same environment.
4. Define any Destination options such as selecting dependent artifacts.
5. Review Summary & Execute the migration or save the migration definition to an XML file.

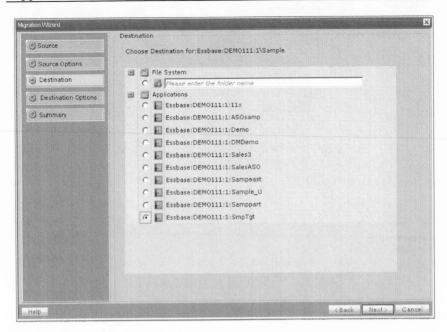

The saved migration definition file contains all the information about a migration (source, destination, artifacts for migrations, export and import options) and can then be used to automate migrations or is updated to execute the migration into a disconnected Shared Services environment. The migration definition file is in XML format.

Life Cycle Management Reports

The Life Cycle Management tools have reporting capabilities to assist in the management of LCM activities. The Migration Status Report provides migration status, migration date and time, and total number of artifacts migrated. The Compare Report provides comparison information of artifacts based on file dates. The Audit Report displays user LCM activities and must be configured prior to use.

Life Cycle Management Utility - Command Line Utility

The Life Cycle Management Utility is a command-line utility that provides an alternate way to migrate artifacts from source to destination. Lifecycle Management Utility can be used with a third-party scheduling service such as Windows Task Scheduler or Oracle Enterprise Manager.

```
C:\WINDOWS\system32\cmd.exe                                    _ □ X

C:\Hyperion\common\utilities\LCM\9.5.0.0\bin>dir
Volume in drive C has no label.
Volume Serial Number is 7CED-1D75

Directory of C:\Hyperion\common\utilities\LCM\9.5.0.0\bin

12/15/2008  08:40 PM    <DIR>          .
12/15/2008  08:40 PM    <DIR>          ..
12/15/2008  08:40 PM             2,490 hsslcmutility.bat
12/15/2008  08:40 PM             3,151 hsslcmutility.sh
12/15/2008  08:40 PM             1,437 invokeCLU.bat
12/15/2008  08:40 PM             8,190 Utility.bat
12/15/2008  08:40 PM             6,703 Utility.sh
               5 File(s)         21,971 bytes
               2 Dir(s)  10,441,723,904 bytes free

C:\Hyperion\common\utilities\LCM\9.5.0.0\bin>_
```

Conclusion

Life Cycle Management provides a powerful set of tools that can be used to facilitate many administrative tasks within an Oracle EPM Environment:

- Application migrations with cross-product artifact dependencies
- Security migrations
- Edit Shared Services Registry data
- Configuration of Oracle EPM System products in a mixed-release environment
- Enable or disable Secure Socket Layer (SSL) connections
- Perform other manual configuration changes
- Backup & Recovery (not intended for data)
- Bulk security updates
- Import and export artifacts for editing purposes
- Edit a single artifact
- Version control

In summary, Life Cycle Management is a big step forward for configuration and change management processes for the Oracle EPM System products.

Appendix E:
ODI and EPM

By Kelli Stein, interRel Consulting

Introduction to ODI and EPM

ODI is a data integration tool that moves data across multiple systems. It has officially replaced Hyperion Application Link (HAL) as the tool to load Planning, Essbase and HFM metadata and data. You may sometimes hear it referred to as Sunopsis; this would be because like many of Oracle's products it was obtained through an acquisition.

All processes within ODI are based on metadata within the source and target systems. A really important and exciting feature of ODI is that actual data is not stored in ODI, only metadata, mappings, connection parameters and translations required to move the data from one system to the other.

One of the first challenges of understanding ODI is learning all of the new terminology. Oracle thankfully uses terms most information system technologists are familiar with, but it does sometimes use these words uniquely.

Let's start with discussing the term metadata. Metadata is data about data. For example suppose you have a field in a relational database that stores Customer, metadata would include things such as the field length (20) and data type (string). Metadata is not the actual value that is stored for Customer (John Doe).

The next question to answer is how is ODI used with EPM? As we mentioned earlier ODI is used to interface data across systems. In the EPM space, examples would include: load dimensions to Planning, HFM and Essbase from a flat file or a relational database, load data to these applications, export Essbase outlines, etc.

Thankfully when ODI became the official tool to replace HAL they included knowledge modules (we will discuss this term later) that provide the following functionality:

	Planning	Essbase	HFM
Metadata discovery & model creation	✓	✓	✓
Load data	✓	✓	✓
Load Metadata	✓	✓	✓
Extract data	X	✓	✓
Extract metadata	X	✓	✓
Other	Refresh to Essbase	Calc, post and pre MaxL scripts	Consolidate

X indicates functionality that is not supported in the current release.

The following diagram is an example of a sequential data integration process that can be accomplished with ODI. The dimensions Accounts and Entities are loaded to Planning, HFM and Essbase. The Customer dimension is loaded to Essbase only. The last step is to load Forecast, Actual and Sales data. Once the data is loaded a MaxL script can be executed to allocate and aggregate data.

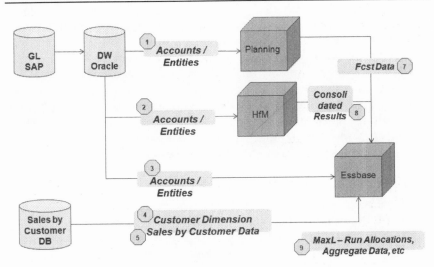

The ODI architecture has several applications that work together to provide a seamless data flow across technology independent platforms.

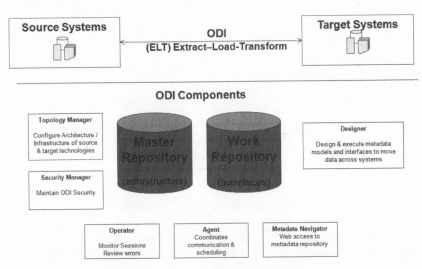

ODI uses two types of repositories: a Master repository and Work repository which are relational databases that store ODI configuration (similar to the BI Repository for EPM).

The Master repository stores information that is configured in Topology Manager and Security Manager and version information from Designer.

The Work Repository stores the mapping and interface information created with Designer. It also stores the Operator information. It is possible to have multiple work repositories but each environment can only include one master repository.

Topology Manager is the application used to configure connection information for source and target technologies. This would include parameters such as server name, user id and password, connection strings, driver references, etc.

Security Manager is the tool used to create users, profiles and roles. It is separate from Shared Services. You can assign access to objects, methods and servers. In layman's terms you can lock it down to each item or you can do it role-based (metadata admin, security admin, interface designer, etc)

Designer is the application used to design and execute metadata models and interfaces.

Agent(s) is a java service that is placed on one or multiple servers as the listening mechanism for enabling communication between multiple technologies and ODI.

Operator is the application that contains status and log information about each job that is executed.

Metadata Navigator is a web based tool that allows business or technical users to maintain metadata about the source or target systems and field. They can also trigger and monitor jobs from this interface.

Oracle Data Profiling and Quality is another tool available when you install ODI. This tool provides more advanced capabilities for data cleansing and data enrichment in the source and target systems. Data cleansing examples include removing duplicates and parsing fields. Data Enrichment examples include user driven rules.

ODI Deployment

It is possible to have different configurations of ODI. The design of Topology Manager is such that you can have one master repository that points at all servers within a company network, including development, test and production. The advantage of this configuration is that you set up the connection parameters for all systems that will be used only once. This provides you the ability to take data from production and load it to development and vice versus. However, typically you would see three or more work repositories: one for development, one for test and one for execution only in production.

Many IT managers cringe at the idea of a production application talking to a development application. Therefore, another common configuration is to have one master repository for development, a separate one for test and a final one for production, all linking to their own work repository. This follows a more traditional and conservative approach which keeps objects completely isolated.

Dev	Test	Prod
• Master Repository	• Master Repository	• Master Repository
• Work Repository (s)	• Work Repository (s)	• Work Repository (s) **(Execution Only)**

Topology Manager – A little more in-depth

To access Topology Manager, from the Start menu select Oracle >> Oracle Data Integrator >> Topology Manager. Again, think of topology manager as the ODI infrastructure layer that supports all of the other components. Many users want to skip this part all together and move onto Designer but it is essential to understand the topology layer.

Let's dive into some more terminology that is important in Topology Manager. There are multiple objects within Topology Manager.

The **physical architecture** includes the connection and driver information for each data storage system that will ultimately be the source or target of the interfaces.

Within the physical architecture, the gold database level is a technology. ODI comes out of the box with drivers and predefined configuration options for these technologies.

The blue database level is a data server. A data server is considered any technology that can store data. That could include a file folder, a relational database or an Essbase server, etc.

The next layer down is referred to as the physical schema layer. A physical schema is considered an instance of the data server. For example within an Essbase data server, each application is considered its own physical schema. In Planning, the Planning server is the data server and each Planning application is a physical schema.

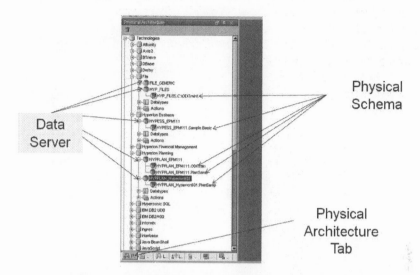

The required information to configure and use a data server is the computer name, user and password information. Please note: references to computer names should be fully qualified or ensure the host file on the ODI server where the agent is located refers to the computer name specified in this definition.

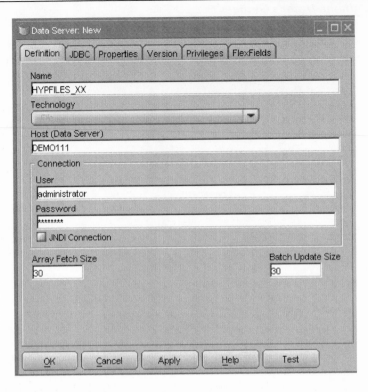

The connection string and driver reference is also specified on the JDBC tab.

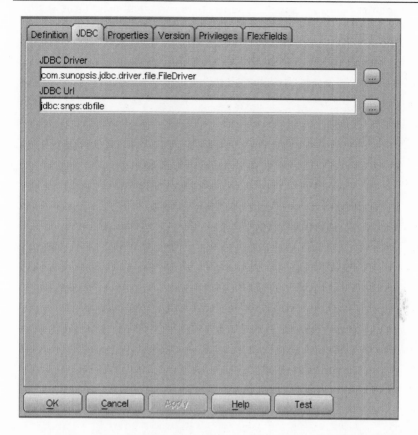

Once the physical architecture has been defined the next object to consider is the Logical Architecture. The Logical Architecture is the functional view of the physical architecture. This is what is referenced at design time. For example you may want to pull customers from the sales and marketing relational database to build the customer dimension in Essbase. Physically the S&M database has been split into three instances of a structurally identical database. (Structurally identical means they have the same tables, field names, field lengths, logic, etc.) There may be three instances because of performance reasons or storage reasons. When designing the interface in ODI, to pull the customer data, all three sources look the same from a metadata point of view. You only need to create this interface once by using the Logical architecture reference. At execution time you select which of the three physical databases to pull from.

The set up of the Logical Architecture looks similar to the Physical Architecture without all of the connection and driver parameters. In the Logical Architecture, a logical schema is set up for each physical schema in the Physical architecture.

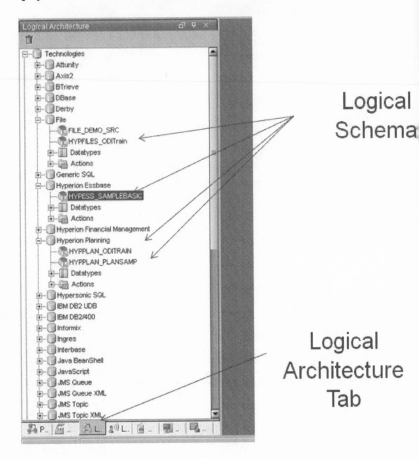

So the next question is, how does ODI know which physical architecture is relevant to each logical architecture? This is through an object called the Context.

In the Customer example we discussed earlier, you would have:

Physically:
Customer database 1
Customer database 2
Customer database 3
Logically:
Customer database

Context:
Customer db on db1
Customer db on db2
Customer db on db3

Another example of this concept is using the dev, test, prod model:

Physically:
Sample Basic – Dev
Sample Basic – Test
Sample Basic – Prod
Logically:
Sample Basic
Context:
Sample Basic on Dev
Sample Basic on Test
Sample Basic on Prod

When you design the interface you simply select Sample Basic. When you execute the interface you select the Context "Sample Basic on Prod" which tells ODI which environment to update.

Agents are another important concept to discuss related to Topology Manager. Both a physical and a logical agent are used to facilitate the communication between ODI and other servers. Similar to the architecture layers, the physical agent specifies the machine name. You can also set up options to perform load balancing and span sessions across multiple servers. One very important concept related to Agents to mention is that there are two types, a listener agent and a scheduler agent. The listener agent can be used in environments where jobs will be executed manually in designer. If the user is going to schedule jobs, they must configure the scheduler agent. Both types of agents should be run as a service in the background.

Languages are the final concept to discuss. Within ODI Topology, each technology uses a language to receive and give commands. For example, when writing queries to pull data from a Relational Source, you use SQL. Languages within ODI can be modified and updated for all technologies specified.

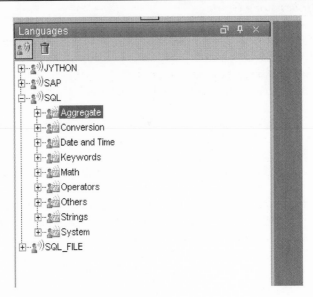

Design Time with Designer

Designer is the application that is used to define the interface, mappings and models. To access Designer from the Start menu select Oracle >> Oracle Data Integrator >>Designer.

Every object within Designer is contained within a Model or a Project. Models are the metadata for your source and target systems. Projects are the integrations that move data from your source and target systems. Within a project you can have:

- Interfaces
- Packages
- Procedures
- Variables
- Knowledge Modules

As a reminder, the Designer module stores this information in a work repository, it references the topology and the security information defined in the master repository.

Knowledge Modules

Let's start with Knowledge Modules. Knowledge Modules (KMs) are components with built in knowledge (functions and logic) that connect technologies to ODI. Similar to HAL Adapters, but many more connection options. KMs connect to the technology, extract data from it, transform the data, check it, integrate it, etc.

There are different types of Knowledge Modules:

- LKM (Loading Knowledge Modules) are used to extract data from the source database tables and other systems (files, middleware, mainframe, etc.).
- IKM (Integration Knowledge Modules) are used to integrate (load) data to the target system.
- CKM (Check Knowledge Modules) are used to check that constraints on the sources and targets are not violated.
- RKM (Reverse Knowledge Modules) are used to perform a customized reverse-engineering of data models for a specific technology.
- JKM (Journalizing Knowledge Modules) are used to create a journal of data modifications (insert, update and delete) of the source databases to keep track of the changes.
- SKM (Service Knowledge Modules) are used to generate the code required for creating dataservices.

To utilize a Knowledge Module within ODI, select the Projects tab. Right-click on the Knowledge Modules item (contained within the individual project) and select Import. Typically the available knowledge modules are stored within the OraHome1 directory under the impexp folder.

You can find a complete list of KMs at http://www.oracle.com/technology/products/oracle-data-integrator/10.1.3/htdocs/documentation/oracledi_km_reference.pdf.

Models

Models contain the metadata for source and target systems. RKM's are used to extract the metadata information from a source or target system. The below picture is a reverse engineered model for a Hyperion Planning application.

In the picture you notice that it translates the multidimensional format of planning into a more table friendly format. Each dimension has a set of columns that can be updated with an ODI interface. For each column, parameters such as field type and length are set during the reverse process.

Once a model has been configured for both the source and target system, an interface can be created. An interface is the object which loads one target data store with data from one or more sources, based on business rules implemented as mappings.

Projects

Within a project there are multiple objects that are created and grouped within Folders. Folders include Packages, Interfaces, Procedures, Variables, Sequences, User Functions and Knowledge Modules.

The interface is typically the first item to configure. All objects can typically be created or edited by right-click on the object name and using the appropriate selection from the menu. Initially, the source and target models are placed into their respective window frames in the interface designer. The expression editor is used to map the source and target columns. Columns with identical names are automatically mapped for ease of use.

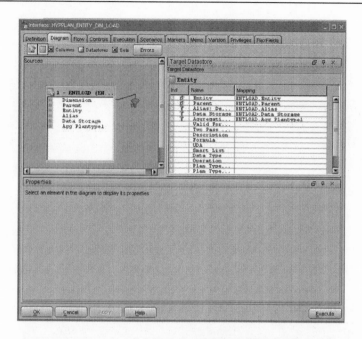

More options are available in the panel below, select the target column. From here you can access the expression editor, indicate whether the logic should be applied on the source or target, select whether the system should perform an insert or an update.

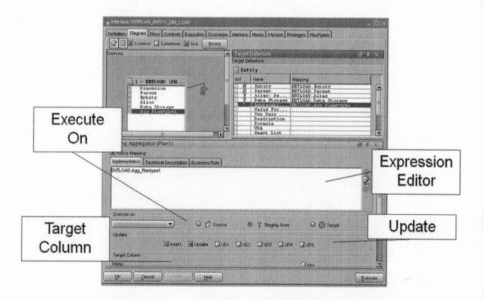

Filters can be applied to the source system by dragging the field into the gray area. A yellow funnel will appear indicating a filter has been applied. An example of a filter would be to extract all entities that have a prefix of "Fin" from the source system.

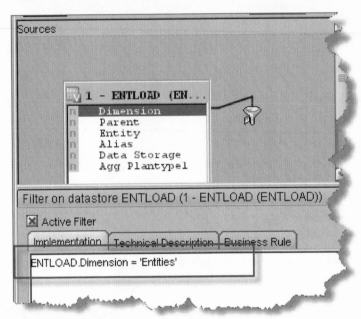

The illustration above only includes one source, but ODI provides the ability to join multiple sources and map them to a single target. This is useful in situations where some information is stored in the data warehouse and a user provides you another set of information in a file. As you can see below, advance joins can be applied.

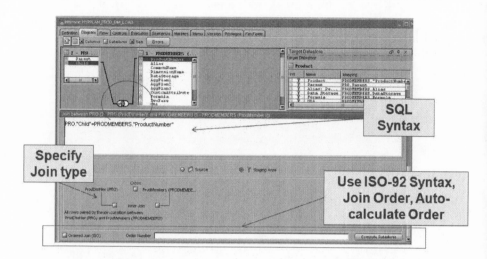

The Expression Editor can be opened in a separate window and provides more functionality. You can drag and drop columns, include variables, update the sql manually (ie. Append prefix to the column) and check syntax. The syntax follows the language of the source or target. However, it does allows you to apply sql to non sql sources that have been joined with a sql source.

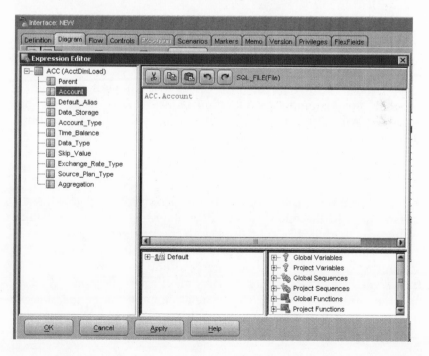

Once all mappings and translations are complete, it is time to move onto the Flow tab. The flow tab depicts a graphical view of what is occurring in the interface. By clicking on each object, you are provided a list of options.

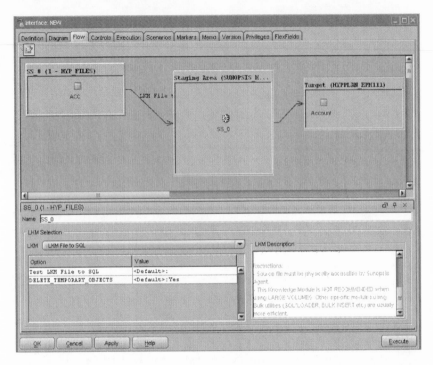

Each Knowledge Module comes with a predefined set of options. For example, the Planning IKM includes an option that specifies "sort the data in parent child format before loading". Behind the scenes this includes the SQL necessary for that to occur. As you can see from the above picture, the flow tab illustrates the source, knowledge module used to take data from one place to the next.

If you pay close attention to the picture above you will see a staging area in the middle of the flow diagram. ODI has a default temporary staging area that ships with the product. It is referred to as the Sunopsis_Memory_Engine. You have the option to use a staging area or bypass the staging area and send data straight to the target. However, in most cases you will need to pump the data to a temporary location for the translations and mappings to occur properly. With the EPM Suite of products you must use the staging area. However, it is not recommended to use the Sunopsis Memory

Engine when you have large volumes of data going through the interface. At this point you would want to create a separate staging area that you can allocate space to and manage database settings for optimal performance.

Once the flow options have been set, you can execute the job directly from this window.

You will always be prompted with a message that says session started. Then the place to go and look is the Operator.

The Operator

The Operator logs information about jobs in a hierarchical format of Sessions, Steps and Tasks. It is grouped and can be filtered by Physical Agent, Keywords, Date, Sessions, Status and User.

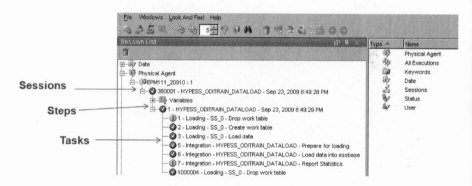

A plethora of information is kept about each session. You can find who submitted, what context was used, what code was run, if it was successful, etc. You can even restart and stop jobs from the Operator.

Error Logs

In the interface on the flow tab, error trapping and log files can be specified. This should be used to trap records and error messages that have not flown through to the target system.

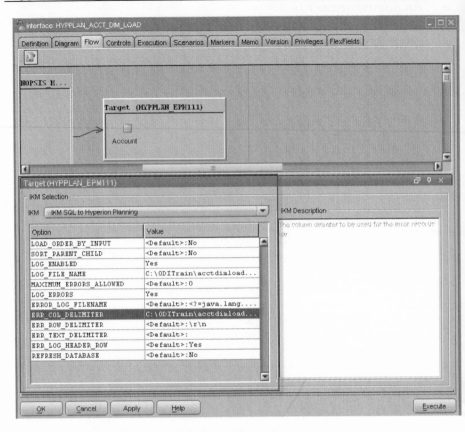

Another location to look for error or processing information is on the execution tab within the Operator. Typically in the message box, if there is a system error, it will be captured here. The Description tab will tell you more information about the series of steps and functions that are called during the execution.

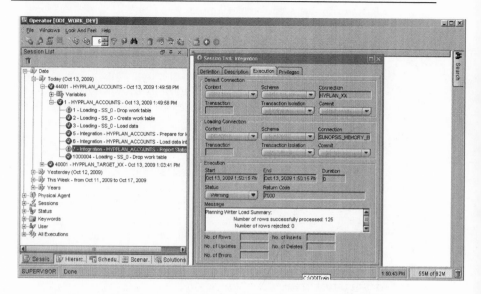

We should forewarn you that reading errors, trapping errors and understanding the messages from ODI can be the most challenging obstacle to overcome when learning the product. The more familiar you are with the source and target technologies, the easier it becomes to translate the technical "gobbly gook" to something meaningful.

Automation

The ODI objects Packages, Scenarios and Variables all come into play when it is time to automate or string multiple steps (interfaces) together. A package can include multiple interfaces, OS commands, Procedures, and variables. Variables can be used to pass in a parameter (month, file name, etc.) Once a package has been created a Scenario is generated and can be scheduled. Reminder: the Agent must be running as a scheduler agent!

There is also a batch utility that can be used to run an ODI Scenario. Use StartScen.bat in the \\..\OraHome_1\oracledi\bin directory. This would be useful if your organization has another scheduler that is used and supported in-house. It is also useful if you have a series of IT personnel that feel more powerful using the "black screen".

Shortlist of Steps

To summarize, let's recap the list of steps to create a source to target data integration with ODI:

1. Define and configure Topology.
   a. Physical Architecture
   b. Logical Architecture
   c. Map through a Context
2. Before you start building an interface you:
   a. Import Knowledge Modules into the project
   b. Create your Metadata Models

Then in the interface you:
3. Define your source and target
4. Define the mapping and translations (business rules)
5. Define the flow requirements
6. Execute

To automate execution, you will need to create and work with packages, procedures, variables, and sequencing.

Real Life Tips

As always we like to pass along some time saving tips to our readers. Tip #1: Use the 10.1.3.5 release! No patching is required for Essbase, Planning, and HFM. You can find this version at http://www.oracle.com/technology/software/products/odi/index.html.

Tip #2: Design before you build!

- Whiteboard the Topology before configuring in ODI
- Standardize naming conventions for topology components
- Incorporate as many error logs and error trapping processes as possible.
- Consider using a staging area instead of the Sunopsis Memory Engine. This will allow performance optimization and error resolution.
- If the source is a relational database, perform as many translations in a view as possible.
- Instead of loading Essbase Data with ODI KM, write a MaxL to load data to Essbase and add it as an OS Command step in the ODI package.
- Plan extra development time; the learning curve is steep as ODI is more complex than HAL.

This concludes our brief overview of ODI and EPM applications.

Appendix F:
Kickin' Old School with HAL

By Heather Wine, interRel Consulting

Yes, HAL (*Hyperion Application Link* not that computer that kills people in the movie *2001*) still works just fine with EPM 11 so those of you who were worried can breathe a sigh of relief. As you may already be aware, HAL is not the dimension creation tool of choice for EPM 11. However, knowing that many administrators have come to know and love HAL, we'll spend some time showing you the very basics as a tribute to a classic.

Note! HAL is officially unsupported by Oracle as of June, 2010. In other words, if you're using it and something breaks or HAL shuts off your life support and forces you out an airlock, you're on your own. You have been warned.

HAL can be used to load metadata or data to Hyperion applications like Essbase or Planning. There are far better ways to load data (directly to Essbase, for instance) so we'll concentrate on metadata maintenance.

Note! The latest version of HAL for install is 9.3 but this version works against EPM 11.

HAL allows you to create a "data flow" between the source and target using a visual diagram. HAL loads from a variety of sources including, but not limited to, a flat file or a SQL source creating a one-time load or a repeatable process. You can also automate your project by building adapter process files, deploying the processes to a Windows platform, and then running the processes outside of HAL.

First, let's define some key HAL terminology.

- Adapter: The basic elements of a flow diagram. Typically a data source (like a flat file or SQL source) or application (like Planning).
- Flow Diagram: A visual diagram of connected adapters. All work is done within a flow diagram (connecting the text file to the Planning application).

- Project: A single flow diagram or multiple flow diagrams make up a project. Projects can be saved and re-used just like you would any other file.
- Adapter Library: Visual menu of the available adapters. See below for a screen shot of the adapter library.

- Port: Data flows between the adapters using connections to ports. Ports can be input ports which receive data, output ports which send data, or inout ports which send and receive data.

After connecting to HAL, the window below appears. You can choose to create a new flow diagram (and therefore a new project) or open an existing project. For our discussions here, we'll create a new flow diagram:

You can now consider yourself an artist with a blank canvas. What you see is a blank flow diagram:

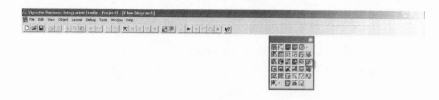

Note!

Mouse over the adapters and a tool tip will display the adapter name.

Drag and drop the Planning adapter from the adapter library into your flow diagram. This will bring up the Planning adapter properties window where you'll enter or choose the proper information related to Planning:

- o Server
- o Application
- o User name
- o Password

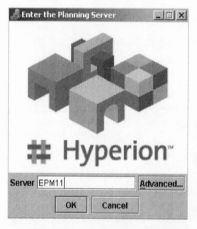

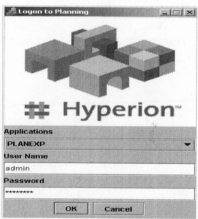

The Planning properties can now be altered. Name your adapter and give it a description on the General tab:

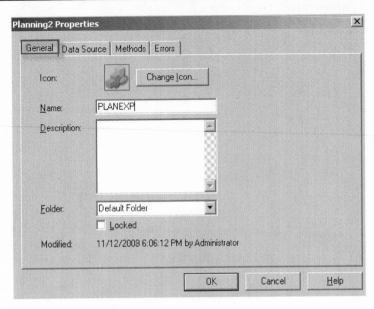

The Data Source tab provides the server and application connection information. If changes are needed to the Data Source (server or application) choose the Refresh option on the Methods tab:

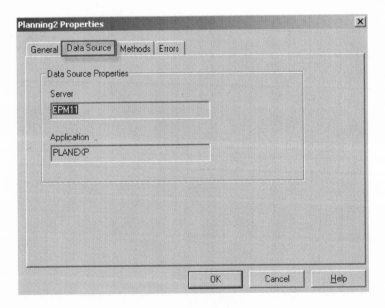

Select the dimension to be updated and the load order on the Methods tab:

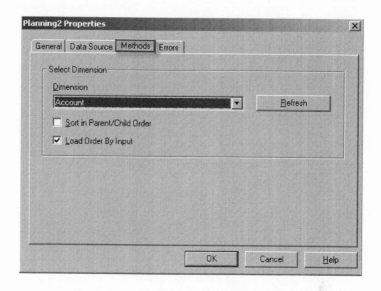

Note! Avoid Sort in Parent/Child Order in HAL if possible as this option can be slow. Instead, try to sort before you get to HAL.

Specify the location of the error file and exception log on the Errors tab. The exception file shows the records that failed to load while the error file shows the reason for failure and the status including how many records loaded and how many failed.

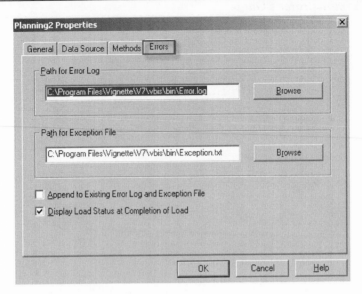

Note!

If your project has multiple flow diagrams, use a different naming convention for each file or choose the option to Append to the Existing Error Log and Exception File. This will give you visibility to all errors.

The adapter is now added to the flow diagram. Different input ports are available for connection depending on the dimension selected in the methods tab during set-up. The ports shown below should look familiar - they are the same as the dimension build properties in Planning:

Account	⟷
Parent	⟷
Alias: Default	⟷
Valid For Consolidations	⟷
Data Storage	⟷
Two Pass Calculation	⟷
Description	⟷
Formula	⟷
UDA	⟷
Smart List	⟷
Data Type	⟷
Operation	⟷
Account Type	⟷
Time Balance	⟷
Skip Value	⟷
Exchange Rate Type	⟷
Variance Reporting	⟷
Source Plan Type	⟷
Plan Type (Plan1)	⟷
Aggregation (Plan1)	⟷
Plan Type (Plan2)	⟷
Aggregation (Plan2)	⟷
Plan Type (Plan3)	⟷
Aggregation (Plan3)	⟷

The only required ports for new member creation are the parent and the dimension, in this case Account. Default values are used to populate all other ports (fields). The only required port for existing member edits is the dimension, Account. Any other ports connected will override the current values.

The default setting when using HAL is update/move which means members will be moved to a new location if a different parent is used in the parent port. Members will not be deleted unless specified in the Operation port.

Note!

CAUTION – if your source no longer contains a parent, all level 0 members will be moved to the new parent but the original parent will NOT be deleted in Planning. This could cause problems if the parent is a stored member that is populated through an aggregation because the data will not be cleared.

The next step is to connect these input ports to another adapter with output ports. There are many adapters that can be used like the Essbase adapter, ODBC adapter, a flat file, or many others. We'll concentrate on the flat adapter. Below is a sample flat file that was created in Excel and saved as a CSV file. You'll notice this file doesn't contain all dimension properties so the default settings will be used wherever they are not defined.

parent	child	alias	storage	agg	Account Type	Variance Reporting	Time Balance	Plan Type 1	Plan Type 2	Plan Type 3
Account	NetInc	Net Income	Dynamic Calc	~	Revenue	Non-Expense	Flow	1	0	0
NetInc	Revenue		Dynamic Calc	+	Revenue	Non-Expense	Flow	1	0	0
Revenue	400100	Product Revenue	Store	+	Revenue	Non-Expense	Flow	1	0	0
Revenue	400200	Service Revenue	Store	+	Revenue	Non-Expense	Flow	1	0	0
NetInc	Expense		Dynamic Calc	+	Expense	Expense	Flow	1	0	0
Expense	600100	Payroll	Store	+	Expense	Expense	Flow	1	0	0
Expense	600200	Travel	Store	+	Expense	Expense	Flow	1	0	0

Drag and drop the flat file adapter 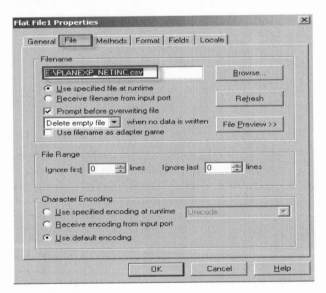 into your project to bring up the properties tabs. Provide the flat file path and other properties related to the file in the File tab. Don't forget that like the other adapters, you can name your adapter on the General tab.

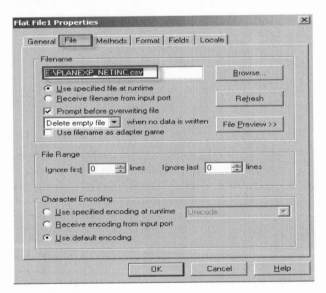

Define the file type, field delimiter, reading options, and error handling on the Format tab:

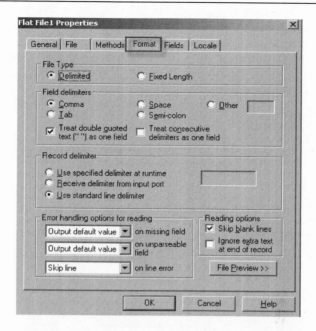

On the Fields tab, each field (output port) can be named either manually by overwriting the Name or by using the first line in the file. You can also preview the file to ensure it parses correctly on the Fields screen by selecting File Preview.

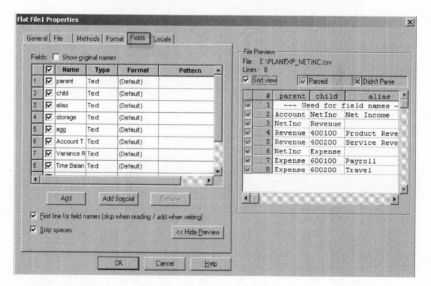

Now that you've added the flat file adapter to your project, you can connect the ports between the two adapters one of two ways. If your flat file contains the same port names as the Planning adapter, click the small circle in the upper right-hand corner of the Output adapter and drag it to the small circle in the upper right-hand corner of the input adapter. This action will connect all ports with the same name. The screen shot below, shows four ports connected this way.

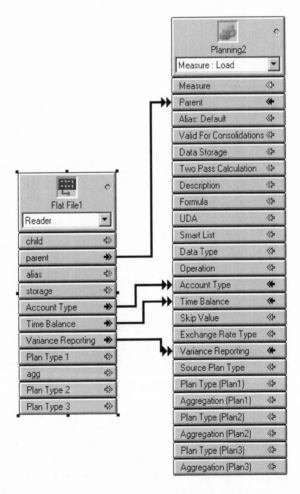

The remaining ports can be connected by linking the output port directly to the input port. Click the arrow to the right of the output port and drag it to the arrow to the right of the appropriate input port. The screen shot below shows all ports connected. Notice

the direction of the arrow between the two adapters shows the flow
of data from the flat file to Planning.

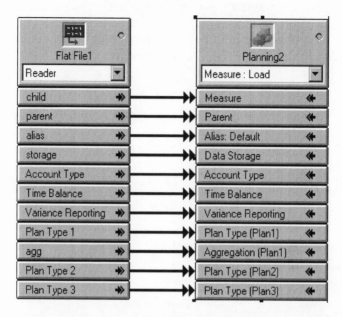

We are sure you are wondering how we got the lines
between adapters so straight and only have the connected ports
showing on the Planning adapter. Here's the trick: right-click on
the Planning adapter and choose the option to Hide Unconnected
Ports. Now, for lining up the adapters perfectly, first, you have to
have A-type tendencies. Next order your flat file the same way as
the Planning adapter ports. Finally, just move the adapters until
they are lined up. For the non A-Type personalities, you're safe
with messy data flows.

Technically this is all that's needed to load a flat file into
Planning. Of course, you can always enhance your project by
adding a variable adapter to pass the server, database, user name,
and password Planning information. You can also expand this
project by adding flow diagrams for each dimension in Planning.
Since we are just concentrating on the basics we'll leave it as is for
now. If we were to talk about all HAL features we would be here for
a lot longer than either of us is willing.

Click the play icon ▶ to run the flow diagram. If a
variable adapter, with the Planning connection information, is not
included in your flow diagram, you will be prompted to enter the

user name and password. Once the process is complete, a dialog box, similar to the one below, appears stating the results of the load:

Turn off animation for better performance.
Debug>Animate

Note!

Rejected records are viewable in the exception file and error log (remember this location is specified in the Errors tab of the Planning properties). Loaded records are viewable in Planning:

Name (8 Total)	Alias (Default)	Data Storage	Security	Attributes	Plan Type
Account		Never Share			1,2,4
NetInc	Net Income	Dynamic Calc			1
Revenue		Dynamic Calc			1
400100	Product Revenue	Store			1
400200	Service Revenue	Store			1
Expense		Dynamic Calc			1
600100	Payroll	Store			1
600200	Travel	Store			1

For additional information on HAL, refer to the System 9.2 documentation for HAL. Also note that the Hyperion specific adapters (Essbase and Planning) have special help files that can be accessed within the adapter itself.

Appendix G:
Planning & Crystal Ball

By Troy Seguin, interRel Consulting

One of the new features in the next release of Planning will be its interaction with Crystal Ball. Crystal Ball is a leading tool used to model risk in business.

MODELING RISK

Nothing is better than experience. If a person has 20 or 30 years of experience he will probably have a very good idea what will happen in the next year given the current environment. However, there aren't very many people with this level of experience and they probably won't be working in the Budgeting and Planning department of your company. So what do you do if you don't have decades and decades of experience and you are tasked to come up with an accurate prediction of the next year's budget? That's where tools like Crystal Ball can help.

Risk vs. Uncertainty

Throughout business, as well as the rest of our lives, we must make decisions in the presence of uncertainty. But what exactly is uncertainty? Many people get the definition of risk and uncertainty confused. Let's look at the differences using an example. Let's assume that you are given a standard pack of playing cards. You know that there are 13 hearts, 13 clubs, 13 spades, and 13 diamonds. You are asked to draw one card. If you draw a diamond, you will win $1. What is the likelihood that you will draw a diamond? Since there are 52 cards in a deck and 13 diamonds, you have a chance of 13/52 or 25% to win a dollar. This is an example of probabilities and risk. You know that you are taking a risk to win $1 and that you have a 25% chance to win.

Now in the next scenario, assume you are given a stack of cards. You have no idea what type of cards. They could be playing cards, flash cards, or even tarot cards for all you know. You are still asked to draw a card and are told that you will win $1 if you draw a diamond. However, you don't even have the information to calculate a percentage of success. This is an example of uncertainty.

Reducing Uncertainty

Understanding the uncertainties that exist allows us to make better decisions. Let's illustrate this using our wolverine juggling business. Let's assume that the wolverine juggling business has really taken off and you are now looking to expand into other sports. The 2 main sports that you would like to start are badger wrestling and porcupine riding. Initial investments would cost $1 million for either venture. Also, your analysis says that they would both provide an average profit of $2 million. However, there are a lot of common skills with badger wrestling (obviously) and the range of values for profit is [$0, $3 million]. You don't know as much about porcupine riding so the profit falls in the range [$-1 million, $6 million]. Even though you have a chance to make more money porcupine riding, there is a great deal more uncertainty in the porcupine riding venture. Thus, the more predictable choice would be to start a badger wrestling business.

CRYSTAL BALL

The hard part now is to start calculating risk and determining your uncertainties. Fortunately, Crystal Ball makes this a lot easier. Crystal Ball works just like any other Excel add-in. There is a drop down menu to run different predictive modeling calculations. It's also very easy to upgrade existing Excel models to Crystal Ball applications. There are 3 main areas that Crystal Ball uses to build predictive models: Optimizer, Predictor, and Simulations.

Optimizer

Most Excel based models have a number of variables that you can change that affects the outcome of the model. In many budget models, a number of controllable factors will have an effect on the end result of the model. For example, investments in marketing will affect Sales figures. Usually, there are a large number of variables whose values you can change. Ideally, the people making the models would be able to find the perfect mix of values for these variables that will maximize profit. This is easier said than done. Usually, the only tool that modelers have is to manually change each variable and check the end result. This gets boring and tedious really fast. Optimizer automatically runs through all of the possible combinations of values of these variables and picks the combination that will optimize the end result.

Predictor

Predictor uses Time Series Analysis to predict variables that you cannot control. Examples of this would be inflation or oil prices. Predictor will look at historical data for these variables and make predictions based on patterns that emerge from the data. There are a number of sophisticated algorithms that Crystal Ball uses to do this and it will automatically choose the algorithm that is the best fit with the data. However, you do have the ability to choose which algorithm to use. This option works really well if you have a lot of clean historical data.

Simulations

Simulations feature is Crystal Ball's version of Monte Carlo Analysis. Monte Carlo Analysis is a term that I have heard used a lot. However, most of the people that I've heard use the term don't seem to have a clear intuition about what it is. Since this is a book on Planning, you have heard the term "What If" analysis. Monte Carl analysis is What If analysis on steroids.

Let's review the concept of What If analysis. Usually you have a budget model set up with a few variables that represent numbers that you don't have a lot control over. So a lot of times people will say things like "What if I sell 5000 units this month instead of 3000?" or "What if I sell 500 units?" How will this affect profits? To do this in a model is simple enough. You just change you units sold variable from 3000 to 5000, run the model, and look at the profit. You then change you units sold variable to 500, run the model, and look at the profit again. This gives you a little information but it can be a slow tedious process.

Monte Carlo analysis takes this concept a step further. Keeping the same example, you would say "I know my units sold will be somewhere between 500 and 5000 units." Crystal ball will then run a number of simulations randomly picking numbers in that range and recorded the resulting profit. You specify the number of simulations. It seems most people run around 10000 simulations. Once the simulations run, you then have a report that graphs the different profit values and the percentage they occurred. This allows you to start asking questions like "Based on these simulations, what chance do I have of making any kind of profit?"

CRYSTAL BALL AND PLANNING

The following group of screens shots shows an example of when Crystal Ball would be useful in a Sales Revenue model. In this case, sales managers were given sales goals by upper management.

Carol is a sales manager who has just received her sales goals for the following year. The total amount is $382 million. This seems kind of high to her.

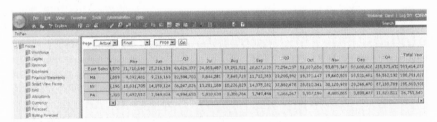

She looks at the Actual sales for FY09 and sees that they total $353 million. "What!!??" she says to herself. "How am I supposed to increase my sales by almost $30 million next year?" In the old days, she would go say her boss and yell and scream that this is a ridiculously high goal. This approach is usually extremely uncomfortable and often counterproductive. She remembers that she recently got Crystal Ball installed with her Planning client and decides to change tactics.

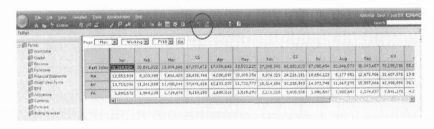

She clicks on the "Open in Smart View" icon to export the web form in Excel.

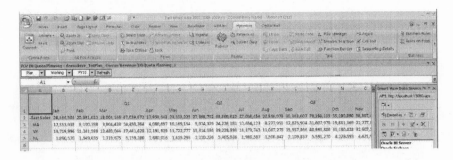

In Smart View, she wants to do 2 things. First, she would like to predict what her sales will be in the next year using Predictor. Secondly, she wants use Simulations to show the likelihood of achieving a goal of $382 million.

Using Smart View, she retrieves 3 years of monthly historical data from the Planning database.

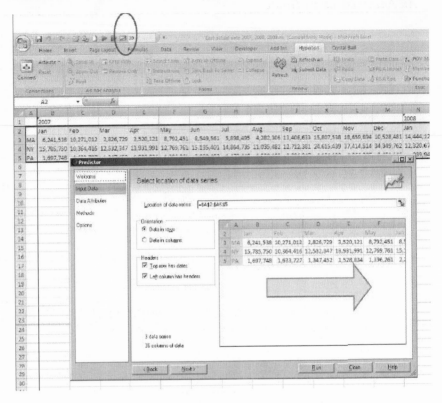

She then clicks on the Predictor icon to open up the Predictor wizard. The first screen is used to select the cells that contain the historical data.

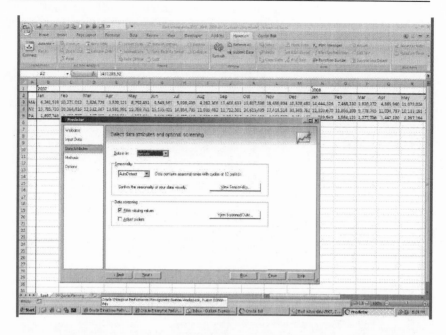

The next screen describes the periods and any seasonality that might occur in the data. Note that you have the option to let crystal automatically detect seasonality.

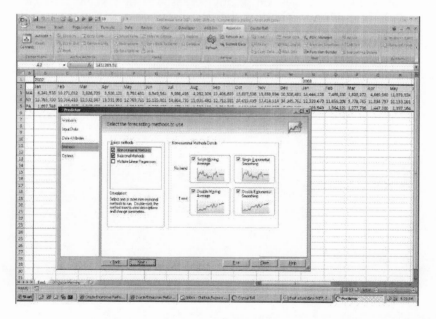

The next screen shows the forecasting methods that are available to you. Again, Crystal Ball automatically detects the best one but it also allows you to choose one yourself.

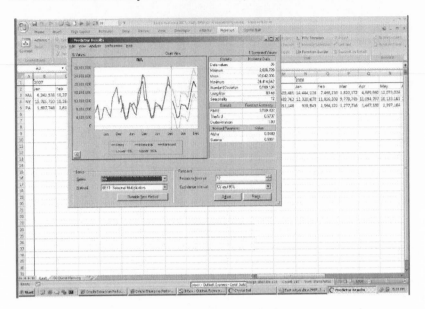

The next screen graphs the forecasted data for you. On the graph itself, the vertical black line represents the present. The past data is to the left of the line and the predicted data is to the right. The green line to the left of the vertical black line is the graph of the historical data. The blue line to the left of the vertical black line is the trend line created by the forecasting logic. The blue line to the right of the vertical black line is the forecasted values based on the forecasting logic. The dotted red lines to the right of the vertical black line represent the possible range of values of the forecasted data.

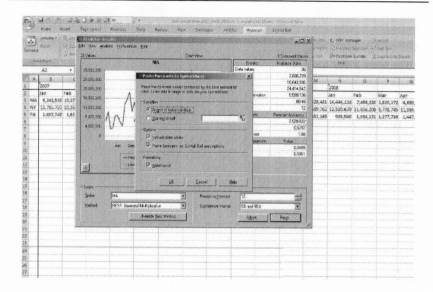

Clicking on the Paste button brings up the Paste Forecast to Spreadsheet dialog box. You can specify how you would like the predicted numbers onto the spreadsheet.

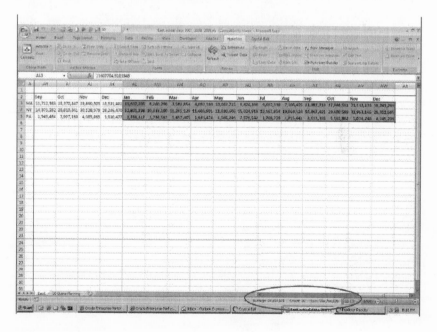

The cells holding the forecast values are highlighted in green. The sum of the cells is $366 million. This represents the more achievable goal for Carol to make.

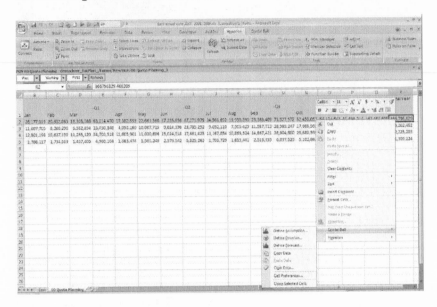

To determine the chances of making the $382 million goal, right-click on the cell representing total sales for the year. Select Crystal Ball>>Define Forecast.

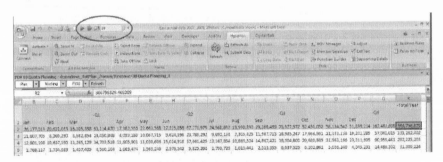

The cell will turn blue. There is the text box with the number 10 in it. This tells Crystal Ball to run 10 simulations. Change that to 10000. Click on the green play button.

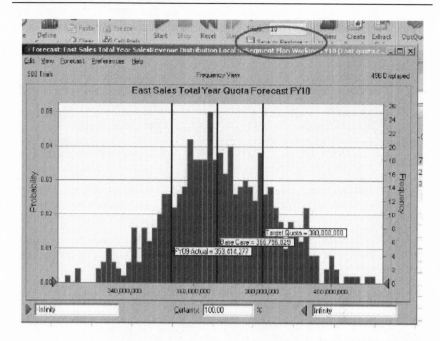

After 10000 trials, you will see a report like this. This shows all of the sales outcomes that occurred during the 10000 trials. Carol wants to see what her chances are of making her quota of $382 million.

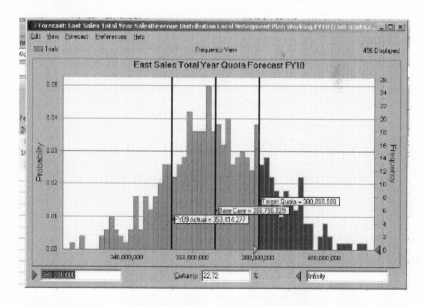

In the box at the lower left side of the report, she types in 380,000,000. This is telling Crystal ball to show the percentage of trials where the outcome of annual sales was between $380 million and infinity (i.e. where the sales was greater than $380 million). The percentage is in the center box labeled certainty. This shows that Carol roughly has a 22.72% chance of achieving the sales goal given to her by management.

Now, based on this analysis, Carol has a much more reasoned, logical argument for her boss to lower her sales goal. She can give a goal that she thinks will be success ($366 million). She can also present her chance of achieving her sales goal in the current environment. She could always go to her boss and ask for more support to help her achieve her goal. This support could be in the form of more marketing or more sales personnel.

We hope this introduction has shown you the exciting possibilities of improving the forecasting process with Planning and Crystal Ball.

Appendix H:
OTHER STUFF

Don't stop reading now; you've only got 2 more pages. This appendix has some helpful notes for consideration along with a "don't miss" finale.

NOTE ON THIS BOOK

We've tried to be as detailed as possible but if we described every single click or button, you'd be 100 years old before you were ready to use Planning (and at that point, Hyperion would probably not even be an independent company but rather bought by some totally awesome firm like Oracle and Hyperion's CEO would be replaced with a really great guy like Larry Ellison, who if he's looking for an heir apparent should contact me at eroske@interrel.com). So we don't mention the fairly obvious tasks and buttons. For example, if there is a Close button, we probably skipped defining what this button does. Cancel means Cancel (doesn't save anything that you just did). Nothing tricky there.

NOTE ON PLANNING VERSIONS

Our objective is to teach you how to use Oracle Hyperion Planning from an administrator perspective. While this book is based on version 11, most of the content in this book applies to version 9.3.1. We've tried to highlight the new 11 features that aren't available in 9.3.1. Some of these features include: Smart Slices and Reporting Designer in Smart View, View Member Formulas, Attach Documents to a Data Form, and Hide / Show Rows and Columns.

WHAT ABOUT MULTI-CURRENCY?

You'll only find high level information on Planning's out-of-the-box functionality for multiple currencies in this book. Why, you may be asking. First, let's review what happens when you enable an application for multi-currency. Two additional dimensions are added to the Planning application, HSP_Rates and Currencies.

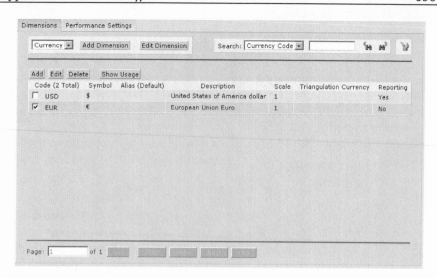

Two currency calc scripts are automatically created in the Manage Database process. The copy rates scripts copy the exchange rates to account members. The conversion scripts execute the currency conversion for accounts and entities at level zero members in the database.

With these dimensions, defined exchange rates and currency calc scripts, you control the following:

- Which currencies an application uses
- How currencies display in reports and data forms
- How one currency is translated into another currency
- Whether a third currency (also known as a triangulation currency) is used for converting between currencies
- When currency conversions occur

While this currency conversion process certainly works, we recommend developing your own logic for currency conversion. Planning Currency Conversion has a series of problems (versus the custom XREF cube of rates method). First, two added dimensions (HSP_Rates and Currencies) are added where only one dimension is really required. Not only does this balloon the potential size of your cube, it makes it difficult for your users to do ad-hoc analysis against your Planning application.

Second, this design can be slow. The currency conversion scripts that Planning writes take much longer than custom scripts. For example, when interRel replaced the built-in HP currency conversion at a large global retail client with a custom solution, the calc times went down from over 100 hours to under 3 minutes. Yes, that's a 99.95% improvement.

Finally, the Planning multi-currency design makes it difficult optimize your cube. The built-in method stores rates at the top member of all of your dimensions. Because of this, you can't dynamically calculate the top member of your dimensions (that would otherwise not require calculation). This can seriously affect aggregation time.

Now that said, have we ever used the built-in method? Sure. In two cases: 1) A customer had a very small application where it was going to run really quickly anyway and 2) a customer wanted to enter numbers in both local and reporting currencies in a single data form and then have the data form save action run the calculation between the currencies automatically.

In general, the drawbacks of the built-in multi-currency conversion may warrant a custom currency conversion solution unless you have a pretty small application.

FINAL SONG

Spoiler Alert! Our musical ends with the CFO giving himself a big bonus when actuals exceeded the plan numbers. Aquaman received a promotion when he proved he could be really useful. And most importantly, despite attempts by Dr. Dementor, Eddie and Penny finish the plan and reunite and are married in Las Vegas at the Annual Budgeteer's Conference.

We'd like to dedicate our last song to our fearless leader at Oracle, Larry Ellison. Sing along if you know the lyrics (parody of *Mickey Mouse Club Theme*).

ALL

WHO'S THE LEADER OF THE CLUB
WHO MAKES THIS MERGER A WIN WIN?

L A R R Y E L
L I S O N

LARRY!
ELLISON!
LARRY!
ELLISON!

HE'LL TAKE THIS COMPANY HIGHER THAN JOHN GLENN!
(GLENN, GLENN, GLENN)

COME ALONG AND SING THE SONG
WE'LL SAY WE KNEW HIM WHEN,

L A R R Y E L
L I S O N

(Signs held up spelling letters as each word is sung.)

ORACLE!
EPM!
ORACLE!
EPM!

SINGLEHANDEDLY
YOU'LL KILL S.A.P.!

HEY THERE, HI THERE, HO THERE,
WHAT A GREAT RIDE IT'S BEEN

L A R R Y E L
L I S O N

(Ending theme, much slower.)

NOW IT'S TIME TO SAY GOODBYE
TO OUR DEAR HY-PER-I-ON.

L A R
(Spoken by Penny) ARE WE SURE THIS ISN'T A BIG MISTAKE?

R Y E L
(Spoken by Eddie) 'ELL IF I KNOW, BUT IT'LL BE FUN.
L I S O N

INDEX